Re-forming Judaism

Re-forming Judaism

Moments of Disruption
in Jewish Thought

EDITED BY

Rabbi Stanley M. Davids
and Leah Hochman, PhD

CCAR
Press

CENTRAL CONFERENCE OF AMERICAN RABBIS
NEW YORK · 2023/5783

Unless otherwise noted, Torah translations are from *The Torah: A Modern Commentary,
Revised Edition*, ed. W. Gunther Plaut (CCAR Press, 2006), and other biblical translations are from *Tanakh: The Holy Scriptures* (Jewish Publication Society, 1985).

Published by Reform Judaism Publishing, a division of CCAR Press
Central Conference of American Rabbis
355 Lexington Avenue, New York, NY 10017
(212) 972-3636 | info@ccarpress.org | www.ccarpress.org

Library of Congress Cataloging-in-Publication Data
Names: Davids, Stanley M., editor. | Hochman, Leah, editor.
Title: Re-forming Judaism: moments of disruption in Jewish thought /
  edited by Rabbi Stanley M. Davids and Leah Hochman, PhD.
Other titles: Reforming Judaism
Description: New York: Central Conference of American Rabbis, 2023 / 5783.
  | Summary: "Throughout Jewish history, revolutionary events and
  subversive ideas have burst onto the scene, transforming everything in
  their path. Re-forming Judaism seeks to explore these ideas--and the
  individuals behind them--by delving into historical disruptions that led
  to lasting change in Jewish thought"-- Provided by publisher.
Identifiers: LCCN 2023013381 (print) | LCCN 2023013382 (ebook) | ISBN
  9780881236095 (trade paperback) | ISBN 9780881236101 (ebook)
Subjects: LCSH: Judaism--History. | Jewish philosophy--History. |
  Judaism--Essence, genius, nature. | Reform Judaism--United
  States--Essence, genius, nature. | Jews--History--Philosophy.
Classification: LCC BM160 .R42 2023 (print) | LCC BM160 (ebook) | DDC
  296.09--dc23/eng/20230414
LC record available at https://lccn.loc.gov/2023013381
LC ebook record available at https://lccn.loc.gov/2023013382

Cover art: Chaim Soutine, *The Philosopher* (1921)

Design and composition by Scott-Martin Kosofsky
at The Philidor Company, Rhinebeck, NY

Printed in the United States of America
10 9 8 7 6 5 4 3 2 1 0

Contents

Acknowledgments ix

Introduction: Thinking about Continuity and Disruption xiii
Rabbi Stanley M. Davids

Part One: Biblical Considerations

1. The Disruptive Prophets: Linking Action and Intention 3
Kristine Henriksen Garroway, PhD

2. 586 BCE: Defeat and the Emergence of Jewish Peoplehood 17
Jacob L. Wright, PhD

Part Two: Rabbinic Disruptions

3. Christianity: A Pauline Revolution 35
Rabbi Joshua D. Garroway, PhD

4. Persecution, Martyrdom, and Divine Justice:
How the Afterlife Came to Be 49
Rabbi Candice Levy, PhD

5. "They Are Israel": Nonbinary Gender Then and Now 65
Gwynn Kessler, PhD

Part Three: Medieval Constructions

6. The Radical Rationalist: Maimonides Reshapes
Rabbinic Discourse 83
Tamar Ron Marvin, PhD

7. The *Zohar* Transformation:
A New Understanding of Torah, God, and Humanity 99
Rabbi Lawrence A. Englander, DHL

8. Sabbatianism: Convulsions and Creativity   113
   Rabbi Stanley M. Davids

9. Jewish Thought in the North African Sephardic Diaspora:
   Continuity and Change   131
   Michal Ohana, PhD

Part Four: Modern Deliberations

10. Haskalah in Berlin: Moses Mendelssohn, Immanuel Kant,
    and the Foundations of Reform Judaism   147
    Yoav Schaefer

11. Breaking the Chain: The Radical Thought
    of Rabbi Samuel Holdheim   165
    Michael A. Meyer, PhD

12. Sephardism and Modernity: Jewish Communities in Flux   179
    Rabbi Marc D. Angel, PhD

13. The Pittsburgh Platform of 1885:
    The American Reform Rabbis' Declaration of Independence   197
    Rabbi Kari Tuling, PhD

14. Power, Pragmatism, and Peoplehood:
    Mordecai Kaplan's Radical American Judaism   211
    Rabbi Michael Marmur, PhD

Part Five: Contemporary Innovations

15. The Breakup: Rethinking American Jewish Literary History   229
    Adam Rovner, PhD

16. Liturgy as an Instrument of Intellectual Change:
    Between Comfort and Disruption   245
    Rabbi Sonja K. Pilz, PhD

17. Reform Jewry Sings a New Song: Disruptions and Innovations   261
    Cantor Evan Kent, DMA

18. The Gender Revolution: Disruptions of Jewish Feminism   279
    Rabbi Elyse Goldstein

19. Moving Beyond Post-Holocaust Theology:
Critical Theory as a New Paradigm   295
Rabbi Jason Rodich

20. Holocaust Testimony: Listening, Humanizing, and Sacralizing 305
Stephen D. Smith, PhD

21. Inclusive Judaism: A Vision for the Future   319
Rabbi Nora Feinstein

Afterword   327
Leah Hochman, PhD

Contributors   335

Acknowledgments

Rabbi Stanley M. Davids

הַדֶּרֶךְ אֲרֻכָּה הִיא וְרַבָּה מְאֹד, אֲבָל אֲנִי לְבַד צוֹעֵד. הַלְלוּיָהּ.

I USED TO SING that song as a teenager. "The way forward is very long, but it's okay because I am marching by myself. Hallelujah." I wasn't much into collaboration and partnership back then. I can do quite well, I thought, just by working things out on my own.

The way to bring an important book to life is amazingly long and very challenging. And doing it alone is more often than not self-defeating. Along the path toward maturity, I came to understand that partnership and collaboration are not only critically important, but also personally enriching.

CCAR Press has been consistently supportive of my work. Rabbi Hara Person had the patience and wisdom (and more patience) to teach me the basics and to inspire me to continue. Rafael Chaiken picked up Hara's mantle after my second book was published and has been willing to sharpen what I have learned and to give me unfailing support and guidance in this, my third undertaking. Rabbi Sonja K. Pilz, PhD, was my regular and wonderful go-to person during the gestation of this volume, and Rabbi Jan Katz was able to step in as a source of great wisdom and skill—not just in moving matters forward, but in calming me down when things would become a bit more complicated than I had expected. Her editorial skills and her friendship are simply amazing.

When we needed expert translations of Hebrew texts into English, Rabbi Yoni Regev volunteered his services. He is family to me.

I needed an informal kitchen cabinet to help take a poorly articulated dream and work it into a viable proposal. Howard Adelman, PhD; Rabbi Joshua D. Garroway, PhD; Rabbi Tamara Cohn Eskenazi, PhD; Yoav Schaefer; Rabbi Lawrence A. Englander, DHL; and Rabbi Joseph

Skloot, PhD, all helped to sharpen the focus, to suggest topics and scholars, and to share their growing enthusiasm for the project.

The missing piece was a full partner. I am not well-trained in Jewish intellectual history. Paraphrasing Amos, I am neither an academic nor the offspring of an academic. This book became a reality only once Dr. Leah Hochman accepted my invitation for us to be coeditors. Leah is not only a world-class scholar, deeply knowledgeable about Jewish intellectual history, but also a close reader of texts and one who would know which scholars to invite to contribute to our volume. Honest, open, wise, and endlessly patient, Leah spent our first month of collaboration teaching me what I had to know if we were to go forward. Though she was forced to juggle many obligations and to handle difficult challenges with which life has confronted her, I could not have had a better partner—a partner who has become a valued friend.

מִכֹּל שֶׁתָּפָי הִשְׂכַּלְתִּי.

I have gained so much from my partners.

The scholars who authored the chapters in this book are of course possessed of profound scholarship. They are exemplary individuals who were willing to take time away from their professional burdens to contribute. I thank them for bringing together a lifetime of specialized study with the notion of evolution through disruption.

But what I truly never expected was how much I was privileged to learn from their thoughts and accumulated knowledge. I would read a first draft over so as to make edits and to offer suggestions. And then, I would read that draft again just to absorb what contemporary scholarship has to say about so many topics that are significant to me.

כִּי הֵם חַיֵּינוּ וְאֹרֶךְ יָמֵינוּ.

For they are my life and the length of my days.

I acknowledge with profound gratitude the gift of my precious friend M. Howard Jacobson in support of this book, in memory of his beloved wife Frances Jacobson, z"l.

It has been a long road, a road that began shortly after both my wife, Resa, and I emerged from prolonged stays in the COVID isolation wing of the UCLA Hospital. We both learned many things from that experience, an experience that has not been free of lingering consequences. Gilroy Chavez, our at-home caregiver, continues to be a key person in our recovery.

I gratefully dedicate this exploration of disruption and evolution to my beloved Resa; to our children, Ronn and Nicole Davids; Shoshana Dweck; and Dr. Aviva and Jason Levin; and to our grandchildren, Elizabeth and Hannah Davids; James, Joshua, and Gabriel Dweck; and Zeke, Mya, and Cole Levin.

And to whatever emerges from the disruptions of our own day.

Leah Hochman

This book is like an elephant: it has had a long gestational period, had a community of protective and productive members, and carries with it long, rich, deeply felt memories. I am grateful to the many people who turned what seemed like an eternal becoming into an actual being.

First, thank you to our contributors, who responded to our initial inquiries with curiosity and excitement and who remained patient with the many interruptions of pandemic, illness, loss, staffing, and professional obligations. Each author responded to our queries, suggestions, deletions, and insertions with grace, acumen, and deep integrity, and their final versions reflect a rich, deep, and wide-ranging approach to the study of global, historical, spiritual, and intellectual Jewish experience.

Second, thank you to the CCAR editorial team, led by Rafael Chaiken and ably assisted by Chiara Ricisak, Debbie Smilow, and Raquel Fairweather-Gallie. Rabbi Sonja K. Pilz, PhD, was the first shepherd of this project; she brought vision and deep love to the subject. When Rabbi Jan Katz stepped in as the editorial DH, she brought her kind, unerring eye, genuine interest, graceful honesty, and persevering integrity to bring the project to its completion. And the ninth inning addition of the deeply committed and generous editorial hand of Rabbi Annie Villarreal-Belford was the home run we needed to complete the series. We are grateful also to our copy editor Debra Hirsch Corman, our proofreader Michelle Kwitkin, and our book designer Scott-Martin Kosofsky.

Third, I am deeply grateful to my coeditor Rabbi Stanley M. Davids, who turned an idea into a committee, that committee into a group of contributors, and those contributors into a sweeping study of centuries of Jewish experience. This book is Stan's baby. He has been generous and open, patient and curious, willing to push and be pushed, steadfast in his commitment and determined at every turn. The book would not exist without Stan's devoted attention to the people, the ideas, and the disruptions within it. My thanks to him for sticking with it and with me.

Fourth, I turn to my son, Levi, who has remained a beacon of light during an extremely dark time. Many hours were stolen from him in completing this project. He met the challenges of an overtired, grumpy, caffeinated parent with great aplomb and insisted on helping me think through big ideas and editorial conundrums. He has faced worldwide crises and familial disruptions with a matter-of-fact generosity that astounds me. My gratitude for his loving, insightful, and funny self knows no bounds. I hope someday he will read these essays, see the threads of productive disruption, and use the many lessons in this volume to help him as he continues to better the world.

The gestational period of this book has been extraordinarily difficult for me professionally and personally. In addition to the global and local catastrophes of pandemic, war, famine, and natural disaster, I mourn the loss of friends who, normally, I would have the occasion to thank for buoying my spirits, asking probing questions, feeding my body and my spirit, and providing key insights. My life and the world is a much poorer place for the absences of Dr. Sharon Gillerman, z"l, Larry Gray of blessed memory, Hattie Pearson of blessed memory, and Cathee Weiss, z"l— friends and colleagues from Hebrew Union College–Jewish Institute of Religion who have passed away since I joined this project. And the hole left by the passing of my mother, Linda Potter Hochman, z"l, in March 2022 represents a disruption like none other. I miss her terribly. I know she would have been proud without measure. It is to her memory that I dedicate this work.

Introduction:
Thinking about Continuity and Disruption

Rabbi Stanley M. Davids

IT IS MORE THAN A BIT frightening to think about what our lives would be like today without the Global Positioning System (GPS). How would we ever manage to get from "there" to "here" without it? We don't need to understand GPS in order to use it. There is a high probability that we will arrive amazingly close to our intended destination with little effort on our part. We don't need to consider that GPS arose out of military considerations and that it currently is controlled by the newest branch of the US military, the Space Force. We don't need to understand its operating system. We just input our destination and off we go.

Not so when attempting to navigate the world of ideas. Of course, we can always enjoy at a superficial level great achievements in art, music, philosophy, and literature without fully understanding their origin stories. But we cannot fully respond to those ideas that animate our lives, that enrich our appreciation of human creativity, without first understanding the nature of their journey through intellectual history. How did they get here from there? What events and individuals contributed to the formation and then the evolution of those ideas? If we do not understand that journey, then we will not be ready to effectively engage with newly emergent ideas that are already at work all around us, shaping our tomorrows.

Adherents of Liberal, Reform, and Progressive Judaism hold that the system of faith, thought, and practice that they embrace today is the authentic outcome of a pattern of growth, emergent disruptions, and the creative adaptation of ideas, practices, and beliefs first articulated thousands of years ago in the Hebrew Bible. To be clear: in no sense is liberal Judaism the only possible outcome of the astonishing array of disruptions that have impacted Judaism as it continues to shape much of what we know today as Western civilization. Some of those disruptions, in fact, have led us in directions that are far distant from the intellectual and spiritual space currently occupied by most twenty-first-century Jews. We study those disruptions and our responses to them in this book not as a prideful act of asserting our proper place in Jewish history, but rather to help prepare our entire community for the inevitable arrival of new and perhaps even greater disruptions and their attendant challenges. Our authors, collectively and individually, have demonstrated that the path from the ancient Middle East to contemporary liberal Judaism is most certainly neither linear nor predetermined. We ask our readers not only to dispassionately understand what forces were at play that led us to where we are today, but also to be prepared with courage, faith, and wisdom to continue our people's nonlinear progress into a beckoning yet clouded future. The following comment regarding innovation offers a necessary cautionary note: "Over the years, there has been a widespread tendency in the innovation literature to make the assumption that innovation is always good. Yet . . . innovation does not necessarily benefit society at large. Innovation may often be of the 'destructive creation' type . . . that is, innovations benefiting the few at the expense of the many—rather than the supposedly more desirable 'creative destruction' type (which may destroy a few incumbents but to the ultimate benefit of society as a whole)."[1]

Pedro Ramos Pinto notes that a developmental view of history can be a very useful tool in clarifying how we got here from there.[2] Useful, but not sufficient. In the following chapters, our emphasis is on the study of radical discontinuity or disruption, while still making room for continuity. To understand the past and to contemplate the future, disruptions must be given their due. In this way, examining the past with an open lens can be of practical use in shaping the future.[3]

Zoltan Boldizsar Simon points out that the eminent philosopher of science Thomas Kuhn and others believed that the study of paradigm shifts—that is, of disruptive changes—promotes an excellent way to explore the human experience and warned that the search for deep continuities, along with a willful disregard of radical discontinuities, may lead to intellectual blindness.[4] While it is true that innovation and disruption may both be intentional, calculated, and purposeful, more often than not their appearance onto the public stage is serendipitous, unintentional, and inadvertent. Kuhn offers that those disruptions and innovations are rarely the product of the gradual accumulation of insights and data. Rather, it seems that something out of the ordinary unexpectedly appears: some person or group offers attractive or challenging new ways to help us comprehend and respond to the central questions of our existence.[5] It could be a new way to think, to believe, and to respond to the power structures or dominant intellectual insights of the day or perhaps a new way to comprehend emergent, inchoate social or natural forces. "Something out of the ordinary" begins to invite us to see our lives as if through a new lens and can provide us with new and useful ways of acting and believing.

When a disruption occurs, in proper Hegelian fashion it arouses dramatic opposition.[6] That opposition can find its expression in apologetics, polemics, and disputations; it can result in state power exerting brutal physical, communal, and intellectual repression, as well as in the emergence of a genre of secular, religious, or philosophical literature in which the case for vigorous opposition is made. Though winners and losers can only be crowned by history, the outcome of the clash of such forces inevitably changes both the source of the disruption and its target. Throughout Jewish history, nonlinear zigs or zags entered our cultural history and awaited their inevitable encounter with whatever would become the next disruption.

Institutionalists of all political, ideological and denominational stripes—those who are committed to showing that even though many things seem to have changed, in fact nothing of significance has changed—resist by their very nature emerging disruptions. They will argue: It is obvious that what is happening in our own day was foreseen by those who came before. Didn't our patriarchs and matriarchs, our prophets and our teachers, embed within their acts and teachings precisely what we are confronting today? Don't our revealed texts actually contain within them those hidden messages, hints, and allusions that not only embrace and absorb the disruptions in advance but also firmly attach them to the infrastructure of traditional faith and institutions? One who openly asserts that substantial changes must be made to the status quo is declared by the holders of power to be a *kofer b'ikar*, one who

denies a core principle.[7] It is better for the institutionalist to deny publicly that any changes have ever been made rather than to go on to live
with an unfamiliar and unwelcome new reality.

We acknowledge that there are many institutionalists in our midst—
that is, those who still hold fast to their own hard-earned certificates of
authenticity and absolute authority; at the same time, there are also others among our people who struggle to find traction between institutionalists and those who intentionally find the need and the will to embrace
what the disruptions have to teach us.

Those who initiated, who were early adopters, or who became adherents of the disruption responded with a varied range of reactions. Some
were anxious to maintain a degree of common ground with the institutionalists so as to preserve what they considered to be a meaningful connection with the feeder roots of tradition while nevertheless dramatically
pruning, trimming, and reshaping the crown or the canopy of the new
growth. They knew that their actions must carry strong indicators of
identity with what came before; yet, without embracing aspects of the
disruption that they treasure, they might cease to speak to the world.

Others were like Elisha ben Avuyah (Acher), who felt driven to cut the
very roots of the tradition and to enter the gardens of other traditions.[8]
The disruption becomes so dominant for them that there is no space,
no sunlight, no nurturing soil for what had come before. For them, the
ancient trees no longer are capable of bearing new fruit. Something new
must emerge, something far more congruent with the latest insights of
faith, thought, and science. Perhaps unable to totally disassociate themselves from that which the institutionalists hold dear, such people may
compensate by becoming vigorous, uncompromising opponents of that
which had once given meaning to their lives.

Still others, who acknowledge and embrace the disruption, openly and
consistently accept the most daunting challenge of all. They know that
there is no place for them among the institutionalists. Sensing the power
of the disruption and the truth it carries, they know that fundamental
change is necessary. Many old forms and structures must be discarded,
even though the very essence of what was once treasured might be fatally
damaged in the process. Some of the core values that were once deemed
irreplaceable will be repudiated. Some long-standing certainties will be

declared false, while other ideas once deemed to be utterly irreconcilable with the world that they knew will now be embraced and enshrined. The process has been described as follows: "A rupture opens up a new space in place of the shattered status quo. It clears away illusions about an old order no longer fit for purpose and makes way for what has been incubating to emerge in clearer form. Above all, a rupture from the past demands choices about the foundations of the future."[9]

We cannot examine disruptions as if displayed on a chronological spreadsheet. Retrospectively, it is obvious that most disruptions have antecedents. How our people responded to acts of crushing hatred and devastating assault in one generation is inevitably shaped and grounded by how such events were dealt with in earlier times. How our people respond to attractive, compelling new ideas today reflects at least some aspect of how we responded to such invitations in the past. How we have overthrown or submitted to religious authority in the past and how we have previously forced ourselves to choose between making changes or being pushed aside by historical forces beyond our control inevitably have an impact on how we respond to the flood tides of change in our own day.[10]

History is not neat or tidily arranged. Disruptions that brought the end to certain cultures and civilizations then became forces for the birthing of new cultures. Moreover, disruptions that possessed enormous impact in one century in some places might very well not manifest their presence in other places until centuries have passed. It was therefore not sustainable to attempt to assemble this book in a chronological fashion. Neither could we follow the well-trodden path of arranging our ideas according to the "great person" approach. The great person behind a major disruption could be Benedict Spinoza, Samuel Holdheim, Shabbetai Zvi, or Mordecai Kaplan. However, it is more than difficult to connect a single great person to disruptions such as the emergence of a unique Sephardic culture in North Africa, approaches to understanding our sacred literature through a feminist or queer lens, or building a robust response to the collapse of a sustainable Jewish identity when we have been forcibly separated from the institutions of our national sovereignty. Thus, it was also not sustainable to attempt to assemble this book according to great people. We were left with a hybrid approach, focusing at times on disruptions that seemed to flow from history, alongside those disruptions that were not emergent from the flow of history but rather from great people who embodied a disruption.

We were aware that we had to be selective, if only because of the exigencies of publication. Not every disruption could possess its own chapter. Disruptions occurring in our own day were set aside if it is too early to properly understand their impact. We did seek out a single chapter that would bring together those important disruptions that we reluctantly left out, such as the obviously significant impact that the growing number of Jews of Color will bring to our people and our future, the dramatic shift in understanding about who is considered to be a Jew, or the emerging consensus that in human biology the binary view of gender is woefully deficient.

Our work has not been haphazard nor without purpose. We begin with reconceptualizing the impact of the destruction of the First Temple, which shaped the final editing of the *Tanach* and the very nature of the structure of Jewish life and key concepts such as theodicy. We gaze at the biblical texts through queer theory and feminism and discover how much we have failed or refused to see for the past twenty-two hundred years. We look again at Paul to see the impact of radical discontinuity on postbiblical and Rabbinic Judaism. To push back at so much of the ever-so-conventional Ashkenazic manner of understanding disruptions, we drill down into Sephardim and Sephardism and throw open the window onto disruptions emerging from North Africa.

Some disruptions are more consequential and more enduring than others. There is no denying the tidal waves of changes that flowed, intentionally and unintentionally, from the creation of the *Zohar* and the refocusing of Jewish mysticism, along with the radical philosophical explorations of Spinoza and Mendelssohn. In the midst of an era of dramatic climate change, communal strife, and deadly plague that collectively led to pervasive fear, uncontrollable change, and relentless anxiety, it surely was no surprise to see another messianic claimant burst forth onto the Jewish scene in the mid-seventeenth century. What might be a surprise is to consider the relationships between the followers of Shabbetai Zvi and those of nineteenth-century Reform Judaism. Samuel Holdheim, Martin Buber, and Mordecai Kaplan were astonishingly radical sources of disruption. We have not yet come near to absorbing the worlds that they tore down, the worlds that they longed to return to, and the future that they most intentionally sought to re-form. New theologies are crafted, opening the door to yet more disruption.

Disruptions continued to emerge from and impact our liturgy and the music that accompanies our worship: from unaccompanied *chazanut* to organs to guitars to worship texts that reflect a constant struggle to discover continuity and contemporaneity; from shtetls to neo-Byzantine sanctuaries to summer camps. How do disruptions stay anchored even while they move on the chaotic tides of change?

Studying our historical disruptions leads to critical questions. Can we embrace disruption while holding fast in more than a pro forma manner to precious continuity? Can there be a future without a coherent past? Can there be a future without an openness to disruption? Will our tradition ultimately be re-formed into obsolescence? What lies beyond the next corner? None of these questions has straightforward answers.

Readers of this book need not feel compelled to read the text straight through. Each chapter stands alone, even as each chapter struggles with similar challenges across the ages. Some of our readers will themselves become authors of the next disruptions. Others will find comfort in being institutionalists, committed to strengthening continuity. And still others will awaken to changes that they never saw coming and that they don't quite understand. We welcome them all.

NOTES

1. Jan Fagerberg, Ben R. Martin, and Esben S. Andersen, eds., *Innovation Studies: Evolution and Future Challenges* (London: Oxford University Press, 2013), 9.
2. Pedro Ramos Pinto, "History Manifested: A Commentary on Continuity, Disruption and the Production of History," *European Review of History* 22, no. 5 (2015): 835–38.
3. The physical design (interior and exterior) of synagogues, the tasks and purposes of synagogues, the push and pull between "synagogue," "temple," and "center," and the shifting roles of clergy all were dynamically impacted by sociological, philosophical, historical, and theological disruptions that arose from many sources—some interrelated, while others were not. Being open to the powerful and not necessarily positive disruptions of the past can

better prepare us to be thoughtfully prepared for disruptions that are already emerging all around us today.

4. Zoltan Boldizsar Simon, "History Manifested: Making Sense of Unprecedented Change," *European Review of History* 22, no. 5 (2015): 819–34.

5. See Thomas Kuhn, *The Structure of Scientific Revolutions* (Chicago: University of Chicago Press, 1962).

6. As the nineteenth-century German philosopher Georg Hegel showed us in his theory of the dialectic: every disruption arouses its dramatic opposite—a conflict to be resolved through the crafting of a synthesis.

7. The term *kofer b'ikar* is used throughout Rabbinic writings to designate one who through action or speech denies the very essence of Judaism—namely, the existence and role of God. In that sense, one who denies the divine origin of Torah or who insists on the human right to contradict or deny select values of Torah would be a *kofer*.

8. The most interesting albeit novelized story of Elisha ben Avuyah may be found in Milton Steinberg's *As a Driven Leaf*. A great rabbinic scholar born ca. 70 CE, Elisha came to embrace a worldview that his colleagues deemed heretical.

9. Nathan Gardels, "Rupture: A Convergence of Breaking Points Demands Choices about the Future," *NOEMA*, April 2, 2022. Available online at www.noemamag.com/rupture/.

10. We need only look to our chapters on Paul, Shabbetai Zvi, Moses Mendelssohn, and Samuel Holdheim to feel the anxiety and passion of those who sought to overthrow the past and its authority in whole or in part so as to embrace a new understanding of truth and meaning.

PART ONE

Biblical Considerations

I

The Disruptive Prophets
Linking Action and Intention

Kristine Henriksen Garroway, PhD

THE BIBLICAL PROPHETS have very different personalities and play different roles within Israel's historical memory.[1] Moses is the leader who sees God *panim al panim*, "face to face." Nathan is the court prophet who acts as King David's conscience. Amos is a shepherd and gardener who draws on his profession to speak to the people in their own language. Their role as prophets, however, unifies them.[2] They are the voice box of God to human beings, and in their respective roles of messenger, the prophets disrupt. They shake up the status quo and point the people Israel in new directions. While there are many different moments of prophetic disruption, this chapter will examine the first two instances of prophetic disruption, both of which challenged the Israelites to live differently.

Disruption One: Moses and the Covenant at Sinai

Like all prophets, Moses was chosen to act as God's mouthpiece (Exodus 3–4).[3] Moses, however, is special and given a place of privilege within Jewish tradition. He facilitates the covenant with Israel and the giving of the law at Sinai. While this moment might not seem like a disruption, it is. Prior to the Sinai experience, Israel was a group of people that had common ancestors (the Patriarchs and Matriarchs), who each had individual covenants with God (Exodus 2:24–25). By the time of Moses, the Israelites had been living in the land of Egypt long enough for an entire generation to die and a new one to arise (1:1–8, 12:40). Exodus 12:38 notes that when the Israelites left Egypt, they did so along with a mixed multitude of people. The group that arrives at Sinai and receives the covenant is diverse. This group moves from a ragtag band of people to a unified nation seemingly in a matter of minutes. The moment they declare, "We will do, and we will obey" (24:7),[4] they enter into a new status. This status is the first prophetic disruption. Moses presented God's covenant to the Israelites and their lives changed. No longer was each person for himself—for herself—or for themselves, but at that moment a group coalesced, bound both to each other and to God through their shared covenant and a common set of laws.

The covenant and the laws therein are reiterated in three different biblical books: Exodus, Leviticus, and Deuteronomy.[5] Exodus 19:5–6 provides a sort of CliffsNotes to the entire covenant: "Now then, if you will obey Me faithfully and keep My covenant, you shall be My treasured possession among all the peoples. Indeed, all the earth is Mine, but you shall be to Me a kingdom of priests and a holy nation." The biblical phrasing is constructed in technical legal language nuanced in the syntax of classical Hebrew. A conditional particle "if" (*im*) opens the condition, which is followed by a doubling of the verb, meant to give emphasis to the statement that follows. The Plaut translation renders that repeated Hebrew verb *sh'ma* as "obey Me faithfully," the same word used in the central monotheistic prayer Jews put in their mezuzot and recite during morning and evening prayer services: "Hear, O Israel, the Eternal is our God, the Eternal is One" (Deuteronomy 6:4). But here in Exodus 19:5, *sh'ma* is not an imperative to listen. Rather, it appears paired with the preposition "in" (the letter *bet*) and the word for "voice," an idiom that specifically means "to obey." In other words, at the covenantal moment, Israel agrees emphatically to obey, not merely to listen to God's voice. This emphasis is the first part of the conditional agreement. The second part requires the Israelites to keep the covenant. The result will be that the people will be God's treasured people, a kingdom of priests and a holy nation—that is, Israel will be the recipients of covenantal blessing.

Exodus 20 contains the Ten Commandments, after which the remainder of the laws are given (Exodus 21–23). These laws are referred to by biblical scholars as the Book of the Covenant, *Sefer HaB'rit* (24:7).[6] Notably, the first laws that follow the Ten Commandments concern the correct way to offer sacrifices. God says, "Make for Me an altar of earth and sacrifice on it your burnt offerings and your sacrifices of well-being, your sheep and your oxen; in every place where I cause My name to be mentioned I will come to you and bless you" (20:21). This law will become important later as a linchpin to be undone by the prophets of the eighth century BCE. When presented with the covenantal expectations, Israel responds with the famous dictum *Naaseh v'nishma*, "We will do, and we will obey" (24:7). Here then is the first time Israel is presented with laws, mitzvot, which they must follow in order to stay in the covenantal relationship.

The Book of Deuteronomy, written in the seventh century BCE, reiterates the conditions of the covenant.[7] Instead of employing a subtle grammatical syntax, the Deuteronomy text couches the covenant in the same structure as a treaty between political allies.[8] Ancient Near Eastern treaties had six general parts: a preamble, historical prologue, stipulations (laws), blessings and curses, public reading and deposition, and witnesses. Scholars have noted these different sections in Deuteronomy as well.[9] Like the Book of the Covenant, the Deuteronomic Law Code offers benefits for keeping the covenant: if Israel keeps the commandments, "loving the Eternal your God and serving [God] with all your heart and soul," God "will grant rain . . . [and] provide grass in the fields for your cattle—and thus you shall eat your fill" (Deuteronomy 11:13–15).[10] In keeping the covenant, that is, fulfilling the stipulations of the laws, the Israelites will prosper in the Promised Land. Deuteronomy appears strikingly similar to ancient Near Eastern treaties, which clearly state that if one party fails to uphold their end of the treaty, that is, if they fail to keep the laws established by the treaty, they effectively break the covenant, and a terrible fate will befall the transgressive party. And indeed, Deuteronomy presents a bleak picture for Israel should they fail to uphold their covenant with God. Not only will their land not be blessed, but they will also be cursed in everything they do. Their land will be struck with calamity, panic, pestilence, sickness, disease, drought, and warfare; the curses go on for fifty-four verses! (28:15–68). Most notably, God will cause a nation to come from afar, who will show no mercy, to scatter the people of Israel to the ends of the earth (28:49–50, 64). Breaking the covenant will result in the desiccation of the Promised Land, a loss of national autonomy, and *galut* (exile). Thus, Israel has every motivation to do the mitzvot, that is, to keep the covenant.

The Sinaitic covenant was revolutionary. The laws in Exodus and Deuteronomy brought together a ragtag group of people and bound them to one another both politically and theologically. This national peoplehood was guaranteed not only to thrive, but to live in the Promised Land as long as they upheld the covenant. Exodus and Deuteronomy address the civil side of the covenantal agreement in detail. Leviticus, for its part, further expounds on how a group of people bound by certain theological obligations needs to comport itself in order to uphold the covenant. The Book of Leviticus can be broken up into two sections, the Priestly Code (Leviticus 1–16) and the Holiness Code (Leviticus 17–26).[11] The theology behind the laws in the Priestly Code is concerned with how purity and impurity affect the sanctuary. In these laws, the sanctuary is contaminated by Israel's moral and ritual violations, and it must be purified by an offering of the High Priest (16:3–22). In the Holiness Code, however, pollution comes not from singular moral or ritual violations that pollute the Temple, but rather pollution comes from violation of the covenant. For example, laws concerning incest, idolatry, and breaking Shabbat are not just an affront to God; they are a direct means for dismissal from the Promised Land. Unlike people, for whom t'shuvah is possible, "the polluted land cannot be expiated by ritual, and hence the expulsion of its inhabitants is inevitable."[12] For example, the text in Leviticus makes it very clear that sacrificing one's children to Molech pollutes the land. There is no possible ritual that can be done to reverse or atone for that sin, and so the offending person shall be put to death (20:2).

Indeed, throughout the Holiness Code, individuals are called to remain holy by keeping the covenant. Leviticus 19 specifically exhorts Israel to keep all the laws listed by linking Israel's privileged presence in the land to their status as God's holy people: K'doshim tih'yu ki kadosh ani Adonai Eloheichem, "You shall be holy, for I, the Eternal your God am holy" (19:2). Leviticus 18:24–29 explains that the prior inhabitants of the land were kicked out because they were abhorrent and brought iniquity to the land: "Thus the land became defiled; and I called it to account for its iniquity, and the land spewed out its inhabitants" (18:25). References explaining the connection between sin and expulsion from the land have led scholars to propose that Leviticus was composed no earlier than the Babylonian exile in the sixth century BCE.[13] This dating of Leviticus will become important when we consider the third moment of prophetic disruption.

While the contents of the laws in Exodus, Leviticus, and Deuteronomy differ, they are all understood conceptually to be rules and regulations by which Israel needs to abide to be a people in covenant with their God. If the first moment of prophetic disruption led to the creation of the covenant, the second moment of disruption challenges the people in their practice of the covenant.

Disruption Two: Alterations to the Covenant in Light of Impending Exile

The next point of prophetic disruption comes when the people Israel face a major military threat from the great Mesopotamian empires of the Assyrians and Babylonians in the eighth to sixth centuries BCE. Some historical context will prove vital for understanding the work of the prophets who came after Israel settled into its territory. According to the biblical text, after Israel arrived in the Promised Land, they set up a monarchy, first ruled by King Saul, and then by David and Solomon. This period is called the United Monarchy. After the death of Solomon, his son Rehoboam's rule was contested, and the kingdom split into two. The kingdom to the north was called the Kingdom of Israel (or Northern Kingdom), and the kingdom to the south the Kingdom of Judah (or Southern Kingdom).[14] Each kingdom had its own capital and places for worship. The Temple of Jerusalem in the south functioned as the focal point for Judeans, while the Israelites in the north split their worship between shrines at Dan and Bethel.[15] During the late eighth century and into the seventh century BCE, the Assyrian and later Babylonian armies began to move west with their eyes set on Egypt, conquering along the way the lands and people down the Mediterranean coast. The Northern Kingdom fell to the Assyrians with the defeat of their capital city of Samaria in 722 BCE. Judah's strength was tested in 701 BCE as the Assyrians pushed further south, destroying the important fort of Lachish and besieging the capital of Jerusalem.[16] The Southern Kingdom withstood this incursion and remained standing until the Babylonian army came and destroyed the Temple in 586 BCE.

The message of the prophets operating during the Divided Kingdom echoes this historical reality of bifurcation and competition. To borrow a phrase from a later prophet, Daniel, they "see the writing on the wall" and they shout their warnings (Daniel 5:1–31). The prophets did not, however, say to gather the men of military age, stockpile weapons, and prepare for war. No, the prophets sought to cut off the enemy before they even reached the land. According to the prophetic theology, the reason that the Assyrians and Babylonians would be able to approach was because the people were sinning; they had broken the covenant and were now about to feel the repercussions of that decision. All the curses laid out in Deuteronomy were about to become real. The way to stop the impending war was by returning to the covenant.

The prophets of the eighth century BCE were dramatic. Their texts are full of creative cries for change and warnings for the people to repent of their wicked ways lest evil befall them. Cries of woe fill the pages of their prophecies. Consider the rhetoric of Amos. His book opens with a popular rallying cry ("The Eternal roars from Zion!" [Amos 1:2]) as he proclaims calamities for the surrounding nations (Amos 1–2). The Philistines are called out for their evil deeds, followed by the Phoenicians, the Ammonites, and the Moabites. One can almost feel the frenzied crowd cheer along as Amos castigates the enemies of Israel. But then Amos delivers his zinger. After drawing in his captive audience, he proclaims disaster will befall Judah and Israel because they, too, sin (2:4–16). Fire will rain down on Judah and devour the strongholds of Jerusalem. Israel's warriors will be defeated, and they will run away on the day of battle. Like Amos, the other prophets of the eighth century BCE—Isaiah of Jerusalem, Hosea, and Micah—try desperately to turn the hearts of the people. But people rarely want to hear they are in the wrong, and this is an important point, for embedded in the disrupting prophetic message is a confusing trope that the people tried to twist to their own ends. Put in the most basic terms, the prophets clearly state that God no longer desires sacrifices, which seems to contradict the laws found in the covenant (e.g., Exodus 20:21).

The first place the trope appears is in the Book of Samuel. When conquering the neighboring Amalekites, King Saul disobeys God's directions and spares the best of the Amalekite sheep and oxen. Then Saul denies his actions to Samuel, who dryly responds, "Then what . . . is this bleating of sheep in my ears, and the lowing of oxen that I hear?" (I Samuel 15:14). Saul's response is that he brought the animals to sacrifice to God (15:15). His response is tantamount to saying, "I know what God wants and it is not what you, Samuel (the prophet), say. God desires sacrifices and I brought the best thing to sacrifice." God is not pleased. Samuel responds, "Does the Eternal delight in burnt offerings and sacrifices as much as in obedience to the Eternal's command? Surely, obedience is better than sacrifice, compliance than the fat of rams. For rebellion is like the sin of divination, defiance, like the iniquity of teraphim. Because you rejected the Eternal's command, God has rejected you as king" (15:22–23). This narrative becomes the paradigm of what will come. Every other time the prophets speak these words, they hyperlink back to this narrative. The prophets are saying to the people: You think you know what God wants (sacrifices and the other mitzvot), and you are wrong.

Speaking in the days of Uzziah, Jotham, Ahaz, and Hezekiah (ca. 760–720 BCE), Hosea minces no words in his admonition against sacrifices. The setting of his prophecy is the Northern Kingdom, and his message applies equally to Israel and Judah. Based on the superscription to his book (Hosea 1:1), he speaks at a time when the Northern Kingdom has either fallen or is about to fall to the Assyrians. He states, "For I [God] desire goodness, not sacrifice; obedience to God, rather than burnt offerings" (6:6). Though he is direct about what God does not want, the rest of Hosea's message is oblique. What does it mean to be good and obey God, if not to offer the sacrifices required by the covenant? The answer is not immediately clear.

Isaiah, son of Amoz, speaks sometime in the last half of the eighth century BCE.[17] He directs his comments toward Jerusalem and the Kingdom of Judah. He, too, reiterates this trope and lays out the many things that God does not want:

> "What need have I of all your sacrifices?" says the Eternal. "I am sated with burnt offerings of rams, and suet of fatlings, and blood of bulls; and I have no delight in lambs and he-goats. That you come to appear before Me—who asked that of you? Trample My courts no more; bringing oblations is futile, incense is offensive to Me. New moon and sabbath, proclaiming of solemnities,

assemblies with iniquity, I cannot abide. Your new moons and fixed seasons fill Me with loathing; they are become a burden to Me, I cannot endure them." (Isaiah 1:11–14)

Not only do we learn what God does not want, but Isaiah asks a very strange rhetorical question: Who asked you to do these things? To the average listener the answer would not make sense: God is the one who asked for sacrifices and offerings (Exodus 20:21). God told the people to come to the Temple three times a year and to bring gifts and sacrifices (Deuteronomy 16:16–17). Rosh Chodesh, the celebration of the new moon, was also to be celebrated with sacrifices and gifts (Numbers 28:11–15). But here God calls them assemblies of iniquity and a burden. God says to stop trampling (i.e., visiting) God's courts (i.e., the Temple). Why?

Amos prophesizes during the days of Uzziah (ca. 760 BCE). Noting the ambiguity of the term "Israel," his message applies equally to both kingdoms as he prophesies "concerning Israel" (Amos 1:1). His use of the trope provides more information: "I loathe, I spurn your festivals, I am not appeased by your solemn assemblies. If you offer Me burnt offerings—or your meal offerings—I will not accept them; I will pay no heed to your gifts of fatlings. Spare Me the sound of your hymns, and let Me not hear the music of your lutes. But let justice well up like water, righteousness like an unfailing stream" (5:21–24). Like Hosea and Isaiah, Amos notes that God does not want sacrifices, or festivals or assemblies, that is, the pilgrimage festivals and holidays (e.g., Exodus 23:15–18; Leviticus 23:5–6; Deuteronomy 16:1–17). Instead, God desires justice and righteousness.

In a similar vein, Micah, prophesizing in Judah during the latter half of the eighth century BCE, states, "[God] has told you . . . what is good, and what the Eternal requires of you: only to do justice and to love goodness, and to walk modestly (humbly) with your God" (Micah 6:8). Only in Micah do we get a full understanding of what is wrong. The prophets use the trope in question to tell the people that what they think they know about what God wants (sacrifices and the other mitzvot) is flat-out wrong. What God wants is a pure heart. God wants people who act morally, ethically, and righteously. The disruption they present comes into clearer focus: people must not act according to *keva*, the set actions; they must act with *kavanah*, the right intention. It is not enough to follow the letter of the law; they need to also be ethical people. They must not knowingly one day cheat the poor or give bribes to a judge and the next day offer a guilt sacrifice. For the prophets—speaking in the name of the Divine—such actions are duplicitous and not acceptable.

Yet, not wanting to change their ways, to be shown they have been mistaken, the people clung to their sacrifices. And so, destruction came, first to the Northern Kingdom and then to the Southern, and the people were exiled to the lands of Assyria and Babylon. The warnings of the preexilic prophets were not heeded; accordingly, the Israelites faced the loss of political autonomy while the leadership was exiled.

Conclusions: The Continued Prophetic Cry

The tension that developed surrounding the consequence of the prophets and the proper adherence to the laws ebbed and flowed throughout history. Born in a subsequent exile, Rabbinic Judaism grabbed on to the *keva* of the law and developed a large body of literature that explicated halachah. Rabbinic Judaism has come to stand for what Judaism looked like in the years after the close of the biblical canon.[18] As for the relevance of the prophets, at some point during the early first centuries CE, public reading of Torah was outlawed.[19] In its place, Jews began reading from the prophets in synagogue. When exactly the haftarah was set in stone is not known. This moment might be understood as another prophetic disruption as readings from prophets replaced the texts of Torah, including the Book of the Covenant, Deuteronomic Law Code, and Levitical Law Code. Could it be possible that the prophetic texts continued and reinforced their covert and overt messages of *kavanah* over *keva*? Of course, the prophetic texts were chosen for the haftarah for their thematic links to the various *parashiyot*. The knowledgeable Jew in synagogue would know that the words of the prophets they were hearing were really code for the words of Torah. In this respect, we might question whether the prophets really succeeded in replacing the Torah and its laws.[20] It is certainly tantalizing to think so.

It was not until the turn toward modernity, with the advent of prophetic Judaism in the late eighteenth and early nineteenth centuries, that the prophets again found their voices heeded.[21] The concept of prophetic Judaism has deep ties to contemporary Reform Judaism. It champions the universalist, ethical proclamations of the prophets over and against the rigid confines of halachah that have come to characterize Rabbinic Judaism and the more orthodox branches of contemporary Judaism. Peter Berkowitz of the Hoover Institute notes that prophetic Judaism resonates with Reform Jews who seek to connect with a part of their religion that reflects their liberal and democratic ideals.[22] Prophetic Judaism, championed by Rabbi Abraham Joshua Heschel, represents a movement away from the laws and legalism of Torah toward something more meaningful, a *kavanah* the early prophets would recognize as deep commitment to morality and conscience.

While there are ways to find meaning within the mitzvot, for many Reform Jews the antiquity of and embedded misogyny within the laws render them incontrovertibly at odds with the sensibilities of modernity. Instead, many find ways to express their Judaism through "Jewish values" rather than mitzvot. Here we might think of the many bet mitzvah[23] projects in which students volunteer at homeless shelters (welcoming the stranger), raise money for the underprivileged (taking care of the widow, orphan, and stranger), or raise awareness for an environmental cause (care for the earth). Such projects are often favored in liberal congregations over and against projects wherein an individual commits to take on one of the 613 mitzvot, where one might journal what it is like to keep kosher for a month, wear a *kippah* or tzitzit in public, or commit to keeping Shabbat. The tension that exists today between actions driven by values and actions driven by adherence to mitzvot is not new. While we might understand it today as epitomized by two extremes, that of prophetic Judaism and Orthodox Judaism, it is the result of a disruption that arose long before and remains embedded in our sacred texts.

NOTES

1. The references and commentary within this essay are drawn from a mix of commentaries on the prophets, some leaning more toward the scholarly and arcane. For the interested lay reader, accessible information on the individual prophets and their messages can be found in the introduction to each prophetic book found in the following sources: Adele Berlin and Marc Zvi Brettler, *Jewish Study Bible* (Oxford: Oxford University Press, 2004); Victor

Matthews, *The Social World of the Hebrew Prophets* (Grand Rapids, MI: Baker Academic, 2012); and the well-loved work *The Prophets* (New York: Harper & Row, 1962) by Abraham Joshua Heschel.

2. Matthews, *Social World of the Hebrew Prophets*, 19–37.

3. Each prophet has a call narrative. Moses's call narrative is the longest, whether this is because he is the first or the most important is hard to say. The call narrative includes the following elements: (1) a theophany, (2) a demurral or refusal, (3) God's resolution to the prophet's excuse, (4) an assignment of a mission, and (5) a sign (Matthews, *Social World of the Hebrew Prophets*, 39–40).

4. Author's translation. Unless otherwise noted, all other translations are from Plaut or NJPS.

5. The relationship between these laws has been the subject of inquiry since the Talmud. Were the laws meant to stand alone, be replacements of that which came before, or revisions of older laws? For a discussion of the Sinai covenant and law, see Joseph Blenkinsopp, *The Pentateuch: An Introduction to the First Five Books of the Bible* (New York: Doubleday, 1992), 183–228. Furthermore, the question arises as to whether Moses received some or all of the laws at Sinai, since the Book of Leviticus suggests that he received some laws in the Tent of Meeting. A traditionalist approach to this question cites the Talmud: "Rabbi Yishmael says, 'The generalities were spoken at Sinai, and the specifics at the Tent of Meeting.' Rabbi Akiva says, 'Both the generalities and the specifics were [first] spoken at Sinai. They were reiterated at the Tent of Meeting and stated a third time at the steppes of Moab'" (Babylonian Talmud, *Z'vachim* 115b).

6. For a discussion of the dating of the Book of the Covenant and the relationship to other ancient Near Eastern laws, see Carol Meyers, *Exodus*, New Cambridge Bible Commentary (New York: Cambridge University Press, 2005), 181–87 and sources therein.

7. John Collins, *A Short Introduction to the Hebrew Bible* (Minneapolis: Fortress Press, 2007), 86.

8. Elements of earlier Hittite treaties, as well as contemporary Assyrian vassal treaties of Esarhaddon, were used as a frame for the Book of Deuteronomy. See Collins, *A Short Introduction*, 84–86; Moshe Weinfeld, *Deuteronomy and the Deuteronomic School* (Winona Lake, IN: Eisenbrauns, 1992), 59–157.

9. See in Deuteronomy the preamble (1:1–5), historical prologue (1:6–4:9), stipulations (5:1–26:19), blessings and curses (27:1–28:68), reading and deposition (31:9–29), and witnesses (32:1–47), according to Collins, *A Short Introduction*, 84.

10. This section of the text is included in the second paragraph of the *Sh'ma*.

11. For an overview of Leviticus, see Jacob Milgrom, *Leviticus 1–16*, Anchor Bible Commentary (New Haven, CT: Yale University Press, [1998] 2009),

28–128; Baruch Levine, introduction to *The JPS Torah Commentary: Leviticus* (Philadelphia: Jewish Publication Society, 1989), xi–xli.

12. Milgrom, *Leviticus 1–16*, 49.

13. Levine comments on the link between land pollution and exile (Levine, *Leviticus*, 123). For an overview of the various positions regarding the dating of Leviticus, see Levine, *Leviticus*, xxix–xxx.

14. Archaeological evidence for the existence of the United Kingdom is still being sought. Evidence of the Divided Kingdom is much more abundant. On the correlation between the biblical text and historical events, see Eric Cline, *Biblical Archaeology: A Very Short Introduction* (Oxford: Oxford University Press, 2009), especially Chapter 8.

15. Dan and Bethel and the shrines located there represented the northern and southern extents of the Kingdom of Israel (I Kings 12:25–30).

16. The events of 701 BCE were enshrined on the walls of King Sennacherib's palace at Nineveh. These reliefs can be seen in the British Museum. A replica of the walls showing the siege of Lachish can also be seen in the Israel Museum.

17. Christopher B. Hays, "The Formation of the Book of Isaiah in Its Ancient Near Eastern Contexts," *Hebrew Bible and Ancient Israel* 6, no. 1 (2017): 1–6; David Petersen, *The Prophetic Literature: An Introduction* (Louisville: Westminster John Knox, 2002), 47–50.

18. The Mishnah was closed in the year 200 CE, while the Babylonian Talmud was finished sometime in the fifth century CE.

19. On the tradition of reading Torah in services, the recitation of haftarah, and the use of haftarah when Torah was outlawed, see Michael Fishbane, *The JPS Bible Commentary: Haftarot* (Philadelphia: Jewish Publication Society, 2002), xix–xxxii.

20. *Pirkei Avot* is a collection of ethics, morals, and teachings. It is part of the Mishnah. The texts of *Pirkei Avot* concern many of the same aims as those of the prophets of the eighth century BCE, guiding the people Israel toward proper behavior. Yet, the sayings in *Pirkei Avot* are those of the early Rabbinic voices rather than the prophets themselves.

21. While the origins of mystical Judaism can trace their roots to the prophetic texts, the texts were not read for their insights into ethical teachings, but rather as a guide for how to come closer to God. Daniel Matt, *The Essential Kabbalah: The Heart of Jewish Mysticism* (San Francisco: Harper Collins, 2007); Pinchas Giller, *Kabbalah: A Guide for the Perplexed* (New York: Continuum, 2011).

22. See Peter Berkowitz on prophetic Judaism, https://tikvahfund.org/library/prophetic-judaism.

23. Bet mitzvah is used here as the gender-inclusive term.

FOR FURTHER READING

Berlin, Adele, and Marc Zvi Brettler. *The Jewish Study Bible*. Oxford: Oxford University Press, 2004.

Blenkinsopp, Joseph. *The Pentateuch: An Introduction to the First Five Books of the Bible*. New York: Doubleday, 1992.

Cline, Eric. *Biblical Archaeology: A Very Short Introduction*. Oxford: Oxford University Press, 2009.

Collins, John. *A Short Introduction to the Hebrew Bible*. Minneapolis: Fortress Press, 2007.

Fishbane, Michael. *The JPS Bible Commentary: Haftarot*. Philadelphia: Jewish Publication Society, 2002.

Giller, Pinchas. *Kabbalah: A Guide for the Perplexed*. New York: Continuum, 2011.

Hays, Christopher B. "The Formation of the Book of Isaiah in Its Ancient Near Eastern Contexts." *Hebrew Bible and Ancient Israel* 6, no. 1 (2017): 1–6.

Heschel, Abraham Joshua. *The Prophets*. New York: Harper & Row, 1962.

Levine, Baruch. *The JPS Torah Commentary: Leviticus*, xi–xli. Philadelphia: Jewish Publication Society, 1989.

Matt, Daniel. *The Essential Kabbalah: The Heart of Jewish Mysticism*. San Francisco: Harper Collins, 2007.

Matthews, Victor. *The Social World of the Hebrew Prophets*. Grand Rapids, MI: Baker Academic, 2012.

Meyers, Carol. *Exodus*. New Cambridge Bible Commentary. New York: Cambridge University Press, 2005.

Milgrom, Jacob. *Leviticus 1–16*. Anchor Bible Commentary. New Haven, CT: Yale University Press, [1998] 2009.

Petersen, David. *The Prophetic Literature: An Introduction*. Louisville: Westminster John Knox, 2002.

2

586 BCE
Defeat and the Emergence
of Jewish Peoplehood

Jacob L. Wright, PhD

THE YEAR 586 BCE marks the most dramatic disruption in Jewish history.[1] In the preceding decade, Babylon had besieged Jerusalem, and the Kingdom of Judah had suffered many deaths and deportations. But now the defeat was absolute and unmitigated. As the capital was breached and burned, its palaces and holy places were looted and then razed to the ground. Most of the elites were either executed or exiled, while much of the remaining population—having survived years of military conflict and the disease and famine that accompanied it—vacated their homeland and sought refuge in neighboring lands.

The suffering during these years would have been intense, yet Jewish communities have faced much more traumatic violence over the millennia. What makes 586 BCE so pivotal is not the intensity of the injury, but the corpus of writings and a new collective identity that emerged in response to it. This was the moment that Judeans became Jews, and without it, there would be no Jewish history, or Jewish thought—or other moments of disruption that reshaped this collective identity and produced new corpora of writings.

The corpus of writings from the disruption of 586 BCE—what Jews call the *Tanach*, Christians the "Old Testament," and academics the "Hebrew Bible"—responded to a revolutionary new question: What does it means to be a people—not a kingdom, city, clan, or ethnicity, but *a people*? In other words, we are talking about a political community that embraces many different cities, clans, ethnicities, etc. and may have kingdoms in their collective past but that now—thanks to new institutions and survival strategies—does not depend on statehood and territorial sovereignty.

In wondering what it means to be a people and how a people can not only survive but also flourish under foreign rule, the biblical authors discovered a new collective identity that was foundational for the work of the Rabbis after the destruction of the Second Temple. This identity— what we may call "peoplehood"[2]—is crucial to understanding Judaism's distinctive character as well as its manner of survival from antiquity to the present.

Exodus from an Old Order

The story of Judah's recovery from the Babylonian devastation is not one of a phoenix rising from the ashes, liberating itself from foreign bondage, and restoring what had been demolished. Instead, we witness the gradual exodus from an old order and the creation of something altogether new.

Prior to the radical disruption in 586 BCE, kings like David, Solomon, and Hezekiah had defined the destinies of Judah's families and clans, its cities and towns, and its Temple and priests. In its constitution and function, the kingdom resembled its rivals throughout the region: state and society worked together like well-oiled machinery whose primary purpose was to preserve a political order with the palace at its center. What held together competing communities was their shared duty to the throne, not covenantal commitments to their God and to each other. Collective identity was demarcated in terms of physical borders with forts and garrisons. A Judean was thus one who lived in Judah. The Jew had yet to be invented.[3]

When the Kingdom of Judah fell, there was little left either in structure or ideology that could reconstitute its clans and communities. As the mother of invention, necessity forced survivors to turn their attention elsewhere as they struggled to build a new existence. In both the Diaspora and their homeland, they now lived in "shadows of the empire," owing allegiance to a foreign king. Without a Davidic dynasty to define their destinies, the Judean clans and communities initially went their separate ways.

Current critical evaluations of biblical and external sources yield a new understanding of what brought some of those clans and communities back together for the first time in this new post-monarchic period.[4] Central to these developments was the message of an otherwise unknown prophet from the sixth century named Haggai. Pointing to the ruins of the Temple in Jerusalem, the prophet declared:

> Is it a time for you to dwell in your paneled houses,
> while this House [i.e., the Temple] is lying in ruins?
> Now thus said *YHVH* of Hosts:
> Consider how you have been faring!
> You have sowed much and brought in little;
> you eat without being satisfied;
> you drink without getting your fill;
> you clothe yourselves, but no one gets warm;
> and one who earns anything, earns it for a leaky purse. . . .
> Go up to the hills and get timber, and rebuild the House;
> then I will look on it with favor and I will be glorified—said *YHVH*.
> (Haggai 1:4–6, 8)[5]

What is most significant about Haggai's words is seemingly trivial: the use of the plural "you" in his address (something lost in translation). Haggai spoke to "this people" (*haam hazeh*) as a whole, not solely to their leaders.

This is a remarkable development. The construction of temples in the ancient world was conventionally the duty of monarchs, as the building of Solomon's Temple also illustrates. In Haggai, however, we see the community coming together and building on their own.

To be sure, facts on the ground were often demoralizing. The new Temple, completed in 515–516 BCE, was but a humble replica of its former glory, and the economy did not take a sudden turn for the better, as Haggai had promised. Yet this construction project, even though it was modest, catalyzed the growth of a new communal self-understanding, and what set it all in motion were the spoken words of an otherwise unknown prophet.

The population of Judah would go on to initiate other building ventures, such as the repairs of Jerusalem's ramparts during the days of Nehemiah.[6] As they participated in these communal projects, they began to think—and write—in new ways about their past, about their place in the world, and about what it means to be a people.

A National Narrative for North and South

What unifies our history? What thread connects the dismal present to our illustrious past? Without our fearless kings, formidable cities, valorous warriors, and all the glory and grandeur they brought to us, who are we? At the same time prophets were inspiring Judeans to rebuild through their spoken word, scribes in their midst were busy composing and compiling a corpus of biblical writings that addresses these foundational questions. And just as their communities rebuilt among the ruins and razed foundations of a bygone era, these scribes worked by collecting and expanding materials that they inherited from earlier generations.

Since the ninth century BCE, two small kingdoms had existed side by side in Canaan's central hill country: the Northern Kingdom of Israel and the Southern Kingdom of Judah. In 722 BCE the Assyrian Empire destroyed Samaria, the capital city of the Northern Kingdom, and transformed it into an imperial province without a native king. For centuries the Northern Kingdom had overshadowed its Southern neighbor. Once it was gone, Davidic dynasts ruling in Jerusalem seized the opportunity to expand their influence in the region, taking the prominent place that Samaria had vacated. Judah managed to hold on for over a century, and it was during this politically volatile period, following the Assyrian conquest of Israel in 722 BCE, that some of the most important biblical writings emerged.[7]

The biblical account of Israel's and Judah's shared history begins with the creation of the world in Genesis and ends with the destruction of Jerusalem in the Book of Kings. This composite work, which I call the "National Narrative," evolved over the ages from smaller, originally independent pieces.[8] Generations of anonymous scribes collected these pieces, embroidered them with new details, and wove them into an elaborate literary tapestry.

The National Narrative portrays the relationship between the two kingdoms, Israel and Judah, and their tragic ends. It not only blends their separate stories; it also sets them in relation to an earlier "United Monarchy" from the time of David and Solomon (ca. 1000 BCE). But its most significant achievement goes beyond this political unity, imagining a people that evolved from an extended family and existed for many generations before the emergence of the monarchy and the establishment of a centralized state.

As readers, we follow the biblical story from the evolution of that family to the formation of two kingdoms. But as historians, we discover that at the beginning there was not one family or one nation, as the Bible portrays it, but a wide array of unrelated clans that would later populate these two kingdoms. In their efforts to consolidate one people from these two kingdoms, the biblical writers traced these clans back to common ancestors.

Scholars are now confident that much of what became the National Narrative originated in the Northern Kingdom of Israel.[9] After its downfall, scribes began to collect the fragments of their past and piece them together to tell stories of their people. These are familiar tales of a family becoming a nation and of liberated slaves migrating to a new land. Although Northerners composed the earliest drafts of these tales, much of their poignancy and power is due to the work of Southerners who, in response to their own traumatic defeat and disruption, created a larger narrative by connecting the disparate pasts of Israel and Judah.

The National Narrative as we know it is therefore a work from the North that has been filtered through, and decisively shaped by, the experience of the South. North and South had long been divided, and what propelled the composition of this work—and for that matter, much of the Bible—is a vision that the populations of these two conquered kingdoms could, in fact, be one people.

Admitting Defeat

According to the Italian Jewish writer Primo Levi, being a survivor is about bearing witness to the past, not consigning it to oblivion.[10] The testimony is painful for those living in a new age. Life is easier if the trauma is forgotten. Nevertheless, the biblical authors saw themselves as descendants of past generations and their mistakes. As they fashioned a grand monument to their own defeat, they also forged a template for a new identity.

Drafted in anticipation of and then in reaction to the nation's political demise and downfall, the National Narrative from Genesis to Kings tells the story of a people, its deity, its territories, and the various communities and institutions that comprised it. Even when celebrating liberation and triumph, this narrative resists nostalgia for forfeited glory by asserting the nation's culpability for its tragic fate.

This work does not have a happy ending. Its conclusion describes Judah's destruction and exile (II Kings 25), and it has nothing to say about the period of reconstruction that followed. The narrative begins with inspiring promises and auspicious triumphs: the foundation of a family in Genesis, the liberation of a nation in Exodus, and the conquest of Canaan in Joshua. Yet things go awry thereafter: the nation abandons its founding charter, and after generations of enervating conflict, decides it wants for itself a monarchy—"like the nations around us" (I Samuel 8:5). The account underscores the trials and tribulations that David and Solomon had inflicted on the nation. Later, the monarchy cleaves into two competing kingdoms, which wage war with each other for generations. Eventually the Assyrian and Babylonian armies conquer these two states and deport their inhabitants. In the end, nothing remains.

Such is the biblical version of Israel's and Judah's history, and this National Narrative comprises the first half of the Hebrew Bible (from Genesis to the Book of Kings). This account of a people's past is exceptional for the ancient world, not only in its length and subject matter but also in its basic structure. The pattern of most inscriptions begins with defeat and ends in triumph. The biblical narrative presents the opposite, with the liberation and success at the beginning and destruction and downfall at the end.[11]

The prophetic writings (Isaiah, Jeremiah, Ezekiel, etc.) not only make the downfall of the two kingdoms the centerpiece of their penetrating discourses; they place responsibility for it squarely on the people. By identifying the sins of the past, they lay out survival strategies for the future.

Defeat, life in exile, and national restoration are also formative themes in the final section of the canon (the *K'tuvim*, or "Writings"). The books in this collection depict the consequences of defeat and lay out means of living in a new age of foreign rule. Lamentations mourns and protests the disaster that its five poems graphically portray. Daniel and Esther envision life in exile. Chronicles recounts the story of the nation's rise and fall, albeit from a very different perspective. Ezra-Nehemiah tells of exiles returning to Judah and rebuilding the ruins of Jerusalem; this restoration proceeds, however, in the shadow of foreign hegemony. The order of the Psalms follows the nation's history, with the final ones expressing hope for return and restoration. The Book of Job describes individual loss and adversity in a manner that mirrors the nation's collective experience.

The only works that do not relate explicitly to defeat are Proverbs, Ecclesiastes, and the Song of Songs, but these works are important parts of the project of peoplehood by focusing on interpersonal relations.

The Bible's attention to defeat is truly remarkable. Most ancient societies consigned their downfall to oblivion, and with few exceptions, the vanquished vanished from the historical record.[12] In the cases of Israel and Judah, imperial armies brought an end to the ancient folkways that defined life in those kingdoms. But instead of denying or diminishing their defeat, the biblical authors turned that existential disruption or rupture into an opportunity to pursue something new and more enduring.

The Primacy of Peoplehood

The Bible represents an interweaving of two master narratives. There is the familiar monarchic story, familiar because of its ubiquity in human civilization. It lingers on the exploits of the great men (and occasionally, great women) who have defined history—their architectural achievements, their military triumphs, and the powerful states they created.[13] The second, however, is something altogether new and unique: the people's story. With it, the biblical authors undercut the monarchic story and made their most enduring contribution. While acknowledging the benefits of statehood, they relegated it to a supporting role and insisted on the *primacy of peoplehood*.

The biblical authors articulated, for the first time in history, a cardinal political distinction: the nation and the state are two separate entities.[14] Affirming the priority and primacy of the former, it removes any doubt that Israel (including both North and South) could still be Israel even when it lost its territorial sovereignty and was dispersed abroad.

By virtue of a covenant with their God, Israel had become a people (i.e., nation) long before it established a kingdom (i.e., state). Although this narrative runs counter to what we know today about Israel's political evolution, the biblical authors wanted their readers to understand that with the help of their narrative and the divine laws embedded in it, a vanquished and exiled population can unite and flourish as a nation when imperial domination prohibited the reestablishment of the sovereign state.

The Bible does not cast aspersions on statehood per se. To the contrary, the critiques by the scribes who produced this corpus reflect their solicitude for a state that is properly governed.

Statehood still has a purpose—namely, to serve and protect the nation. It is a means to an end. When it becomes the end and crowning glory, it swallows up the nation so that nothing remains when it is conquered.

A basic truth that the Bible illustrates across its many chapters is that all states end up either being conquered or collapsing under their own weight. Statehood may be the ideal. But in a world dominated by superpowers, native sovereignty is not a given for a small nation. The Bible formulates an alternative to statehood—a Plan B. What its authors deemed to be most urgent, and what occupied their attention, is the constitution for a new form of political community that could persist through the repeated rise and fall of kingdoms.

As a project of peoplehood, the formation of the biblical corpus is unprecedented. Nowhere else in the ancient world do we witness an effort—and such an elaborate and collaborative effort at that—first to document and depict one's own defeat and then to use that narrative history as a means of envisioning a new model of community, one that was more resilient to political misfortune and that could rise above deep social divisions.

The biblical authors were guided by the intuition that their communities would survive conquest by imperial powers when all their members could claim a piece of the pie, when they had not only a spiritual vision that unified them, but also material incentives to participate in the life of a larger political community that they called *B'nei Yisrael* ("the Children of Israel," or "Israelites"). The foundation for their new project was a body of writings that they collected, edited, and expanded to create an exceptionally rich corpus of literature that attracted communities of readers and formed them into a people of the book.

Working with stylus and scroll, they created what we may call a movable monument, and the fabric and texture of what they produced is an important part of their agenda. Their model of community embraced diversity, an ideal exemplified in the weaving together of competing ideologies and perspectives, diverse sets of laws, conflicting narratives, disparate ancestors, rival territories, and so on. Although the Bible is heavily redacted, it does not speak with a single voice. Instead of one view, the biblical authors set forth a common text.

A New Theater for Public Life

In the post-monarchic period (as noted about Haggai in the sixth century BCE), building activities assumed the formative role previously exercised by battles and war efforts as the central stage of communal collaboration. This shift marks the beginning of what was to become (and remain until the present) a centerpiece of Jewish life: collective building projects and individual philanthropy, with the names of the sponsors and contributors publicly displayed and commemorated (see, for example, the lists of names throughout Ezra-Nehemiah). This choice of a new theater for public life—building sites instead of battlefields—was not a natural one; it owed much to the initiatives of communal leaders like Haggai and Nehemiah, but even more to the nameless scribes who shaped the biblical corpus.

In the days of Haggai, scribes were fleshing out the Book of Exodus with passages that promoted ideals of volunteerism. The passages imagine an ideal past when the Israelites, during the Exodus from Egypt, come together to construct a dwelling, or Tabernacle, for *YHVH* (Exodus 25–40). As a communal undertaking, it marks their first achievement as a nation after their liberation from bondage.

In this imagined past, the people contribute to the construction on their own accord. Moses does not need to apply pressure or make threats; he simply summons the nation's members to donate precious objects: "Everyone who is of a willing hearted shall bring them. . . . And let all among you who are wise/skilled come and make all that *YHVH* has commanded" (Exodus 25:2, 35:10). The call is heeded widely: "And they came, both men and women, as many as were of willing heart . . .

and all brought brooches and earrings . . . and all sorts of gold objects" (35:21–22).[15] The response is so enthusiastic that Moses must order the people to stop coming.

The attention to women in these texts and other postexilic texts is noteworthy. In comparison with war efforts, building projects offered more opportunities to participate in public life. As when a sparsely populated ship sets sail on stormy seas, all hands were needed on deck. Not only were women's contributions necessary for the survival of their communities; they also had much to teach men about collaborating and flourishing in a world in which the cards were stacked against them. As the National Narrative presents, Israel owes its origins to a collaborative effort of generations of women—from the Matriarchs of Genesis to the women in the first chapters of Exodus (the midwives, Moses's mother and sister, and the Pharaoh's daughter) who work together to undermine a genocidal decree (Exodus 1–2).

In the liturgy of later Jewish synagogues, the story of the Tabernacle in Exodus came to be read with the story of how King Solomon, centuries later, built the Temple. The combination of these epochal episodes should cause one to compare and contrast: on the Torah side, the people as a whole (including both men and women) came together to build the Tabernacle in the wilderness; in the Book of Kings, a male monarch built the Temple at the pinnacle of political power. One was achieved through voluntary action, the other by conscripting labor with the arm of the state.

Sociologists make a basic distinction between conscription and volunteerism: kings and states conscript bodies and resources; communities and nations volunteer their time and donate their resources. A nation exists only to the extent that groups are willing to come together for voluntary collective action.[16] With this goal in mind, the biblical authors created a past that long precedes the palace. Their elaborate narrative of the nation's beginnings in the wilderness portrays the Israelites, soon after their liberation from bondage in Egypt, coming together to build a dwelling for the deity who had delivered them from their affliction.

The impoverished community in the province of Judah, which was struggling to rebuild this deity's dwelling after imperial armies had torn it to the ground, should know that their project has an ancient precedent. What they were doing now is what their ancestors had done long ago at Mount Sinai, at the moment it all began. In their literary labor of constructing this grand narrative, the biblical authors refashioned and reframed their community's physical labor—and the general tedium of this post-monarchic age—as a new, and auspicious, chapter in the nation's ongoing story.

From Ezra to the Rabbis

The end of the Hebrew Bible as we have it resumes the National Narrative after the rupture of 586 BCE. It begins with the rise of the new Persian Empire. It culminates in the time of Ezra and Nehemiah in the fifth century BCE, a period recognized today as pivotal for the formation of the Torah and the Bible as a whole. According to Ezra-Nehemiah (the biblical book that depicts this period of the reconstruction after the exile), the inhabitants of Judah not only rebuilt the Temple, but also reoriented and united themselves around a shared text. Having restored Jerusalem's walls under Nehemiah (Nehemiah 1–7), the people gather around the book of the Torah that a priest and scribe named Ezra introduces publicly (Nehemiah 8).

It is at this point in the biblical story that the focus on peoplehood comes most explicitly to the fore, with the Torah at its center. The scribes responsible for Nehemiah 8 keep their attention focused on the people: the people ask Ezra to bring the book of the Torah; and the people respond to the reading. When Ezra opens the book (or scroll), all the people—men, women, and those with understanding—rise, and after a blessing is pronounced, they respond "Amen, Amen!" Then they all bow and prostrate themselves "before *YHVH*" (Nehemiah 8:6). They all listen attentively to the reading that Ezra and his associates read and expound. This emotion-laden day ends with celebration "because they understood the words that [Ezra and others] had imparted to them" (8:12).

As this highly symbolic account continues, the community learns to read on their own. First, the leaders gather around Ezra on the following day. Later, they are reading and studying without his help and also carrying out the teachings that they discover in it. The text is firmly in their hands, and together they have embraced a groundbreaking paradigm for their future as a people (Nehemiah 8:13–18).

Many today may find it difficult to appreciate the dramatic significance of this account. Ritual reading of a sacred text is not unusual for many of us. But the reason why that is so is that this account and the wider book of Ezra-Nehemiah have directly informed the shaping of Rabbinic Judaism. The practice so familiar to us was born at this juncture. What we witness in the scene depicted in Nehemiah 8 is nothing less than the birth of "the People of the Book," with a new approach to education that informs this text-based identity.

Conclusions

In grappling with the consequences of defeat, the authors of our biblical texts envisioned a new ideal: peoplehood. And in doing so, they resorted to something no army could eradicate: language and the power of the written word. We saw how the words of the prophet Haggai inspired the survivors to rebuild, vesting power in the community as a whole, with scribes from this community curating a corpus of writings as a center of the community.

The writings these survivors produced in response to crisis and disruption have been read and studied for millennia. These facts bear witness to the truth of Bulwer-Lytton's maxim that "the pen is mightier than the sword."[17] Across the globe, communities of readers, inspired by the Bible's model of community, have established robust and durable identities that could sustain their members in the bleakest of circumstances.[17] Likewise, influential political thinkers have found in the Bible alternatives to the political status quo—forms of political community that assign power to *the people* as a whole rather than to monarchies, aristocracies, and ecclesial institutions. These historically decisive developments deserve our renewed attention in a time of great instability and uncertainty.

It was only during the post-destruction period that our ancestors, having forfeited autonomy and territorial sovereignty, needed to create for themselves a space in a foreign empire. The space they carved out is not so much territorial-political as it is social, one demarcated by practice and behavior. The tools they used for demarcating this social space are texts.

Why and how did defeat spark off a project of peoplehood in Israel and Judah but did not do the same elsewhere in the ancient world? We can only hypothesize.[18] One thing seems clear: it is not because unique intuitions (such as "monotheism") reverberated throughout the societt ies of Israel or Judah. Rather, the biblical corpus represents the work of a handful of anonymous, countercultural thinkers who pushed against the status quo and sought real, pragmatic truths that could sustain their communities in a world governed by foreign powers.

Consider, by contrast, the case of the great world empires that conquered Israel and Judah. "Look on my Works, ye Mighty, and despair!" Such protestations notwithstanding, "nothing beside remains," as Shelley points out in his *Ozymandias*. The written records of Assyria, Babylon, and Persia were left buried in the ashes until they were recovered through archaeological excavations in recent times. These texts were abandoned because they represented solely the perspective of states and temples and ruling elites, all of which perished together with their societies. Moreover, until recent excavations, we knew of many small kingdoms and peoples throughout the ancient Near East only because the Bible mentions them.

My appreciation of the Bible as a project of peoplehood departs significantly from the academic consensus, which still takes its cue from the groundbreaking work of the influential German scholar Julius Wellhausen (1844–1918). In a world ruled by empires, Wellhausen insisted, there could be no nations, only religions. Even so, the religion of the Bible was not what it once was; it had evolved from "its original and natural role" in the kingdom. The symbiosis of the national and the spiritual ceased, and in the process, religious life assumed a monotone, rational, legalistic character.

While Wellhausen did much to advance our understanding of the Bible and its origins, he was deeply misguided, I would suggest, when it came to interpreting his findings. Rather than stripping Israel of its political character and reducing it to a religious sect, the biblical authors responded to military defeat by demonstrating that their vanquished communities could, even without a king, still be a diverse and dispersed, yet unified, people.

What we witness in the Bible, then, is the genesis of a nation, not its death and replacement by "religion," as Wellhausen supposed. Of course, rituals and religious activities played an important part in this project of peoplehood, but in reducing the complexity of the biblical corpus to the realm of religion, scholars have neglected its most distinctive and important features toward building peoplehood.[19]

NOTES

1. I want to thank Rabbi Stanley M. Davids, Dr. Leah Hochman, and Rabbi Tamara Cohn Eskenazi, PhD, for their very helpful feedback on the drafts of this chapter.
2. On Jewish peoplehood, see the diverse publications and perspectives curated by the Center for Jewish Peoplehood Education: https://jpeoplehood.org.
3. Shaye J. D. Cohen, *The Beginnings of Jewishness: Boundaries, Varieties, Uncertainties* (Berkeley: University of California Press, 1999). Much of what Cohen shows for Rabbinic developments are found already in Ezra-Nehemiah, the biblical book that describes how Judeans became Jews; see Tamara Cohn Eskenazi, *Ezra*, Anchor Bible Commentary (New Haven, CT: Yale University Press, 2023).
4. See the range of studies on these developments in Oded Lipschits and Manfred Oeming, eds., *Judah and the Judeans in the Persian Period* (Winona Lake, IN: Eisenbrauns, 2006).
5. Author's translations.
6. I explore the formation of this work in my book *Rebuilding Identity: The Nehemiah Memoir and Its Earliest Readers* (Berlin: De Gruyter, 2004).
7. See discussion in Reinhard G. Kratz, *Historical and Biblical Israel* (Oxford: Oxford University Press, 2016); and Carly Crouch, *The Making of Israel* (Leiden: Brill, 2014).
8. I treat the formation of this narrative in my forthcoming book *Why the Bible Began: An Alternative History of Scripture and its Origins* (Cambridge: Cambridge University Press, 2023). See also Jacob L. Wright, *War, Memory, and National Identity in the Hebrew Bible* (Cambridge: Cambridge University Press, 2020); and *David, King of Israel, and Caleb in Biblical Memory* (Cambridge: Cambridge University Press, 2014).
9. See Daniel Fleming, *The Legacy of Israel in Judah's Bible* (Cambridge: Cambridge University Press, 2012).
10. Primo Levi, *Survival at Auschwitz* (New York: Simon & Schuster, 1996) originally published in Italian as *Se questo è un uomo* in 1947 and translated into English in 1959.
11. See discussion in Jacob L. Wright, "The Commemoration of Defeat and the Formation of a Nation in the Hebrew Bible," *Prooftexts* 29 (2009): 433–72.
12. See Jessica H. Clark and Brian Turner, *Brill's Companion to Military Defeat in Ancient Mediterranean Society* (Leiden: Brill, 2018).

13. This monarchic narrative provided the point of departure for messianism in later Judaism and especially in Christianity.

14. I introduced this point in my essay "The Commemoration of Defeat" (n. 13) and developed it throughout *David, King of Israel* (n. 10).

15. Homi K. Bhabha, *Nation and Narration* (London: Routledge, 1990); see especially Ernest Renan's lecture "What Is a Nation?" from 1882, which is republished and interpreted in this volume on pages 9–22.

16. *Richelieu; Or the Conspiracy* (1839), act 2, scene 2.

17. Fernando F. Segovia and Tat-siong Benny Liew eds., *Colonialism and the Bible: Contemporary Reflections from the Global South* (Lanham, MD: Lexington Books, 2018).

18. I explore this question at length in my forthcoming book *Why the Bible Began* (see note 8, above).

19. On the influence of Wellhausen's paradigm of religion replacing state/nation, see the introduction and conclusion to my *War, Memory, and National Identity in the Hebrew Bible* (see note 8, above), 1–11 and 247–250.

PART TWO

Rabbinic Disruptions

3

Christianity
A Pauline Revolution

Rabbi Joshua D. Garroway, PhD

WHY DO BAD THINGS happen to good people? A timeless question that hardly seems out of place in a collection of essays about disruptions in the history of Jewish thought. But what has it to do with the present subject, the theology of Paul? In fact, this question provides a natural starting place for such an investigation, for in order to make sense of Paul, one must first make sense of Jesus; to make sense of Jesus, one must reckon with ancient apocalypticism; and to understand apocalypticism, one starts with the question "Why do bad things happen to good people?"

Ancient Jews struggled with the apparent injustice of God, just as we do today. Among the most well-known solutions to the problem was afforded by the author of Deuteronomy, who famously insisted that bad things do not, in fact, happen to good people. To the extent that goodness is measured by a Jew's obedience to the commandments of God, God rewards good people and punishes the bad—without exception. Obedience to God merits fertility, long life, abundance, and security, while disobedience results in barrenness, famine, illness, and ruin. If it seems as though a good person is suffering, rest assured the suffering is warranted. Bad things do not happen to a person who is truly good.

Many modern Jews find this notion of theological quid pro quo unconvincing, even offensive. So did many ancients. In Job and Ecclesiastes, the Hebrew Bible preserves two such defiant voices. Job offers the story of an obedient man who nevertheless suffers terribly at God's hands. Ecclesiastes proclaims more matter-of-factly that Deuteronomy has it wrong: "There are righteous people who receive what is due for

the wicked, and wicked people who receive what is due the righteous"
(Ecclesiastes 8:14).[1] Unfortunately, neither book has much to say about
why people appear to suffer undeservedly. God is just, they insist, even as
they acknowledge that human experience indicates otherwise.

Beginning in the second century BCE, an alternative viewpoint
emerged among Jewish thinkers who had become frustrated with the
ongoing subjugation of Jews to foreign nations. Their concern was less
the unjust suffering of individuals than the unjust suffering of Israel.
Even if the sack of Jerusalem in 586 BCE had been warranted because of
the nation's sins, they reckoned, surely the punishment had lasted too
long. By the beginning of the second century BCE, Jerusalem had passed
from the control of Babylonians to the Persians to the Greeks. Given
these centuries of dispossession, how could anyone continue to say that
God was treating the Jewish people fairly? Their answer to this question
was as simple as it was bold: God cannot be accused of treating Jews
unfairly because God, in fact, is not in control of the world—at least not
now. God had ceded control centuries ago to evil, demonic forces that
currently govern the world through evil human minions like the Babylonians, Persians, and Greeks. Explanations for why God relinquished
control and whether God did so voluntarily varied among these thinkers,
but they all agreed that God's lengthy absence had allowed the world to
go to pot: wicked nations were prospering while God's nation, Israel,
was not.

Hope soothed the despair, however. Unbearable as the current state
of affairs had become, these thinkers assumed that divine redemption
was on the horizon. One day soon, they figured, God would return tri-
umphantly to topple the demons on high and, in turn, execute justice
on earth by overthrowing foreign kingdoms, gathering the dispersed of
Israel, and restoring the nation to native rule in its own land. This political redemption would be part and parcel of a cosmic redemption for the
entire world, in which God would raise the dead, judge humankind, and
consign each person to everlasting life or everlasting death as deserved.
It would be the end of the world as we know it.

Such thinkers are known today as apocalyptics, from the Greek for
"revelation," because they often presented their predictions about the
end as if they were revelations made earlier to ancient figures. The oldest

such "apocalypse," chapters 7–12 in the biblical Book of Daniel, epitomizes the genre. Composed between 167 and 164 BCE, shortly before the death of Antiochus IV Epiphanes, the author of Daniel claims to relate a revelation delivered long ago to the sixth-century prophet Daniel. The visions describe the death of Antiochus IV and the unprecedented global turmoil to follow. The angel Michael will appear and bring history to an end. The dead will be raised, judged, and given their just deserts, with those fortunate enough to pass muster "[shining] like the stars forever and ever" (Daniel 12:3).

Whatever prompted the author of Daniel to compose an apocalypse in response to the tyranny of Antiochus (and hypotheses about the origins of apocalypticism are legion), many similar works appeared over the next three centuries.[2] Their titles are not familiar to most Jews—I Enoch, IV Ezra, II Baruch, the War Scroll, for example—but they are studied extensively by historians who specialize in Judaism of the late Second Commonwealth, because apocalyptic thinking became prevalent in that era. And it never really went away. Rabbinic literature, too, is peppered with apocalyptic statements and grand expectations about a future redemption, even if such ideas are generally overshadowed by a focus on Jewish law and scriptural interpretation. Today, apocalypticism is more commonly associated with Christianity than with Judaism, and for good reason. As we shall see in what follows, the man whose ministry gave root to Christianity was an apocalyptic Jew. So were his followers. So, too, was Paul, the man whose ideas did more than anything else to transform an apocalyptic Jewish movement into the religion of Christianity we recognize today.

The Jesus Movement

Apocalyptic thinking in the first century CE was not limited to educated elites with the knowledge and wherewithal to compose literature. It prevailed among the masses as well. The first century witnessed several popular movements headed by figures who proclaimed that a cosmic redemption for the Jewish nation was in the offing. A certain Theudas, for example, is said to have led a band of followers to the Jordan River in the mid-40s CE, where he planned to part the river miraculously, as Joshua had done, and then lead his army into the Promised Land to displace the Romans, just as Joshua had ousted the Canaanites.[3] Having learned of the uprising, the Roman governor sent a cavalry to capture the would-be insurgents. Theudas himself was beheaded. A decade or so earlier, an apocalyptic prophet called John also set up shop on the banks of the Jordan. He became known as "the baptist" (from the Greek *baptizō*, "to immerse") because he encouraged the throngs who flocked to him to immerse in the river as a demonstration of their repentance in advance of history's final hour.[4] His head was taken, too—and famously displayed on a platter—but not before he made the acquaintance of a young Galilean named Jesus of Nazareth, who had come to the Jordan to be baptized and to hear the prophet's preaching.

Soon, Jesus set off to begin his own ministry in the Galilee. He gathered disciples numbering twelve, probably in anticipation of the restoration of the twelve tribes of Israel, and with this band he traveled from village to village healing the sick, exorcising demons, and preaching about the dawning of a kingdom of God. The message was thoroughly apocalyptic: God was about to reenter history, annihilating evil forces on high and upending the dominant powers below—namely the rich, the powerful, and the Roman.[5] Such a message was dangerous. However peaceful was his ministry, and there is little evidence to suggest that he advocated insurrection, leaders knew that proclamations about a coming kingdom in which the fortunes of the poor and powerless would be reversed could spark riots in a heartbeat, especially when multitudes gather. When Jesus came with his disciples to celebrate Passover in Jerusalem, a time when political unrest might be expected, the Roman governor Pontius Pilate thwarted a potential fiasco by doing away with him.

As everyone knows, however, the story does not end there. Unlike Theudas, John the Baptist, or the other apocalyptic figures of the first century, the disciples of Jesus came to believe that God had raised him from the dead. They would later claim that Jesus "appeared" to them following the crucifixion.[6] What this means is hardly clear, however. Did Jesus appear to them face-to-face in the flesh? In dreams? In states of ecstasy? As a vision in the heavens? It is impossible to know. What matters is that the disciples genuinely believed that God had raised Jesus from the dead, and they felt compelled to make sense of the experience. They did so in apocalyptic terms. Jesus died and rose, they figured, because Jews had been unprepared for the final judgment. Had God ushered in the kingdom of God during the ministry of Jesus, no Jew would have passed muster, condemned as they are by their sins. By raising Jesus from the dead, God made it possible for Jews to rectify their standing before God through an act of baptism in which they, like Jesus, can die and be reborn anew. In this reborn spiritual state, forgiven of their sins and having received the gift of the Holy Spirit, they would stand prepared when Jesus returns imminently to judge the world.[7]

The task was tall, therefore, and time was short. The disciples felt compelled to spread the word to as many Jews as possible in the few weeks, months, or maybe years that remained. Thus, the Jesus movement began, first in Jerusalem and then spreading northward to Damascus and Antioch.[8] Within a short time, the audience for the message expanded. The disciples and their deputies began to invite not just Jews but also gentiles to be baptized. Why attention turned to non-Jews remains a matter of historical controversy. Some have said it happened because the message was largely falling on deaf ears among Jews. After all, a messiah who dies ignominiously on a cross was hardly the triumphant redeemer Jews were expecting. Others say that a consideration of the implications for gentiles of Christ's death and resurrection was inevitable because Diaspora synagogues were so filled with non-Jews, such as spouses, friends, and religious seekers. Still others contend that the apocalyptic spirit of the new movement led ineluctably to a universalistic scope. Seeing as the prophets of yore, like Isaiah, had envisioned the day when "the many peoples shall go and say: 'Come, let us go up to the Mount of the Eternal'" (Isaiah 2:3), the disciples figured that the end times they anticipated could not materialize until some number of gentiles acknowledged the sovereignty of the Jewish God.

It was in connection with this so-called mission to the gentiles that Christianity as we know it emerged, and smack in the center of this outreach a brilliant, stubborn, relentless Jew named Paul.

Paul

Though born in Tarsus, a city on the northeast corner of the Mediterranean Sea, Paul was residing in Damascus when Jews first arrived there (ca. 35 CE) heralding Jesus as the Messiah. He took exception to this proclamation, by his own account hounding its supporters for spreading the scandalous notion of a crucified messiah.[9] The persecution turned out to be short-lived. For reasons that elude historians—he says he experienced a revelation—Paul came to believe what he had so recently deemed preposterous, that God indeed had raised Jesus from the dead and that Jesus was therefore God's messiah, or Christ.[10] Braced by this new belief, Paul became a man possessed. He ventured along the northeastern Mediterranean rim proclaiming the glorious news of Jesus's death, resurrection, and imminent return and beseeching gentiles to transform themselves through baptism and to put their trust in the saving power of the Jewish God.

The campaign was not so radical at first. Alongside Barnabas, a leader in the Damascus congregation, Paul set off to find open-minded gentiles in and around what is today southeastern Turkey. The pair's objective was essentially Jewish proselytism. They sought to persuade gentiles (who probably were already associated in one way or another with local synagogues) that the time had come to make the momentous decision to join the Jewish community in earnest. Through Jesus, they said, the God of Israel had revealed that history would conclude shortly and that only baptized Jews endowed with the Spirit would pass the final judgment. Gentiles ought therefore to become baptized and join the ranks of God's people Israel. For men, of course, this meant circumcision; for all, it meant submitting to the yoke of the Torah and obeying its commandments. For five or six years, Paul and Barnabas preached this message in Syria, Cilicia, and Lycaonia. Their precise whereabouts and the extent of their success during these years are difficult to determine because the evidence available for reconstructing Paul's life, namely his seven letters now preserved in the Christian New Testament, stem from a later period.[11]

More specifically, they were written after 42 CE, the year when Christianity as we know it originated.[12] What happened in that fateful year? Put simply, Paul radically revised his understanding of what God had accomplished through Christ. Whereas previously he had considered baptism into Christ's death and resurrection as a *complement* to established markers of Jewish identity such as descent from a Jewish father, circumcision, and obedience to the laws of the Torah, Paul came to see baptism rather as an *alternative* to them. Where for several years he had required the gentiles he baptized to become Jews—that is, to join the covenant of Israel through circumcision (for men) and Torah observance—he began to insist that such practices were entirely inappropriate. The Torah, Paul now believed, had run its course. In the brief, final phase of human history inaugurated by Christ's resurrection, gentiles could achieve the righteousness necessary for salvation only through the spiritual transformation conferred at baptism. To submit to circumcision or the yoke of the Torah thus constituted an affront to the saving power of God demonstrated through Christ.

What prompted this dramatic change in the message Paul delivered to his gentile charges? Paul attributes the turnabout, as he did his shift from persecutor to believer, to a revelation from Christ, but the historian can nonetheless imagine a few other possibilities. Jewish commentators have often cynically suggested that Paul was motivated by the desire to make his message more appealing. Paul was the consummate salesman, it is said, and convincing gentile men to undergo circumcision was a tough row to hoe. By disconnecting baptism from circumcision and from other Jewish behaviors that were viewed negatively in the wider Greco-Roman world, Paul aimed to secure a larger following.

I have argued alternatively that Paul may have been motivated more so by a genuine concern for inclusivity, especially with respect to women.[13] First-century Judaism struggled to imagine the possibility of a female proselyte. The phenomenon of conversion to Judaism had emerged a century or two earlier, and for male candidates the tradition possessed a ready-made ritual for marking the transition from gentile to Jew, namely admission to the covenant through circumcision, just like for an infant boy. No such ritual existed for women interested in joining a Jewish community. Texts from this period are notoriously vague about whether women can become proselytes and how such a deed might be accomplished. Eventually, of course, the Rabbis would institute immersion as the decisive ritual. In my view, Paul may have beaten the Rabbis to the punch. Urged on by his conviction that the end was nigh and bewildered by an ability to conceptualize the incorporation of gentile women into the God's end-of-times elect, Paul might have been led to the idea that baptism supersedes circumcision precisely because of the latter's universal applicability.

However he came to this point of view, the ever indefatigable Paul spent the next decade trekking further westward—to Philippi, Thessaloniki, Athens, and Corinth—to preach the novel message of salvation through Christ for gentiles *without* circumcision or Torah observance. In making his case, Paul did not rely on the authority of his alleged revelation alone. His surviving letters exhibit the deft and sophisticated interpretations of biblical passages he deployed when instructing his congregations. He relied heavily on the patriarchal narratives and various statements from the prophets. Of crucial importance, for example, was the prelude to the covenant of the pieces (Genesis 15:1–5) in which God reckons "righteousness" to Abraham because he "has faith" in God's promise of future progeny.[14] For Paul, this moment established forever the relationship between God and humanity: whoever has faith in God's promises is reckoned righteous before God. Everything that transpires subsequently in Israelite history is, according to Paul, beside the point. Circumcision was commanded two chapters later as a symbol of the covenant, but this circumcision merely confirmed rather than established Abraham's worthiness before God. The Torah was delivered four hundred years later, but its laws hardly altered the standard for righteousness already established with Abraham generations and centuries before. With the arrival of Christ, the single "offspring" of Abraham mentioned in Genesis 12:7, Abrahamic faith had been reintroduced into the world and was available to all. Just as God deemed Abraham righteous when he trusted in the life-giving power of God, so, too, in the final judgment will God deem righteous anyone who trusts in the saving power of God revealed through Christ.[15]

This reevaluation of Israelite history had profound implications. On the one hand, it undermined the traditional understanding of Jewish identity as determined by descent from the Patriarchs. On Paul's reckoning, God's elect people was not composed of individuals who could trace their origins back to Abraham, Isaac, and Jacob. Abraham had but one offspring of significance, namely Christ, and therefore genuine descent from Abraham could be claimed only by a person who became united with Christ through baptism. Once "in Christ," an individual's actual pedigree became irrelevant. In Christ, "there is no longer Jew or gentile," as Paul puts it in the famous baptismal formula of Galatians 3:28, "for all of you are one in Christ Jesus"; as such, a gentile no less than a Jew might properly be called the "seed" and the "heir" of Abraham.

The implications for the ongoing authority of the Torah's commandments were no less drastic. By asserting that the Torah constituted a secondary addendum to the covenant of faith established between God and the Patriarchs, Paul made the Torah into a temporary and conditional provision that could be removed once the historical circumstances that gave rise to it had passed away. To clarify this point, Paul used as a metaphor the ancient *paidagogos*, or "pedagogue." A *paidagogos*, often a slave, was the member of an aristocratic household tasked with supervising the behavior of boys before they came of age. Working alongside a *didaskalos*, the instructor who provided education, the *paidagogos* enforced the discipline that would ensure the boys grew into proper patrician men; he was something like a middle school vice-principal or perhaps a strict nanny. And, like a nanny, the *paidogogos* became superfluous once the children reached adulthood. By comparison, Paul contends, for centuries the Torah served a custodial function by regulating the behavior of the Israelites and ensuring the community would last long enough to give rise to Christ. With the advent of Christ, however, the regulations of the Torah became unnecessary. Its ceremonial rites such as dietary laws and circumcision were no longer useful, while its worthy moral directives would naturally be observed by anyone imbued with the Spirit through baptism. It should come as no surprise that undermining the distinction of Jewish descent and the authority of the Torah did not go over well with many of Paul's peers. Recall that Paul spent several years following his call to Christ participating in the early missions that required circumcision and Torah observance for gentiles. Many of the leaders in those missions did not agree with Paul's decision to remove these criteria for admission. Indeed, some were downright furious, and around the year 51 CE, Paul was summoned to Jerusalem by Peter, James, and other leaders of the congregation in Jerusalem to account for the rogue message he had been preaching for almost a decade.

The historical importance of this conference at Jerusalem, and even more so the ensuing confrontation at Antioch, cannot be underestimated.[16] Paul won the day in Jerusalem, securing from Peter and James the authorization to continue his unique mission among the gentiles.

Whatever rapprochement was achieved did not last long, however. Several months later Paul was sojourning with the congregation in Antioch when Peter, who was also visiting, determined that uncircumcised gentiles, despite their baptism, should not be allowed to eat alongside Jewish believers at communal meals. Such gentiles might be saved when Christ returns, Peter reckoned, but they remained gentiles nonetheless, and as such their full participation in the community was inappropriate. Paul berated Peter openly, insisting that any ongoing distinction between baptized Jews and gentiles on the basis of descent or circumcision defied the achievement of Christ on the cross. Peter seems nevertheless to have won the day at Antioch, as even Paul's longtime partner Barnabas joined Peter and the other Jews in separating from uncircumcised gentiles.

A fierce contest ensued. Peter and James dispatched emissaries from Antioch and/or Jerusalem to visit the communities Paul had founded and to persuade the gentiles in them to be circumcised and to undertake Torah observance despite what Paul had told them. Paul, for his part, ran the same race. He returned to his communities and even gathered in new ones—northern Galatia and Ephesus, at least—proclaiming that faith and baptism alone suffice to grant a person entry into the elect people of God. All but one of Paul's extant letters were composed during this roughly five-year period, which explains why they are chock-full of Paul defending his credentials and his ideas, maligning his rivals, and beseeching his gentile readers to accept his unique understanding of the Christ event.

How this contest ended is shrouded in mystery, as are any details regarding the end of Paul's life. The New Testament Book of Acts, composed around 100 CE, reports that Paul eventually made his way to Rome, where later Christian traditions say that Paul accepted the martyr's death. These claims are more likely the stuff of legend. The last of the extant letters Paul wrote is probably the New Testament Book of Romans, which he sent probably from Corinth, likely in the mid- to late 50s CE. All we can say is that his subsequent silence suggests that sometime soon thereafter, Paul died.

After Paul

The man died, but his teaching endured. Paul's interpretation of the death and resurrection of Jesus, in its general contours at least, would ultimately become the foundation of medieval Christianity, both Roman Catholicism and Eastern Orthodoxy. While various expressions of Christianity vied for predominance until the fifth century, the church that ultimately prevailed embraced the key tenets of Paul's theology, namely that the God of Israel sent his son, Jesus Christ, to die and rise again as a fulfillment of the covenantal promises to the Patriarchs; that the ceremonial and ritual commandments of the Torah, in the wake of the resurrection, had become obsolete; and that God's elect people no longer comprises the physical descendants of Israel, the Jews, but rather the spiritual descendants of the Patriarchs determined by faith.

The triumph of this Pauline Christianity was hardly inevitable. We have seen already that Paul himself struggled with rivals who supposed that the ceremonial commandments of the Torah remain in effect after Christ—that baptized believers, whether Jew or gentile, are nonetheless obligated to observe the laws regulating diet, Sabbath, circumcision, and the like. Practitioners of such a "Jewish Christianity," as it is often labeled by modern historians, remained active well into the second century and possibly later. Christian groups calling themselves Ebionites or Nazoreans, for example, acclaimed Jesus for his unsurpassed obedience to the Torah rather than his supernatural origins or sacrificial death, and they saw in Jesus a source of inspiration for a life conducted in strict adherence to the Torah's laws.

Formidable as such Jewish Christians were, an even fiercer competitor to Paul's legacy in the second century came from believers who sought to purge the vestiges of Judaism from Christianity. Followers of Marcion (d. ca. 160) or Valentinus (d. ca. 160), for example, held that Jesus was sent by a God far superior to the God of the Jews. The God of the Hebrew Scripture, they argued, was an inferior deity who created our hostile, miserable world, whereas true salvation comes from the knowledge afforded by the superior deity, the true God of the universe, through God's son, Jesus. Such Christians not only rejected the supremacy of the Jewish God, but they also discarded as worthless most or all of the Jewish Scripture. Marcion famously produced a work called the *Antitheses*, in which he juxtaposed the sayings of Jesus to (allegedly) inferior precursors in the Jewish Scripture. He also drew up a bowdlerized version of the Gospel of Luke that eliminated all references to the Hebrew Bible.

Paul would scarcely have approved. Recall that Paul's proclamations about the obsolescence of the ceremonial laws do not constitute a rejection of either the God of Israel or the authority of the Jewish Scripture. On the contrary, Paul insists that the God of Israel is the only God (I Corinthians 8:4), the "living and true God" (I Thessalonians 1:9) who fulfilled the covenantal promises to the Patriarchs through the reconciliation afforded by his son, Jesus. He insists likewise that the Jewish Scripture remain authoritative; indeed, he routinely draws upon the Torah and the Prophets to bolster his claims. What changed for Paul was simply the way the sacred texts should be interpreted, which is at all times and in all ways through the interpretive lens of Christ's death and resurrection. After all, Paul explains, in Christ "the righteousness of God, attested by the Law and the prophets, has been made manifest" (Romans 3:21).

The Pauline theology that eventually found expression in Orthodox Christianity thus constitutes something of a middle path in terms of its relationship to the Jewish tradition from which it emerged. Had Christianity followed the lead of James, Peter, the Ebionites, or the Nazoreans, it might ultimately have become indistinguishable from late ancient Judaism, just another Torah-observant community with a peculiar admiration for one great Jew of the past. Had it followed the lead of Marcion, Valentinus, or the later Gnostics, it might well have become so removed from Judaism—with a different God and different scriptures—that it never would have come to be understood as possessing any relationship to Judaism at all. As it stands, however, medieval Christianity followed Paul. It preserved the God of Israel as God the Father, one person in a triune Godhead, and it preserved the Jewish Scripture, turning it into an Old Testament that anticipates the New.

As such, Christianity developed into a biblical religion that has been and always will be tethered to the other revolution in biblical religion that arose in late antiquity, Rabbinic Judaism. Where Christianity, following Paul, came to view the Hebrew Scripture through the lens of Christ and the writings of the New Testament, the Rabbis considered them through the lens of the Oral Torah. As any student of medieval and early modern Jewish-Christian relations knows well, this shared ancient heritage, until recently, led mostly to competition, animosity, and persecution. Developments in Jewish-Christian relationships since the middle of the last century nonetheless indicate that a new era may be upon us, one in which the familiarity between these two biblical religions breeds mutual admiration and esteem rather than contempt.

NOTES

1. This, and all other biblical passages, are the author's translation.
2. For an accessible introduction to Jewish apocalyptic thought and literature, see John J. Collins, *The Apocalyptic Imagination: An Introduction to Jewish Apocalyptic Literature*, 3rd ed. (Grand Rapids, MI: Eerdmans, 2016).
3. An account of Theudas appears in the writing of the first-century Jewish historian Josephus, *Jewish Antiquities, Volume IX: Book 20*, trans. Louis H. Feldman, Loeb Classical Library 456 (Cambridge, MA: Harvard University Press, 1965), 20:97–98.
4. Accounts of John the Baptist appear in all four canonical gospels of the New Testament—Matthew, Mark, Luke, and John—as well as in Josephus (*Jewish Antiquities*, 18:116–19).
5. For an accessible introduction to the problem of ascertaining historically reliable information about Jesus of Nazareth and his ministry, see Helen K. Bond, *The Historical Jesus: A Guide for the Perplexed* (London: T&T Clark, 2012).
6. I Corinthians 15:1–11.
7. In this sense, the initiatory rite of baptism in early Christian circles differed from ritual immersion as it was typically practiced by Jews in the late Second Temple period. For Jews, immersion in water was a routine experience designed to cleanse bodies or utensils defiled by ritual impurity. For Christians, immersion was a one-time event that marked the ontologically transformative entrance into the Christian community. In this sense, Christian baptism resembled the rite of immersion later enjoined by the rabbis for proselytes to Judaism. For more on the issue of immersion in early Christian and Jewish circles, see Joshua D. Garroway, "Engendering Judaism: Paul, Baptism, and Circumcision," in *Paul the Jew: Rereading the Apostle as a Figure of Second Temple Judaism*, ed. Gabriele Boccaccini and Carlos A. Segovia (Minneapolis: Fortress, 2015), 219–43.
8. The terms "Christian" and "Christianity" have come to be seen as anachronistic when applied to figures or ideas prior to the second century CE. Hence,

here, "the Jesus movement" in lieu of "Christianity"; below, "believers" or persons "in Christ" in lieu of "Christians."

9. Paul refers to his own harassment of the earliest followers of Jesus in Galatians 1:13–14, 23.

10. "Christ" comes from the Greek word *christos*, meaning "anointed." The Hebrew word for "anointed" is *mashiach*, which gives us the word "messiah."

11. New Testament scholars widely agree that Paul wrote at least seven of the thirteen letters attributed to him in the New Testament. These "undisputed" letters are Romans, I and II Corinthians, Galatians, Philippians, I Thessalonians, and Philemon. The remaining six are known as the "disputed" or "contested" epistles, because many scholars—indeed, most scholars in the case of some letters—consider them to be pseudepigraphic. A helpful introduction to the study of Paul's letters is Calvin J. Roetzel, *The Letters of Paul: Conversations in Context*, 6th ed. (Louisville, KY: Westminster John Knox, 2015).

12. It should be noted that the argument being pursued here reflects my own recent proposal, which has not—yet?—received wide acceptance in New Testament scholarship. See Joshua D. Garroway, *The Beginning of the Gospel: Paul, Philippi, and the Origins of Christianity* (Cham, Switzerland: Palgrave Macmillan, 2018). The predominant assumption remains that Paul all along discouraged baptized gentiles from observing the ceremonial requirements of the Torah. Whether Paul developed this idea from the start or five to six years into his missionary career, as I am proposing here, has no impact on the broader claims of this essay.

13. Garroway, *Beginning of the Gospel*, 72–73.

14. When we first meet Abraham in Genesis 11–12, he is called Abram. After God renews the covenant and commands circumcision (Genesis 17:4–14), God changes Abram's named to Abraham. This essay uses Abraham throughout so as to avoid confusion.

15. Paul offers the arguments in the preceding and ensuing two paragraphs in Galatians 3:1–29.

16. Paul describes the conference at Jerusalem in Galatians 2:1–10 and the incident at Antioch in Galatians 2:11–14.

4

Persecution, Martyrdom, and Divine Justice
How the Afterlife Came to Be

Rabbi Candice Levy, PhD

THE BABYLONIAN TALMUD, *Taanit* 31a, relates the following vision of the afterlife:

> Ulla of the city of Bira'a said in the name of Rabbi Elazar: In the future, in the end of days, the Holy One, blessed be God, will arrange a dance of the righteous, and God will be sitting among them in the Garden of Eden, and each and every one of the righteous will point to God with their finger, as it is stated: *In that day, they shall say: This is our God; we trusted in God, and God delivered us. This is the Eternal in whom we trusted; let us rejoice and exult in God's deliverance!* (Isaiah 25:9).

According to this text, the world-to-come is one where God is manifest and the ultimate reward of the righteous is that God will be revealed to them. In this text and others, the Sages imagine that humans will be granted the ability to behold God and understand divine justice in the afterlife. This Talmudic ideation of the afterlife suggests that the Sages are struggling with the inscrutability of divine justice and the imperceptible presence of God. Consequently, the afterlife functions to rectify the Rabbis' dilemma and to envision a time or world where that dilemma no longer exists. Although the notion that the afterlife can provide a corrective to a world that seems devoid of divine justice has roots in the Second Temple period, the Rabbis have a particular formulation of the afterlife. In this chapter, I demonstrate how the afterlife emerges as a response to the disruption of religious persecution and how the Rabbis deploy it to uphold divine justice, while also raising fundamental questions about its inscrutability and the perceived absence of God in this world.

The Hebrew Bible, as a whole, does not evince an expectation of an existence after death, certainly not in the doctrinal sense that later emerges in both Judaism and Christianity.[1] Nonetheless, postbiblical Jewish literature is rife with depictions of ascents to heaven, postmortem judgment and recompense, the survival of the soul beyond the expiration of the body, and the eventual resurrection of the dead. The shift in eschatological expectations from the biblical belief in the absolute finality of death to a Rabbinic belief in life after death[2] can be explained in several ways: external factors, such as cultural and religious influences facilitated by exile and dispersion, altered political and social landscapes, as well as internal factors, such as the need to respond to the theological crisis precipitated by subjugation and religious persecution.

The increased eschatological preoccupation within Jewish literature of the Second Temple period can be understood as a response to the religious persecution experienced by Jews under Antiochus IV in the second century BCE.[3] While retribution theology[4] had provided a response for exile and the destruction of the First Temple,[5] that model would prove insufficient when Jews were forced to contend with the profound theological dilemma posed by the death and suffering of the righteous, *precisely for their faith in God and adherence to the commandments.* Consequently, Daniel 12 introduces the idea of the resurrection of the dead as an attempt to vindicate God's justice and affirm the validity of the Torah and its covenantal promises:[6]

> At that time, the great prince, Michael, who stands beside the sons of your people, will appear. It will be a time of trouble, the like of which has never been since the nation came into being. At that time, your people will be rescued, all who are found inscribed in the book. Many of those that sleep in the dust of the earth will awake, some to eternal life, others to reproaches, to everlasting abhorrence. And the knowledgeable will be radiant like the bright expanse of sky, and those who lead the many to righteousness will be like the stars forever and ever. (Daniel 12:1–4)

Theodicy is a central element in many texts of the Hellenistic period. While the texts maintain the belief in divine justice on a communal and individual level, they often defer divine judgment and recompense for the individual until death, to account for the reality of injustice. In doing so, these texts maintain that the death and suffering of the righteous are not an indication of God's abandonment of the people, but that true reward and punishment are reserved for the afterlife. This tendency is on full display in II Maccabees 7 and IV Maccabees 16, which present a mother and her seven sons as willing martyrs who embrace death not only as a more palatable option than the transgression of biblical law, but also because their death will bring them recompense and vindication after death.[7] The texts reflect an important transition as they draw upon established notions of retribution theology and collective judgment, while also affirming a belief in an afterlife.

The ascension of Antiochus, and his seizure and desecration of the Temple, prompted questions about the omnipotence of God. The Maccabees texts affirm the power and omniscience of God by framing the persecution as a punishment for the collective guilt of the people. However, they also maintain that Antiochus will be subject to divine judgment, and the righteous will be vindicated and recompensed for their loyalty to God and the Law in the hereafter. In recounting the story, the author of IV Maccabees states, "Here lie buried an aged priest and an aged woman and her seven sons, because of the violence of a tyrant who wished to destroy the way of life of the Hebrews. They vindicated their nation looking to God and enduring torture even to death. Truly, the contest in which they were engaged was divine, for on that day virtue gave the awards and tested them for their endurance. The prize was immortality in endless life" (IV Maccabees 17:9–12). IV Maccabees presents a firm conviction that a blessed afterlife awaits the mother and her sons, and that their suffering is not devoid of meaning, but rather serves a purpose in expiating the collective guilt of the people.

If the belief in the afterlife provided meaning for the martyrs and those who survived the Antiochan persecution, it is not surprising that these ideas would be deployed during another period of religious persecution, under the Roman emperor Hadrian in the second century CE. This instance of persecution came on the heels of two failed revolts against Rome and the destruction of the Second Temple. It was a time of subjugation and humiliation under the Romans, who regarded their victories as a triumph over the Israelite God. To many Jews, the failure of the Bar Kochba Revolt in 132–135 CE shattered their messianic hopes and expectations for restoration, and the ensuing persecution by the Romans suggested a withdrawal of God that necessitated a response. It is against this backdrop that the Rabbis simultaneously question and affirm divine justice. Rabbinic texts on the martyrdom of the sages in the post–Bar Kochba period often include the phrase *zo Torah v'zo s'charah?* (this is the Torah and this is its reward?), which is uttered incredulously by the Rabbis when reality flies in the face of the biblical promises of long life and prosperity as rewards for the observance of Torah.[8]

If the imperceptibility of God and the inscrutability of divine justice pose a problem for the Rabbis of the second century CE, it is telling that their justification of God is given light through the interpretation of the last speech of Moses in Deuteronomy 32:4. *Sifrei D'varim* 307 finds Moses standing on the precipice of death while the Israelites are about to enter the Promised Land without him. Moses opens his final oration with an unequivocal statement about the absolute justice of God. "The Rock!—whose deeds are perfect, yea, all God's ways are just; a faithful God, never false, true and upright indeed" (Deuteronomy 32:4). It is against this backdrop that the Rabbis present not only their conception of divine justice, but also a remarkable attempt at theodicy, which hinges on the afterlife. What distinguishes this text is that it bears signs of an underlying anxiety concerning the absolute justice of this system, as it culminates in an account of martyrdom and the observation, by none other than Moses, that sometimes divine justice is anything but just.[9] The Rabbis' willingness to concede the experience of divine injustice distinguishes the Rabbinic articulation of divine retribution from other texts that grappled with similar circumstances, such as the Books of Maccabees.

Sifrei 307 offers a number of interpretations of Moses's proclamation that God is just, and that divine justice is perfect. The midrash begins with the idea of the perfection of Creation, as the text paints a portrait of a God who is intimately involved with humans. God the Creator is likened to an artist[10] who fashions every individual in a precise and calculated way. The midrash dismisses any questions about the perfection of human design, stating "there is not a single person who will look [at themselves] and say, 'If only I had three eyes, if only I had three hands, if only I had three legs, if only I walked on my head, if only my face were turned backward, how becoming would it be for me.'"[11] However, as Chaya Halberstam points out, it is entirely possible that three eyes or hands would be more beneficial than two.[12] This is the first indication of doubt regarding divine justice, which the midrash resolves by making a distinction between human vision and perceptibility and that of the Divine.

The next section of *Sifrei* 307 transitions from the idea of the perfection of Creation, "God's workmanship is perfect," to the perfection of divine justice, "God's dealings are perfect." Though the midrash affirms the impeccability of divine justice, it provides a number of examples that suggest otherwise:

> God's dealings with all those who come into the world are perfect, and there is not even a single cause to criticize God's deeds. There is not a single person who will look and say, "Why were the people of the generation of the flood drowned? Why were the people of the Tower [of Babel] scattered from one end of the earth to the other? Why were the people of Sodom swept away by fire and brimstone? Why did Aaron assume the priesthood? Why did David assume the monarchy? Why were Korach and his congregation swallowed into the earth?"[13]

Ironically, the midrash attempts to illustrate the perfection of divine justice with examples that one might consider to be instances of divine *in*justice, involving the suffering of innocents, overly harsh punishments, and rewards to those who may have been undeserving of them. The repeated, categorical denial of any cause to find fault with God, followed by examples that indicate otherwise, alludes to an awareness of such cause, even if the Rabbis are unwilling to make it explicit. Ultimately, the Rabbis resign themselves to the fact that they simply are not privy to the way in which divine justice works, but they are willing—perhaps needing—to believe that there is justice to be found, even if it is indiscernible. The midrash stresses timing as a fundamental difference between divine and human justice, and though the delayed nature of divine retribution creates an illusion of inequity, divine justice is still operative. By deferring the administration of justice to the world-to-come, the midrash reinforces the expectation of divine justice but divests us of the expectation that it will be manifested in this world.

Whereas the midrash previously emphasized the perfection of God's deeds, the third section of the midrash focuses on the deeds of humankind; more precisely, it focuses on the unparalleled ability of God to see the entirety of an individual's deeds. The midrash contends that delayed retribution is what allows God to deliver perfect justice, as it is based upon the context of an individual's lifetime of deeds rather than on an immediate, quid pro quo basis. "This midrash not only invokes the afterlife, or world-to-come, as the location of God's true justice, but it positions this world as a complete *reversal* of justice—a way station in which individuals receive the opposite of their deserved recompense. The wicked are rewarded in this world for any good deed they may have done so that they can be punished exclusively in the world-to-come; the righteous are punished for every minor transgression so that their future reward will be untainted."[13] Consequently, the circumstances of an individual's life in this world should not be taken as an indication of their merit nor of the absence of divine justice. On the contrary, the *Sifrei* posits that since one cannot reap rewards in both domains, divine justice can *never* be perceived in this world.

This idea is also illustrated in the Babylonian Talmud, *Sanhedrin* 101a, when Rabbi Akiva laughs upon seeing Rabbi Eliezer on his deathbed. He explains, "In all the time I have seen my master, his wine does not turn to vinegar, his flax is not smitten, his oil does not spoil, and his honey does not become liquid; I said, perhaps, God forbid, my master has already received his [reward in this] world. But now that I see my master in sorrow, I am happy." Troubled by the implications of Rabbi Eliezer's prosperity in this world, Rabbi Akiva is comforted by Rabbi Eliezer's suffering, which, however tragic, reassured him that his teacher would indeed have a share in the world-to-come. The reversal of justice and the role of theodicy in the world-to-come is evident here, as the promise of the afterlife not only alleviates the anxiety caused by the suffering of the righteous, but it also assigns a necessary redemptive function to that suffering. The midrash continues to detail a postmortem judicial process, which culminates in the justification of God's judgment by each individual:

When a person departs from this world, all of their deeds are
brought forth and specified before them. They say to [the individ-
ual], "Such and such you have done on such and such day, do you
confirm these matters?" and [the individual] says, "Yes." They
say to them "Sign," as it is said, "It shall be sealed by the hand
of every person so that all people shall know God's deeds" (Job
37:7), and the individual justifies the judgment and says, "I have
been judged well."

The midrash reinforces the Rabbinic belief in the transparency of
divine justice and its accessibility to humans in the afterlife. The individual affirms the divine decree and justifies God once they are afforded a
holistic view of their life and deeds and the ability to understand God's
ways after death. The fulfillment of divine justice in the afterlife and the
justification of God is an ongoing theme of this midrash, which begins
with Moses's statement in Deuteronomy 32:4 and culminates in the last
section of the midrashic text, which details the martyrdom of the second-century sage Rabbi Chanina ben Teradyon, in the aftermath of the
Bar Kochba Revolt.

As with the account of the mother and her seven sons in the Maccabees texts, Rabbi Chanina and his family willingly accept death and suffering rather than submit to religious persecution. Despite the *Sifrei*'s
repeated claims that there is no cause to question any of God's dealings
with humanity, the midrash's account of Rabbi Chanina and his family
does provide such a cause, since there is no suggestion of their guilt in
the text. While Rabbi Chanina and his family are confident that they will
be vindicated, the rabbis who witness these events are forced to confront
their beliefs about divine justice, and they express doubt about the justice
of God, even as they affirm it:

When [the Romans] captured Rabbi Chanina ben Teradyon,
they decreed upon him that he would be burned with his Torah.
They said to him, "It has been decreed that you will be burned
with your Torah," [whereupon] he invoked the verse "The Rock,
God's deeds are perfect" (Deuteronomy 32:4). They said to his
wife, "It has been decreed that your husband will be burned and
that you will be killed," [whereupon] she invoked the verse "a

God of faith, without fault." They said to his daughter, "It has been decreed that your father be burned, your mother killed, and that you will perform labor," [whereupon] she invoked the verse "great in counsel and mighty in deed, for Your eyes are open"[14] (Jeremiah 32:19).

Rabbi [Judah the Prince] said, "How great are these righteous persons that in their time of sorrow they brought forth three verses to justify the divine decree, something that is unparalleled in all the Scriptures." The three of them directed their hearts and justified the divine decree upon themselves.

A philosopher approached his prefect and said to him, "My master, do not let your mind become unsettled on account of the fact that you have burned the Torah, for it has returned to its place of origin, its father's home." He replied to him, "Tomorrow you will share their fate." The philosopher replied, "You have brought me good tidings, for tomorrow my share will be with them in the world-to-come."

This account of martyrdom presents us with several responses to the matter of religious persecution, which suggests the Rabbis' underlying anxiety that they are hard-pressed to adequately resolve this theological dilemma. Rabbi Chanina and his wife invoke Moses's words and justify God unequivocally and without any doubt. However, the midrash offers us two other responses through the daughter and the philosopher.

The daughter invokes Jeremiah 32:19, which serves as a promise to Israel and a warning to her enemies, thereby allowing the Rabbis to rebut Roman claims that the God of Israel had been vanquished.[15] Through Rabbi Chanina's daughter, the Rabbis echo the Maccabees texts and argue that God is not only present, but also fully aware of what is happening and will ultimately restore justice. The belief in this absolute truth is demonstrated by the fact that the philosopher—a gentile—submits to the authority of God rather than to his own prefect.[16] Thus, the afterlife serves to offset the imbalance of power, allowing the Rabbis to maintain the promises of restoration and redemption prophesied by Moses and Jeremiah and negate Roman claims of supersession.

The Rabbinic doubt is also resolved through the statement of the philosopher, who affirms the actualization of divine justice in the afterlife.

Per Halberstam, the philosopher "becomes the mouthpiece for the rabbis, protesting against the prefect, and invoking a truly compassionate God, who lavishes reward in the world-to-come upon those who suffer the cruelty of the tyrants on earth."[17] The midrash, perhaps unable—or unwilling—to champion a God who appears to disregard justice so readily, introduces the idea of the world-to-come as a panacea for the anxiety and doubt that this episode elicits. The *Sifrei* itself notes that the absolute justification of the divine decree by Rabbi Chanina and his family was exceptional and unparalleled, implying that most persons would not be capable of this, nor could they realistically be expected to do so. Perhaps the Rabbis were aware that such injustice was untenable and fundamentally unsustainable. Hence, the promise of the afterlife provides the Rabbis and their adherents with the means to accept injustice and suffering in this world. Unlike Rabbi Chanina, who could go to his death without question, the midrash tells us that the philosopher accepts his fate and that of Rabbi Chanina because of his conviction that the world-to-come awaits them.[18] Perhaps the afterlife also allows the Rabbis to make sense of a world where justice is seemingly absent, so that they too can justify the divine decree.

The imminent death of Moses and its underlying cause as a consequence of the striking the rock in Numbers 20 is suggested by the motif of the rock within the exegetical context of *Sifrei* 307. The midrash ends with a final justification of divine justice, even as it acknowledges that it remains unknowable even to Moses:

> When Moses came down from Mount Sinai, the people of Israel gathered upon him and said to him, "Our master, Moses, tell us, what is the principle of justice in heaven?" Moses responded, "I do not tell you that it is to acquit the innocent and make the guilty liable, but rather even if the matter is reversed, 'a God of faith and without fault.'"

Despite being the sole individual who was granted direct access to God, Moses was not able to understand divine justice.[19] Ultimately, Moses justifies God even as he concedes that God may be *un*just. Perhaps this is the reason why Moses refers to God as "the Rock" in Deuteronomy 32:4. As Moses justifies God, he also recalls the rock that he struck in Numbers 20 and the injustice of his denied entry into the Promised

Land. The severity of Moses's punishment for such a minor infraction is troublesome for the Rabbis,[20] which brings the question of divine justice to the forefront. Given all of this, Moses's statement acknowledging that sometimes divine justice may appear to be inverted is understandable. Yet, even so, "God's deeds are perfect" (Deuteronomy 32:4).

The motif of the rock in Exodus 33,[21] Deuteronomy 32, and *Sifrei* 307, three texts that simultaneously reveal aspects of God while maintaining that God is essentially unknowable, is quite telling. Just as a rock is solid, enduring, and yet impenetrable, so too is God, according to the midrash. The concurrent admission of injustice and faith in divine justice that is prevalent throughout the *Sifrei* is encapsulated in *Mishnah Avot* 4:15, "We do not have within our grasp [an explanation] for the prosperity of the wicked, nor for the suffering of the righteous."

The Rabbis were profoundly aware of injustice, yet they repeatedly negate the arbitrariness of suffering and any hint that it may indicate a rupture with God. They preferred to admit their ignorance of the ways of God, owing to the limits of human perceptibility, rather than concede the expectation of divine justice. The Rabbinic engagement in theodicy was essential to the relevance of the nascent Rabbinic tradition and its ability to withstand the challenges it faced, both internally and externally. Among the variety of responses to suffering, the displacement of the locale of retribution from this world to the afterlife enabled the Rabbis to confront and respond to unjust suffering and the perceived absence of God and divine justice in this world.

We have seen that a belief in the afterlife emerges as a consequence and response to the disruption caused by religious persecution. These moments of severe disruption forced Jews to confront the theological dilemma prompted by their inability to reconcile established beliefs in the covenantal promises of God with the reality of their experience. Exile and the exposure to other cultures paves the way for the entry of such a belief into Jewish thought, and the trauma of religious persecution demands a response that is articulated in Hellenistic Jewish literature and refined by the Rabbis. On an individual and collective level, the afterlife functions to provide a response to the perceived withdrawal of God and the absence of divine justice. It is therefore quite revealing that when the Rabbis imagine the afterlife that awaits the righteous, they envision that it will be a time where God will be perceivable and known to humans. The righteous who have suffered unjustly and have had to endure the absence and withdrawal of God from their midst will dance joyously around God. After a lifetime where they have been unable to see God and have struggled to understand God and divine justice, they will be able to point directly to God and say, "This is our God, for whom we have waited" (Isaiah 25:9).[22] Thus, the afterlife grants them the very thing that tests and challenges them, and their reward is to be at peace, at one—*shaleim*—with God.

Notes

1. On the contrary, much of the biblical literature reflects a belief in the finality of death and the cessation of life upon the death of the individual. See, for example, Psalms 49:6–13 and 146:2–4. With regard to passages like Ezekiel 37 that seem to suggest a resurrection of the dead, it is unclear that they reflect a widespread belief in the afterlife or resurrection of the dead.

2. This development is reflected in the evolution of the term *olam* as referring to nonspecific, cyclical time to its subsequent use with the modifiers *hazeh* (this) and *haba* (the coming/future) to designate a specific time and space. The Hebrew Bible does not attest the use of *olam* to designate "world" as a physical space as it is frequently used in later apocalyptic and Rabbinic texts and in the New Testament. See Ernst Jenni, "'Olam, עולם," in *Theological Lexicon of the Old Testament*, ed. Ernst Jenni and Claus Westermann (Peabody, MA: Hendrickson, 1997), 204–47; "Das Wort 'Ōlām Im Alten Testament," *Zeitschrift für die Alttestamentliche Wissenschaft* 64, no. 1 (1952); H. D. Preuss, "'Olam, עולם; 'Alam עלם," in *Theological Dictionary of the Old Testament*, ed. G. Johannes Botterweck, Helmer Ringgren, and Heinz-Josef Fabry (Grand Rapids, MI: Eerdmans, 1974).

3. John Collins suggests that the expectation of the resurrection arises as a solution to the problem of the persecution of the righteous during the Maccabean era and cultural trauma experienced by the Jews. The ascents to heaven and ideas of the resurrection reflected in texts of the era "offered an alternative reality in its visions of hidden places and life beyond death." John J. Collins, "The Afterlife in Apocalyptic Literature," in *Judaism in Late Antiquity: Part Four: Death, Life-after-Death, Resurrection and the World-to-Come in the Judaisms of Antiquity*, ed. Alan J. Avery-Peck and Jacob Neusner (Leiden: Brill, 2000), 127.

4. This is a central theme of Deuteronomy and the prophetic literature, where divine justice operates by granting retribution on the basis of merit and the ability to uphold the covenantal laws.

5. The destruction of the First Temple and exile by the Babylonians had been foretold by the prophets and explained through the lens of the covenant at Sinai, such that the Israelites' idolatrous practices violated the commanded loyalty to *YHVH*, thereby causing the withdrawal of God and the destruction of the Temple as God's abode. See Deuteronomy 31:17–18.

6. Although the Book of Daniel is set in the sixth century BCE, it was composed in the second century BCE against the backdrop of the Antiochan persecution of Jews.

7. This story is also recounted in the Babylonian Talmud, *Gittin* 57b, where the Rabbis identify the mother as Hannah and set the story during the Hadrianic persecutions of the second century CE.

8. See, for example, Babylonian Talmud, *B'rachot* 61b and *M'nachot* 29b; Jerusalem Talmud, *Chagigah* 2:1; and the minor tractate *S'machot* 8:12.

9. It should be noted that while the *Sifrei* grapples with unjust suffering and its implications for divine justice, the midrash never expresses its doubts concerning the latter explicitly. Nevertheless, as I will demonstrate, the text bears signs of doubt and anxiety about the nature of divine justice.

10. As a play on the word *hatzur*, הצור —the rock—which the Rabbis interpret as *hatzayar*, הצייר—the artist.

11. All sections of *Sifrei* 307 are author's translations.

12. "The midrash here might be subtly implying that perhaps we could imagine a more perfect, more able human body, but that nonetheless we must know with conviction that God has given us what is right and just, no more and no less; that creation is perfect, despite what one might imagine to the contrary" (Chaya T. Halberstam, *Law and Truth in Biblical and Rabbinic Literature* [Bloomington: Indiana University Press, 2010], 136).

13. Halberstam, *Law and Truth in Biblical and Rabbinic Literature*, 139.

14. The verse continues, "to all the ways of humanity, so as to give to [i.e., repay] each person according to their ways and according to the fruit of their deeds."

15. Jeremiah 32 lends itself to the present context since it depicts the Babylonians as instruments of God, who delivers Israel and her cities to them as a result of Israel's sins. Hence, the Babylonian conquest, like that of the Seleucid king and Rome, is not an indication of God's defeat. Rather, these events are part of a divine plan and Israel's covenantal destiny.

16. In the Babylonian Talmud, *B'rachot* 61b, Rabbi Akiva's executioner is also promised a share in the world-to-come for speeding up Rabbi Akiva's death and lessening his suffering.

17. Halberstam, *Law and Truth in Biblical and Rabbinic Literature*, 142. Halberstam cites Christine Hayes, who has argued that "rabbinic authors introduce or exploit the presence of *minim* (i.e., heretics or sectarians) and Romans... in order to voice and thus grapple with their own ambivalence and radical doubt" (142).

18. It is important to note that the world-to-come is not presented as a reward for martyrdom. The afterlife allows them to integrate their reality with the biblical tradition of divine justice and adhere to a God whose justice was not always apparent.

19. An aggadah from the Babylonian Talmud, *B'rachot* 7a, recounts that Moses requested three things from God, among them to understand the ways of God. The text concludes with the following statement from Rabbi Meir: "Two [requests] were granted to him and one [request] was not granted to him. As it is said, 'And I shall show favor upon whom I show favor' (Exodus 33:19)—even though they may not be worthy—'and I will show mercy upon whom I show mercy' (Exodus 33:19)—even though they may not be worthy." Rabbi Meir interprets Exodus 33:19 to demonstrate the apparent arbitrariness of divine justice but points out that the statement is immediately followed by God's declaration that no person can see God and live (Exodus 33:20), which implies that while the ways of God are inaccessible to the living, they are accessible in the world-to-come. *Sifrei D'varim* 357, interpreting Deuteronomy 34:10, maintains that though Moses's request to see God was denied while he was living, he would be able to see God in the afterlife.

20. See, for example, *M'chilta D'Rabbi Shimon ben Yochai, Va-eira* 6:2; *B'midbar Rabbah* 19:13; *D'varim Rabbah* 11:10; *M'chilta D'Rabbi Yishmael, Amalek* 2; *Tanchuma, Chukat* 11; *Sifrei D'varim* 26.

21. In Exodus 33:21–23, Moses's request to see God is denied, but he is instructed to stand on a rock where he will be able to glimpse the back of God.

22. Author's translation.

FOR FURTHER READING

Avery-Peck, Alan J. "Death and Afterlife in the Early Rabbinic Sources: The Mishnah, Tosefta, and Early Midrash Compilations." In *Judaism in Late Antiquity: Part Four: Death, Life-after-Death, Resurrection and the World-to-Come in the Judaisms of Antiquity*, edited by Alan J. Avery-Peck and Jacob Neusner. Leiden: Brill, 2000.

Basser, Herbert W. *In the Margins of the Midrash: Sifre Ha'azinu Texts, Commentaries, and Reflections.* Atlanta: Scholars Press, 1990.

Berger, Peter L. *The Sacred Canopy: Elements of a Sociological Theory of Religion.* New York: Anchor Books, 1990.

Blenkinsopp, Joseph. "Deuteronomy and the Politics of Post-Mortem Existence." *Vetus Testamentum* 45, no. 1 (1995): 1–16.

Botterweck, G. Johannes, Helmer Ringgren, and Heinz-Josef Fabry, eds. *Theological Dictionary of the Old Testament.* Grand Rapids, MI: Eerdmans, 1974.

Boustan, Ra'anan S. *From Martyr to Mystic: Rabbinic Martyrology and the Making of Merkavah Mysticism.* Mohr Siebeck GmbH & Company K, 2005.

Boyarin, Daniel. "Between Intertextuality and History: The Martyrdom of Rabbi Akiva." In *Intertextuality and the Reading of Midrash*. Bloomington: Indiana University Press, 1994.

Boyce, M. *Zoroastrians: Their Religious Beliefs and Practices*. London: Routledge, 2001.

Braiterman, Zachary. *(God) after Auschwitz: Tradition and Change in Post-Holocaust Jewish Thought*. Princeton, NJ: Princeton University Press, 1998.

Bremmer, J. N. *The Early Greek Concept of the Soul*. Princeton, NJ: Princeton University Press, 1983.

———. *The Rise and Fall of the Afterlife: The 1995 Read-Tuckwell Lectures at the University of Bristol*. London: Routledge, 2002.

Cohn, N. R. C. *Cosmos, Chaos and the World to Come: The Ancient Roots of Apocalyptic Faith*. 2nd ed. New Haven, CT: Yale University Press, 2001.

Collins, John J. "The Afterlife in Apocalyptic Literature." In *Judaism in Late Antiquity: Part Four: Death, Life-after-Death, Resurrection and the World-to-Come in the Judaisms of Antiquity*, edited by Alan J. Avery-Peck and Jacob Neusner. Leiden: Brill, 2000.

Costa, J. *L'au-Dela Et La Resurrection Dans La Litterature Rabbinique Ancienne*. Leuven: Peeters, 2004.

Elman, Yaakov. "Righteousness as Its Own Reward: An Inquiry into the Theologies of the Stam." *Proceedings of the American Academy for Jewish Research* 57 (1990): 35–67.

———. "The Suffering of the Righteous in Palestinian and Babylonian Sources." *Jewish Quarterly Review* 80, no. 3/4 (1990): 315–39.

Friedman, Richard Elliot, and Shawna Overton. "Death and Afterlife: The Biblical Silence" in *Judaism in Late Antiquity*. Edited by Alan J. Avery-Peck and Jacob Neusner. Leiden: Brill, 2000.

Gillman, Neil. *The Death of Death: Resurrection and Immortality in Jewish Thought*. Woodstock, VT: Jewish Lights, 1997.

Halberstam, Chaya T. *Law and Truth in Biblical and Rabbinic Literature*. Bloomington: Indiana University Press, 2010.

Hallote, Rachel S. *Death, Burial, and Afterlife in the Biblical World: How the Israelites and Their Neighbors Treated the Dead*. Chicago: Ivan R. Dee, 2001.

Hammer, Reuven. "A Rabbinic Response to the Post Bar Kochba Era: The Sifre to Ha-Azinu." Paper presented at the Proceedings of the American Academy for Jewish Research, 1985.

———. *Sifre: A Tannaitic Commentary on the Book of Deuteronomy*. Yale Judaica Series. New Haven, CT: Yale University Press, 1986.

Herr, Moshe David. "Persecutions and Martyrdom in Hadrian's Days." *Scripta Hierosolymitana* 23 (1972): 85.

Jenni, Ernst. "Das Wort 'Ōlām Im Alten Testament." *Zeitschrift für die Alttestamentliche Wissenschaft* 64, no. 1 (1952): 197–248.

Jenni, Ernst, and Claus Westermann. *Theological Lexicon of the Old Testament.* Accordance electronic edition, version 2.1. ed. Peabody, MA: Hendrickson, 1997.

Johnston, Philip. *Shades of Sheol: Death and Afterlife in the Old Testament.* Downers Grove, IL: InterVarsity Press, 2002.

Katz, Steven T. "Man, Sin, and Redemption in Rabbinic Judaism." In *The Cambridge History of Judaism.* Vol. 4, *The Late Roman-Rabbinic Period,* edited by Steven T. Katz, 925–45. Cambridge: Cambridge University Press, 2006.

Klein, Ernest. *A Comprehensive Etymological Dictionary of the Hebrew Language for Readers of English.* New York: Macmillan, 1987.

Kraemer, David. *The Meanings of Death in Rabbinic Judaism.* London: Routledge, 2000.

———. *Responses to Suffering in Classical Rabbinic Literature.* New York: Oxford University Press, 1995.

Levenson, Jon D. *Resurrection and the Restoration of Israel: The Ultimate Victory of the God of Life.* New Haven, CT: Yale University Press, 2006.

Nickelsburg, George W. E. "Judgement, Life-after-Death, and Resurrection in the Apocrypha and the Non-Apocalyptic Pseudepigrapha." In *Judaism in Late Antiquity,* edited by Alan J. Avery-Peck and Jacob Neusner. Leiden: Brill, 2000.

———. *Resurrection, Immortality, and Eternal Life in Intertestamental Judaism and Early Christianity.* Expanded ed. Harvard Theological Studies. Cambridge, MA: Harvard University Press, 2006.

Rajak, Tessa. *Dying for the Law: The Martyr's Portrait in Jewish-Greek Literature.* The Jewish Dialogue with Greece and Rome. Edited by Tessa Rajak. Leiden: Brill, 2001.

Sasse, H. "Αιων." Translated by Geoffrey William Bromiley. In *Theological Dictionary of the New Testament,* edited by Gerhard Kittel. Grand Rapids, MI: Eerdmans, 1964.

Schofer, Jonathan. "Protest or Pedagogy? Trivial Sin and Divine Justice in Rabbinic Narrative." *Hebrew Union College Annual* 74 (2003): 243–78.

Segal, Alan F. *Life after Death: A History of the Afterlife in the Religions of the West.* New York: Doubleday, 2004.

Setzer, Claudia. "Resurrection of the Dead as Symbol and Strategy." *Journal of the American Academy of Religion* 69, no. 1 (2001): 65–101.

Urbach, Efraim E. *The Sages, Their Concepts and Beliefs.* Publications of the Perry Foundation in the Hebrew University of Jerusalem. Jerusalem: Magnes Press, Hebrew University, 1975.

Van Henten, Jan Willem, and Friedrich Avemarie. *Martyrdom and Noble Death: Selected Texts from Graeco-Roman, Jewish, and Christian Antiquity.* London: Routledge, 2002.

5

"They Are Israel"
Nonbinary Gender Then and Now

Gwynn Kessler, PhD

DECADES OF FEMINIST, queer, and trans scholarship have established that biblical constructions of gender are less stable than we might first realize.[1] Nevertheless, the biblical gender landscape presents male and female as exhaustive gender ("sex") categories.[2] Marc Brettler writes, "The Bible only recognizes two sexes: male and female." Brettler proceeds, by way of contrast, to invoke the presence of the categories *tumtum* and *androginos* in Rabbinic literature as evidence that while presumably people who exceed the confines of binary gender were known to exist, "they were ignored by the biblical authors."[3]

Indeed, if we take biblical binary gender as a starting point, the mere mention of *tumtum v'androginos* across Rabbinic sources from the third century CE forward provides strong evidence not only of a disruption but also a rupture in the ways biblical and Rabbinic authors wrote about bodies and gender; only the latter acknowledged genitalia and bodies beyond a male-female binary frame.[4] Faced with the knowledge of bodies that exceed the limitations of rigid, binary gender on the one hand and with the knowledge that biblical sources do not acknowledge such people on the other, Rabbinic sources did what they often do: rewrote Scripture in order to reflect their very existence. In other words, they denied any apparent disruption through the creation of midrash. In doing so, Rabbinic sources not only incorporated nonbinary gender people into the community of Israel, but they also insisted they were always already there in the beginning—*in Scripture.*[5]

This chapter first presents Rabbinic sources that situate nonbinary gender bodies within the community of Israel as if they always existed, which they did. It highlights the places where halachic discourse expands beyond a male-female binary gender frame inherent in, and inherited from, biblical sources to include these bodies as part of the people of Israel. Much of the chapter remains focused on this initial Rabbinic "disruption" of biblical gender categories through the introduction of the novel Rabbinic phrase *tumtum v'androginos*.[6] However, toward the end, I also consider ways that contemporary disruptions of binary gender, better thought of as further expansions of gender, touch across time to behold a usable past and to fortify a Jewish future beyond "beyond binary gender."

From Binary Biblical Bodies to Rabbinic Incorporation of Nonbinary Gendered Bodies

The Hebrew Bible readily appeals to the categories man (*ish*) and woman (*ishah*) and male (*zachar*) and female (*n'keivah*) as if they represent exhaustive gender categories. By their repeated mentions of men and women, husbands and wives, sons and daughters, etc., biblical sources not only reflect but actively construct gender within a hetero-patriarchal, male-female binary frame—a framing that simultaneously divides between men and women, naturalizes hetero-procreative impulses, and enshrines male privilege and power.

Beyond beginning with myths about male and female created simultaneously (Genesis 1) and woman fashioned from man (Genesis 2), the Hebrew Bible presents bodies as either male or female based on physiological characteristics. For example, Leviticus 12 assigns a newborn infant's gender based on genitalia, and it then prescribes different periods of birth impurity if a woman gives birth to a male child or a female child. The text represents the possibilities as exclusively *either* male *or* female. Likewise, Leviticus 15 delineates different periods of impurity that result from genital discharges for men and women, again representing men and women as exhaustive gender embodiments.

Rabbinic sources, in contrast, expand the biblical binary construction of gender. By incorporating *tumtum v'androginos* in numerous sources, they expose the Bible's binary construction of gender as partial instead of exhaustive. Man and woman, or male and female, as well as sons and daughters, are insufficient; they do not accurately reflect the diversity of gendered embodiments.

Tumtum v'Androginos

The phrase *tumtum v'androginos* enters into the earliest Rabbinic sources in the tannaitic period (first and second centuries CE). Lacking biblical precedent both linguistically and conceptually, *tumtum v'androginos* first appears, with notable frequency, across the tannaitic corpus: in midrashic compilations (*M'chilta, Sifra, Sifrei*), the Mishnah, and the *Tosefta*.

Although much recent scholarship, following medieval Talmudic commentators, distinguishes between the terms *tumtum* and *androginos* as if they are always and everywhere clearly demarcated, differentiated embodiments, the vast majority of tannaitic sources (and even many traditions in the Babylonian Talmud) make no clear, consistent distinctions.[7] Instead of reading through the lens of later sources, which increasingly distinguish between *tumtum* and *androginos*, in this chapter I foreground how the novel Rabbinic phrase *tumtum v'androginos* itself disrupts binary constructions of gender.[8]

Centering the phrase *tumtum v'androginos* allows us to see more readily how it functions as a novel Rabbinic gender category alongside the gender categories of male/man and female/woman. It also shifts us away from a potential pitfall I see looming in the focus on fixing the definitions of and distinctions between *tumtum* and *androginos* based on a selective reading of a minority of traditions from Rabbinic sources.[9] By reifying the meanings of *tumtum* and *androginos*, we are creating another binary at the precise point and through the very vehicle through which Rabbinic sources challenge binary constructions of gender. This binary, consisting of one who has an "excess" of genitalia (*androginos*) and one who has a discernible "lack" (*tumtum*), has flattened Rabbinic sources, and bodies, across different time periods and occluded development and disagreement across the corpora. In addition, it has led to a privileging in terms of disproportionate treatment of *androginos* over that of *tumtum*, one that is not shared by the primary sources.[10] Again, the majority of primary sources, especially those extant in tannaitic midrashic compilations and the Mishnah, use the phrase *tumtum v'androginos* without making distinctions.

Scholars will no doubt continue to parse Rabbinic sources for distinctions between *tumtum* and *androginos*. These are vital endeavors that will continue to shed light on Rabbinic constructions of gender in general and should expand, instead of flattening, our understandings of *tumtum* and *androginos* in their particularities. Here, however, I bring forward *tumtum v'androginos* itself, highlighting the ways that this phrase functions in tannaitic, midrashic, and Mishnaic sources as a Rabbinic category for bodies that exist outside the categories man/male and female/woman. My operating definition is that *tumtum v'androginos* is a novel Rabbinic phrase that functions as a category for "nonbinary gendered bodies." However, I leave the phrase *tumtum v'androginos* untranslated, to replicate the language of the tannaitic sources. Although perhaps initially awkward, I believe it to be a productive strategy to disrupt the traditional and consensus readings that approach these sources as if *tumtum* and *androginos* are always and everywhere static embodiments distinguishable from each other. However, as a category, *tumtum v'androginos* is distinguished from and outside of the Rabbinic categories of male/man and female/woman.

Tannaitic Midrashim

As mentioned previously, not only is the phrase *tumtum v'androginos* lacking in the Bible, but the language is also uniquely Rabbinic. Although it is used as a self-evident categorization throughout tannaitic midrashim, midrashic sources do not offer definitions beyond what the words might convey. Definitions and descriptions have accrued through inferences from the possible meanings of *tumtum* and *androginos* based on scant evidence (*Mishnah Y'vamot* 8:6 in particular) and other elaborations.

What is clear from midrashic sources is that *tumtum v'androginos* connotes those who are excluded from the scriptural words "man/male" and "woman/female" and who are neither assimilable nor reducible to a binary gender frame. Despite being categorically excluded from and unassimilable to man/male and woman/female, *tumtum v'androginos* is included in halachic discourse and considered obligated to perform most mitzvot that are discussed. In the following paragraphs, I present some textual examples from midrashim that establish *tumtum v'androginos* as a Rabbinic gender category that exists to recognize and incorporate nonbinary gendered bodies—that is, those bodies beyond a fixed male-female binary—into the collective community of Israel.

Extant midrashic sources (*Sifra*, *Sifrei*, and *M'chilta*) appear to use the phrase *tumtum v'androginos* without exception; they do not treat *tumtum* or *androginos* separately.[11] These sources never ask whether *tumtum v'androginos* are male or female or whether they should be categorized as man/male or woman/female. The assumption of each text, even its underlying logic, is that by definition, they are not male/man or female/woman and cannot be subsumed under either category. The very words used in the Bible for male (*zachar*) and man (*ish*), female (*n'keivah*) and woman (*ishah*), and their corollaries do not include *tumtum v'androginos*. In other words, *tumtum v'androginos* are, by definition, not man/male and not woman/female.

Leviticus 12:2–5 delineates varying lengths of birth impurities dependent on whether a woman gives birth to a male or female infant. The biblical text presents gender as binary, clearly assignable, and finite. Yet, the *Sifra*, a tannaitic midrashic compilation on the Book of Leviticus, acknowledges bodies beyond either male or female. Leviticus 12:2 states, "When a woman brings forth seed and gives birth to a male [*zachar*], she shall be impure as at the time of her condition of menstrual separation."[12] This is followed by Leviticus 12:5, "If she bears a female [*n'keivah*], she shall be impure for two weeks as during her menstration." In the *Sifra*, interpreting the mention of the word "female" in Leviticus 12:5, the text states, "'And when she gives birth to a female.' From the word female I only know female, from where do I know *tumtum v'androginos* are included [in the biblical commandments upon a woman to observe periods of birth impurities and then bring a sacrifice upon their birth]?" The text continues, "Scripture states, 'And when a woman gives birth (*teled*).' This matter [of birth impurities] depends only on birth (*teled*) [not on gender]."[13]

The *Sifra* expands biblical gender categories from binary to beyond. Second, it establishes that *tumtum v'androginos* are distinct from "female," mentioned in Leviticus 12:5, as well as from "male," mentioned in Leviticus 12:2. *Tumtum v'androginos* are not subsumed under either "male" or "female," and indeed, they are categorically excluded from the scriptural words "male" and "female" in this text. Their incorporation requires a

different scriptural word precisely because *tumtum v'androginos* are categorized as and defined by being not "male" and not "female." Here,
the word *teled* (she gives birth) establishes that *tumtum v'androginos* are
outside binary biblical gender and yet acknowledged, known, and recognized by biblical authority—God, according to the Rabbis.

Another tannaitic tradition likewise excludes *tumtum v'androginos*
from the scriptural words "sons" (*banim*) and "daughters" (*banot*), again
demonstrating that *tumtum v'androginos* is a novel Rabbinic category
for bodies that exist beyond binary gender. *M'chilta D'Rabbi Yishmael*, a
midrashic compilation on the biblical Book of Exodus, interprets Exodus 21:4, "If his master gave him a wife, and she has borne him sons or
daughters, the wife and her children shall belong to the master." The
M'chilta states:

> *If she has borne him sons or daughters.* I know only sons and daugh-
> ters. From where do I know this about *tumtum v'androginos* [that
> they too belong to the slave's master]?
> Scripture states *the wife and her children.* In each case [whatever
> their gender]." (*M'chilta D'Rabbi Yishmael, Mishpatim* 2)[14]

In this midrash, "her children" (*viladeha*) provides the scriptural opening for the Rabbinic text to read *tumtum v'androginos* into Scripture. And
here, *tumtum v'androginos* are excluded from the scriptural words "sons"
and "daughters," but they are included in the word "her children."

One last example from midrash demonstrates that *tumtum v'androginos*
is a category excluded from the biblical words "man" (*ish*) and "woman"
(*ishah*). *Sifrei B'midbar* interprets Numbers 5:6, "When a man or woman
shall commit any sin that people commit, to do a trespass against the
Eternal, and if that person be found guilty."[15] The following verse obligates those who are found guilty to confess and make restitution. Posit-
ing an apparent redundancy in this verse because it mentions both "man
or woman" and then "if that person" (*hanefesh hahi*), the text reads:

> *If that person be found guilty.* Why does Scripture mention *and if
> that person is guilty*?
> Since Scripture states *man or woman*, I know only man or woman.
> From where do I know [that if *tumtum v'androginos* commit a tres-

pass they too are obligated to confess and make restitution]?
Scripture states *and if that person is guilty*. (*Sifrei B'midbar, Naso* 2)

Again, *tumtum v'androginos* are excluded from the categories man or woman but included by virtue of the scriptural use of "that person."

In each of these examples, what defines *tumtum v'androginos* is that they are neither male/man nor female/woman. The midrashim work by explicitly excluding *tumtum v'androginos* from the biblical words that mean man/male and woman/female as well as sons and daughters. This is consistent across all tannaitic midrashic sources. And, in almost all those sources, an apparent redundancy located in a proximal word or in a similar verse elsewhere is mobilized to include *tumtum v'androginos* in the commandment being discussed. Bodies categorized as *tumtum v'androginos* are thus incorporated into the community of Israel because, as Rashi will succinctly summarize almost a thousand years after *tumtum v'androginos* enter the Rabbinic corpus, "they are Israel" (Rashi's commentary to Babylonian Talmud, *Arachin* 4a).

Now, asserting that *tumtum v'androginos* are Israel does not mean that they are equal to those at the top of Rabbinic expressions of Israel's power or hierarchy—those who are categorized as free, adult, unblemished men with full cognitive ability.[16] As we have seen, the sources are unanimous that *tumtum v'androginos* are *not men/male*. Moreover, there are commandments that *tumtum v'androginos*, being *not men*, are not obligated to perform. These are the commandments to appear before God at the Temple three times a year (Exodus 23:17, 34:23; Deuteronomy 16:16) and to be evaluated according to the monetary amount ascribed to men and women to give to the Temple (Leviticus 27).

It is unclear why these two commandments are exceptions to the strong tendency to include *tumtum v'androginos* in halachic obligations.[17] For my purposes here, however, it is important to point out that excluding *tumtum v'androginos* from these halachic obligations is not the same as excluding them from halachah, or "Jewish law," tout court. In fact, the halachic discussion *includes* them—as not male and not female— asserting their very existence in the face of biblical silence. For example, *M'chilta D'Rabbi Yishmael* interprets Exodus 23:17, "Three times a year all your males shall appear before the Sovereign, the Eternal": "Your males" excludes the women, and "all your males" excludes *tumtum v'androginos*

(*M'chilta D'Rabbi Yishmael, Mishpatim* 20). The halachic construction of gender here, as in the texts cited above, is not confined to binary male or female genders. There is another category that Rabbinic sources must address: nonbinary gendered bodies, or *tumtum v'androginos*.

To sum up, tannaitic midrashic sources supplement binary biblical constructions of gender. No longer are bodies divided between male and female only, but alongside halachic discussions of the categories male and female, there is another category: *tumtum v'androginos*. The Rabbinic acknowledgment of nonbinary gendered bodies brings with it, and necessitates, a new halachic category, *tumtum v'androginos*, precisely because they are defined as not male/man and not female/woman—outside binary gender.

Mishnah

The Mishnah uses the phrase *tumtum v'androginos* ten times and does so as if it is self-evident.[18] Though there are a few Mishnaic texts that appear to differentiate between *tumtum* and *androginos*, I do not think that they outweigh the majority of texts, especially given that the exceptional texts are almost always stated as minority opinions.[19] In the examples below, I focus on the majority positions where *tumtum v'androginos* is used as an additional gender category, alongside the categories of man/male and woman/female.

We saw above that the *Sifra* supplemented Leviticus 12's binary gender categories by discussing infants born who were not male or female. *Mishnah Nazir* 2:7 states, "[If a man says:] Behold, I am a *Nazir*[20] when there will be a son to me, and a son is born to him, behold he is a *Nazir*. [If] a daughter [is born to him] or *tumtum v'androginos*, he is not a *Nazir*. If he said: [I will be a *Nazir*] when I see that I have a child [*valad*], even if a daughter, or *tumtum v'androginos* is born to him, behold he is a *Nazir*."[21] As in the midrashic sources, which read the words *teled* (she gave birth) and *viladeha* (her children) as locating the inclusion of nonbinary gendered infants in the category of "child/offspring," this Mishnah appeals to the word *valad*, which is not gender-specific. Again, *tumtum v'androginos* are outside the categories male (son) and female (daughter). The text raises no concern or judgment about *tumtum v'androginos* offspring; in contrast, it naturalizes them. The concern, rather, is that the man making the vow use correct, precise language in obligating himself to be a *Nazir*. And, as with the *Sifra* text, *tumtum v'androginos* sits simultaneously alongside and outside of son and daughter, as an additional gender category.

Mishnah Bikurim 1:5 obligates *tumtum v'androginos* to bring first fruits to the Temple, stating: "The guardian, and the agent, and the slave, and the woman, and *tumtum v'androginos* bring [first fruits] but do not recite (Deuteronomy 26:10) [as free Israelite men do], since they cannot say *the land that You, God, have given me*." Since, according to the Bible, God divided the land among the Israelite men by tribes, *tumtum v'androginos*, defined by being not men, cannot utter those words. Here again, *tumtum v'androginos* are neither men, nor are they women, who are listed separately in this mishnah.²² However, as a recognized halachic gender category that stands outside male and female, they are obligated to bring first fruits.

Another example where the Mishnah clearly categorizes *tumtum v'androginos* outside of binary gender, outside of man/male and woman/female, is in *Mishnah Arachin* 1:1, which discusses commandments laid out in Leviticus 27:2–8 about donations to the Temple: "All [Israel] evaluate others [according to the fixed biblical *erech* amount] and are evaluated [according to the fixed biblical *erech* amount], and make vows [to donate the monetary worth] and are vowed about [regarding their monetary worth]: priests, Levites, and Israelites, women and slaves. And, *tumtum v'androginos* make vows and are vowed about and evaluate others, but they are not evaluated because no one is evaluated except 'male,' read literally, and 'female,' read literally."²³ The intricacies of this mishnah need not detain us. At its most basic level, however, this mishnah deals with a substantial issue: who counts as Israel?²⁴ Here again, *tumtum v'androginos* appear as squarely outside the categories of men/male and women/female and as a distinct halachic gender category. And, here again, *tumtum v'androginos* are integrated into halachah precisely as neither men nor women. Men and women are obligated in all four types of vows listed in this mishnah, while *tumtum v'androginos*, being not male and not female, are only obligated to three out of the four.

In all Mishnaic texts where the phrase appears, *tumtum v'androginos* functions as a category of gender that supplements and remains outside of the categories male and female. Even in the rare Mishnaic texts that mention *androginos* without *tumtum* and discuss the *androginos*'s penis, they are outside the category of "men."[25] For example, according to the *tanna kama* (the anonymous, majority opinion) in *Mishnah Shabbat* 19:3, an *androginos* infant is not circumcised on the eighth day if it falls on Shabbat, while typically healthy male infants are. Rabbi Y'hudah, however, permits the *androginos*'s penis to be circumcised. The task before us, however, is to understand that Rabbi Y'hudah is not deeming this infant male by virtue of their penis. He is simply voicing his individual opinion that for any healthy infant who has a penis, circumcision is permitted on Shabbat.[26] The Babylonian Talmud, commenting on this mishnah, puts it this way: "Not in all matters (alternatively, nor categorically) did Rabbi Y'hudah say *androginos* is male" (Babylonian Talmud, *Shabbat* 136b). We must also remember that in the Mishnah itself, there's never any reason to even think *androginos* is male, as tannaitic texts over and over insist that *tumtum v'androginos* are not male and not female.

Even *Mishnah Shabbat* 19:3, understood in the context of near-unanimous tannaitic midrashic and Mishnaic teachings that *tumtum v'androginos* are not male and not female, beckons us to see constructions of gender beyond binary bodies and binary genitalia. This infant has a penis and is not male and not female. *Mishnah Shabbat* 19:3 is a counter-text to *Tosefta Shabbat* 15:9, which does not mention *tumtum v'androginos* as it blithely proclaims that circumcision occurs "at the place from which a child is assigned male or female."

Mishnaic texts, as we have seen with midrashic texts, consistently supplement binary constructions of gender through the category of *tumtum v'androginos*. Both sets of sources disrupt binary biblical constructions of gender and compel us to see Rabbinic constructions of gender as working beyond a male-female binary as well. Moreover, all of these texts obligate (or exempt) *tumtum v'androginos* from mitzvot explicitly as nonbinary gendered bodies who are (part of) Israel. *Tumtum v'androginos* are neither male nor female, and as nonbinary gendered bodies, from the selected texts I've presented here, we see that their births matter (*Mishnah Nazir* 2:7), they are commanded to bring first fruits to the Temple (*Mishnah Bikurim* 1:5), and their bodies are counted and valued (*Mishnah Arachin* 1:1). According to *Mishnah Arachin* 1:1, the bodies that comprise Israel—*tumtum v'androginos* included—are valued according to "market value," the value one would be sold for on the slave market. Of course, we, instead, are obligated to recognize the real value, the pricelessness, of each and every body.

From "They Are Israel" to We Are Israel

In the material above, I have presented the Rabbinic category of *tumtum v'androginos* as a disruption of a rigid, binary construction of gender pervasive in the Hebrew Bible. I have also interrupted traditional and scholarly approaches to *tumtum* and *androginos* by focusing on how the phrase *tumtum v'androginos* itself functions as a novel Rabbinic gender category that exists alongside, but not subsumed by, male and female gender categories. I've also suggested that tannaitic sources offer us historical precedent for disrupting fixed gender/sex based on the presence of particular genitalia (*Mishnah Shabbat* 19:3). All of this contributes to the recognition that Jewish sources have long recognized nonbinary gendered bodies, accounted for them, and counted them as part of Israel.

And yet, recognition and acknowledgment of bodies categorized as *tumtum v'androginos* are not sufficient. Even as Rabbinic sources recognize male and female gender as insufficient and incomplete, the sources, with their sorting and sourcing of bodies, are not enough. I have creatively embraced Rashi's statement "They are Israel" in ways that make a statement about language, speech, pronouns, self-proclamations, and self-creations. At the same time, I have used the language of "nonbinary gendered bodies" to draw attention to some overlap and simultaneously signal significant difference between then and now.

Nonbinary gendered bodies are not the same as self-identifying as trans, gender nonconforming, or nonbinary gender. Some might be comforted by some overlap; others will be at best indifferent. I have been both, other, and more.

Throughout Rabbinic sources, *tumtum v'androginos* are silenced bodies categorized by others, without bothering ever to ask or even deigning to animate such bodies with speech.

In the end, "They are Israel," is not the same as "We are Israel." And, yet, we most certainly are—and always have been.

Notes

1. Among contemporary biblical scholars who have engaged in gender and queer theories, see, for example, Robert Goss and Mona West, *Take Back the Word: A Queer Reading of the Bible* (Cleveland: Pilgrim Press, 2000); Ken Stone, *Queer Commentary and the Hebrew Bible* (London: Sheffield Academic Press, 2001); Deryn Guest et al., *Queer Bible Commentary* (London: SCI Press, 2006); Ken Stone and Theresa Hornsby, *Bible Trouble: Queer Reading at the Boundaries of Biblical Scholarship* (Atlanta: SBL Press, 2011); Rhiannon Graybill, *Are We Not Men? Unstable Masculinity in the Hebrew Prophets* (Oxford: Oxford University Press, 2016).

2. This chapter is written from a perspective central to queer theory, which challenges the notion that biological sex can be understood as separated from constructions of gender. I use the word "gender" instead of "sex" throughout in order to convey that understandings of biology are influenced by cultural assumptions. See Judith Butler, *Gender Trouble: Feminism and the Subversion of Identity* (New York: Routledge, 1990).

3. Marc Brettler, "Happy Is the Man Who Fills His Quiver with Them (Ps. 127:5): Constructions of Masculinities in the Psalms," in *Being a Man: Negotiating Ancient Constructs of Maculinity*, ed. Ilona Zsolnay (London: Routledge, 2016), 198–99. See also Amy Kalmanofsky, *Gender-Play in the Hebrew Bible: The Ways the Bible Challenges Its Gender Norms* (London: Routledge, 2016).

4. It is important to note, however, that the exclusive binary construction of gender in the Bible is itself a departure from and disruption of other ancient Near Eastern literatures, which did record nonbinary gendered bodies. See, for example, Uri Gabbay, "The Akkadian Word of 'Third Gender': The Kalu (gala) Once Again," in *Proceedings of the 51st Rencontre Assyriologique Internationale at the Oriental Institute of the University of Chicago, July 18–22, 2005*, ed. Robert D. Diggs, Jennie Myers, and Martha Tobi Roth (Chicago: Oriental Institute of the University of Chicago, 2008); Ilan Peled, *Masculinities and Third Gender: The Origins and Nature of an Institutionalized Gender and Otherness in the Ancient Near East* (Munster: Ugarit-Verlag, 2016); Saana Svard and Maretti Nissinen, "(Re)constructing the Image of the Assinnu," in *Studying Gender in the Ancient Near East*, ed. Saana Svard and Agnes Garciea-Ventura (University Park, PA: Eisenbrauns, 2018), 373–411; and Sophus Helle, "Only in Dress? Methodological Concerns Regarding Non-Binary Gender," in *Gender and Methodology in the Ancient Near East: Approaches from Assyriology and Beyond*, ed. Stephanie Lynn Budin et al. (Barcelona: Edicions De La Univesitat de Barcelona, 2018), 41–53.

5. For a lengthier discussion, see Gwynn Kessler, "Rabbinic Gender: Beyond Male and Female," *A Companion to Late Ancient Jews and Judaism: Third Century BCE to Seventh Century CE*, Naomi Koltun-Fromm and Gwynn Kessler, eds. (Hoboken, NJ: Wiley Blackwell, 2020).

6. *Tumtum* is commonly understood as a person who has indeterminate genitalia or one who lacks discernible genitalia, and *androginos* (a Greek loan word literally combining the words "man" and "woman") is commonly understood as a person who has a penis (man) and a vagina (woman). That said, this chapter shifts our focus away from these fixed definitions of *tumtum* and *androginos*, which have arisen from a small selection of sources and minority opinions expressed within them, and focuses instead on the use of *tumtum v'androginos* without distinguishing between the terms.

7. See, for example, Babylonian Talmud: *Nazir* 13a; *Y'vamot* 99b; *Sanhedrin* 66a, 85b; *Arachin* 2a, 4a–5b; *T'murah* 11a, 24b; *Nidah* 28a–b, 40a. *B'chorot* 41b–42b explicitly grapples with distinguishing between the categories *tumtum* and *androginos*. The efforts expended here, attempting to distinguish the categories, suggest cautiousness in assuming facile distinctions across texts of different time periods.

8. I do not include sources from the *Tosefta* except toward the end of this chapter. Although the majority of Toseftan sources use *tumtum v'androginos*, the compilation also has a number of traditions that posit distinctive halachic rulings for *tumtum* and *androginos* people. I consider *Tosefta Bikurim* 2:3–7, which is often presented as the "seminal" text, as a post-tannaitic interpolation into the *Tosefta*. However, even if it is tannaitic, its unique, exceptional framing should not determine our understanding of *tumtum v'androginos* across all Rabbinic sources.

9. Even the minority of traditions that separate *tumtum* and *androginos* in Mishnaic sources are presented as a minority opinion attributed to an individual *Tanna*. See Mishnah *Shabbat* 19:3; *Y'vamot* 8:6; and *Parah* 5:4.

10. See, for example, Charlotte Fonrobert, "Gender Duality and Its Subversions in Rabbinic Law," in *Gender in Judaism and Islam: Common Lives, Uncommon Heritage*, ed. Firoozeh Kashani-Sabbet and Beth Wenger (New York: New York University Press, 2014); Marianne Schleicher, "Constructions of Sex and Gender: Attending to Androgynes and Tumtumim through Jewish Scriptural Use," *Literature and Theology* 25, no. 4 (2011): 422–35; Max Strassfeld, "Translating the Human: The Androginos in Tosefta Bikurim," *Transgender Quarterly Review* 3, no. 3–4 (2016): 587–604; and Sarra Lev, "A Creation Sui Generis: The Evolution of a Concept," in *From Scrolls to Traditions: A Festschrift Honoring Lawrence H. Schiffman*, ed. Stuart S. Milller et al. (Leiden: Brill, 2021), 325–249. The disproportionate emphasis whereby *androginos* has come to dominate is due to the placement of *Tosefta Bikurim* 2:3–7 as the "seminal" source." However, this is an exceptional source, which uses language otherwise unattested in extant tannaitic sources.

11. The one extant tannaitic midrashic source where *androginos* appears outside of *tumtum v'androginos* is interpolated from *Mishnah Shabbat* 19:3. See *Sifra*,

Tazria 1:5, in *Sifra deVei Rav: Hu Sefer Torah Kohanim*, ed. I.H. Weiss (Vienna: J. Scholssberg, 1862), 58c. On the *Sifra's* frequent use of Mishnaic sources, see H. L. Strack and Gunter Stemberger, *Introduction to the Talmud and Midrash*, trans. and ed. Markus Bockmuehl (Minneapolis: Fortress Press, 1996), 262–63.

12. Author's adapted translation.

13. *Sifra, Tazria*, manuscript Vatican 66, in *Sifra or Torat Kohanim according to Codex Assemani LXVI*, ed. Louis Finkelstein (New York: Jewish Theological Seminary of America, 1956), 61 (corresponds to Weiss 58d). See also Babylonian Talmud, *Nidah* 40a.

14. *M'chilta D'Rabbi Yishmael on Exodus*, ed. H. S. Horovitz and A. Rabin (Frankfurt am Main: J. Kauffman, 1928–31; reprint, Jerusalem: Shalem Books, 1997), 250.

15. Author's translation.

16. They can, however, be priests, because this is an inherited status, which grants *tumtum v'androginos* some privileges over non-priestly men (e.g., eating *t'rumah*). See *Mishnah Y'vamot* 8:6; Babylonian Talmud, *Y'vamot* 99b; *Tosefta Y'vamot* 10:2; *Tosefta T'rumot* 10:18.

17. While both of these commandments are connected to the Temple, it is not the case that *tumtum v'androginos* are excluded from all Temple-related commandments. According to *Sifrei D'varim* 301, *tumtum v'androginos* are obligated to bring first fruits to the Temple, though they cannot utter the accompanying biblical verse as men would (see *M'chilta D'Rabbi Yishmael, Mishpatim* 20; *Mishnah Bikkurim* 1:5). According to *Sifra B'chukotai*, although *tumtum v'androginos* are not evaluated according to specific *erech*, vows of evaluation, to be donated to the Temple funds, they are able to make such evaluations of men and women to donate, and they are eligible for other monetary vows to be donated to the Temple (see *Mishnah Arachin* 1:1). See also Babylonian Talmud, *Arachin* 4a, which obligates *tumtum v'androginos* to bring guilt offerings.

18. See Mishnah: *Bikurim* 1:5; *Chagigah* 1:1; *B'chorot* 6:1; *Nazir* 2:1; *Arachin* 1:1, *T'murah* 2:3, 5:2; *Nidah* 3:5; *Zavim* 2:1; and *Parah* 10.

19. In *Mishnah Shabbat* 19:3, *Y'vamot* 8:6, and *Parah* 5:4, *androginos* is mentioned distinguished from *tumtum*; in each of these sources, the statements are presented as minority opinions, usually attributed to Rabbi Y'hudah. *Mishnah Bava Batra* 9:2 is the only tannaitic midrashic and Mishnaic source that mentions *tumtum* without *androginos*, though the Parma manuscript adds *androginos* in the second clause. *Mishnah Bikurim* 4, which is a parallel to Babylonian Talmud, *Bikurim* 2:3–7, was not included in earliest manuscripts of the Mishnah; the Jerusalem Talmud does not comment on it in *Masechet Bikurim* or elsewhere.

20. A *Nazir* is a person who takes a Nazirite vow (Numbers 6:1–21), voluntarily vows to abstain from drinking wine and cutting their hair, and also vows to maintain ritual purity for a certain amount of time.

21. Read according to ms. Kaufman and Cambridge T-S E 91 (*genizah* fragment), https://web.nli.org.il/sites/nli/Hebrew/collections/jewish-collection/Talmud/Pages/default.aspx?IsByManuscript=False&Im_Ms=1723&Fr_Co=2&Fr_Tr=27&Pe_code=002&Mi_code=07&Li_code=-1.

22. It is grammatically plausible, and seems quite likely to me, that *tumtum v'androginos* often connotes one category, which is presented as parallel to the other single categories: guardians and agents; slaves and women; and *tumtum v'androginos* people. At the same time, the language differs slightly insofar as each other category is presented as a collective singular with a definite article (*haapotropos, v'hashaliach, v'ha-eved, v'ha-ishah*), but then the text switches to *v'tumtum v'androginos*. The term *tumtum v'androginos*, as well as *tumtum* and *androginos*, never appears with a definite article. This is true throughout the extant Rabbinic corpus, including the Talmuds. In halachic contexts, plural forms are also never used. See *Mishnah Chagigah* 1:1, where the text uses either plural forms or definite articles for all other categories except *tumtum v'androginos*. The grammatical uniqueness of the phrase is apparent there. See also *Mishnah Arachin* 1:1. There is one use of the plural *tumtumin* in the context of a midrashic interpretation in the Babylonian Talmud (unparalleled in amoraic midrashim), which states that Abraham and Sarah were *tumtumin* (Babylonian Talmud, *Y'vamot* 64a).

23. I am translating according to the text of *Mishnah Arachin* 1:1 in ms. Kaufmann, which reads "*zachar vadii* and *n'keivah vadii*." See Sokoloff (1992 s.v. vadii): "in reality (i.e., understand the word literally)." Cf, for example: *Mishnah P'sachim* 9:2; *Tosefta Sotah* 4:4 (Lieberman); *Vayikrah Rabbah* 34:8. *Mishnah Arachin* 1:1 is usually translated as "certain" or "definite" male and female, reading vadai as the opposite of safek (uncertain). Note that the manuscript spells *vadai* as ודיי rather than ודאי, which we have rendered here as *vadii*. However, neither the Mishnah nor tannaitic midrashim ever use the word *safek* in reference to *tumtum v'androginos* (or *tumtum* or *androginos*).

24. See Jane Kanarek, "Rewriting *Arakhin*: Women and Tannaitic Vows of Valuation," *AJS Review* 40, no. 2 (November 2016): 261–77.

25. *Mishnah Shabbat* 19:3 is the only text that explicitly mentions that an *androginos* has a penis. That an *androginos* has a penis and vagina is inferred from *Mishnah Y'vamot* 8:6.

26. See Jerusalem Talmud, *Shabbat* 19:3:17b; *Chagigah* 1:1:76b; *Y'vamot* 8:1:9a.

PART THREE

Medieval Constructions

6

The Radical Rationalist
Maimonides Reshapes Rabbinic Discourse

Tamar Ron Marvin, PhD

"FROM MOSES TO MOSES, there was none like Moses." This folk saying, written as an epitaph on the traditional site of the grave of Moses Maimonides (Rambam), expresses the great reverence with which he is regarded.[1] Originating in the Middle Ages, the saying playfully suggests that Maimonides is on par with the biblical Moses. Today, Maimonides's influence continues to shape Jewish life across the diverse array of Jewish communities. His works are lovingly probed in yeshivot and consulted curiously by secular seekers. But Maimonides was also a radical thinker who garnered strident criticism in his lifetime and set off waves of controversy thereafter. He sought to encapsulate Jewish law in an accessible guide, which he called *Mishneh Torah*, "a second Torah,"[2] imposing order upon the messy, meandering conversations of the Talmudic rabbis. At the head of this work, Maimonides placed *Sefer HaMada* (*The Book of Knowledge*), integrating the received wisdom of Jewish tradition with the rational philosophy of Aristotle. The tension between the dialectical exuberance of traditional Jewish discourse and Maimonides's quest to systematize Jewish law and belief underlies all subsequent Jewish thought.

Between al-Andalus and Egypt

His whole life, Maimonides referred to himself as "Moses, the son of Maimon, the Spaniard" (Moshe ben Maimon HaSefaradi). This is the name visible in his autograph signature, which has come down to us from the Cairo Genizah.[3] In his self-conception, Maimonides was rooted in a community that saw itself as descended from "the Jerusalemite exile community of Sepharad" mentioned by the prophet Obadiah (Obadiah 1:20).[4] His formative years were spent in Córdoba, the jewel of al-Andalus, where he was born approximately 1138. His father, Maimon, was a judge in the rabbinical court; Maimon had been educated in the Lucena academy of the renowned Joseph Ibn Migash, a student of the famed Talmudist Isaac al-Fasi (Rif), both of whom his son would consider his greatest intellectual influences.[5]

Sometime in his early adulthood, in about 1159, Maimonides was impelled, like many other Andalusi Jews, to flee with his family due to the intolerant policies of the Muwahhidun (Almohads), Berber Muslims from the Maghrib (present-day Morocco), who had invaded the weakened city-states of Muslim Iberia.[6] He spent seven years in Fez, an odd choice for a family fleeing the Muwahhidun, as it was their capital. According to the near-contemporaneous account of Ibn al-Qifti, a Muslim historian who included an entry on Maimonides in his encyclopedia of philosophers, the Maimonides family had been compelled to convert to Islam.[7] Further evidence for this is conjectural, and the claim is contested. What we know is that Maimonides made notably empathic halachic rulings regarding forced converts.[8] While still in Fez, Maimonides trained to become a physician and began writing one of his key works, the *Commentary on the Mishnah*.[9]

This chapter of Maimonides's life is one that has, until recently, been less examined. Sarah Stroumsa has suggested that Maimonides's experiences in Fez under Muwahhidun rule were formative upon his thought.[10] In particular, the Muwahhidun emphasis on the absolute unity of God and on doctrinal purity in general is echoed in Maimonides's strident indictment of anthropomorphizing God (for example, understanding God as having a body or emotions) and his adoption of fundamental principles of belief for all Jews. Another influential aspect of Muwahhidun thought was the significance it placed upon primary sources of law (*usul*). This was reflected in the legal compendia of the school of Ibn Tumart, which, unlike those of the Maliki tradition they supplanted, do not record disagreements among scholars or chains of transmission. Consider, in light of this, Maimonides's account of his methodology in crafting a code of Jewish law: "I . . . intently studied all these works, with the view of putting together the results obtained from them in regard to what is forbidden or permitted, clean or unclean, and the other rules of the Torah—*all in plain language and terse style*, so that thus the entire Oral Law might become *systematically known to all, without citing difficulties and solutions or differences of view,* one person saying so, and another something else—*but consisting of statements, clear and convincing.*"[11]

Around 1166, when Maimonides was nearing thirty, the family settled in Fustat (Old Cairo).[12] Quickly recognized as a scholar and leader, Maimonides was tasked with communal responsibilities, particularly in rendering difficult legal decisions. From this period until the end of his life, Maimonides produced important responsa (especially impactful upon the Jewish community in Yemen), which often reveal a more pragmatic and sensitive side to the intellectual philosopher. He was even promoted briefly to the office of *ra'is al-yahud,* the Jewish representative to the Muslim government, usually reserved for well-connected locals.[13] Soon after settling in Fustat, Maimonides completed the *Commentary on the Mishnah* and almost immediately began work on his masterpiece, *Mishneh Torah,* a comprehensive law code, around 1168.

Maimonides worked on *Mishneh Torah* for close to a decade. During this time, the extended family was supported by Maimonides's beloved younger brother David, a merchant. In 1177, disaster struck when David was drowned, along with the family fortune, in the Indian Ocean. Maimonides records that he endured a year of debilitating depression following David's death.[14] Years later, he wrote, "Close to eight years have now elapsed and I still mourn for him, for there can be no consolation.... He has departed to his eternal life and left me confounded in a strange land. . . . Whenever I come across his handwriting in one of his books my heart turns within me and my grief reawakens."[15] In addition, the circumstances of his brother's death meant that the financial support of the family now fell upon Maimonides. Building upon his earlier training, he began working as a physician and was soon awarded the office of physician to the vizier. In this capacity, Maimonides worked grueling days in the palace followed by hours of service, both medical and halachic, to the Jewish community. In a letter he wrote to his eager young protégé and translator, Samuel Ibn Tibbon, Maimonides describes his packed schedule. Still, during this period, Maimonides found time to produce medical works as well as his major work of philosophy, *The Guide for the Perplexed,* in which he set out to reconcile human reason with revealed tradition by explaining difficult passages in Scripture. It was translated by Ibn Tibbon from Judeo-Arabic into Hebrew in the year of Maimonides's death, 1204.

Constructing Creed

Although only fragments remain, we know that a precocious Maimonides wrote commentaries on several orders of the Babylonian Talmud, as well as a digest of the Jerusalem Talmud modeled after al-Fasi's.[16] Something significant shifted in Maimonides's thinking between his youthful Talmud commentaries and the time in Fez that he picked up his pen to write the *Commentary on the Mishnah*. He desired to return to the Mishnah as the source of the law, obviating the *shakla v'tarya* (back-and-forth) of the Gemara, the discursive and dialectical Rabbinic commentary on the Mishnah that constitutes the bulk of the Talmud. In so doing, Maimonides decentered the Talmud and positioned the Mishnah as the core source of law. His approach did not minimize the authority of the Talmud, which Maimonides readily affirmed.[17] Still, his emphasis on the Mishnah was audacious; like the *Amoraim*, he could engage in a generative process from the unadulterated source, the Mishnah.

The *Commentary on the Mishnah* also served for Maimonides as a testing ground for his growing perception that belief in particular truth propositions was required of Jews. The first place this occurs is in *Sh'monah P'rakim* (*The Eight Chapters*), his introduction to *Pirkei Avot*, a unique tractate of the Mishnah dealing with ethics. In this mini-treatise, Maimonides explores the characteristics of the soul, advocating for a "golden mean" balancing between different needs and desires, a theme to which he would return throughout his work. The *Sh'monah P'rakim* is also an integration of Jewish tradition with ideas and methods culled from medieval Aristotelianism, the science of his day. Medieval Aristotelian traditions, which included Neoplatonic works misattributed to Aristotle, was, in Maimonides's cultural context, mediated heavily through the commentaries of the Muslim philosopher Ibn Rushd (Averroes, 1126–98). Although such knowledge was external to Jewish tradition, Maimonides would insist, "One should accept the truth from whatever source it comes."[18] The insertion of Aristotelianism into an introduction to a traditional text like *Pirkei Avot* shows that Maimonides saw non-Jewish and Jewish wisdom as complementary, even required, for a full understanding of Torah.

The second place in the *Commentary on the Mishnah* where Maimonides inserted systematic theology is in the special introduction he wrote to *Perek Chelek*, the tenth chapter of Tractate *Sanhedrin*, which opens with the declaration, "All Jews have a share in the world-to-come" (10:1). The Mishnah proceeds to list three exceptions: one who denies the resurrection of the dead, one who denies the divinity of the Torah, and the heretic (*epikoros*).[19] It is here that he presents his Thirteen Principles of Faith. The theological propositions that Maimonides describes as normative and incumbent upon every Jew are belief in (1) God's existence, (2) God's unity, (3) God's incorporeality, (4) God's eternality, (5) the prohibition of idolatry, (6) the existence of prophecy, (7) the special prophetic status of Moses, (8) the divinity of the Torah, (9) the authenticity of the Torah, (10) divine omniscience, (11) divine reward and punishment, (12) the existence of a future messiah, and (13) the resurrection of the dead.[20]

Menachem Kellner notes that prior to Maimonides, the Jewish sense of *emunah*, "faith," usually refers to "belief in," an emotive loyalty or trust, as evoked in the commonly said phrase "I believe in you." Maimonides's innovation is to integrate an essentially Aristotelian way of thinking into *emunah*, transforming it into "belief that," intellectual assent to a truth proposition, as evoked in the common phrase "I believe that to be true."[21] The chasm he opened between "belief in" and "belief that" is one into which real people can really fall; failure to comply intellectually with the Thirteen Principles of faith has dire consequences. In Maimonides's conception, a heretic forfeits their Jewish personhood: "When all these principles are perfectly understood and believed in by a person, *they enter into the community of Israel*. . . . But if a person doubts any of these principles, *they leave the community*, denies the fundamental, and is called a . . . heretic (*epikoros*). . . . One is required to hate them and destroy them."[22] That not only means that a person is eschatologically barred from the world-to-come, as per *Mishnah Sanhedrin* 10:1; it has implications for that person's membership in the Jewish community of this world too.[23] On the ground, however, such questions were largely ignored.[24]

Mishneh Torah opens with a section called *Sefer HaMada* (*The Book of Knowledge*), serving as a preliminary section of theology and science that Maimonides considered prerequisite for proper understanding of the law. It begins with principles of the Torah and continues with ethics, scientific information needed to understand God's world, laws of Torah study, an extended disquisition on the nature of the prohibition on idolatry, and the laws of *t'shuvah*, "repentance." *Sefer HaMada* begins, "The basic principle of all basic principles and the pillar of all knowledge is to realize that there is a First Being who brought every existing thing into being."[25] Note Maimonides's language here: on the one hand, God is described in Aristotelian terms as the First Being (or First Cause); on the other hand, it is God and Creation that are the most basic principle of existence. In the third chapter, we are faced with something surprising— an explanation of basic concepts in medieval astronomy—while chapter 4 treats the four elements, the soul, and epistemology. Maimonides makes a powerful statement here that rational understanding is the basis of the ideal practice of the law.

Maimonides's philosophical magnum opus is the evocatively titled *Guide for the Perplexed*, a beacon for rationally minded Jews for the past nine hundred years.[26] Unlike its precursor, Saadyah Gaon's *Sefer Emunot V'Dei-ot* (*The Book of Doctrines and Beliefs*, 933 CE), the *Guide* was not systematically organized. In fact, Maimonides was at pains to emphasize that due to the sensitivity of the subject matter, "you should not ask of me here anything beyond the chapter headings. And even those are not set down in order or arranged in coherent fashion in this treatise, but rather are scattered and entangled with other subjects that are to be clarified. For my purpose is that the truths be glimpsed and then again be concealed from the vulgar among the people."[27] The *Guide* has since been scoured and analyzed by generations of scholars. Shlomo Pines created an analytical table of contents that seeks to unscramble Maimonides's "chapter headings";[28] Leo Strauss famously suggested that Maimonides was impelled by socioreligious forces to hide his true beliefs, which were radically Aristotelian.[29] But the *Guide* retains its enigmatic nature. One of its most powerful ideas is the paradoxical tension of what has been called the *via negativa*, the impossibility of describing God, even as the core task of the human being is to achieve intellectual understanding of the Divine. The *Guide* has meant that Jews have a powerful precedent for reconciling tradition with secular knowledge and a guide to approaching serious questions with both faith and curiosity.

Systematizing Rabbinic Discourse

The theological work Maimonides began in the *Commentary on the Mishnah* was developed further in the *Sefer HaMitvzot (Book of Commandments)*, which is crucial to understanding the revolutionary moves that he makes in *Mishneh Torah*.[30] In it, Maimonides explains the fourteen rules by which he determined which commandments would count toward the traditional 613 commandments said to be included in the Torah.[31] He answers such questions as the following: How do we decide what is a Torah law and what is a Rabbinic law? What happens if there are too many commandments—which ones count? He criticizes previous attempts to enumerate the commandments, especially those of the geonic *Halachot G'dolot*, which he viewed as inconsistent and misleading. Maimonides then describes each commandment according to his own system, rearranged in two major divisions, positive commandments ("you shall") and negative commandments ("you shall not"). Importantly, he includes in these what might be called commandments of thought, beliefs that are required of Jews. This list would form the backbone of *Mishneh Torah*.

In *Sefer HaMitzvot*, Maimonides also crafted what was in effect a programmatic introduction to *Mishneh Torah*. It was brazen: "Such was my goal to be in this work: brevity with completeness—so that the reader thereof might encompass all that is found in the Mishnah and Talmud, *Sifra*, *Sifre*, and *Tosefta*, and more than that, all the decrees and ordinances of the later *Geonim*," Maimonides writes.[32] He continues with a remarkable claim about *Mishneh Torah*: "In short, outside of this work there was to be no need for another book to learn anything whatsoever that is required in the whole Torah, whether it be a law of the Scriptures or of the rabbis."[33] Maimonides also made a deliberate decision to write in Mishnaic Hebrew, "so that it should be easily understood by most of the people."[34] His goal was to make his law code accessible to Jews across the known world.

In the *Mishneh Torah*, Maimonides developed a unique taxonomy, arranging the 613 precepts of *Sefer HaMitzvot* into thematic units different from those of any previous halachic compendium. This organizational strategy allowed him to detach halachah from the order of the Mishnah by creating his own sui generis orders and chapters. He first divided the totality of the law into fourteen thematic treatises that he termed *s'farim*, "books," including, for example, *Sefer Z'manim* (Book of Occasions) and *Sefer N'zikin* (Book of Torts). Here a comparison to the organizational scheme of the Mishnah (and the Talmud based upon it) is instructive. The Talmud, too, is composed of *s'darim* (orders), which in some cases overlap with the *s'farim* of *Mishneh Torah*. For instance, the Talmud's *Seder Mo-eid* covers holidays and other appointed times on the Jewish calendar, as does *Mishneh Torah*'s *Sefer Z'manim*. This is not always the case, however: *Mishneh Torah*'s *Sefer Kinyan* (Book of Acquisition) has no analogue in the Talmud. Maimonides's highest taxonomic level, with fourteen categories, allows for more specificity than does the Talmud's. This constituted a bold reconceptualization of Rabbinic law. No one before or since has used the categories named by Maimonides.

Maimonides further subdivided each book of *Mishneh Torah* into sections. For instance, the laws pertaining to Passover are to be found in *Sefer Z'manim* under the section *Hilchot Chameitz Umatzah* (Laws of Leaven and Matzah). These sections also evince bold creativity. In the Talmud, the laws of Passover are mostly to be found in Tractate *P'sachim*. However, its primary topic is not Passover as it is observed by Jews at home, but the laws of the paschal sacrifice. In recognition of this, Maimonides bifurcated Tractate *P'sachim*. He placed the laws of the paschal sacrifice in *Sefer Korbanot* (Book of Sacrifices) under the section called *Hilchot Korban Pesach* (Laws of the Passover Sacrifice). Meanwhile, the laws of Passover observance, such as ridding one's home of leavened goods and holding the seder meal, are placed in *Sefer Z'manim* under *Hilchot Chameitz Umatzah*.[35] In this manner, Maimonides created a from-the-ground-up reconfiguration of laws that govern everything from a Jew's daily life to the functioning of an ideal halachic state. It took the work of many commentators to reconstruct Maimonides's sources; it was Joshua Boaz Baruch, a Spanish exile living in Italy in the sixteenth century, who created the extensive cross-references necessary to connect the Talmud text to Maimonides's rulings.[36] *Mishneh Torah* is a well-conceived repository of the entirety of Jewish legal tradition, but it accomplishes this at the cost of detachment from Rabbinic modes of organizing knowledge, the legacy of centuries of oral transmission.

Maimonides's reconceptualization of Rabbinic law did not, ultimately, win out. The *Mishneh Torah* surely remains a core text without which no consideration of the law can be made. To a large extent, however, the imprecise orders of the Talmud maintained their hold over traditional Jewish learning.[37] It was Jacob ben Asher who created the organizational scheme that was widely adopted. Written around the turn of the fourteenth century in Christian Spain, his code was titled *Arbaah Turim*, meaning "the four rows"—that is, of gemstones in the High Priest's breastplate. As its name implies, it consists of just four broad sections: *Orach Chayim*, on prayer and holidays; *Yoreh Dei-ah*, on everyday ritual law; *Even HaEizer*, on family law; and *Choshen HaMishpat*, on torts and business law.[38] *Arbaah Turim*, commonly referred to as the *Tur*, omits theoretical areas of halachah that Maimonides was mindful to include, such as the Temple service and the messianic age. The *Tur* would serve as the basis of the *Shulchan Aruch* by the Sephardic Yosef Karo, which, with the added glosses of the Ashkenazic Moses Isserles, became the comprehensive code of Sephardic and Ashkenazic Jews alike with its publication in the sixteenth century.[39]

What made the *Tur*'s conceptual scheme more successful than that of *Mishneh Torah*? Was this a case of *habent sua fata libelli*—books have their own destinies? It would seem that three key factors contributed to the *Tur*'s preeminence. First, it was pragmatic, covering only actionable areas of law. The first two sections were addressed to community rabbis, while the last two were designed for use by judges in rabbinical courts. Second, it included sources and paid particular attention to the positions of later authorities, including those that its Sephardic author had received from his Ashkenazic father. Third, the *Tur* was easier to navigate. These factors all point to what was extraordinary about Maimonides's code: *Mishneh Torah* was ambitious, aiming for universality and eternity; it was bold, asserting its rulings as the definitive position; and it was complex, using original categories to reconstruct the multifarious body of Rabbinic law.

Maimonideanism and Its Discontents

Critical response to Maimonides's innovations began in his own lifetime. The first, and arguably most enduring, was the criticism leveled against *Mishneh Torah*'s lack of sources—in effect, Maimonides's refusal to show his work and explain how he had arrived at his rulings.[40] Among the most pointed are the *hasagot* (critical glosses) of Abraham ben David (Raavad), a contemporary of Maimonides, who writes, "He aimed to improve, but made no improvement; for he abandoned the path of all authors who preceded him; they supported their contention by quoting authority. Moreover, there are matters concerning which the *Geonim* disagree. This author comes and selects the opinion of one in preference to another; why should I rely on his choice, when an opinion does not please me, or when the dissenting party is unknown to me, and is probably not competent to take issue on a question? This is nothing but sheer arrogance."[41] Raavad is also critical of Maimonides's theology. Regarding Maimonides's strict incorporealism and labeling of those who anthropomorphize God as heretics, Raavad writes, "Why would he call such a person a heretic, when those greater and better than him believed this idea based on what they saw in scriptures?"[42] This is not to say that Raavad disagrees with Maimonides; he indicates that he personally considers the views he defends mistaken.[43] Raavad insists, rather, that creed is not regulated by halachah. This points to one of the great paradoxes of the Maimonidean legacy: although Maimonides was, as we have seen, open to "the truth from whatever source it comes" and a proponent of philosophy and human reason, by insisting on correct theological beliefs, he also created a hard boundary, excluding those who failed to adhere to them.

The authority wielded by Maimonides as his eminence grew would draw socially based criticism in the East, particularly from the legacy institutions of the *gaonim* in Baghdad, but more significant is Maimonides's reception in the Christian Mediterranean communities of Iberia, Provence, and Italy. It was here that arose a philosophical culture termed Maimonideanism, the adoption of Maimonides's worldview, with its emphasis on mastery of halachah through codified rulings in order to allow for higher physical and metaphysical studies. Alongside intensive study of the *Guide* and *Mishneh Torah*, Maimonideans produced prodigious works of philosophy as well as allegorical-philosophical scriptural commentaries—some of which were delivered as public sermons. Among the exemplars of Maimonideanism are Menachem HaMeiri, Levi ben Gershom (Ralbag), and Joseph Ibn Kaspi; even critics of Aristotelianism, like Chasdai Crescas, Joseph Albo, and Isaac Arama, were steeped in Maimonideanism and attempted their own formulations of theology in relationship to his.

The backlash to Maimonideanism, especially the study of philosophy exemplified by the *Guide for the Perplexed*, became open controversy on several occasions in the thirteenth and early fourteenth centuries. Each time, letters written back and forth between Mediterranean communities, in some cases including northern France, record communal deliberation over the study of Greco-Islamic philosophy. The two most acute controversies occurred in the 1230s and again in the early years of the fourteenth century. The controversy of the 1230s drew in one of the towering figures of the period, Moshe ben Nachman (Ramban; Nachmanides), whose response is notably complicated. On the one hand, Nachmanides placed himself squarely in the camp of Maimonides's defenders. At the same time, he expressed reservations about philosophy and its potential misuse.[44] At the height of this controversy, Jewish informers notified mendicant friars of heresies contained in the *Guide*.[45] The reaction was swift: copies were burned publicly in Montpellier in 1232. This event shook the Jewish communities of Provence and Aragon and tamped down the controversy. A similar objection to the radical implications of Maimonidean thought was raised in 1304 by another scholar in Montpellier, who sought the involvement of Solomon Ibn Adret (Rashba), the eminent successor to Nachmanides in Barcelona. A flurry of correspondence followed, resulting in a ban of excommunication promulgated in Barcelona against anyone who studied philosophy before the age of twenty-five or taught to the underaged. The ban, however, was toothless. Moreover, the Barcelona ban never intended to regulate Jewish belief, choosing instead to focus on a curricular matter.

A Maimonidean Legacy

Maimonides casts a long shadow over subsequent Jewish discourse. The conceptual Eastern European tradition of Talmud study relies upon analysis of Maimonides's legal work—as does the robust tradition of Sephardic halachic *p'sak* (legal decision). Any Jewish philosopher writing after Maimonides writes in relationship to him, an exquisitely specific anxiety of influence. His ideas have become prayers on the lips of Jews worldwide, committed to memory in singsong. His precepts draw red lines through Jewish communities, defining the boundaries of identity, likely in ways he could not have imagined. Whether in the university hall or the *beit midrash*, Maimonides is an unflagging presence and constant influence.

And yet the law does not usually go according to Maimonides.[46] In this, *Mishneh Torah* fails its essential task, to standardize Jewish law. Far from stemming Talmudic dialectic, Jewish culture teemed with Talmud learning in the years following the publication of *Mishneh Torah*, producing endless legal commentaries, including numerous commentaries on *Mishneh Torah* itself. In the philosophical realm, Maimonides's disquisitions into subjects like (geocentric) astronomy are irrelevant; his fervent quest to reconcile Aristotle's eternal universe with the Bible's created universe subsided in its passion. It was not philosophy but Kabbalah that was to win the hearts and minds of world Jewry in the centuries after Maimonides's death. It exploded in popularity in early modernity as a system of meaning that animated Jewish life anew. Maimonides's only son, Abraham, would take the path of the mystic.

It is, rather, Maimonides's prodigious mastery of traditional Jewish knowledge and radical willingness to reconstruct it systematically that make him such a significant and enduring figure for Jewish culture. Maimonides insists on finding reasons and meaning, on seeking core principles and right actions. He never shies away from grappling with the most perplexing questions that arise in a Jew's inner life, which, though differing in their particularities through the course of time, ever remain intellectual points of tension crying out for answers.

NOTES

1. The earliest record of the saying is found in the introduction to the thirteenth-century *Shaar HaShamayim* by Isaac Ibn Latif, a philosophical commentary on Ecclesiastes, which has been published in a critical edition by Raphael Cohen (Jerusalem: Magnes, 2015). The earliest record of Tiberias, Israel, as the burial place of Maimonides is in Ibn al-Qifti (thirteenth century); see below for more on Ibn al-Qifti's account of Maimonides's life.
2. Author's translation.
3. For reasons that are not entirely clear, the *genizah* (storage room for worn-out holy texts) of the Ben Ezra Synagogue in Fustat (Old Cairo) collected a massive array of texts of all kinds written by Jews, which were never buried

and survived for over a thousand years. They were rediscovered in the late nineteenth century and have since yielded rich knowledge about Jewish life in the Islamic Mediterranean, including the rediscovery of texts that had been lost for hundreds of years. For an account of the discovery and impact of the Cairo Genizah, see Adina Hoffman and Peter Cole, *Sacred Trash: The Lost and Found World of the Cairo Geniza* (New York: Schocken Books, 2016).

4. The biblical "Sepharad" was widely understood by medieval Jews to refer to what we today call Spain.

5. See Maimonides's statement in *Mishneh Torah, Sefer Mishpatim, Hilchot Sh'eilah Ufikadon* 5:6, where he writes, in a rare attribution, "Thus ruled my teachers [*rabbotai*], Rabbeinu Joseph HaLevi [Ibn Migash] and his teacher of blessed memory [al-Fasi]." As Ibn Migash died when Maimonides was still a young child, he clearly makes this statement as an expression of his intellectual training.

6. The Muwahhidun conquered Córdoba in 1148 from the Murabitun (Almoravids), an earlier Berber dynasty, when Maimonides was still a child of about ten years of age, meaning that the Maimon family lived under Muwahhidun rule for over a decade before moving to Fez.

7. Ibn al-Qifṭī, *Tar'ikh al-Hukama*, ed. Julius Lippert (Leipzig, 1903; reprint, 1999), 392–93.

8. In the responsum known as the *Epistle on Martyrdom*; in Itzhak Shailat, ed., *The Letters and Essays of Moses Maimonides: A Critical Edition of the Hebrew and Arabic Letters of Maimonides*, 3rd ed., 2 vols. (Jerusalem: Ma'aleh Adumim, 1995), 1:57.

9. Prior to the *Commentary on the Mishnah*, Maimonides had produced several works, including a treatise on logic attributed to him, although the attribution is contested. On his Talmudic commentaries, see below.

10. Sarah Stroumsa, *Maimonides in His World: Portrait of a Mediterranean Thinker* (Princeton, NJ: Princeton University Press, 2009), 53–72.

11. Introduction to *Mishneh Torah*, in *A Maimonides Reader*, ed. Isadore Twersky, Library of Jewish Studies (New York: Behrman House, 1972), 39–40, emphasis added.

12. Fustat was near al-Qahirah (New Cairo), the seat of the Fatimid, then the Ayyubid, government.

13. Maimonides held the office of *ra'is al-yahud* only briefly, from 1171 to 1172, almost certainly due to his relative lack of social connection. He was appointed *ra'is* again at the end of his life, after he had become an established member of Egyptian Jewish society. See Moshe Halbertal, *Maimonides: Life and Thought*, trans. Joel A. Linsider (Princeton, NJ: Princeton University Press, 2014), 45–46.

14. *Mishneh Torah, Sefer Shof'tim, Hilchot Eivel* 13:1; Maimonides's description of

his mental state following David's death is in his letter to Pinchas HaDayan, in Shailat, *Letters* 2:444–45. This is pointed out by Halbertal, *Maimonides*, 59.

15. Letter to Yefet HaDayan, in *Shailat, Letters*, 1:228–30; cited in Halbertal, *Maimonides*, 59–60, in the translation of L. Sitskin, *Letters of Maimonides* (New York: Yeshiva University Press, 1977), 73.

16. On the commentaries to the *Bavli*, see Herbert A. Davidson, *Moses Maimonides: The Man and His Works* (New York: Oxford University Press, 2005), 140–44; on *Hilchot HaY'rushalmi*, see Halbertal, *Maimonides*, 18. Surviving fragments of both have been published in the twentieth century.

17. See, for instance, *Mishneh Torah, Sefer HaMada, Hilchot Y'sodei HaTorah* 4:13.

18. Introduction to *Sh'monah P'rakim*, in Twersky, *Maimonides Reader*, 363. This idea is elaborated in *Mishneh Torah, Sefer Z'manim, Hilchot Kiddush HaChodesh* 17:24, in which Maimonides advances his theory that wisdom once held by Jewish sages was lost and transmitted via an alternate route by the Greeks. On this theory, found in the works of many medieval Jewish thinkers, see Abraham Melamed, *The Myth of the Jewish Origins of Science and Philosophy* [in Hebrew] (Jerusalem: Magnes, 2010).

19. Maimonides spends time in the introduction to *Perek Chelek* developing the term *epikoros*, which he connects to the root *p-k-r*, "to be free of restraint"; this is not necessarily the view of the Mishnah, which also knows the *epikoros* as one who disrespects Torah scholars. For the present purposes, "heretic" is a serviceable translation.

20. The Thirteen Principles first appear in Rambam's commentary to *Mishnah Sanhedrin* 10:1.

21. Menachem Kellner, *Must a Jew Believe Anything?*, 2nd ed. (London: Littman Library of Jewish Civilization, 2006), 12–13.

22. Introduction to *Perek Chelek*, translated in Kellner, *Must a Jew Believe Anything?*, 53–54 (with author's modifications and emphasis added).

23. Maimonides's theological stance is complicated by his own written legacy, in which he explicitly states that there are things he promotes merely as effective policy and not as truths. This is required to promote social order, public welfare, and personal uprightness in ordinary people. For instance, before listing the Thirteen Principles, Maimonides explains that he is writing "in order to teach those with no training in theology, a subject which not every man can understand" (introduction to *Perek Chelek*, in Twersky, *Maimonides Reader*, 417).

24. See Menachem Kellner, *Dogma in Medieval Jewish Thought: From Maimonides to Abravanel* (Oxford: Oxford University Press, 1986), 66, and *passim*. One way in which the Thirteen Principles were disseminated widely is through liturgical poetry. The most successful of such compositions are *Yigdal* and *Ani Maamin*, which were composed later in the Middle Ages.

25. *Sefer HaMada*, Chapter 1, Twersky, *Maimonides Reader*, 43.

26. So problematic was the *Guide* to traditional Jewish thought that already in the Middle Ages, kabbalists began circulating the myth of its forgery, and anti-rationalists denounced it to the mendicant friars, leading to its public burning in Montpellier, France, in 1232, on which, see below.

27. Introduction, *Guide of the Perplexed*, in Twersky, *Maimonides Reader*, 238. Rather, according to Maimonides, "the first purpose of this treatise is to explain the meanings of certain terms occurring in books of prophecy" (Twersky, *Maimonides Reader*, 236).

28. Maimonides, *The Guide of the Perplexed*, trans. Shlomo Pines, 2 vols. (Chicago: University of Chicago Press, 1963).

29. For example, the idea that Maimonides actually believed in the eternality of the universe in some form, as per Aristotle. See Leo Strauss, *Persecution and the Art of Writing* (Chicago: University of Chicago Press, 1952).

30. This work was culturally superseded by more widely circulated works based upon it, including *Sefer HaChinuch*, which accepted Maimonides's enumeration of the commandments but arranged them according to the weekly Torah portions, and the *Sefer Mitzvot Gadol* (known by its acronym, *S'mag*).

31. On the establishment of the 613 commandments, their enumeration prior to Maimonides's version, and his puzzling adherence to the traditional number, see Albert D. Friedberg, *Crafting the 613 Commandments: Maimonides on the Enumeration, Classification and Formulation of the Scriptural Commandments* (Boston: Academic Studies Press, 2013), 13–26.

32. Introduction to *Sefer HaMitzvot* (Twersky, *Maimonides Reader*, 426). In the introduction to *Mishneh Torah*, he specifies the sources he was including and obviating as "the Talmud itself—the Babylonian as well as the Palestinian—the *Sifra*, the *Sifre*, and the *Tosefta*" (Twersky, *Maimonides Reader*, 39).

33. Introduction to *Sefer HaMitzvot* (Twersky, *Maimonides Reader*, 426).

34. Introduction to *Sefer HaMitzvot* (Twersky, *Maimonides Reader*, 426). Maimonides had written the *Commentary on the Mishnah* and *Sefer HaMitzvot* in Judeo-Arabic (Arabic written in Hebrew characters), the lingua franca of the Jews of the Islamic world, the standard language for philosophy from the time of Saadyah, and his own native spoken language.

35. Maimonides also divided each section into chapters, then into individual laws. Before each subject area, he enumerated how many and which commandments from *Sefer HaMitzvot* are included in the subject area. For example, in the book *Sefer Z'manim*, the section *Hilchot Chameitz Umatzah* includes eight commandments (three positive and five negative). The section consists of nine chapters, each consisting of some ten to twenty laws.

36. Baruch's work, entitled *Ein Misphat Ner Mitzvah* (The wellspring of justice, the lamp of commandment), includes cross-references to major halachic codes.

37. It was the tosafists of France and Germany in the eleventh and twelfth centuries who compared the different places in the Talmud where a given topic was addressed—an enterprise of which Maimonides was not aware.

38. Within the four categories of the *Tur*, subjects were broken down into areas similar to Maimonides's secondary division into sections, but these are generally referenced by section number (*siman*) and paragraph.

39. Nevertheless, even *Shulchan Aruch* has not succeeded in accomplishing the goals Maimonides set for *Mishneh Torah* of serving as a single reference of Jewish law alongside the Torah. Nor has the widespread acceptance of *Shulchan Aruch* allowed it to supplant the study of Talmud and the voluminous responsa literature. On the genesis and impact of *Shulchan Aruch*, see Isadore Twersky, "The *Shulḥan 'Arukh*: Enduring Code of Jewish Law," *Judaism* 16 (1967): 141–58.

40. The work of reading sources back into the rulings of *Mishneh Torah* was undertaken by commentators beginning in the Middle Ages, providing explanations, cross-references, and sources.

41. Introduction to *Hassagot to Mishneh Torah*, translated in Joseph Sarachek, *Faith and Reason: The Conflict on the Rationalism of Maimonides* (Williamsport: Bayard, 1935), 68.

42. Critical gloss to *Mishneh Torah, Sefer HaMada, Hilchot T'shuvah* 3:7.

43. See the end of the gloss to *Mishneh Torah, Sefer HaMada, Hilchot T'shuvah* 3:7.

44. David Berger, "How Did Nahmanides Propose to Resolve the Maimonidean Controversy?," in *Me'ah She'arim: Studies in Medieval Jewish Spiritual Life in Memory of Isadore Twersky*, ed. Ezra Fleischer (Jerusalem: Magnes, 2001), 135–46.

45. The mendicant movement in Christianity arose as a popular movement espousing poverty and charity and was quickly subsumed and deradicalized by the Roman Church. The friars, most prominently the orders of Franciscans and Dominicans, channeled their fervor into scholarship, including Hebrew scholarship, and became involved in intra- and intercommunal debate, particularly in regard to heresy. The shift in perception of Jews incepted by the mendicant movement and developed throughout the thirteenth century was to profoundly change the position of Jews in Christian Europe, viewing Jews not as a despised but tolerated minority but as having abrogated their adherence to Mosaic law through loyalty to the Talmud and hence targets for conversion.

46. Here the exception proves the rule: the Jews of Yemen do traditionally follow the rulings of *Mishneh Torah*, but they are notably distinguished among worldwide Jewries for this practice.

7

The *Zohar* Transformation
A New Understanding of Torah, God, and Humanity

Rabbi Lawrence A. Englander, DHL

There's Trouble in Synagogue!

IN THIRTEENTH-CENTURY SPAIN,[1] a troubled rabbi witnessed what he perceived to be the aberrant behavior of a growing number of congregants. He recorded his shock:

> I have seen people who used to occupy themselves with Torah and the teachings of the Rabbis, day and night. And they served God with a full heart, as is appropriate. And then, one day, scholars of secular wisdom asserted themselves against the Eternal, and Satan was among them. They strayed from the source of living waters by engaging in these texts, until they abandoned the teachings of the Torah and the commandments.
>
> According to their alien thinking, they considered the teachings of the Rabbis to be falsehood. There was no spirit of God within them, so that they cast aspersion on their former selves. . . .
>
> I have seen them during the festival of Sukkot, standing in their place in the synagogue and watching the devout circling the Torah scrolls with their lulavs. They laughed with scorn and said that these people were fools, lacking in understanding, while they themselves had no need for lulav or etrog. They contended, "Doesn't the Torah tell us to take the lulav and etrog to fulfill the verse, *You shall rejoice before the Eternal seven days* (Lev. 23:40)? You think that these trinkets will cause us to rejoice? Silver and gold will do better!" They added, "Do you think that God *needs* our

blessings? All this is vanity!" ... They take up these secular books and claim, "This is the Torah of truth." ...

As a result, so much Torah has been forgotten among the Jewish people—until God awakened a different spirit, and people took up the good advice to return to God, and to understand matters within the words of the Rabbis, in the gradual awakening that they experienced.[2]

The troubled rabbi was Moshe de Leon (ca. 1240–1305), and he was reporting most likely about his community in Guadalajara in north central Spain. Among the few details available about his early life, it is known that he studied Maimonides's *Guide for the Perplexed* in the 1260s. Shortly afterward, while wandering through Castile, he made the acquaintance of several kabbalists. He began to delve into Jewish mysticism and was particularly influenced by the writings of Joseph Gikatilla.[3] Regarding the Kabbalah as a means to preserve and enrich Jewish tradition, he then identified the "scholars of secular wisdom," to whom he refers in the above text, as those intellectuals who had studied the works of Moses Maimonides and had come to the conclusion that ritual observance was inferior to the philosophical quest for divine truths. Although this approach may have refined their intellect, it resulted in a serious detachment from the Jewish community. De Leon resolved to find a way to bring these wayward individuals back into the fold—in a way that would appeal to them.

And he found it! When he writes that "God awakened a different spirit," de Leon himself provided the initiative by gathering a circle of mystics who had commenced literary activity in the middle of the thirteenth century. The efforts of this "Chavraya"[4] culminated in the publication of the *Zohar* (meaning "splendor" or "radiance"), which to this day is the classical work of the Jewish mystical tradition, the Kabbalah.

From his home in Guadalajara, de Leon circulated the first strata of the *Zohar*, claiming that the author was the second-century rabbi Shimon bar Yochai. De Leon himself had already published several mystical works under his own name, including *Sefer HaRimon* cited above, but it had been a long-established practice to publish under a pseudonym in order to lend more authority—and popularity—to the text.[5] Initially there was some skepticism regarding the authenticity of the *Zohar*. The kabbalist Isaac ben Samuel of Acre heard about the *Zohar* during his travels. He journeyed to Spain in 1305 and met Moshe de Leon at a fair in Valladolid. De Leon told him that he was in possession of an "ancient book written by Shimon bar Yochai" and that, if Isaac would accompany him back to his home in Avila, he could see the document for himself. By the time Isaac arrived, Moshe had died; but Isaac heard a rumor that a wealthy townsman had offered to marry his son to the deceased's daughter in exchange for the original manuscript, which de Leon had allegedly been copying. However, both the widow and the daughter had denied knowledge of any such manuscript, claiming that they had only seen de Leon writing on his own. It is not clear to what extent Isaac challenged the claim of ancient authorship, since his evaluation is not quoted until the fifteenth century, and then only partially.[6] But at any rate, the contemporary skepticism was short-lived. "Soon, however, the light shadow of scandal that had fallen upon its publication and initial appearance in the world of literature, the enigma of the illegitimate birth of a literary forgery, disappeared and was forgotten. Very slowly but surely the influence of the *Zohar* grew."[7]

By exploring de Leon's method, which I call the "*Zohar* Transformation," we shall see how the *Zohar* presented a radically new understanding of the Torah—a view, the *Zohar* claims, that embraces philosophical inquiry but goes even beyond it. The *Zohar* Transformation aimed to succeed in bringing many scoffers back into the community.[8]

Historical Background

The first half of the thirteenth century was a period of prosperity for Iberian Jewry. The Muslim Almohad dynasty had lost political and religious control of Castile and Aragon, where the majority of Jews lived. As the new Christian rulers took power, they relied upon Jewish leaders to lend their expertise during the interregnum and appointed them to trusted positions as court advisors. To reward their loyalty, "Jews were invited to establish their residences in quarters abandoned by, or forcibly taken away from, the Muslims."[9] As a result of the favorable treatment, Jewish artisans and merchants flourished.

However, this period of stability was short-lived. The elevation of Jews was resented both by the Catholic Church and by an emerging Christian middle class. By the time Alphonso X became king of Castile in 1252, he began to implement restrictive measures upon the Jewish community. In 1279, he imprisoned Jewish tax collectors. In 1281, on a Sabbath, he arrested a group of Castilian Jews and demanded a ransom for their release. In 1293, a vote of the Castilian Cortes forbade Jews from owning real estate. Jews were required to wear distinguishing garments; restrictions were imposed upon synagogue building, and additional taxes were levied upon them.

As a further blow, the church itself joined this offensive against the Jews. "The newly introduced preaching friars and inquisitorial courts embarked upon ambitious schemes to convert the large religious minorities in the country. These efforts, which had led to the dramatic disputation in Barcelona [between Moses Nachmanides and Pablo Christiani] in 1263, were crowned at times with considerable success."[10] These measures, which had entered Aragon a few decades earlier, now penetrated into Castile. Even though Jews lived in the same towns as their Christian neighbors and spoke the same language,[11] they were increasingly regarded as outsiders who denied the truths of Christianity. The Jewish community faced disruption as different options presented themselves. Some chose to convert to Christianity. Others maintained their faith and communal bonds but felt more and more like exiles and pariahs. A number of Jews who had studied the teachings of Maimonides, as we noted above, opted for a more intellectual expression of Judaism and distanced themselves from their congregations. Jewish grandees ingratiated themselves through their wealth and even consorted with non-Jewish women. Many feared that the community was on the verge of collapse.[12]

The Zoharic Response

But adversity can often spur fertile intellectual and spiritual activity. The authors of the *Zohar* realized that they would have to appeal to this increasingly diverse population and give them a reason to remain faithful. Since the Torah had always been the living center of Jewish life, they developed a new and creative way to understand Torah, a way that would inspire their readers to return to its teachings and follow its traditions. They drew from previous authors whom Gershom Scholem terms "theosophic-Gnostic" mystics,[13] thinkers who claimed that the Torah contained secret teachings that were accessible only to initiates. The Chavraya of the *Zohar* refined this doctrine and sought to bring Kabbalah to a wider readership.

The following passage provides an insight into the methodology of the *Zohar*:

> Rabbi Shim'on said:
>
> Woe to the human being who says that Torah intended to present a mere story and ordinary words! For if so, we could compose a Torah right now with ordinary words and more laudable than all of them. . . . But all the words of Torah correspond to the following pattern. . . .
>
> Come and see: There is a garment visible to all. Those fools, when they see someone in a good-looking garment, look no further. Yet the significance of that garment is the body; the significance of the body is the soul.
>
> Corresponding to this pattern, Torah has a body—and words of Torah called "bodies of Torah." This body is clothed in a garment, namely stories of this world. Fools of the world look only at that garment, the story of Torah. Those who know more do not look at the garment, but rather at the body under that garment. The wise—servants of the supernal King, those who stood at Mount Sinai—look only at the soul, root of all, real Torah! And in the world that is coming, they are destined to gaze upon the soul of the soul of Torah.
>
> Come and see: So it is above—there is a garment, body, soul, and soul of soul. The heavens and their host are the garment. Assembly of Israel is the body who receives the soul, *Tif'eret Yisra'el* (the Beauty of Israel), so She is the body for the soul. The soul that we have mentioned is *Tif'eret Yisra'el*, who is real Torah. The soul of soul is the Holy Ancient One—and all are linked to one another.
>
> Woe to the wicked who say that Torah is merely a story! They look at this garment and no further. Happy are the righteous who look at Torah properly! (Zohar 3:152a)[14]

Through this analogy of the human figure, this passage identifies two layers of Torah that would be known to the philosophical intelligentsia:

1. The narratives, symbolized by the garment.
2. The laws of halachah, known in Rabbinic literature as *gufei Torah*, "bodies of Torah."

The *Zohar* then adds a third layer, which it terms the *n'shamah*, "soul." This term refers to mystical insight through which the *Zohar* evolves a radically new understanding of the relationship between God and humanity.

To understand this new relationship, we may delve into the realm of modern psychology. Our human condition is that we regard ourselves as incomplete.[15] There is always more knowledge to pursue, more love to give, more answers to seek. To use a modern image, our life is like a jigsaw puzzle with pieces missing. If we are religious, we reach out to God to aid us in finding those missing pieces.

Thus far, Rabbinic literature and medieval Jewish philosophy would agree. But the next step is a Zoharic innovation. If we are created in the image of God, and if we have this sense of incompleteness, then God, too, must feel incomplete. And just as we reach out to God in search of wholeness, so does God reach out to humanity to attain completion. In the *Zohar*, the two parties meet through a ladder of ten divine potencies called *s'firot*.[16] Divine energy flows through these *s'firot* from God to humanity, and through our actions we recycle that energy back to the divine realm, thereby enabling divine power to grow and evolve. This Zoharic innovation can be construed as a "cryptic meta-midrash" on the *Tanach*. In order to understand the *Zohar*, the reader must first be conversant in Bible and Rabbinic literature, to which the *Zohar* then adds its unique layer.[17]

An example of this dynamic is provided in the following discussion about the Blessing after Meals. This discourse begins with a narrative in which two rabbis are on a journey and stop at an inn. As they sit down to dine, they meet a young boy who appears to be ignorant; but when they engage him in conversation, he delivers the following teaching:[18]

> If there are three [who have eaten together], the Rabbis ruled that one says, "Let us praise of whose bounty we have eaten"—let us merge our intentions in giving blessing since "we have eaten of

God's bounty," of that food which God apportions to sustain the world.

When the others reply, they allude to the upper world: "Blessed [*baruch*] be the one of whose bounty we have eaten and by whose goodness we live." Now they have indicated that specific level from which all food comes, by saying "Baruch." Who is Baruch?—the king with whom there is peace, the supernal King, from whom all blessings flow....

Thus the respondents mention the specific source [of blessing], something which the leader does not say. What is the explanation? It is because this upper world, which is Understanding [*Binah*], pours out blessing initially to the two lower cherubim—namely, right and left, Lovingkindness [*Chesed*] and Power [*G'vurah*]. Therefore, these two are specified [by the respondents] in order to indicate that upper level. The leader, who is in the middle, takes all from both sides. From here onward the leader says the blessing, indicating place and level, and thus they become cheerful together in great peace. (*Zohar, Midrash HaNe-elam to the Book of Ruth* 87c)[19]

Here the *Zohar* employs the mystical technique of theurgy, which Melila Hellner-Eshed defines as "the conscious intention of the human being to influence the world of the divinity through deeds and consciousness . . . to fulfill a desire to participate in the great work of rectification (*tikkun*) of the world of humanity, and its redemption through the rectification of the divine world."[20] The theurgic process, therefore, is reciprocal: by influencing the divine realm, the mystics serve to bring integration not only to their own world, but to God as well.

In this passage, the theurgic process is activated through the responsive introduction to the Blessing after Meals. With proper intent, the mystics are able to unite the *s'firot* and thus enable the divine energy to flow into their lives. As a professor of mine once put it, "When we *express* a blessing, we *impress* blessing into the world."[21]

Thus far, one may suspect that the mystics of the *Zohar* were a contemplative group who eschewed worldly concerns. On the contrary, they were deeply concerned with the injustices of their society and applied their teaching to social justice:

The share of the Holy Blessed One consists in gladdening the poor as best as one can. For . . . the Holy Blessed One comes to see those broken vessels [as divine creatures who are in need of sustenance]. Entering their company and seeing they have nothing to celebrate, God weeps over them. Then God ascends to destroy the world!

Many members of the [angelic] Academy come before God and plead: "Master of the universe: You are called Compassionate and Gracious. May Your compassion be aroused for Your children."

God answers them, "Don't the inhabitants of the world realize that I based the world solely on love? As it is written, 'I said, the world shall be built on love' (Ps. 89:3). By this the world endures." The angels on high declare before God, "Master of the universe: Look at so- and-so who is eating and drinking his fill. He could be generous with the poor, but he gives them nothing!"

The Accuser comes, claims permission, and sets out in pursuit of that human being. (Zohar 1:10b)[22]

In thirteenth-century Spain, the wealthier classes were becoming indifferent to the less fortunate members of the community. Yitzchak Baer relates that "the *Zohar* also inveighs against other lewd practices which were apparently common among the urbane aristocracy if its day. . . .

The author of the *Zohar* was conscious of the social conflicts which flared up during this period within the Jewish communities, and his heart was with the poor and lowly."[23] Other socially responsible Jewish leaders expressed their condemnation of such behavior, yet the *Zohar* adds that the shirking of one's charitable duties provokes not only communal disappointment but divine retribution as well.[24]

By employing the system of *s'firot* to teach a new understanding of Torah, the *Zohar* Transformation gave its followers a radically new theology. Instead of the remote, impassive God of rationalist philosophy, the God described in the *Zohar* yearns for a closer relationship with humanity. In turn, the mystics' quest for God allows for greater human initiative in addressing the concerns of their society. As David Blumenthal states, "As God grants man [*sic*] more power, not only over the world but over Himself, man must face the responsibility that goes with that power."[25]

Aftermath of the Zohar Transformation

The century following the publication of the *Zohar* was fraught with danger and tragedy for Iberian Jewry. When Jews were expelled in 1492 from their holdings in the Iberian Peninsula, bringing to an end centuries-long culture, literature, and liturgy, many Jews took the teachings of the *Zohar* along with them in their exile to other lands. Moshe Idel writes that "a distinctive feature of particularistic Kabbalah was the continuous transmission of Kabbalistic lore from masters to students; thus, Spanish Kabbalah did not disappear with the destruction of its stronghold, but was preserved, transmitted, and elaborated by the offspring of the exiles and their disciples."[26]

Other heirs of Spanish Jewish thought competed with the *Zohar* Transformation. Within the kabbalistic tradition itself, the ecstatic Kabbalah of Abraham Abulafia (1240–92) appealed to those seeking an internal mystical experience by employing a mantra-like technique of letter combinations.[27] However, the *Zohar* seemed best able to meet the challenges of a shattered Jewish world; its teachings acknowledged the disruption within both the divine and human realms and offered a means of response through ritual, study, and compassionate acts. The Zoharic approach found fertile soil in Turkey, whose *millet* system[28] allowed for the Jewish community to close ranks against a threatening outside world.

The *Zohar* Transformation also flourished north of Jerusalem, where a community of mystics gathered to extend its teachings. Within a few decades after the expulsion, Rabbi Moshe Cordovero formed a tight-knit circle of mystics in the northern town of Safed. His successor, Rabbi Yitzchak Luria, nullified the injunction against studying Kabbalah before the age of forty[29] (he himself died at the age of thirty-eight) and sought to make Kabbalah a more popular discipline by showing how proper conduct could ultimately bring about the redemption of his exiled people. Through study, prayer, and social activism, the Safed mystics taught that human beings had the potential to perform *tikkun*—restoration and repair—by releasing divine sparks into the universe. These efforts would contribute toward the unification of the world, of humankind, and of God. To this very day, the term *tikkun olam* is part of the basic vocabulary of Jews worldwide.

The *Zohar* Transformation continued to influence later movements. Beginning in Renaissance Italy, a Christian Kabbalah developed, which later influenced such figures as Gottfried Leibniz and William Blake. The rise of Chasidism in eighteenth-century Eastern Europe applied the doctrine of divine *s'firot* toward understanding aspects of human character. In the early twentieth century, Rabbi Avraham Yitzchak Kook intuited a divine imperative for the Jewish people to return to their homeland in Israel; this return would engender a global *tikkun*, ushering in the messianic age.[30]

We can speculate on how the *Zohar* Transformation might aid us in facing contemporary challenges within the liberal Jewish world. Synagogues and Jewish communal institutions are witnessing a retreat from their teachings and activities. Whereas the medieval critics of de Leon's time scorned what they believed to be the childish rituals in the sanctuary, many of today's scoffers don't even show up. Can we adapt the methods of the *Zohar* Transformation to attract our own fellow Jews back into the fold?

For us, however, the methodology will have to be different. Whereas the *Zohar* authors developed a new approach to Torah and disseminated that approach in literary form, our generation of transformers must first pay attention to what the "scoffers" are already doing. So let's allow one of them to speak for herself:

> The old Jewish guard—what's often referred to as the organized Jewish community—has two main concerns: the *future* of the Jewish people and the future of the Jewish *people*. Two different senses of the same problem, that is. The first sense is the future generations of Jews, us young'uns who are supposedly being "lost"—assimilating, intermarrying and, perhaps most disturbing to the old guard, not joining the established religious institutions that allow us to be counted as "affiliated" Jews. The second sense is the future of the *idea* of the Jewish people as one, unified people.
>
> There's certainly reason to be concerned with the future of the Jewish people in both senses, but there's also reason to think that problem #1 is actually taking care of problem #2. The young and diffuse next Jewish generation may be comprised largely

of individuals doing their own thing, but when doing their own Jewish thing, they are more likely to seek out an accepting community and to eschew the traditional denominational labels that have done much more to divide than to unite the Jewish people.[31]

Rebecca Honig Freidman is giving us a new understanding of the Jewish people—one that has been accentuated by the recent period of COVID-19 pandemic. The synagogue may no longer be the central institution of communal Jewish life; in fact, there may not be *any* central place. Therefore, to bring Jews back into the fold, it will be necessary to meet them where they happen to be—in restaurants, living rooms, and internet chat rooms. We might think of this new approach as the "Networking Transformation."

And once we meet them, what is it that we should teach? It is doubtful that the theurgic technique will attract them, since it smacks too blatantly of magic. And although the stress on human initiative may be appealing, it is doubtful what proportion of Jews today will seek to pair that initiative with divine power. Yet just as the *Zohar* Transformation appealed to its generation by revealing an inner, mystical layer of Torah, so our current generation must seek a "hook" to make Torah relevant today. Although no one has yet discovered a winning formula, we may at least speculate on what ingredients that formula should contain.[32] In a world in which the only constant is change, the *Zohar* teaches that Torah conveys a meaning that is timeless, in that we must settle for nothing less than *tikkun* in our striving for justice, peace, and enlightenment in our world. Moreover, the Jewish people has a unique contribution to make toward this effort through a blend of ethical, spiritual, educational, and cultural elements—a blend that is different for each individual but that can be shared with fellow Jews in community.

Adapting to new conditions while maintaining ancient traditions is part and parcel of the Jewish historical experience. In the Mishnah, at the end of *B'rachot* 9:5, the text cites Psalm 119:126, "It is time to act for *Adonai*; they have nullified Your Torah." While most of the Rabbis interpret this to mean that Jewish tradition must be preserved despite trends toward apostasy or assimilation, Rabbi Natan offers a different interpretation. He reverses the two parts of the verse: "Nullify Your Torah *because* it is time to act for *Adonai*." The Zohar Chavraya addressed the disruption of their time by following Rabbi Natan's advice: to preserve tradition by transforming it. That approach may well succeed yet again!

NOTES

1. Although the name "Spain" had not yet come into existence at this time, this name, as well as "Iberian Peninsula," will be used when referring to more than one kingdom.

2. Moshe de Leon, *Sefer HaRimon*, in Elliot R. Wolfson, *The Book of the Pome-granate: Moses de Leon's Sefer Ha-Rimmon* (Providence, RI: Brown Judaic Studies; Atlanta: Scholars Press, 2020), 391–92, https://doi.org/10.2307/j. ctvzgb92b.

3. For more details, see Gershom Scholem, *Kabbalah* (Jerusalem: Keter; New York: Quadrangle, 1974), 432–34.

4. Gershom Scholem had earlier identified Moshe de Leon as the sole author of the *Zohar*; see his *Major Trends in Jewish Mysticism* (Jerusalem: Schocken Books, 1941), 190–96. Later, however, Yehuda Liebes claimed that the text of the *Zohar* was the product of several minds; see his *Studies in the Zohar* (Albany: State University of New York Press, 1993), 88–90. The character of this circle will be explained further below.

5. There are several instances of pseudepigraphical works within the Jewish mystical tradition itself. For example, *Sefer Yetzirah* (written sometime between the fourth and sixth centuries) is attributed to Abraham (see Aryeh Kaplan, *Sefer Yetzirah: The Book of Creation* [Northvale, NJ: Jason Aronson, 1995], xii). *Sefer HaBahir* (twelfth century, Provence) is attributed to the first-century rabbi N'chunya ben HaKanah (see Aryeh Kaplan, *The Bahir* [New York: Samuel Weiser, 1979], iii).

6. Isaac of Acre's comments were quoted by Abraham Zacuto in his book *Sefer Yuchasin*. See Gershom Scholem, *Major Trends in Jewish Mysticism* (New York: Knopf, 2011), 190–91. Also Boaz Huss, *The Zohar: Reception and Impact* (Cambridge: Cambridge University Press, 2020), 239–40.

7. Gershom Scholem, *Zohar: The Book of Splendor* (New York: Schocken Books, 1963), 8. For a more cynical appraisal of Moshe de Leon, see Heinrich Graetz, *History of the Jews* (Philadelphia: Jewish Publication Society, 1967), 4:11–14.

8. Similar to the passage from *Sefer HaRimon* above, the *Zohar* also refers to the danger of the forgetting of Torah. See *Zohar* 3:58a.

9. Salo W. Baron, *A Social and Religious History of the Jews* (New York: Columbia University Press; Philadelphia: Jewish Publication Society, 1965), 10:119.

10. Baron, *Social and Religious History*, 10:141–42.

11. During the early part of the Christian reconquest, the rulers relied upon the Jews' expertise in Arabic dialects to aid in the transition of power. Once the new rulers had ensconced themselves, these services were no longer required.

12. See Arthur Green, introduction to *The Zohar: Pritzker Edition*, trans. Daniel C. Matt (Stanford, CA: Stanford University Press, 2004), lxviii–lxix, where the above historical outline is presented. See also Yitzhak Baer, *A History of the Jews in Christian Spain* (Philadelphia: Jewish Publication Society, 1978), 1:111–37.

13. See, for example, Scholem, *Kabbalah*, 52–57.

14. Translated by Daniel Matt, *The Zohar: Pritzker Edition* (Stanford, CA: Stanford University Press, 2014), 8:518–21.

15. See, for example, Paul Kollarackal, "Embracing the Incomplete," Humans and Nature, September 23, 2015, https://humansandnature.org/embracing-the-incomplete/.

16. Many diagrams of the *s'firot* can be found online. For example, see "Kabbalah: The Ten *Sefirot* of the Kabbalah," Jewish Virtual Library, https://www.jewishvirtuallibrary.org/the-ten-sefirot-of-the-kabbalah.

17. For the contemporary reader, this hierarchy can be compared to crossword puzzles. One must first be conversant in the English language to solve "definition crosswords" found in many newspapers and magazines. However, a step above this is the "cryptic crossword," which employs rules of its own. In order to solve these cryptic puzzles, knowledge of the first two levels is essential.

18. This story is one of many examples in which a seemingly ignorant person— for example, a young lad (known as *yanuka*) or a camel driver—is discovered to be the repository of great mystical wisdom. This may be the *Zohar*'s way of teaching that some individuals have an intuitive talent for revealing mystical insights.

19. Translated by Lawrence A. Englander, *The Mystical Study of Ruth: Midrash HaNe'elam of the Zohar to the Book of Ruth* (Atlanta: Scholars Press, 1993), 129–30.

20. Melila Hellner-Eshed, *A River Flows from Eden: The Language of Mystical Experience in the Zohar* (Stanford, CA: Stanford University Press, 2009), 10.

21. Professor Uriel Tal, *z"l*, heard at a lecture during my student days at Hebrew Union College–Jewish Institute of Religion, Cincinnati, in the mid-1970s.

22. Translated by Matt, *The Zohar: Pritzker Edition*, 1:71.

23. Baer, *History of the Jews in Christian Spain*, 262–63.

24. The sin of not speaking out against injustice is a common theme in Jewish texts—see, for example, Babylonian Talmud, *Avodah Zarah* 18a; and Maimonides, *Mishneh Torah, Hilchot Sh'vitat Yom Tov* 6:18. The *Zohar* was not unique in leveling this criticism but gave it special focus.

25. David R. Blumenthal, *Understanding Jewish Mysticism* (New York: Ktav, 1978), 157.
26. Moshe Idel, "Particularism and Universalism in Kabbalah, 1480–1650," in *Essential Papers on Jewish Culture in Renaissance and Baroque Italy*, ed. David B. Ruderman (New York: New York University Press, 1992), 330.
27. See Ben Zion Bokser, *The Jewish Mystical Tradition* (New York: Pilgrim Press, 1981), 97–106.
28. Under Ottoman law, each religious community was granted autonomy in matters of personal status, such as birth, marriage, and burial.
29. *Mishnah Avot* 5:21.
30. See Daniel Matt, *The Essential Kabbalah: The Heart of Jewish Mysticism* (San Francisco: Harper, 1995), 15–17.
31. Rebecca Honig Freidman, "The Future of the Jewish People—Could It Be Unity?," *Lilith* blog, November 30, 2007, https://lilith.org/2007/11/the-future-of-the-jewish-people-could-it-be-unity/.
32. In what follows, I have drawn from an earlier article that I wrote: Lawrence A. Englander, "In Search of Belonging," *Reform Judaism*, Summer 2011, 48–52.

8

Sabbatianism
Convulsions and Creativity

Rabbi Stanley M. Davids

Sabbatai Tsevi is the redeemer
Beloved Mehmed Tsevi[1]
He is the light of Israel
Sultan Mehmed Tsevi
Truth came to the world
My love Mehmed Tsevi
He is the Shekhinah of Emanation
Beloved Mehmet Tsevi[2]

SHABBETAI ZVI,[3] believed by many to be both the long-awaited messianic redeemer and an incarnate aspect of the Godhead, was born on the ninth of Av, 1626, in Smyrna (today's Izmir). The date fell on a Sabbath; the occasion provided Zvi's first name. Some Jewish traditions held that the Messiah would be born on the Ninth of Av, the date commemorating the destruction of the Jerusalem Temples; this detail played a role in shaping the mythos that embraced Zvi.

Born to an Ashkenazic family, Zvi had a traditional Jewish education, with its heavy focus on Talmud. But even during his early years he displayed profound emotional concerns. In 1642, he took upon himself a rigorous ascetic life, reporting at that time that he was frequently tortured by nightmares. Zvi came to believe that his inner turmoil was the product of the ongoing assault by the *k'lipot*.[4] At the age of eighteen, he began a more serious study of the Kabbalah, in an era in which fascination with mysticism was on the rise. By the time Zvi was twenty, he had already begun referring to himself as the Messiah.

Volcanic periods of exaltation and euphoria and episodes of deep depression both tormented and transformed Zvi throughout his life, and required their own explanations within the polemical encounters of both Zvi's enemies and his followers, the latter known as the *Maaminim*, "the Believers." For example, the Believers asserted that those periods of exaltation were, in fact, periods of heightened illumination and that the periods of passivity were dramatic occasions of *hester panim*, when God hides the divine face. The euphoria would become the setting for new visions, new declarations, and new outrages. The depressions were often accompanied by a crippling passivity, a passivity that would ultimately deprive Sabbatians of the energetic leadership that they required at the worst possible time, when the survival of Sabbatianism itself was at stake.

It was during the euphoria that Zvi would commit or encourage *maasim zarim*, "strange acts"—acts that by their very nature inverted or perverted normative halachah. He would marry a *sefer Torah* under a chuppah to reenact the roles of the bridegroom and bride of the Song of Songs. He would radically reshape the Jewish ritual calendar, including placing the three major festivals on one date, moving the Sabbath to a Monday, and making the Ninth of Av (his birthday) into a joyous occasion. Zvi called women to the reading of the Torah and pledged to make the status of women equal to men.[5] As he declared himself to be outside of and beyond rabbinic legalism, Zvi's followers came to believe that through Shabbetai Zvi ("our king, our sultan, our rabbi") a new Torah was being revealed— one that did not totally negate the "old" Torah, but rather rendered it secondary to the new revelation. This new Torah, referred to as "the Torah of Emanation," would turn away from all materiality until it became a supernal, spiritual Torah, a Torah "of messianic freedom."[6] This assertion marks the point at which holy deeds performed through sins became strongly associated with Sabbatianism. The forbidden became permitted in what Gershom Scholem called a "full-blown antinomian extremism."[7]

Forces of History Prepare the Path

The ongoing debate over which event or events played a significant role in the rise and growth of Sabbatianism is important for those who want to fully understand the nature of the convulsive disruption itself: how a charismatic leader both initiated the disruption and then precipitated its decline.[8] Sabbatianism managed to loosen the bonds of Jewish law and in that way helped set the stage for Enlightenment and post-Enlightenment Judaism.

Following the Alhambra decree of 1492, expelled Sephardic Jews were absorbed into present-day Turkey, North Africa, and southern and western Europe. The shock of the expulsion and the spread of Iberian Jewish culture sent a tidal wave of change throughout Jewish settlements in Europe, North Africa, and the Ottoman Empire.

Lurianic Kabbalah provided the language, the imagery, the yearnings, and the expectations that gave rise to Sabbatianism. The mythology of Lurianic Kabbalah moved redemption from physical exile to the cosmic realm. In such a world, the Messiah was understood as a cosmic redeemer, not one committed to moving earthly existence toward a this-worldly perfection. Lurianic Kabbalah introduced a profound tension between restorative and utopian visions. Thus, according to Scholem, embedded within Lurianic Kabbalah is an opening for embracing an antinomian posture in which the halachah must be broken and rabbinic power weakened.

Kabbalistic doctrine originally focused on redemption as an *individual* matter, not as a collective achievement. *D'veikut* (literally meaning "clinging" and describing an intimate communion with God) was something that the individual could pursue. Jewish mysticism underwent significant changes in focus following the expulsion from Iberia. Now messianism would be paired with individual redemption.

Lurianic Kabbalah gave an immediate answer as to why Israel in exile is the right setting for the fulfillment of the overarching Jewish mission (an approach echoed by the early leaders of American Reform Judaism, as codified within the Pittsburgh Platform of 1885). Wherever Lurianic Kabbalah spread, it also brought with it messianic tensions.[9] Lurianic Kabbalah is a key place from which emerged the idea that a messiah would not be totally free of the power of *k'lipot*. This radical doctrine would play a central role as faithful Sabbatians sought to understand Zvi's unpredictable behavior, his ultimate conversion to Islam, and the implications of his death. This transformation was foundational to Scholem's assertion that "Lurianic Kabbalah provided the background for the Sabbatian movement."[10] Sharply disagreeing with Scholem, Yaacob Dweck asserts,

"Rather than seeing Lurianic Kabbalah as generative of a messianic movement . . . Sabbateanism itself served as the means through which Lurianic Kabbalah spread throughout the Jewish world."[11]

There was a climate crisis at the time of the rise of Sabbatianism, an event that contributed to widespread fear and uncertainty. The Little Ice Age (sixteenth to nineteenth centuries) led to crop failures and to livestock dying off, which in turn led to high unemployment and widespread economic collapse. The seventeenth century has a strong record of intergroup and interpersonal violence, the scapegoating of ethnic and religious minorities, and the spread of disease and social unrest. In Europe, Jews were often targeted as agents of natural disasters, leading some Jews to flee for the more tolerant Muslim Ottoman Empire.

The Thirty Years' War (1618–48) produced more than eight million casualties through battles, famine, and disease. As national boundaries were drawn and redrawn all across Europe, waves of refugees spread across the region. In Ukraine, the Chmielnicki-led massacre of Jews occurred in 1648–49. Tens of thousands of Jews were slaughtered during this horrific period; many others were forced to convert to Christianity or were enslaved. Some three hundred Jewish communities were obliterated.

Finally, Christian millenarianism or chiliasm—the belief that the world-to-come is imminent—was exceptionally strong in the seventeenth century. Christian millenarians believed that the Second Coming of the Christ would initiate a thousand-year period of the rule of the saints in which Satan would be bound in chains, a period to be followed by the Last Judgment and Resurrection. Millenarianism projected a scenario of an end-of-time apocalyptic conflict. It eschewed—like Sabbatianism—moral norms and assumed that faith alone dominated behavioral and social codes.

In his monumental and groundbreaking study of Zvi, Scholem steadfastly resisted any list of possible external triggers as explanation for the rise of Sabbatianism. Instead, he saw Sabbatianism as a uniquely Jewish movement arising from within the Jewish community for reasons directly related to Jewish thought and teachings. For Scholem, Sabbatianism was an effort to transform Judaism in thought and in practice, an effort that was notable for its excesses in both. Scholem unfailingly saw Sabbatianism as legitimately and solely Jewish at its core.[12]

Messianism in Jewish Thought

The messianic idea in Judaism contains a mixture of catastrophe and utopianism. Catastrophes were described by the *Maaminim* as *chevlei Mashiach* (the travails of the Messiah), the suffering that both the Messiah and the world within which the savior was expected to operate were doomed to experience before the end of times. Such ideas were clearly not unique to Jewish thought and were constructed upon a consensus interpretation of the servant passages in Isaiah, especially Isaiah 52 and 53.[13]

It is theoretically possible that whatever helped set the stage for the explosive growth of Sabbatianism in one region might not have directly influenced other regions. But what connected all of the dots was the contagious power of kabbalistic thought and tendencies that crossed all regional boundaries. The city of Safed and its traditions had already begun to spread their influence, and mystical teachings soon enough became intermingled with Sabbatianism even as Sabbatianism flowed across the world. Scholem states that "the kabbalism of the age was the spiritual heritage common to all Jewish communities; it had provided them with an interpretation of history and with a fund of ideas and practices without which the Sabbatian movement is unthinkable."[14] Scholem's assertion regarding the influence of the Kabbalah is not sufficient, however, to totally negate a consideration of a multifactorial background that prepared the way for Sabbatianism.

The Indispensable Prophet

Shabbetai Zvi could no more have succeeded without Nathan of Gaza than could Jesus without Paul of Tarsus. Abraham Nathan ben Elisha Chayim Ashkenazi was born in Jerusalem in 1643. He died in 1680 either in what is today Macedonia or in Skopje, then within the Ottoman Empire. He was a brilliant student, an original thinker, and a profound scholar of Lurianic Kabbalah who has been referred to as a kabbalistic prodigy, and he possessed a powerful, personal magnetism. At the age of twenty, he had an overpowering vision of the heavenly chariot (*merkavah*) with the image of Shabbetai Zvi engraved upon it.[15] During that vision, he came to understand himself to be a prophet, and at the same time, he was mystically delivered the name of Shabbetai Zvi as the Messiah. Two years later (May 31, 1665), Nathan addressed Zvi as "Messiah." Scholars use this meeting as the launch date for the Sabbatian movement. Also in May 1665, Zvi publicly announced that he was the Messiah (a title that was later also bestowed upon him by his third wife, Sarah). Though many Palestinian Jews quickly joined the *Maaminim*, numbers of rabbis across the world just as quickly declared Zvi to be a heretic and put him into *cherem* (exclusion or ban).

Nathan continually received illuminations and heard voices. He exhibited what Shabbetai Zvi never did: "tireless activity, unwavering perseverance without manic-depressive ups and downs, originality of theological thought, and considerable literary ability."[16] Scholem assesses their relationship as crucial to Zvi's popularity. He explains that the "two men complemented each other in a remarkable fashion, and without that combination the Sabbatian movement would never have developed."[17] Perhaps more than Zvi, it was Nathan who generated what was a heretical kabbalism, and it was he who sanctified transgression. As Pawel Maciejko explains in his 2017 study of Sabbatianism, Shabbetai Zvi needed Nathan of Gaza "to explain him to himself."[18]

Analogous but Not Identical

"Nathan was at once the John the Baptist and the Paul of the new Messiah."[19] In every sense, Nathan was perfect for his task.

There is a serious question as to whether Nathan consciously drew upon parallels within early Christianity so as to shape his decision-making, but no definitive proof of this intentionality exists.[20] Scholem "adamantly refused to countenance any suggestion that Nathan of Gaza or any of the other Sabbatian thinkers drew on ideas from the Christianity of their own day."[21] As Scholem notes, "When discussing the Sabbatian paradox by means of which cruel disappointment was turned into a positive affirmation of faith, the analogy with early Christianity (again) almost obtrudes itself."[22] However, it is arguably possible that all messianic revivals by their very nature do share certain factors in common.

Around September 16, 1666, after having been charged by the leadership of the Ottoman Empire with fomenting revolution, Shabbetai took their offer of converting to Islam rather than being executed. He received large cash gifts, a formal position, and was shielded (more or less) and supported (more or less) by Turkish authorities until his death in 1676. It probably never will be definitively known as to what Zvi himself thought of his conversion.

After accepting Islam, Shabbetai Zvi put on the turban, assumed a new name, and took on a mission to encourage Jews to convert to Islam. But Sabbatianism did not simply disappear. It faltered yet endured for many decades. Unlike other messianic movements that preceded the rise of Zvi, Sabbatianism had true extension worldwide. It crossed most political, religious, social, economic, and educational boundaries. At its height, followers of Zvi and adherents to Sabbatianism might have numbered in the hundreds of thousands. Shabbetai Zvi's activities commanded the attention of the news sources of the time, fanning enthusiasm for him and for the messages that he brought.

The Aftermath of Conversion

The strange activities of Zvi along with the Lurianic Kabbalah taught by Nathan of Gaza paved the way for Jewish communities to transition "from mere factual reality to the transfigured reality of the heart."[23] Elijah was said to have walked the streets of Aleppo. Reports were received of visions and miracles and pillars of fire. Many believed that the words of Joel 3:1–4 were being lived out in their day. And elsewhere, the ten lost tribes, armed and ready, were said to be on the march.

The conversion of Zvi, deeply painful and confusing to many, was molded by Nathan of Gaza into a belief that a new world was unfolding and that salvation was drawing near. The crux of the matter was not that Zvi had converted, but rather that there were signs all around for those who could see that the old world itself was dying away. Nathan's assertion that the messianic kingdom had already been established *within* the believers was vitally important in this process. Nathan managed the fraught task of bridging the gap between historic reality and inner experience. He succeeded in moving many Sabbatians to an embrace of a saint who sinned, of an apostate messiah. Shabbetai Zvi had entered upon the lonely path to the *sitra achra* (the other side, the side of impurity, the side of the *k'lipot*). Zvi (Nathan claimed) did this not only as an example for others, but on their behalf. Jews in the seventeenth century had a profound yearning for national redemption. A yearning toward a healthier national existence was woven throughout Sabbatian doctrines: the Exile and the Diaspora had to be brought to an end.

One of the most controversial of Nathan's teaching was that the time had come to replace the study of Talmud with the study of the *Zohar*. A heavenly, spiritual Torah had supplanted the Torah of Moses, and now Nathan advanced the *Zohar* above the Talmud. The timing of this attempt constitutes a crucial reason as to why Sabbatianism did not formally emerge as a religion apart from Judaism. With a spiritual Torah in one hand and a Lurianic approach to the *Zohar* in the other, radical disruption could have been institutionalized. But this opportunity was dashed because Zvi at the worst possible moment was deeply constrained by a period of passivity. He could not escape his own private world; he therefore could not issue a call to action. Some of his followers expected that Zvi would now spark the first major national revival of the Jewish people since Yavneh. It was not to be. But it might have been.

Many explanations were offered for the apostasy. Perhaps it was a sham, an appearance of a reality that was in no way real (a Jewish expression of Docetism).[24] Perhaps it was vital within the teachings of Luria to enter the depths of evil in order to redeem the sparks from *k'lipot*. Nathan, whose teachings still held sway over many out of both respect and fear, had a new revelation: Zvi had to fall as far as possible so as to achieve spiritual redemption. Nathan skillfully assembled biblical texts and put out doctrinal and missionary letters to support his version of the apostasy in a manner and style quite similar to how the crucifixion of Jesus was shaped by proof texts from the *Tanach* and by the Pauline letters. Nathan's work inevitably drove many Jewish scholars of the day to sharply criticize Rabbinic tradition, even if those scholars would not embrace the Sabbatian gospel. Disruption was underway—from within! Even if a realized eschatology was repugnant to many, the critiques had broken into the open. Their impact extended many decades beyond the events of Shabbetai Zvi's life.

Scholem quotes a hymn that he believed was personally quite important to Zvi:

> Oh, my beloved's gone from me
> God's chosen one, Sabbatai Sevi.

Though fallen low and suffering smart
Yet he is closest to my heart.

His faithful servant I remain,
Seek and admire him I would fain
In him I trust, and while I live
May Sabbatai my sins forgive.
My eyes to him in hope I raise:
In his salvation laud and praise.[25]

Frustration, Confusion, Despair, and Hope: Dönmeh

Dates passed and expectations were frustrated. Many rabbis around the Jewish world who had initially embraced Zvi quietly returned to the way that things used to be. They did not renounce or look back. They did not recant. They did not explain. They seemed to shut the door on an alternate universe, resume their prior lives and move forward. Conversions to Islam multiplied in the Ottoman Empire, and there were conversions to Christianity as well in Europe. What began as a Great Awakening dramatically morphed in nature, becoming instead a fundamental and dramatic event that reconfigured the Jewish world.

Nathan traveled widely to strengthen the hearts of Sabbatians, even as there were concerted efforts among his followers and his opponents to suppress all documents connected with Zvi. Over a period of ten years, in a determined effort to contextualize and then to neutralize the forces that were fragmenting and shrinking the Sabbatian base, Nathan promulgated three core theological touchstones: the redemption is not yet complete; the Messiah proved that he is the agent of redemption by descending into the abyss, as an agent and not as its symbol; and the final release of the sparks requires good (in the form of the Messiah) to take on the appearance of evil, to transform into evil and, by doing so, destroy the power of evil. Zvi as the putative Messiah still had much to achieve; Zvi himself must and will battle whatever evil the abyss contains; and the final outcome will appear to his followers to be contrary to their every expectation, until Zvi's intercession will have been completed. These doctrines became the founding beliefs of the Dönmeh.

As official Ottoman support for Shabbetai Zvi waned, imprisonments and exiles marked his last days. He had one last, great illumination in

1676, and then he died on Yom Kippur of that year. Sabbatians referred to his death as an occultation, the temporary removal of a holy person from visible existence. In 1680, Nathan of Gaza died.

From Salonika, Leghorn (Livorno), Amsterdam, London, and Lwów (L'viv) to the West Indies; from Jerusalem and Safed to Smyrna, Gallipoli, Constantinople, the Balkans, North Africa, and Yemen, Sabbatianism grew strong until its flames dimmed and then were finally extinguished by Jacob Frank (1726–91) and his followers.[26]

After Zvi converted to Islam, small groups of the *Maaminim* remained scattered throughout the world, especially in Turkey. Many followed Zvi into Islam, but they still managed to create identities that bridged the worlds of Islam and Judaism. They maintained secret and sacred languages and communicated their "truths" in code, codes that were sometimes written in Rashi script. Because of the closeted nature of their practices and beliefs, they are categorized as crypto-communities and called Dönmeh. The term literally means "turncoats" in Turkish; Jews called them *minim* (sectarians) or *mamzerim* (illegitimates). It was an era in which millenarianism and communities of enthusiasts[27] flourished, and in that sense, the Dönmeh fit in with the passions of their fellow dissenters.

The Dönmeh radically reconceptualized the understanding of "Holy Land." For them, the "Holy Land" was any place where they lived out their new Judaism. Therefore, the tradition of a mitzvah to make *aliyah* was now understood to mean that there was to be no unique physical homeland—Salonika had the same valence as Jerusalem. The separation between men and women in prayer was annulled. Jewish and Muslim festivals were reinterpreted and adapted, and new observances were added to the calendar.

The Dönmeh lived in two parallel worlds, Islam and post-messianic Judaism. They also absorbed elements of Sufism as well as Lurianic Kabbalah. They awaited a Second Coming, which would throw open the gates of a third, infinitely superior world, the spiritual world. Thus, the Dönmeh were not interested in anything connected with the politics of Diaspora existence. Congiz Sisman asserts that Scholem was totally wrong when he saw in Sabbatians a proto-Zionist nationalist movement.[28] He also holds that this Jewish-Ottoman Sabbatian messianic movement "was one of the most striking events in early modern history."[29]

Scholem notes that "the crisis precipitated by the movement which [Zvi and Nathan] initiated may well be regarded as one of the decisive turning-points in Jewish history."[30] The spiritual reality created by the Sabbatians envisaged "a new world which, as yet, it lacked the means of grasping, let alone of adequately conceptualizing."[31] With the full blossom of the Haskalah and its impact upon Judaism less than one hundred years later, Scholem believed that such conceptualization was, in fact, realized. Paradoxically, what also was made possible was the nihilistic transvaluation of religious ethical and moral principles that came to epitomize the Frankist movement.

Maciejko argues that Sabbatianism was a theological, cultural, communal convulsive disruption that, in significant ways, opened the door to early modern Jewish thought. "Sabbatai's messianic allure . . . calls for serious reflection: aside from Jesus, Tsevi was the only Jewish messiah whose gospel gained sufficient momentum to break through the confines of a particular social group or a specific geographic milieu."[32] From Maciejko's perspective, Sabbatianism was not merely a momentary explosion. Rather, it was key to the rise of Zionism and to the secularization of Jewish society. For polemical as well as scholarly reasons, Maciejko's conclusion is still hotly debated.

The Final Convulsion: Jacob Frank

Born in 1726 in the Ukraine, Jacob Frank (d. 1791), strongly influenced by his father's involvement with Sabbatianism, announced himself as the reincarnation of Shabbetai Zvi. Frank, whose primary source of influence was in Podolia, is considered by many as the one who extinguished the last glimmers of the Sabbatian light and brought Sabbatianism to self-annihilation. Scholem considered him to have been "a figure of tremendous if satanic power."[33] Frank preached excess—in sexual behavior, in anti-halachic ritual, in embracing Sabbatian ideology. The movement he sparked sought the annihilation of every religion, of every system of belief, even as its final convulsion resulted in more than twenty-six thousand Jews (including Frank) being baptized into the Catholic Church. Such conversions were seen as part of an ongoing effort to descend into the depths of sin and release the possibility of redemption. Frankists practiced ritual fornication, sexual anarchy, and promiscuity. Not surprisingly, the Frankists aroused serious concern among members of the church hierarchy, and Frank himself was imprisoned as a heretic. He nevertheless was released from prison because his conversion to Christianity was deemed to be fraudulent, and thus he could not properly be convicted of heresy. He lived out his life in comfort.

The Frankists pushed Shabbetai Zvi's commitment to the empowerment of women to a new level. Frank's daughter, Eva, was identified as the supernal "Maiden," who was the only gateway to God. Frank saw the Maiden as the true Holy Virgin, while the Madonna (Holy Virgin and Mother of Christ) was reduced to being the outer shell, protecting the sacred inner core. The Maiden was ultimately identified by Frank as being an expression of the messianic soul. Frank came to believe that the Messiah is necessarily a woman. Eva Frank was venerated as the messianic figurehead. She was the embodiment of both female spirituality and libertine proclivities and thus can be viewed as an icon of the emerging gender revolution.[34] The death of Eva Frank in abject poverty (1816) marked the final collapse of Sabbatianism as a messianic movement.

Sources on Sabbatianism

The Sabbatians published very few books, and those books that we do have conceal more than they reveal. Orthodox opponents of the Sabbatians destroyed whatever original sources that fell into their hands, and the National Socialist invasion of Greece and near destruction of Greek Jewry (1941–43) consumed much of what was left.

Much of the material that does provide background and details regarding Shabbetai Zvi and Sabbatianism in Gershom Scholem's work is based upon Jacob Sasportas's *Sefer Tzitzat Novel Tzvi.*[35] Sasportas (1610–98), a Sephardic rabbi born in Algeria, was Scholem's spirit guide in his study of Zvi. Sasportas was one of the most outspoken of the anti-Sabbatian polemicists ("the most uncompromising and relentless enemy of the [Sabbatian] Movement[36]). His collected writings in the intensely polemical *Sefer Tzitzat Novel Tzvi* (The fading flower of Zevi) is the most significant extant source of Sabbatian teachings and activities. Yet, because of its focus, it emphasizes materials that regard negatively who Shabbetai Zvi was, what he said, how he was received and perceived, and the flaws and deficits of the movement called by his name. The text intentionally omits any materials that possibly might (mis)construe data in Zvi's favor. Sasportas looked on with horror at all that was connected with Zvi. He felt a powerful obligation to warn Jews of its dangers. A biographical study of Sasportas[37] held his view that one of Zvi's most egregious crimes was his threat to rabbinic leadership and his embrace of profound antinomianism, a form of anarchic nihilism.

Sasportas warned about sectarianism; he warned against those who challenged the unity of God and divine revelation. He warned that Sabbatianism was perilously close to Christianity and therefore Shabbetai's death might ignite even greater divisions within the Jewish community. He was himself physically assaulted by some *Maaminim*, and he had to flee for his life. Tishbi views Sasportas as an arrogant zealot in pursuit of his own truth. His polemics at times markedly veered from the truth, and after the book was finished, Sasportas continued to rewrite it as facts on the ground changed.

Reconstructing the history, impact, and implications of Zvi and of Sabbatianism continues to be a challenge. Scholem dismissed Zvi the person, but still saw in Sabbatianism a basis for a secular interpretation of Judaism "that was immanent within Judaism itself."[38] And as a secular Zionist himself, Scholem has long been a target for those who saw in his magisterial effort to understand the impact of Sabbatianism a move to valorize it and to push the roots of modern Zionism back into the seventeenth century.

Many contemporary English-speaking scholars of Jewish thought weighed in to support Scholem's conclusions. Dweck severely castigates those whom he viewed as lacking all scholarly insight on the topic, but who nevertheless wanted to be associated with a project that had "the patina of authenticity."[39] Such people, he believes, were unsuccessfully searching for a way to avoid serious peer review. The current author acknowledges that danger.[40]

Conclusions

Powerfully syncretistic, Sabbatianism was a crypto-Islamic, crypto-Christian, and crypto-Jewish phenomenon.[41] It is as if Zvi's personal enlightenment was far too large, far too substantial, to be bound into any single religious tradition.

Contrary to Scholem, contemporary scholarship holds that Shabbetai Zvi himself was not devoid of originality, nor was his movement just the by-product of the work of Nathan of Gaza or of external historical forces. Zvi embraced a strong, personal relationship with God, a relationship that went far beyond kabbalistic speculation. It was this relationship that allowed him to believe that his *maasim zarim* were neither acts of doctrinal antinomianism nor mere random and irrational acts, but rather an expression of his felt proximity to God. Shabbetai Zvi also insisted that his conversion was not carried out through coercion, but rather that it was an expression of his free will. He offered to the *Maaminim* an accessible God, an accessible world, and a way of belonging to a community of meaning.

There has been a flurry of research recently trying to see what (if any) causal links can be discovered between Sabbatianism, the Haskalah, Chasidism, Reform Judaism, and Zionism. These movements embraced leaders such as the Baal Shem Tov and the Vilna Gaon; Theodor Herzl; and Rav Avraham Yitzchak Kook and Rabbi Menachem Mendel Schneerson, individuals who were fiercely personal, charismatic, and possibly miracle workers. In contradistinction to Scholem, Jacob Katz notes that the "Frankists were the conduit of Sabbatean ideas to the Hassidic camp."[42] Nevertheless, Katz refused to see causal links and conceptual support from Sabbatian doctrine and spirit to the initiators of Reform Judaism, the Haskalah, and modern Zionism.

It's uncertain if these causal links exist at all. Yet, this author clearly discerns that Sabbatianism, the Haskalah, and the beginnings of Reform Judaism and of Chasidism coexisted side by side through at least two generations and that the enemies of any of these forces tended to be opposed to the others as well. These forces were contemporaneous and had "overt and covert points of contact."[43]

Scholem believed that Sabbatian opposition to the orthodoxies of the day made it easier for the *Maaminim* to reject the mitzvot. For Scholem, this was a disaster, a catastrophe that ripped apart the traditional ties binding the Jewish community together and prepared the way for assimilation. This led Scholem to assert that Moses Mendelssohn, Lurianic Kabbalah, and Sabbatianism were somehow linked together in ways that were totally unexpected. For Scholem, assimilation and the Haskalah unfortunately succeeded in accomplishing that which the Sabbatians sought but failed to achieve. There is at least agreement that the contemporary post-Sabbatian world, the world of 2023 and beyond, still bears the impact of the convulsive and disruptive life, acts, and vision of the mystical Messiah and the prophet from Gaza.

NOTES

1. Mehmed Effendi was the name taken by Shabbetai Zvi following his conversion to Islam.
2. This anonymous poem, "Mevlidi Sherif of *Mi Shebeirach*" can be found in "Songs and Poems of the Dönmeh," in *Sabbatean Heresy*, ed. Pawel Maciejko (Waltham, MA: Brandeis University Press, 2017), 53.
3. I have avoided referring to Zvi as a "false" messiah. Such a designation could be understood to signify that Jewish tradition has a broadly accepted definition and description of a "true" messiah. Such an approach not only borders on hubris but could lead to far broader and problematic academic and intercommunal stress. The tradition does not grant Maimonides, for example, a default right to describe what determines a true messiah for anyone other than those who choose to accept Maimonides's authority.
4. *K'lipot*, according to Lurianic Kabbalah, refer to the husks or shells that imprison sparks of the divine light. Through acts of *tikkun* (righteous acts of repair) those sparks can be liberated.
5. There is still much to be learned about Zvi's efforts to bring a "separate but alike" equivalence to the roles of men and women. He acknowledged women's prophetic capacity. He granted women equal opportunity in performing rituals of Judaism. He invited some women to become serious students of the Kabbalah and apparently attributed to such women messianic and divine power. Sarah, Shabbetai Zvi's third wife, was the first public figure to proclaim him as the Messiah. Zvi somehow blended into his visions both orgiastic ceremonies and a stern commitment to chastity.
6. Gershom Scholem, *Sabbatai Sevi: The Mystical Messiah, 1626–1676* (Princeton, NJ: Princeton University Press, [1973] 2016), 323.
7. Scholem, *Sabbatai Sevi*, 163. Further, *nomos* is the Greek word for law. Antinomianism is a rejection of the binding authority of law in matters touching upon morality and ritual. Antinomian tendencies in Judaism are to be found within both rationalist and mystical teachings. Polemicists attacking Sabbatianism found its explicit antinomianism profoundly troubling.
8. See Matt Goldish, *The Sabbatean Prophets* (Cambridge, MA: Harvard University Press, 2004).

9. Scholem, *Sabbatai Sevi*, 67.
10. Scholem, *Sabbatai Sevi*, 27.
11. Yaacob Dweck, introduction to Scholem, *Sabbatai Sevi*, lxi.
12. Scholem's thousand-page book *Sabbatai Sevi* has stood as the definitive work on Zvi for decades.
13. "But he was wounded because of our sins, / Crushed because of our iniquities. . . . / And by his bruises we were healed. . . . / My righteous servant makes the many righteous, / It is their punishment that he bears; . . . / He bore the guilt of many" (Isaiah 53:5, 11–12).
14. Scholem, *Sabbatai Sevi*, 8.
15. The "heavenly chariot" is a tradition based on Ezekiel 1–3, which depicts the divine throne as a chariot and God riding upon it. This material is the most detailed attempt in the *Tanach* to describe God's heavenly domain and is the source of much mystical speculation.
16. Scholem, *Sabbatai Sevi*, 207.
17. Scholem, *Sabbatai Sevi*, 208.
18. Maciejko, *Sabbatean Heresy*, xxv.
19. Scholem, *Sabbatai Sevi*, 207.
20. Early Christianity and early Sabbatianism are analogous movements. Scholem also believed that there was a diachronic relationship between the two movements; though separated by well over one thousand years, they both exhibited mutations and shifts in thought and evolutionary development that were often quite similar to one another. For example, for Shabbetai/Nathan, as with Jesus/Paul, the core emphasis should be on faith rather than on the halachah.
21. Yaacob Dweck, in Scholem, *Sabbatai Sevi*, li. See also Pawel Maciejko, *Sabbatean Heresy*, xxiii. Paraphrasing Avraham Miguel Cardozo, Cordozo's disciple Nehemiah Haym insisted that Nathan went so far as to develop a Sabbatian doctrine of a triune God (xxiii).
22. Scholem, *Sabbatai Sevi*, 795.
23. Scholem, *Sabbatai Sevi*, 417.
24. Docetism is a heterodox doctrine within Christianity, which holds that the historical and bodily existence of Jesus was but a semblance, a phantasm, an illusion.
25. Scholem, *Sabbatai Sevi*, 718.
26. Many of Frank's followers believed that they could achieve direct access to divine revelation. Frank was a Jewish Polish follower of Zvi, who despite his own messianic pretensions eventually decided that the Messiah had to be a woman.
27. Commonly understood to be individuals and groups who claimed direct access to divine revelation.

28. Congiz Sisman, *Transcending Diaspora: Studies in Sabbateanism & Donmes* (Istanbul: Libra Kipatoilik, 2016).

29. Sisman, *Transcending Diaspora*, 96.

30. Scholem, *Sabbatai Sevi*, 928.

31. Scholem, *Sabbatai Sevi*, 798.

32. Maciejko, *Sabbatean Heresy*, xi.

33. Gershom Scholem, *The Messianic Idea in Judaism* (London: George Allen & Unwin; Schocken Books, 1971), 127.

34. To engage in a deeper exploration of these themes, see the brilliant and original writings of Ada Rapoport-Albert. Dr. Rapoport-Albert argues that the role of women in Sabbatianism distinguished it from other messianic and mystical movements; she sees *d'veikut* as a means of personalizing mysticism and asserts that Chasidism arose in reaction to Sabbatianism.

35. The critical edition of this text edited by Isaiah Tishbi is based upon the work of Zechariah Schwarz and published by Mossad Bialik, Jerusalem, 1964. This study is extremely valuable in bringing a contemporary understanding of Sasportas and his work. There was a long and complicated process by which an accurate copy of the original handwritten document made its way into Scholem's hands. The original text was destroyed in the Shoah. The hardest part of understanding the text was the manner in which it references the Kabbalah. When the text was finally ready for publication, it was destroyed in a fire at Schocken Publishing House in Jerusalem.

36. Scholem, *Sabbatai Sevi*, 566.

37. Yaacob Dweck, "Jacob Sasportas and Problems of Discipline in the Ets Haim Yeshiva," in *Religious Changes and Cultural Transformations in the Early Modern Western Communities*, ed. Yosef Kaplan (Leiden: Brill, 2019), 383–92.

38. Yaacob Dweck, in Scholem, *Sabbatai Sevi*, lii.

39. Yaacob Dweck, in Scholem, *Sabbatai Sevi*, lx.

40. For an excellent bibliography of current studies of Shabbetai Zvi and of Sabbatianism, please see Yaacob Dweck's listing on lxii and lxxv, in Gershom Scholem, *Sabbatai Sevi*. For those who wish to explore the documentary underpinnings of Scholem's work, one must begin with *Sefer Tzitzat Novel Tzvi*, by Jacob Sasportas.

41. Maciejko, *Sabbatean Heresy*.

42. Jacob Katz, *Divine Law in Human Hands* (Jerusalem: Magnes Press, 1998), 507.

43. Katz, *Divine Law in Human Hands*, 527.

FOR FURTHER READING

Asch, Sholem. *Sabbatai Zevi*. Westport, CT: Greenwood, 1974.

Carlebach, Elisheva. *The Pursuit of Heresy: Rabbi Moses Hagiz and the Sabbatian Controversies*. New York: Columbia University Press, 1991.

Freely, John. *The Lost Messiah*. Woodstock, NY: Overlook Press, 2001.

Goldish, Matt. *The Sabbatean Prophets*. Cambridge, MA: Harvard University Press, 2004.

Halperin, David J. *Sabbatai Zevi*. Oxford: Littman Library of Jewish Civilization, 2007.

Kaplan, Yosef. *Religious Changes and Cultural Transformations in the Early Modern Western Communities*. Leiden: Brill, 2019.

Katz, Jacob. *Divine Law in Human Hands*. Jerusalem: Magnes Press, 1998.

Maciejko, Pawel. *Sabbatean Heresy*. Waltham, MA: Brandeis University Press, 2017.

Naor, Bezalel. *Post-Sabbatian Sabbatianism*. Spring Valley, NY: Orot, 1999.

Sasportas, Jacob. *Sefer Tzitzat Novel Tzvi*. Edited by Isaiah Tishbi (based upon the work of Zechariah Schwarz). Jerusalem: Mossad Bialik, 1964.

Scholem, Gershom. *Sabbatai Sevi: The Mystical Messiah, 1626–1676*. Princeton, NJ: Princeton University Press, 2016.

———. *The Messianic Idea in Judaism*. London: George Allen & Unwin; Schocken Books, 1971.

Singer, Isaac Bashevis, *Satan in Goray*. New York: Ferrar, Straus and Giroux, 1996.

Sisman, Congiz. *Transcending Diaspora: Studies in Sabbateanism & Donmes*. Istanbul: Libra Kipatoilik, 2016.

9

Jewish Thought in the North African Sephardic Diaspora
Continuity and Change

Michal Ohana, PhD

AFTER THE SPANISH EXPULSION in 1492, Jewish exiles sought refuge in the Ottoman Empire, Western Europe, and North Africa.[1] The influx of Sephardic exiles ushered in a new wave of intellectual activity to the local Jewish community in North Africa. While previous studies have shown their contribution in the fields of halachah, poetry, and historiography, this essay seeks to point out that a new chapter began in the realm of Jewish thought as well. It should be emphasized here that while the contribution of the Sephardic exiles and their descendants was considerable, it did not take place in a vacuum, as North Africa had been a seat of Jewish learning in its own right for centuries prior to their arrival.

Portuguese exiles to Fez brought with them the printing presses used in Portugal and reestablished their workshops there in 1515, thus becoming the first printers in Morocco. However, for reasons not totally clear, the work of these presses did not last long in North Africa and ceased to function at all a short time later, in 1522. As a result, hundreds of original works by North African scholars remained in manuscript form and were never put to press. The cramped and harsh conditions common to Jewish homes threatened the safekeeping of these manuscripts, as did the exposure to the elements, vermin, and moths. Many manuscripts were also lost or destroyed during Berber and Muslim attacks on the Jewish community in times of political turmoil. Moreover, many rabbis did not systematically record their teachings in writing or lacked paper for their work. In fact, they would just jot their insights on the covers of books and in the margins. This was a fascinating process and one that is now receiving scholarly attention.

Without access to printing presses in North Africa, the exiles and their descendants in the sixteenth and seventeenth centuries were forced to seek out printers in Italy and in other places that did have working Hebrew printing presses. This undertaking required great expense for the travel and long stays in foreign lands, above and beyond the already high cost of printing. Therefore, few scholars from the region were ever able to bring their works to print; however, some were successful. For example, Shmuel Hajis traveled in the 1590s from Fez to Venice, where he printed his *Sefer M'vakeish HaShem* (sermons on the weekly Torah portions) and *D'var Shmuel* (commentary on *D'varim Rabbah*) (1596). Similarly, in 1608, Aharon ben Chayim left Fez in order to print his books, *Korban Aharon*[2] and *Midot Aharon* (commentary on Rabbinic midrash). Some authors did not leave North Africa themselves, but their works were sent with emissaries to Jewish communities abroad where a printing press could publish them. In this way, through the efforts of an intermediary, the commentary on *M'gillat Achashverosh* by Zecharya ben Sarok, an exile who settled in Algiers, was published in Venice in 1560. Similarly, in 1599, *Tiferet Yisrael* and *Chesek Shlomo*, the works of Shlomo Duran of Algiers, were brought to press in Venice through the efforts of his student and nephew. Yehudah Uziel (II) of Fez had his essay *Beit Uzieli* (sermons on the weekly Torah portions) printed in Amsterdam with the help of a middleman. Some essays by Vidal Sarfati (II), including *Tzuf D'vash* (Torah commentary), *Otzar Nechmad* (commentary on the Book of Psalms), and *Hatzaat Rut* and *M'gillat S'tarim* (commentaries on the books of Ruth and Esther, respectively), were printed in Amsterdam at the initiative of a family member. Other manuscripts were published hundreds of years after they were first authored. For instance, *Omer HaShich'chah* (commentary on Proverbs), by Avraham Gavishon of Tlemcen, who was born to Iberian refugees in the 1490s, was printed in Livorno in the latter part of the eighteenth century. The rest of the works of Vidal Sarfati (II) were printed in European cities in the nineteenth century. Many other manuscripts were only published in the twentieth century, by authors such as Yosef Almoshnino, Yehudah Kaltz, Yosef Alashkar, Shaul Serero, and Yitzchak Sarfati. Without a doubt, many other manuscripts have yet to be published.

Although no dedicated literature dealing with theological and philosophical issues has been composed by the Sephardic descendants who lived in North Africa, they did indeed produce works that addressed the issues and expressed their views on various topics discussed in medieval Jewish thought. These works shared certain characteristics in form and content. I will describe five here.

The Literary Genre: Commentaries and Sermons

Joseph Hacker noted that contrary to other medieval Sephardic Jewish thinkers, descendants of the exiles who settled within the Ottoman Empire no longer composed independent essays of Jewish philosophy in the manner of Saadyah Gaon's *Emunot V'Dei-ot* (*The Book of Doctrines and Beliefs*, 933 CE), Maimonides's *Moreih N'vuchim* (*Guide for the Perplexed*, 1190), Gersonides's *Milchamot Adonai* (*Wars of the Lord*, 1560), Chasdai ben Abraham Crescas's *Or Adonai* (*Light of the Lord*, 1400), or Joseph Albo's *Sefer HaIkarim* (*The Book of Principles*, 1425). Instead, their works were primarily commentary and often focused on the books of the Bible and on Rabbinic literature. Indeed, Hacker argues that the repeated focus on these texts, which make up the essential annual canon of communal and private study, demonstrates that the primary duty and role for the scholar in his community dictated his scholarly and literary focus. Similarly, Hacker suggests that the many sermon collections published by the descendants of the exiles living in the Ottoman Empire derived from the responsibility those rabbis carried as part of the definition of their position to regularly deliver sermons on Sabbaths, holy days, and special occasions.[3] The well-known Sephardic sermon therefore continued to play an important role among the Diaspora communities following the expulsion. Moreover, in their sermons and commentaries, the descendants of exiles living in the Ottoman Empire addressed many of the essential elements debated in medieval Jewish thought and managed to disseminate their own philosophy through those works.

It seems this description is quite fitting as well for the work of the exiles and their descendants in the North African Diaspora. Like their colleagues in the Ottoman Diaspora, they hardly ever returned to writing independent works of philosophy or thought, but rather focused on prolific writing of commentaries and sermons. Similarly, their works centered on the same biblical and Rabbinic canons. Much like the Jewish scholars of the Ottoman Empire, they were also inspired to write their works as a result of their communal roles. And, like their colleagues in the Ottoman Empire, the exiles and their descendants who settled in North Africa nevertheless addressed different philosophical issues in their homiletical and interpretive works. For instance, there were some who explored the question of human nature through eulogies they delivered or who explored the nature of prophecy in the context of a sermon on a relevant weekly Torah portion. There were others who expressed their perspective on "external or secular wisdom" as they commented on the Book of Proverbs or discussed their astrological views in explicating the conquests of the Land of Israel in the Book of Joshua or in their commentary on the Book of Esther. Shmuel Hagiz, Yehudah Uziel, and Aharon ben Chayim even included a topical index with their works.

It is clear, therefore, that the philosophical teachings of the exiles' descendants in North Africa are neither consistently offered in their essays nor systematically explored in their works. Rather, those who wish to understand the approach or thinking of any of them on a certain issue must read all of their works and blend together all of the various references scattered throughout their writings into a cohesive theory.

Strong Links to Rabbinic Literature

Rabbinic literature occupies a central role in medieval scholarship. For example, the classic Sephardic sermon opened with a quote from a Rabbinic tale, and then additional Rabbinic teachings were integrated into the body of the sermon itself. Citations from and references to Rabbinic tales served to clarify writers' positions as well as to bolster their arguments. Following the printing of the collection of midrash in the sixteenth century, Rabbinic scholars expanded their topics, and a new literature of commentaries on Rabbinic tales, especially on *Midrash Rabbah*, emerged as a new genre. The commentaries were written as guidebooks for the midrash collections through which the authors attempted to lead their readers to a correct understanding of the text; the proliferation of commentaries consequently introduced variances in the text. There were those who conceived of wide-ranging and discursive commentaries that sought to establish a harmonized understanding of the midrash, and others sufficed with brief clarifications of the text in a few words or sentences. Some saw the midrash as a well of philosophical truth and utilized their commentary as the opportunity to debate those issues, while others approached these issues as an aside or only on rare occasions.

A similar strong affinity to Rabbinic literature characterized the works of the exiles and their descendants in the North African Diaspora in the sixteenth to seventeenth centuries. For instance, the vast majority of sermons by Yehudah Uziel, Shaul Serero, Yitzchak Sarfati, Shmuel Hagiz, and Shlomo Duran follow the Sephardic sermon framework described above; they open with a biblical quote, followed immediately by a quote from Rabbinic literature, which is explicated at the end of the sermon. Likewise, throughout the sermons of Duran, Sarfati, Hagiz, Serero, and Uziel, many Rabbinic teachings are utilized as a tool for clarifying a position or bolstering it. The collections of homiletics by Uziel and Hagiz even include an index of Rabbinic teachings discussed throughout the different sermons; whereas Serero, along with Duran and ben Chayim, used sermons not only to point out corruptions in midrashic texts and compare parallel quotes from other Rabbinic collections, but also to make clear what he considered to be the correct version.

Rabbinic literature also served as a tool to clarify positions and confirm arguments in biblical commentaries, as we see in the sixteenth- and seventeeth-century commentaries on the Prophets and Writings by Zecharia ben Sarok, Duran, Sarfati, Aharon ben Chayim, and Serero. The volumes by Duran, Hagiz, and ben Chayim were accompanied by an index of Rabbinic teachings that they had explicated.

A strong affinity to midrashic texts is also expressed in the sparse independent literature composed in the Maghreb; Yosef Alashkar primarily relies on Rabbinic teachings in his book *R'fuat HaNefesh* (Healing the soul, published in the twentieth century), and Duran similarly utilized them in his sixteenth-century essay *Maamar S'udat Mitzvah* (Discourses on the order of commandments).

The interest in Rabbinic literature for its own sake and not merely as a means for clarifying arguments or bolstering positions also took root in the Maghreb. Yosef Alashkar composed a book of commentary on selected Rabbinic aggadot (*Sefer HaTapuach*), whereas Shmuel Hagiz, ben Chayim, and Sarfati composed specific commentaries on midrashic collections (*D'var Shmuel* on *D'varim Rabbah*; *Midot Aharon* and *Korban Aharon* on the *Baraita D'Rabbi Yishmael* and the *Sifra*; *Imrei Yosher* and *Derech HaKodesh* on *Midrash Rabbah* and the *Sifra*). This literary genre also served as the platform for occasionally debating issues in medieval Jewish philosophy, as scholars such as Yosef Alashkar, Shmuel Hagiz, and Aharon ben Chayim laid out their thoughts on diverse issues in the essays mentioned above.

Strong Links to Medieval Sephardic and Postexilic Literature

The flow of knowledge between the medieval Jewish communities in Spain and in North Africa took place through many channels. It seems that the absorption of Spanish exiles in North Africa, including the books with which they were able to escape, significantly increased the flow of knowledge between the two regions.

In their diverse interpretive-homiletical works, the exiles and their descendants in the North African Diaspora displayed a great familiarity with and strong affinity for the medieval Sephardic Jewish philosophical and interpretive literature, such as the works of Saadyah Gaon, Abraham ibn Ezra, Radak, Bachya ibn Pakuda, Y'hudah HaLevi, Maimonides, Yad'aya Hapnini, Nachmanides, Bachya ben Asher, Gersonides, Nissim of Gerona, Chasdai Crescas, Yosef Albo, Yitzchak Arama, Avraham Bibago, Shem Tov ben Yosef ibn Shem Tov, Yitzchak Abarbanel, Avraham Shalom, HaRe'em, and Yosef Yaavetz, as well as many others.

The exiles' descendants in the Maghreb consciously adopted the methods of the Jewish thinkers who preceded them and added to or subtracted from their teachings until they established an interpretive framework that suited them. An examination of the writings of the exilic descendants in the North African Diaspora on topics such as the creation of the world, the nature of prophecy, human perfection, the immortality of the soul, and the status of "external wisdoms" (that is, secular and non-Jewish knowledge) illustrates that the moderate philosophical approach, rather than the radical one, largely influenced their work. At the same time, a study of their writings on topics such as divine providence and the nature of miracles illustrates that the moderate astrological approach continued to influence their thought in parallel.[4]

Alongside this medieval literature, the exiles and their descendants in North Africa became acquainted with interpretive literature composed after the exile in other Diaspora communities. Centers of printing established in the sixteenth and seventeenth centuries in cities such as Venice, Mantua, Amsterdam, Constantinople, Salonika, and Krakow resulted in a wide distribution of books throughout the entire Jewish Diaspora. Disparate Jewish communities became exposed to contemporary literature thanks to emissaries and other travelers, printers among them, who frequently visited different Jewish communities throughout the Diaspora, selling books, trading them, or leaving them on loan so that they might be copied down.

Exilic descendants who operated in Tlemcen, Algiers, and Fez were widely aware of literature printed in Italy and from the Ottoman Empire, especially works written by other exiles. Those works included the writings of Yehudah Muscato, Eliezer Ashkenazi, Yoel ibn Shueb, Avraham Saba, Moshe Elbilda, Yitzchak Adarbi, Moshe Almosnino, Shlomo HaLevi, Yitzchak Karo, Yitzchak Arviv, Yaakov Habib, Shmuel Laniado, Shem-Tov Melamed, Ovadiah Sforno, Shmuel Yafe Ashkenazi, Meir Arama, and others.

Indirect Links to Greek and Muslim Philosophy

In preexilic Spain, Greek and Muslim philosophical and scientific literature was commonly translated into Hebrew, and many commentaries on these sources were written in Hebrew. In contrast, no similar works were found in the Sephardic Diaspora in North Africa. As mentioned, the primary literary output among the exiles and their descendants in the Maghreb was homiletical or interpretive, focusing on the biblical and Rabbinic canon. Among their works, it was rare to find a commentary on Jewish philosophy literature comparable to Y'hudah HaLevi's *Kuzari* or Maimonides's *Guide for the Perplexed*, and certainly not on Greek philosophy or its medieval Muslim interpreters, such as Ibn Sina, al-Farabi, and Ibn Rushd.

Yet, this does not mean that the exiles and their descendants ignored this prolific literature altogether. Rather, they addressed the Greek and

Muslim philosophies selectively in instances where they wished to refute them or, conversely, to utilize their theories to bolster their own argument in some way. When commenting on a complex issue arising out of a text, they preferred Greek or Muslim philosophers.

Thus, when the exiles' descendants in the Maghreb debated the issue of the creation of the world in their essays, they mostly did so while rejecting the Aristotelian conception of the world as positively and necessarily derived from God (in favor of God being an active Creator) while simultaneously adopting Aristotle's proof that the world was not created by chance. In similar fashion, when they addressed the issue of divine providence, they mostly did so by rejecting the Aristotelian denial of individual providence in the sublunar realm. Similarly, when their essays debated the issues of human perfection and the immortality of the soul, they did so while adopting certain elements and rejecting others with reference to the Aristotelian assumption that a person's ultimate end lies in the actualization of their intellect by the rational cognition of truths.

At the same time, the authors felt comfortable making frequent use of terms and definitions coined by Greek philosophy. A few examples among many can be found in Shmuel Hagiz's use of the Aristotelian "four causes" to explain Noah's ark, the justification of circumcision, and the miracles performed during the Exodus from Egypt. Likewise he addressed the definition of "place" in reference to the commandment to build the Temple.[5] Yehudah Uziel explained the creation of the "mouth of the earth" on the eve of the Sabbath (*Mishnah Avot* 5:6) utilizing Aristotle's distinction between "force" and "actor." Similarly, Uziel embraced Aristotle's theory that "a person is by nature a political animal" and used it to explain the contribution of a wife to her husband's life in a wedding sermon he delivered, as well as on other occasions. Shlomo Duran used this same theory and its succinct wording in his commentary on the Book of Proverbs, where he also utilized the Aristotelian theory of natural place. Similarly, Zecharia ben Sarok utilized Aristotle's insights in the *Politics* to explain the character and actions of Ahasuerus, Haman, and Mordecai. Interestingly, Aristotle's *Nicomachean Ethics* was the most widely quoted and mentioned source by the exiles' descendants in the Maghreb.

Nevertheless, it is highly likely that the exiles' descendants' encounter with Greek and Muslim philosophy was second- or thirdhand knowledge mediated through the quotes and summaries of those theories in medieval Jewish philosophical works.

Furthermore, it is possible that in some instances they were not even aware that the origin of some ideas derives from Greek philosophy, because the medieval Jewish philosophical works do not always cite their sources. For example, Shmuel Hagiz used Aristotle's distinction between the three types of love—goodness, utility, and pleasantness—to explain the Rabbinic teaching "From the Torah, and from the Prophets, and from the Writings; [the decree that] a woman [is destined to marry] a [specific] man is from God" (Babylonian Talmud, *Mo-eid Katan* 18b) and the verse "Take your son, your only one, the one you love, Isaac" (Genesis 22:2). Shlomo Duran also explained the Rabbinic teaching using the same Aristotelian theory in his commentary on Proverbs, as well as for other texts. So, too, did Yosef Alashkar in his commentary on Tractate *Avot*. However, it is very likely (though impossible to know for certain) that they only encountered this theory through the work of Joseph Albo on this topic, which does not cite Aristotle as the source for this insight.

It is worth mentioning that among the descendants of Sephardic exiles in the Ottoman Empire, a similarly significant trend diminishing the extent of literary output focused directly on Greek and Muslim philosophy, as well as on translations or commentaries on these works. As mentioned previously, the authorship of the exiles' descendants in the Ottoman Empire's Diaspora was primarily homiletical or interpretive and focused on the Rabbinic and biblical canon of texts. They similarly utilized Greek philosophy and its Muslim interpreters only indirectly. A select few, like Moshe Albilda and Moshe Almosnino, wrote commentaries on Aristotle's *Ethics* or *Physics*. Incidentally, these commentaries were never published.

Links to Zoharic Literature and the Kabbalah of Safed

In North Africa generally, and especially in Morocco, there was a long-standing tradition of engagement with Kabbalah. At times the kabbalist circles gravitated to certain cities, like the kabbalist center in the Draa Valley in Morocco. At the same time, it is known that cultural emissaries who took part in editing the Zoharic fragments in Italy sought to complete their editions based on Zoharic manuscripts from East and North Africa. For instance, Yechiel ben Nissim of Pisa, the famous banker who was involved in the efforts to copy and distribute the Zoharic literature in the first half of the sixteenth century, mentioned that the Zoharic collections from Fez should be sought out.

Moshe Halamish reviewed the dissemination process of the *Zohar* in North Africa and demonstrated that there were some scholars in the area who did not subscribe to the kabbalist school, but nevertheless quoted from it in their essays because they perceived it to be a tannaitic source, and therefore they referenced it as they would other midrashim. This approach aptly captures the attitudes toward the *Zohar* on the part of some of the exiles' descendants mentioned in this study. Their works are categorically not defined as kabbalist literature, yet they regularly quote from the Zoharic literature and relied on it to support their arguments. Some did this frequently, others infrequently, and some quite rarely. They saw in the *Zohar* a tannaitic source and referred to it as the *Midrash Zohar* or *Midrash Rashbi*, and therefore we find expressions like "and on this many Rabbinic midrashim give full expression, particularly the midrashim of the holy Rashbi of blessed memory"; "and here all of these things are hinted at in the *Midrash Zohar*"; and "according to the opinion of the sages, z"l, in particular the sages of the *Zohar*."

Likewise, Boaz Huss argued that the reliance on the *Zohar* and the emphasis on its authority common among sixteenth-century Spanish scholars played an important role in the Spanish exiles' battle to establish a hegemony in their new places of residence. Huss explains that their access to Zoharic texts, their ability to quote from them, and their reliance on the *Zohar* in matters of doctrine and religious practice bolstered their cultural power and aided them in establishing a dominant status.[6] However, I would like to emphasize that their use of kabbalistic literature and their adoption of kabbalist terminology paralleled their use of philosophical literature and the adoption of philosophical terminology, much like the fifteenth-century Spanish movement that strove earlier to harmonize between Kabbalah and philosophy.

Although the exiles and their descendants frequently quoted from the Zoharic literature, there were those who held an esoteric view of the kabbalistic body of knowledge and the *Zohar*. Therefore, at times they chose not to fully explain their thoughts. Rather, they would conclude with statements that limited the kabbalist knowledge to insiders or to those who could complete the knowledge from other kabbalist literature. It is against this background that one should read the advice of Yaakov Gavishon, "In reference to the time required to read the books of Kabbalah and mysticism he said . . . none will sit in her gates other than the learned elders and the Sanhedrin."[7]

Yet, it is worth mentioning that among the scholars' works there is no excessive regard for the *Zohar*'s authority, nor does one find an expression of an approach that sanctifies the non-semantic elements of the *Zohar* or argues that there is a theurgic effect derived from engaging with the *Zohar* or even just memorizing its words. It seems that among the exiles and their descendants in the North African Diaspora (those who were not kabbalists), the *Zohar* was treated as a tannaitic source with unique importance, like an additional Rabbinic midrash, but first among equals.

Toward the end of the sixteenth century, the influence of the kabbalists of Safed grew stronger. Some of the kabbalists from Draa made *aliyah* in the midst of that century to settle in Safed and even attained an important position in its spiritual life. At the same time, emissaries from the Land of Israel to the Maghreb brought with them newly revised kabbalistic literature: for instance, Avraham Azoulai already encountered *Pardes Rimonim* by Moshe Cordovero (Ramak) while he was in Fez. Indeed, the literature composed in North Africa beginning in the second half of the sixteenth century shows reference to the works of Safadian kabbalists, such as Moshe Alsheich, Shlomo Alkabetz, Elisha Gallico, Elazar Azikri, and Shumel Uzida. The descendants of exiles in the North African Diaspora cautiously adopted the methods of their colleagues, the Safadian kabbalists; they added to their teaching or edited and removed from their writings until they reached an interpretation that suited their thought.

Conclusion

The Jewish thought produced in North Africa during the sixteenth and the first half of the seventeenth centuries differs in some ways from the classic medieval pattern: there are no interpretations or translations of Greek or Muslim literature and no independent essays. Yet, the Sephardic descendants in North Africa continued to deal with medieval Jewish thought in their new homeland. They adopted the writings of medieval and contemporary commentators, philosophers, astrologers, and kabbalists and integrated them into their own works as they saw fit. Different genres served them as platforms to forming their outlooks; the noted Sephardic sermon and commentaries to the Bible and ancient Rabbinic texts continued to be favored literary genres—their compositions weaving together biblical and Rabbinic texts, medieval and contemporary literature.

In conclusion, I would like to emphasize that one cannot claim that only one mode of thought prevailed in North Africa during the sixteenth and the first half of the seventeenth—just as one cannot claim that there was only one mode of Jewish thought in Spain before the expulsion. Every one of the rabbis mentioned in this article (not to mention the many omitted for purposes of brevity) had his own unique point of view on various issues. Each thinker in his own way emphasized some aspects of the Jewish theological-philosophical heritage at the expense of others.

NOTES

1. The author and editors would like to thank Rabbi Yoni Regev for his diligence and efficiency in translating this entire chapter from Hebrew.
2. This work was a commentary on the hermeneutical rules of Rabbi Yishmael, also known as Baal HaBaraita, who was a second-century *Tanna* (Rabbinic interlocutor).
3. See Joseph Hacker, "The Intellectual Activity of the Jews of the Ottoman Empire during the Sixteenth and Seventeenth Centuries," in *Jewish Thought in the Seventeenth Century*, ed. Isadore Twersky and Bernard Septimus (Cambridge, MA: Harvard University Press, 1987), 135–95.
4. In the Middle Ages, the understanding that heavenly bodies greatly influenced events on earth was broadly accepted.
5. In his theorizing on the notion of causality, Aristotle posited four distinct ways to describe why an event occurs: material (the source from which something is made, like a statue is made of wood), formal (the form of or in which something is made, like the shape of a statue), efficient (the primary cause of change, like the artist who used the materials to create the statue), and final (the reason or the sake for which something is made). See Andrea Falcon, "Aristotle on Causality," *The Stanford Encyclopedia of Philosophy* (Spring 2019 edition), ed. Edward N. Zalta, https://plato.stanford.edu/archives/spr2019/entries/aristotle-causality/.
6. See Boaz Huss, *Like the Radiance of the Sky: Chapters in the Reception History of*

the Zohar and the Construction of Its Symbolic Value [in Hebrew] (Jerusalem: The Bialik Institute, 2008), 140–78.

7. Muharram Avraham Ben Yaakov Gavishon, *Omar HaShich'chah* [cf. p. 132 above]: *Commentary on the Book of Proverbs* (Jerusalem: Kedem, 1972), 4a.

This chapter was originally published as "Jewish Thought in Fez in the Generations following the Spanish Expulsion," by Michal Ohana, in *Jewish Quarterly Review* III, no. 4 (Fall 2021): 605–21. Reprinted with permission of the University of Pennsylvania Press.

PART FOUR

Modern Deliberations

10

Haskalah in Berlin
Moses Mendelssohn, Immanuel Kant, and the Foundations of Reform Judaism

Yoav Schaefer

IT IS WELL KNOWN that Jewish thinkers were faced with a new set of challenges in the late eighteenth century. In addition to new political, social, and theological challenges, they were forced, for the first time, to reflect upon and justify their religion *philosophically*. To be sure, Jewish thinkers reaching back to Philo in ancient times and Maimonides in the medieval period sought to harmonize Judaism with the major philosophical currents of their time. But in the late eighteenth century, unlike in the premodern world, the beliefs and commitments on which Judaism was based were subjected to scientific and philosophical scrutiny and could no longer be simply taken for granted. From that point onward, Jewish thinkers sought to demonstrate Judaism's compatibility with the principles of Newtonian science and the central tenets of the European Enlightenment, including individual liberty, freedom of expression, religious toleration, and a belief in the power of reason. This process—which came to be known as the Haskalah or Jewish Enlightenment—was especially prominent in Germany, where Jewish thinkers felt compelled to prove the Jews' fitness for emancipation in the final decades of the eighteenth and throughout the nineteenth centuries. While similar processes occurred elsewhere, the Haskalah movement in Germany was particularly important for the development of modern Judaism and produced many of the key religious and intellectual institutions that came to define Judaism in the modern period, including an impressive philosophical tradition.

In what follows, I sketch in broad strokes the emergence of this tradition of modern Jewish philosophical thinking, focusing in particular on two of the most important philosophers for modern Judaism, one Jewish and the other not: Moses Mendelssohn (1729–86) and Immanuel Kant (1724–1804). The first part of this chapter focuses on Mendelssohn's *Jerusalem, or on Religious Power and Judaism* (1783). The second part briefly explores Kant's revolution in philosophy, which undermined Mendelssohn's synthesis of Judaism and philosophical rationalism in his *Jerusalem* and the rationalist philosophy on which it was based. It also focuses on Kant's *Religion within the Boundaries of Mere Reason* (1793–94), in which Kant portrayed Judaism as fundamentally irreconcilable with his ideal of a rational religion. The conclusion reflects on what Kantian philosophy and the challenge it posed to Judaism in the modern period mean for thinking about Judaism today.

Moses Mendelssohn and the Berlin Haskalah

Known as "the German Socrates," Moses Mendelssohn was one of the foremost philosophers of his time as well as a leading figure of the Berlin Haskalah. He also became an important symbol of the religious toleration and freedom of thought characteristic of the German Enlightenment.

Yet, despite his status as a leading figure of the German Enlightenment, Mendelssohn was reluctant to engage in the intense public debates over Judaism and the civic status of Prussia's Jews sparked by Christian Wilhelm Friedrich von Dohm's *On the Civil Improvement of the Jews* (1781). He finally entered the public debate over Jewish political and social integration with his preface to the 1782 publication of *Vindiciae Judaeorum* (Vindication of the Jews), a translation of Rabbi Menasseh ben Israel's famous 1656 appeal to Oliver Cromwell to readmit Jews to England following their expulsion in 1290.[1]

However, Mendelssohn would undertake his most comprehensive defense of Judaism in *Jerusalem*, the first major modern attempt to demonstrate Judaism's compatibility with the leading philosophical ideas of the time. In the first part of *Jerusalem*, Mendelssohn drew on natural rights theory to argue that neither the church nor the state had the right to coerce in matters of individual belief or conscience. Building on themes he had previously elaborated in his preface to *Vindiciae Judaeorum*, especially his opposition to all forms of religious coercion, Mendelssohn sought to both invalidate state discrimination on the basis of religious faith and also undermine the ecclesiastical power of the church. In arguing that the state had no right to impose religious beliefs on its subjects, Mendelssohn not only attempted to secure the conditions of liberty of conscience and religious toleration; he also laid the philosophical foundations for the political emancipation of his coreligionists.

Mendelssohn devoted the second part of *Jerusalem* to demonstrating that Judaism was compatible with both natural theology and the demands of the secular state. He claimed that the fundamental doctrines of natural religion—namely, the existence of God, divine providence, and the immortality of soul—were *"not merely comprehensible to human reason"* but could *"be demonstrated and verified by human powers."*[2] And these "essential truths" necessary for salvation, he argued, were comprehensible to all people at all times through their unaided human reason.

Yet Mendelssohn by no means rendered Judaism's particular historical revelation superfluous. Judaism, he argued, was not a "revealed religion" but a "revealed legislation." Whereas the former is based on universal propositions of reason, the latter referred to historically contingent laws bequeathed by God to a specific group of people for the purpose of their "national felicity."[3] What was revealed to the Israelites at Sinai, Mendelssohn maintained, were particular "historical truths"—laws and commandments—intended for the Israelites alone, not eternal religious truths or doctrines.

It follows from Mendelssohn's argument that there existed no essential conflict between Judaism and natural religion, since what was revealed to the Israelites were not rational dogmas or supernatural truths associated with natural theology, but only specific ritual observances and ordinances relating to the Jewish people's distinctive historical destiny. He maintained that Judaism "boasts of no *exclusive* revelation of eternal truths that are indispensable to salvation" and is entirely in accordance with the basic tenets of natural religion.[4] On Mendelssohn's account, then, Judaism was fully compatible with both the fundamental doctrines of natural religion and the philosophy of the German Enlightenment.

Mendelssohn went on to argue that Judaism's particular revealed legislation comprised two distinct forms of laws: "political laws" pertaining to the national life of the Jews and "ceremonial laws."[5] With the destruction of the Jewish commonwealth in 70 CE, however, the political laws associated with the "Mosaic constitution" were no longer binding. Only the ceremonial laws continued to be obligatory. These ceremonial laws, he alleged, were intended to serve a largely didactic function, reminding those who performed them of the eternal truths of natural religion.[6] They consisted of practical rules for conduct, not rational or metaphysical truths, meant solely for the Jewish people. In this way, Mendelssohn sought at once both to defend the continued validity and religious significance of Jewish law (halachah) and also to demonstrate that Judaism was essentially identical with the fundamental precepts of natural theology. In addition, his important distinction between political and ceremonial laws allowed him to argue that Judaism, as a voluntary association, no longer needed to coerce belief. Once "the civil bonds of the nation were dissolved," he asserted, Judaism ceased to wield coercive power altogether. "Religious offenses were no longer crimes against the state and the religion, as religion, knows of no punishment, no other penalty than the one the remorseful sinner *voluntarily* imposes on himself." No longer political, Judaism "knows of no coercion, uses only the staff [called] *gentleness*, and affects only mind and heart."[7]

Mendelssohn's interpretation of Judaism as a rational religion divested of ecclesiastical authority and fully in harmony with natural theology was meant at least in part as a response to Benedict (Baruch) Spinoza's *Theological-Political Treatise* (1670).[8] Spinoza's *Treatise* not only subjected the Hebrew Bible to intense historical and textual criticism, reduced "divine providence" to the laws of nature, undermined the possibility of miracles, and offered a deflationary account of biblical prophecy; it also contained numerous harsh criticisms of his native religion.

In chapter 3 of his *Treatise*, Spinoza explores the alleged election of the ancient Israelites, arguing that the Hebrews were neither intellectually nor morally superior to other nations. Their chosenness, Spinoza held, referred not to any supernatural election but only to the "enduring [political and material] prosperity of their state."[9] Equal to other nations with respect to both their cognitive powers and their characters, the ancient Israelites were, according to Spinoza, distinguished merely by their political good fortune and their social organization.[10] In such a way Spinoza reduced the Israelites' election to the nature of their ancient political constitution. It followed from this, Spinoza argued, that their election was not eternal but temporal and completely contingent on their political success. Once they lost their political independence, the Israelites were no longer chosen. It was principally due to the hatred directed at them by other peoples as well as separatist practices—especially the ritual of circumcision—that the Jews managed to maintain their diasporic existence.

In the *Treatise*'s fifth chapter, Spinoza turned his attention to Judaism's ceremonial laws. He argued that these ceremonies contained no moral content but served only to promote the stability and continued prosperity of the Hebrew state. The entire Torah, Spinoza insisted, was concerned solely with the ancient Hebrew commonwealth and with the material well-being of its members. Thus, he argued that the law promised only this-worldly rewards—the prosperity of the state and advantages relating to "pleasures of the body"—and threatened "nothing for obstinacy and breaking the covenant except the ruin of their state and the greatest [temporal] disadvantages."[11] Moses introduced religion into the Hebrew Republic, continued Spinoza, in order to persuade the Israelites to perform their "duty [to the state] not so much from fear as from devotion."[12] The law, in other words, served merely to sustain the Israelites' political commonwealth and compel obedience among its inhabitants. For this reason, Spinoza concluded that Judaism's rituals and commandments were no longer valid, since they pertained only to the political and material prosperity of the Israelite polity. With the destruction of the Hebrew Republic, the ceremonial laws became wholly obsolete and superfluous. "There is no doubt that after their state was dissolved," Spinoza asserted, "the Jews were no more bound by the law of Moses than they were before their social order and Republic began."[13]

Although Spinoza's name is mentioned only once in *Jerusalem*, Mendelssohn's book was clearly imagined as a response to his account of Judaism in the *Treatise*. Whereas Spinoza argued that Judaism's apolitical nature made it obsolete and anachronistic, Mendelssohn insisted that it was precisely the depoliticization of the Jewish religion that made it suitable for the modern state. Following the dissolution of the Jewish state, according to Mendelssohn, Judaism had completely lost touch with its political and national past. In such a way Spinoza's account of Judaism supplied the underpinnings of Mendelssohn's vision of the Jewish religion divested of all political characteristics and ecclesiastical authority. But contra Spinoza, Mendelssohn argued that Judaism's rituals and commandments remained valid and binding for latter-day Jews.

And unlike Spinoza, Mendelssohn was thoroughly convinced that there existed no inherent conflict between Judaism and political liberalism. He therefore counseled his coreligionists to adapt themselves to the morals and laws of the states in which they lived and simultaneously continue to observe Judaism's rituals and commandments.[14] Mendelssohn wholeheartedly believed that Judaism was compatible with the modern state, unable to imagine that Jewish ritual observances and commandments could conflict with the duties Jews owed to the states of which they were subjects. If the state could not accommodate Jews and their religion, Mendelssohn argued, it was the fault not of Judaism but of the state. Jews, he held, should be emancipated on the basis of natural rights alone. Were Jews to be compelled to reform their religion in exchange for their rights, such a price would be too high: "If civil union cannot be obtained under any other condition than our departing from the laws which we still consider binding on us, then we are sincerely sorry to find it necessary to declare that we must rather do without civil union."[15] He was thus prepared for Jews to remain unemancipated rather than reform their religion. For Mendelssohn, in other words, it was not Jews and their religion but rather the state that stood in need of reform.

In the book's closing pages, Mendelssohn offered a plea for religious toleration on pluralistic grounds. In response to those who prophesize that someday "there will be only one shepherd and one flock,"[16] he countered, "In order to be under the care of this omnipresent shepherd the entire flock need neither graze in one pasture nor enter and leave the master's house through a single door. This is neither what the shepherd wants nor advantageous to the prosperity of the flock."[17] A union of faiths, Mendelssohn maintained, is neither desirable nor divinely ordained. Should such a thing ever come about, its consequences for reason and liberty of conscience alike would be disastrous. Not a single, universal faith but religious diversity was, in Mendelssohn's words, "evidently the plan and purpose of Providence."[18] With this paean to religious tolerance and pluralism Mendelssohn brought his book to a close.

Mendelssohn's effort to align Judaism with philosophical rationalism and political liberalism was ultimately short-lived. Toward the end of Mendelssohn's life, and especially following his death in 1786, Enlightenment rationalism came under fierce attack from thinkers like Johann Georg Hamman (1730–88), Johann Gottfried von Herder (1744–1803), and Friedrich Heinrich Jacobi (1743–1819). This intellectual assault upon the foundations of Mendelssohn's philosophical worldview was accompanied by increasing opposition to Jewish emancipation, especially in the wake of the French Revolution (1789–99). Taken together, these dramatic upheavals in German intellectual and political life undermined Mendelssohn's attempted synthesis between Judaism and the rationalism and universalism of the German Enlightenment.

But the most significant challenge to both Mendelssohn's rationalistic metaphysics and his apologia for Judaism came from Immanuel Kant, whose *Critique of Pure Reason* (1781) initiated a "Copernican revolution" in philosophy. Even though Mendelssohn admitted to Kant that he had struggled to understand his *Critique*,[19] he was fully aware of its significance for the history of philosophy and the threat it posed to traditional metaphysics, prompting him to refer to the "all-crushing Kant" in his last major work.[20] Even if Mendelssohn comprehended the final death blow that Kant's philosophy dealt to the rationalist tradition to which he was heir, he could not have imagined the challenge it posed to Judaism.

Kant's Copernican Revolution in Philosophy

It is impossible to overstate Kant's significance for the development of modern philosophy. Indeed, it would not be an exaggeration to say that all modern philosophy is in some way a response to Kant. Likewise, no thinker did more to give expression to the ideals associated with the Enlightenment—including a commitment to the freedom of thought and expression, a belief in the equal worth and dignity of all human beings, and a faith in the ultimate authority of reason—than he did. And while the European Enlightenment was by no means a monolithic movement, Kantian philosophy has come to be regarded as representative of Enlightenment thought itself.

In the opening lines of his 1784 essay "An Answer to the Question: What Is Enlightenment?" Kant famously defined enlightenment as *"man's emergence from his self-incurred immaturity. Immaturity* is the inability to use one's own understanding without the guidance of another. This immaturity is *self-incurred* if its cause is not lack of understanding, but lack of resolution and courage to use it without the guidance of another. The motto of enlightenment is therefore: *Sapere aude!* Have courage to use your own understanding!"[21]

Kant thus identifies enlightenment not with a particular set of philosophical or religious views (as had Mendelssohn, for instance), but with a kind of act or process. Enlightenment for him consists simply in subjecting one's beliefs to critical inquiry and reflection. Such a view of enlightenment poses a serious threat to traditional religious dogmas and doctrines, since it rules out any appeal to the authority of a sacred text or divine revelation, on one hand, and to clerical authority, on the other. In fact, Kant considered "religious immaturity" especially injurious to the freedom of thought and expression, going as far as to call it "the most pernicious and dishonorable variety of all."[22]

However, the most serious threat Kant posed to traditional religious traditions, including Judaism, came from his theoretical philosophy. Although an overview of Kantian philosophy is well beyond the scope of this chapter, it is nonetheless possible to outline the main contours of the challenge it presented to the authority of revealed religion in general and to Judaism in particular. The central aim of Kant's *Critique of Pure Reason*—as the title suggests—was to critically examine the faculty of reason and its ability to acquire knowledge *a priori* or independently of experience. Kant was especially concerned with curbing the pretensions of traditional metaphysics and its claim to provide theoretical cognition of supersensible entities—especially of ideas like God, freedom, and the immortality of the human soul—that surpass the limits of possible human experience.

As Kant demonstrated, the world as it appears to us is constructed through a combination of sensory input and innate cognitive categories in our mind. Kant thus argued that the human mind is not merely a passive recorder of empirical reality but that it actively contributes to knowledge by structuring and imposing reality on the sensible world.

He likened his insight that the objects of our cognition must conform to our minds and not the other way around to Copernicus's revolution in astronomy. But since he maintained that all genuine knowledge requires data acquired through the senses, Kant effectively limited the scope of human cognition to empirical reality—to the world of appearances or "phenomena"—while also denying that human beings could have direct knowledge of transcendent entities independent of our cognition of them, that is, of things as they actually exist in themselves (what he called "noumena"). Kant's argument thus amounted to a full-blown critique of the traditional metaphysics to which philosophers like Mendelssohn subscribed, since, as his *Critique* made clear, speculative or theoretical reason could never deliver knowledge of supersensible entities that exceeded the bounds of human cognition.

Kant's moral philosophy presented a challenge to revealed religious doctrines as well. In his *Groundwork of the Metaphysics of Morals* (1785), Kant grounded moral laws not in the will of a transcendent God but in the self-positing will of every rational being. Human beings, according to Kant, as rational moral agents, necessarily willed universal moral laws through their maxims. As he put it:

> If we look back upon all previous efforts that have ever been made to discover the principle of morality, we need not wonder now why all of them had to fail. It was seen that the human being is bound to laws by his duty, but it never occurred to them that he is subject *only to the laws given by himself but still universal* and that he is bound only to act in conformity with his own will, which, however, in accordance with nature's end is a will giving universal law.[23]

For laws to be considered truly moral, Kant argued, they must be self-imposed. The moral agent, in other words, must legislate such universal morals laws for themselves. A moral law would then be "autonomous" rather than "heteronomous," that is, imposed upon the moral subject by their own will rather than by an external authority. Kant's picture of morality thus inaugurated a crucial shift in moral thinking, making the free and autonomous moral agent as opposed to a transcendent God the true author of moral laws. It is not hard to see how Kant's moral philosophy also undermined the cognitive significance of revealed doctrines. He not only denied that a divine revelation could ever be a source of universal moral laws, but his philosophy also implied that revealed doctrines or statues were necessarily *heteronomous* and therefore not moral, since they were based on God's external authority as opposed to principles of autonomous reason.

To be sure, Kant did not deny the importance of religion altogether. In fact, he carved out a central place for religion within his philosophical system, arguing that a belief in God and the immortality of the soul was necessary for morality. Although such beliefs could not be demonstrated on theoretical grounds, since speculative knowledge of that sort necessarily transcended the bounds of human cognition, they could be based on practical, that is, moral considerations. This is the essence of Kant's argument—which he would develop most fully in his *Critique of Practical Reason* (1788)—that religious beliefs could be established on practical and moral rather than theoretical (i.e., abstract philosophical) grounds.[24]

But the profound challenge that Kant's philosophy posed to all revealed religions, including Judaism, should at this point be clear. Roughly, Kant subordinated revelation to reason, the ultimate authority by which all claims must be adjudicated. He challenged religious communities to employ universal standards of argumentation in grounding their claims and beliefs. He argued that religious beliefs and rituals—including sacred Scripture—must be interpreted through a rational and moral lens and that any laws or rituals that could not be accommodated to such an interpretation be discarded. Finally, he held that religious laws and traditions must always be mutable and subject to critical examination, scrutiny, revision, and, if necessary, rejection, since no one should be forced to dogmatically accept views that were proclaimed at a previous time. Together these principles seriously challenged, if not undermined, the basic dogmas and foundations of traditional religious traditions.

Kantian Philosophy and Jewish Religious Reform

It is important to emphasize that Kant's conception of moral theology in the 1780s—the period during which he published his most important philosophical writings—was compatible with a diversity of religious traditions, including Judaism (or at least a reformed version of it). While he sought to place certain rational constraints on traditional religion, Kant did not so much contend that religious beliefs and doctrines had to be abandoned as reformulated along the lines of his philosophy. And though his conception of rational theology may have posed a singular challenge to traditional Judaism, a religion based entirely on a belief in a historical revelation and devoted to a particular people, there was no apparent reason why Judaism was inherently incompatible with the basic spirit of his teachings. Indeed, Kant praised the ethical character of ancient Judaism in his *Critique of the Power of Judgment* (1790).[25]

It should therefore not surprise us that Kant's philosophy set the agenda for leading *maskilim*—Jewish thinkers associated with the Berlin Haskalah—in the final decades of the eighteenth century. In fact, the first efforts to reconceptualize Judaism in the modern period were undertaken by adherents of Kantian philosophy: Saul Ascher's *Leviathan, oder Ueber Religion in Rücksicht des Judenthums* (Leviathan, or Religion in View of Judaism) in 1792 and Lazarus Bendavid's *Etwas zur Charakteristick der Juden* (On the Characteristics of the Jews) in 1793. Convinced that Kant was the most important thinker of the age and that Mendelssohn's defense of Judaism in his *Jerusalem* was no longer adequate, Ascher and Bendavid sought to cast Judaism in the mold of Kant's rational religion.[26] Parting ways with Mendelssohn, they argued that Judaism, in order to become an intellectually respectable religion, had to be reformed. Especially important for these *maskilim* was abolishing Judaism's ceremonial laws on the grounds that it was heteronomous and thus not moral. They also argued on the basis of Kantian philosophy that Jewish rituals or beliefs that either were superfluous to morality or could not be justified on broadly rational grounds had to be discarded. In such a way, these *maskilim* utilized the terminology and principles of Kantian philosophy to introduce unprecedented and far-reaching religious reforms into Judaism in the final two decades of the eighteenth century, at once both anticipating and laying the groundwork for the emergence of the Reform Movement in the early nineteenth century.

Kant's Anti-Judaism

Kant's attitude toward Judaism underwent a dramatic shift in the 1790s, however. It is hard to say for certain what changed Kant's thinking about Judaism in the intervening years between the publication of Mendelssohn's *Jerusalem* in 1783—a book Kant praised[27]—and the publication of *Religion within the Boundaries of Mere Reason* a decade later. One thing that had changed was the political situation in Prussia. Kant's *Religion* appeared at a moment of widespread conservative reaction in the wake of the French Revolution, earning the esteemed professor a royal censure.[28] Some scholars have suggested that Kant's denigration of Judaism was intended as a cipher for the Protestantism of his day, since any criticism of Protestant institutions would have been blocked by Prussian authorities. Perhaps Kant directed his attacks at a safer target, much as Spinoza had criticized Judaism and the Hebrew Bible in order to offer a thinly veiled critique of seventeenth-century Dutch political and religious institutions. Regardless, by the time Kant published *Religion*, his attitude toward Judaism had become highly critical. He now considered Judaism inimical to the rationalism and universalism of his critical philosophy.

The principal task of Kant's *Religion*—his most important work specifically devoted to religious themes—was to formulate a conception of rational religion that accorded with the basic principles of his critical philosophy. And though Kant sought to establish religious principles on a rational basis, he did not hold that the doctrines and beliefs of traditional religion were entirely insignificant. While an ecclesiastical faith could never constitute the foundation of a religion of reason, since that would mean establishing rational religion on grounds that were neither necessary nor universal, such a religion could, given the cognitive limitations of human beings, serve as a historical "vehicle" for spreading rational faith.[29]

Yet if Kant's philosophy in the 1780s seemed broadly compatible with (a reformed) Judaism, in *Religion* he emphatically denied that Judaism had anything in common with his ideal of rational faith. "The *Jewish* faith," he wrote, "*stands in absolutely no connection, i.e. in no unity of concepts* [emphasis added]" with true, moral religion.[30] Kant argued that the kernel of rational religion must be sought in the history of Christianity instead. While he conceded that Judaism may have "immediately preceded" Christianity, Kant claimed that it merely furnished the "occasion" for its founding. By portraying Christianity as a "total abandonment" of Judaism, Kant's *Religion* in fact went far beyond traditional Christian supersessionism, since he held that Christianity not only had supplanted Judaism but was entirely discontinuous with it. He therefore countered Mendelssohn's argument in *Jerusalem* that Christianity was "built upon Judaism, and if the latter falls, it must necessarily collapse with it into *one* heap of ruins."[31] Were Judaism to collapse, Kant's *Religion* implied, it would pose no apparent danger to Christianity, since it rested upon entirely new foundations.

Beyond denying Judaism any substantive connection to his ideal of rational religion, Kant's *Religion* portrayed Judaism as antithetical to the universalism and rationalism of a religion of reason altogether. Following Spinoza, Kant defined Judaism in purely political and secular terms.[32] In his words, "The *Jewish faith*, as originally established, was only a collection of merely statutory laws supporting a political state."[33] This meant, Kant concluded, that Judaism was not truly a religion at all.[34] Moreover, Kant argued that Judaism's political constitution contained nothing but "burdensome ceremonies and observances,"[35] which, since they were necessary for supporting a state, were upheld by "coercive laws."[36] Lacking entirely in ethical content, "*Jewish* theocracy" was concerned exclusively with the imposition of purely civil laws upon the "slavish [Jewish] mind."[37]

Moreover, Kant argued that Judaism, given its this-worldly and political character, was antithetical to morality. Judaism, he insisted, made no claim upon the "moral disposition" of its adherents.[38] Whatever moral content Judaism contained, Kant alleged, was not inherent to Judaism but derived from the influence of Greek philosophy.[39] Kant even went so far as to assert that Judaism denied a belief in the afterlife, something he considered essential to both religious faith and morality. "Whereas no religion can be conceived without faith in a future life," he therefore concluded, "Judaism as such, taken in its purity, entails absolutely no religious faith."[40]

Finally, Kant argued that Judaism's doctrine of election represented a grave moral deficiency. In fact, Kant alleged this doctrine promoted a profoundly misanthropic politics, since according to Kant it implied a deep hatred for all humanity.[41] Given that Judaism "excluded the whole human race from its communion," it is no wonder, he wrote, that Judaism was "treated with hostility by all."[42]

Kant's negative account of Judaism in his *Religion* made it abundantly clear that rational religion must be completely purged of the legal formalism, heteronomy, and clannish tendencies that according to his account were characteristic of Judaism. Or, as Kant notoriously put it in *The Conflict of the Faculties* (1798) several years later, "The euthanasia of Judaism is pure moral religion, freed from all the ancient statutory teachings."[43]

Whether Kant's denigration of Judaism was a strategic move designed to get his writings past the Prussian censors or motivated by a deep anti-Jewish bias, his *Religion* portrayed Judaism as entirely at odds with his vision of rational religion, something that would have far-reaching consequences for German Jewry and its struggle for civic and political integration. Kant's negative picture of Judaism would also shape the attitude of leading post-Kantian German philosophers toward Judaism throughout the nineteenth and early twentieth centuries.

What must be underscored, however, is that it was primarily the philosophical challenge Kant's philosophy posed to Judaism in the 1780s that at once both motivated the efforts of leading *maskilim* to reform their religion in the modern period and also provided them with a conceptual framework for doing so. For if Kant's anti-Judaism in the 1790s portrayed Judaism as completely antithetical to his ideal of rational religion, his philosophy in the 1780s, as we saw above, seemed to hold open the possibility that a reformed Judaism might be broadly compatible with it.

What Does Kantian Philosophy Mean for Judaism Today?

In the nineteenth and early twentieth centuries, Jewish thinkers, Reform and Orthodox alike, often emphasized the deep spiritual affinity between Kantianism and Judaism. As Hermann Cohen, the founder of the Marburg school of neo-Kantianism, wrote in a 1910 essay on the "inner relations between Kantianism and Judaism," "The philosophizing Jew feels as if at home on the soil of Kant."[44] And yet, many scholars today overlook the significance of Kantian philosophy for the development of modern Judaism. One reason for this tendency might be a mistaken assumption about Mendelssohn's continued philosophical importance after the Kantian revolution. Another is that many scholars of Judaism focus primarily on Kant's harsh critique of Judaism in his *Religion* and consequently neglect the positive influence his philosophy exerted over modern Jewish thinkers. Still another reason may be that many scholars assume that the rationalist tradition with which Kant and his followers were associated was eclipsed by other philosophical movements, from Romanticism and German idealism in the nineteenth century to existentialism in the twentieth. As a result, much scholarship on modern Jewish thought has focused predominantly on twentieth-century Jewish philosophers—above all, Franz Rosenzweig, Martin Buber, and Emmanuel Levinas—who turned away from the Kantian tradition and toward more existentialist modes of thought. Yet, there can be no doubt that Kantian philosophy supplied the main conceptual framework by which leading Jewish philosophers conceptualized Judaism in the late eighteenth and throughout the nineteenth centuries. In fact, Jewish thinkers continued to both champion Kant's philosophical legacy and formulate their ideas about Judaism in the spirit of his teachings well into the twentieth century.

Notwithstanding his hostility to Judaism in his *Religion*, Kant's philosophy still has much to offer to Jews and Judaism today. Central to Kant's philosophy of religion, for instance, is his insistence on keeping traditional doctrines and commitments open to investigation and possible change. Not only, according to Kant, is such a willingness to question, revise, and even reject traditional teachings and beliefs morally required, but it is in the political and social interest of religions to do so. This also implies that religious institutions should permit, indeed foster, a spirit of critical inquiry and a robust public sphere, since respect for reasoning and freedom of expression go hand in hand.

Kant also challenges religions to base their teachings and commitments on broadly universalizable grounds. We might agree with Kant's critics that his philosophy leads to excessive universalism and that he discounts the importance of particular beliefs and personal experiences as a result. Nonetheless, his philosophy encourages us to seek reasons for our beliefs and commitments that we can expect other reasonable people to share. In other words, Kant teaches us that when evaluating our beliefs and commitments, we ought to ask ourselves from a place beyond our own particular standpoint whether they are legitimate and worthy of upholding. Regardless of what we personally believe, reasoning, according to Kant, requires that we attempt to base our private beliefs on publicly sharable standards of argumentation rather than on dogma or tradition. It is one of Kant's most important insights, in fact, that reflecting upon our specific beliefs from a more general perspective can often provide a healthy corrective to our own private and necessarily limited standpoint.

Finally, and most importantly, Kant maintains that religion should, above all, be primarily concerned with morality. Even if we do not want to follow him in reducing religion entirely to ethics, Kant calls on religions to reject any teachings or doctrines that are contrary to morality. At the very least, I think he rightly insists that morality should constrain how we interpret and understand traditional texts and beliefs.

In such a way, Kant's philosophy remains as relevant and important for Judaism today as it was at the end of the eighteenth century. To be sure, Kant's fully developed vision of rational religion may have rendered Judaism's specific beliefs and commitments largely irrelevant. Kant may even have looked forward to a time when all sectarian religions would eventually give way to a religion based entirely on rational principles. But Jews do not have to accept the entirety of Kant's conception of rational religion in order to see it as an ideal to be approximated. Kant's religion of reason, in this sense, should be understood less as a rigid ideal and more as a flexible and broad template by which Jews can continually reform their religious tradition, thereby ensuring that it remains intellectually and morally compelling in the long run. Only then will Judaism be able to address each new generation in terms that generation can accept. Only then will Torah, as the Rabbis taught, continue to speak in the language of human beings (Babylonian Talmud, *B'rachot* 31b).

NOTES

1. A translation of Mendelssohn's preface to the translation of *Vindiciae Judae-orum* can be found in *Moses Mendelssohn: Writings on Judaism, Christianity, and the Bible*, ed. Michah Gottlieb (Waltham, MA: Brandeis University Press, 2011), 40–52.
2. Moses Mendelssohn, *Jerusalem, or on Religious Power and Judaism*, trans. Allan Arkush (Waltham, MA: Brandeis University Press, 1983), 89.
3. Mendelssohn, *Jerusalem*, 127.
4. Mendelssohn, *Jerusalem*, 97.

5. Mendelssohn, *Jerusalem*, 128–29.

6. Mendelssohn, *Jerusalem*, 99.

7. Mendelssohn, *Jerusalem*, 130.

8. While Spinoza's *Treatise* was clearly one of Mendelssohn's main targets, the proximate cause for his composition of *Jerusalem* was an anonymously published pamphlet by August Friedrich Cranz entitled *The Search for Light and Right* (1782) and a short postscript by Daniel Ernst Mörschel appended to it.

9. Baruch Spinoza, *Theological-Political Treatise*, in *Collected Works of Spinoza*, vol. 2, trans. Edwin Curley (Princeton, NJ: Princeton University Press, 2016), 115.

10. Spinoza, *Theological-Political Treatise*, 114.

11. Spinoza, *Theological-Political Treatise*, 139, 115.

12. Spinoza, *Theological-Political Treatise*, 145–46.

13. Spinoza, *Theological-Political Treatise*, 142.

14. Mendelssohn, *Jerusalem*, 133.

15. Mendelssohn, *Jerusalem*, 135.

16. John 10:16.

17. Mendelssohn, *Jerusalem*, 135.

18. Mendelssohn, *Jerusalem*, 138.

19 See Mendelssohn's letter to Kant in Kant's *Correspondence*, trans. Arnulf Zweig (Cambridge: Cambridge University Press, 1999), 10:307–8, 190–91.

20. See the preface to Mendelssohn's *Morgenstunden oder Vorlesungen über das Dasyn Gottes* (Morning lessons or lectures on the existence of God) (1785). Mendelssohn was most likely referring to Kant's withering attack on traditional theistic proofs for God's existence in the first *Critique*'s "Transcendental Dialectic."

21. Kant, "An Answer to the Question: What Is Enlightenment?," in *Kant: Political Writings*, trans. H. B. Nisbet (New York: Cambridge University Press, 1991), 8:33–42.

22. Kant, *Political Writings*, 59.

23. Kant, *Groundwork*, in *Practical Philosophy*, ed. Mary J. Gregor (Cambridge: Cambridge University Press, 1996), 4:432–33, 82–83. The emphasis in the provided quote is found in Kant's original writing.

24. See especially Kant, *Critique of Practical Reason*, 5:107–148.

25. Immanuel Kant, *Critique of the Power of Judgment*, trans. Paul Guyer and Eric Mathews (New York: Cambridge University Press, 2000), 5:274.

26. It is important to note that Ascher was not, strictly speaking, a Kantian philosopher, as even a cursory reading of his *Leviathan* plainly reveals. Yet that Ascher, like Bendavid after him, utilized Kantian terminology in *Leviathan* and emphasized the need to abolish Judaism's political constitution in order to make it compatible with central tenets of Kantian philosophy is significant. It suggests, among things, that he recognized both Kant's significance

and the need to make Judaism broadly compatible with his thought. In this sense, Ascher's reliance on Kantian philosophy resembles that of Christian thinkers—often under the influence of Reinhold's *Letters on the Kantian Philosophy* (1786–87)—who emphasized the religious dimensions of Kant's thought and utilized his philosophy toward largely apologetic ends—often in ways that Kant's critical philosophy had in fact invalidated.

27. See Kant's letter to Mendelssohn in Kant, *Correspondence*, 10:343–47, 201–4.

28. Frederick William II's minister of education and religious affairs, Johann Christoph Wöllner, reproofed Kant following the publication of his *Religion*. After Frederick William II's death, Kant no longer considered himself bound by his promise to the deceased monarch to "refrain altogether from discoursing publicly, in lectures or writings, on religion, whether natural or revealed." His last major reflections on religion, *The Conflict of the Faculties*, therefore appeared in 1798.

29. Kant, *Religion within the Boundaries of Mere Reason*, in *Religion and Rational Theology*, trans. Allen W. Wood and George Di Giovanni (New York: Cambridge University Press, 1996), 6:122, 152.

30. Kant, *Religion within the Boundaries*, 6:125, 154.

31. Mendelssohn, *Jerusalem*, 87.

32. Whether Kant derived his characterization of Judaism from Spinoza's *Treatise* remains contested among scholars. On this question, see my "Kant's Anti-Judaism and Spinoza's *Theological-Political Treatise*," in *Spinoza in Germany: Political and Religious Thought across the Long Nineteenth Century*, ed. Jason M. Yanover and Kristin Gjesdal (Oxford University Press, forthcoming).

33. Kant, *Religion*, 6:125, 154.

34. Kant, *Religion*, 6:125, 154.

35. Kant, *Religion*, 6:79, 119.

36. Kant, *Religion*, 6:126, 155.

37. Kant, *Religion*, 6:79–80, 119.

38. Kant, *Religion*, 6:126, 155.

39. Kant, *Religion*, 6:80, 119.

40. Kant, *Religion*, 6:126, 155.

41. Kant, *Religion*, 6:184, 201.

42. Kant, *Religion*, 6:127, 155.

43. Kant, *The Conflict of the Faculties*, in *Religion and Rational Theology*, 7:53, 276.

44. "Innere Beziehungen der Kantischen Philosophie zum Judentum," *Jüdische Schriften* (Berlin: Schwetschke Verlag, 1924), 1:283–305. A translation of this essay can be found in *Hermann Cohen: Writings on Neo-Kantianism and Jewish Philosophy*, ed. Samuel Moyn and Robert S. Schine (Waltham, MA: Brandeis University Press, 2021).

II

Breaking the Chain
The Radical Thought
of Rabbi Samuel Holdheim

Michael A. Meyer, PhD

THE TALMUDIC TRACTATE *Pirkei Avot*, "Sayings of the Fathers," begins with a chain of transmission reaching forward into history from its starting point at Mount Sinai. Jewish spiritual leaders from thence all the way down to the rabbis of the Reform Movement have almost invariably seen themselves as links in that chain. The links might vary in hue, but they insisted on their attachment to the chain. They claimed to be connected to Jewish tradition even as they modified it. Seeking to avoid the charge of sectarianism, reformers argued for continuity and sought to repel the charge of rupture. That was as true of Rabbis Abraham Geiger and Zacharias Frankel in the nineteenth century as it was of Rabbi Leo Baeck in the twentieth. To preserve that continuity, they sought precedent for changes in the past; they spoke of an ongoing reform from ancient times, not of a sudden and fundamental revolution. Aware as they were of rapid change in the current status of the Jews, they feared severing the chain. They began their religious deliberations with the Jewish faith, which they saw as a dynamic but unbroken unity, rather than with the radically altered situation of the Jews themselves, especially in the larger cities, where Jews were caught in a rapidly moving process of integration and acculturation and were separating themselves ever more from the chain of Jewish transmission.

However, within the reforming faction of the German rabbinate there appeared an individual who was willing to cast the chain of transmission aside and begin his religious deliberations not with an evolving Judaism that needed merely to evolve further, but rather with the flesh-and-blood Jews whose situation within non-Jewish society radically separated them from the Jewish religious past. He sought not reform but reformation. He wrote not of a Reform Judaism but of a Reform*ed* Judaism that, like Protestantism, involved the creation of a radically different kind of Judaism with its own set of principles.[1] That individual was Rabbi Samuel Holdheim (1806–60). He was born in the small town of Kempen in Posen (today: Poznan in Poland) and raised as a fully traditional Jew. As his career moved from rabbinates in Frankfurt-on-the-Oder to Mecklenburg-Schwerin, he left his Orthodoxy further and further behind. Finally, he became rabbi of the Reform Congregation in Berlin, the most radical expression of the Reform Movement in Germany. He believed that a rabbi aware of his times had to begin his thinking not with what had come down from the past, but with what existed in the present. And he believed that an abyss yawned between the beliefs and practices of the parents and the worldview of their children. More traditional Jews condemned Holdheim mercilessly for such opinions, yet some of his disruptions became precedents for classical Reform Judaism, while the influence of others stretches down to the present.

In Germany, the Reform Movement, even before Holdheim, had been disruptive of continuity in that for the sake of reform it had begun to employ *Wissenschaft des Judentums* (properly translated as "the critical study of Judaism"), a new approach to the Jewish past. The study of texts that it urged was no longer to be in the manner of the *beit midrash* but in the manner of the university. Instead of understanding Rabbinic works as immutable and to be studied for their God-given content, the new approach sought to understand them within their historical context. For most modern Jewish scholars, however, the disruption this caused was mitigated by a strong apologetic motive. Yes, the texts had to be understood in terms of external influences and the profound changes that the texts and the beliefs and practices based on them had undergone. Yet, one could elide any intellectual or moral problems that they raised by interpreting them in a manner that sacrificed complete historical accuracy and comprehensiveness for the sake of greater acceptability. Thus, if not an objectively obtained historical continuity, at least a moral continuity could be preserved. The past in its totality became the narrower acceptable past.

Samuel Holdheim stood out among his fellow rabbis by refusing to shape the past to meet the needs of the present. For their part, his colleagues chose to be wary of gentile opinion. They did not write a history of Jewish crime in the countryside or focus on elements in Jewish law that were less than edifying. They disregarded or explained away Jewish texts that allowed individuals to break oaths, treated non-Jews differently from fellow Jews, and ascribed embarrassingly lower status to women than to men. They chose instead to pay attention only to those themes in the Jewish past with which they continued to identify, and they made Rabbinic sources seem more modern than they were in fact. Not so Holdheim. He argued that the past was what it was and that honesty required seeing it as such. The Talmudists were not progressives.[2] It was dishonest to prettify Jewish history in the hope that German governments would be more likely to give Jews political emancipation if their ancestors could be pictured as fully trustworthy and morally admirable individuals whose sacred texts were at the least innocuous. Holdheim fully realized that his critique of the Talmud might be used by enemies of emancipation, but he was not therefore willing to forgo what he believed to be the truth. He stood ready to reveal earlier unacceptable ideas even if they militated against the struggle to obtain civil equality. Well aware of possible consequences, he refused to be silenced. He knew "that enemies of emancipation could and would misuse any number of our opinions and proofs for their hostile purposes." Nonetheless, he wrote that he was not afraid "to call a matter by its proper name."[3] Among most fellow rabbis, Holdheim's approach was totally unacceptable. Quite apart from delaying emancipation, they felt his approach would drive alienated Jews further from Judaism and would rupture the emotional relationship that observant Jews had with their tradition. That was put most strongly by the traditionally inclined Jewish historian Heinrich Graetz, who confided to his diary that Holdheim was erasing the reminiscences and diminishing the glory of the Jewish past that had come alive within him.[4] In his *History of the Jews*, Graetz claimed that "since Paul of Tarsus, Judaism had not experienced such an inner enemy, who shattered its inner structure down to the foundations."[5] In short, for religious Jews, Holdheim was soiling the beloved image of an inspiring Judaism that they held dear; in relation to non-Jews, his writings amounted to washing dirty laundry in public.

168 MICHAEL A. MEYER

Ironically, Holdheim's colleagues argued that while his critique was making emancipation more difficult, he was so desirous of gaining it that he was willing to cut chunks out of Judaism so as to make it possible. They held that his practical reforms, in that they minimized religious differences between Jews and non-Jews, were motivated not by religion, but by his unworthy desire for political and social acceptance even at the price of diminishing Judaism. However, Holdheim consistently and strenuously denied that he would ever sacrifice religious principles for the sake of making Jews more desirable citizens. He claimed simply to be a disciple of the outstanding champion of Jewish emancipation in Germany, Gabriel Riesser, who had argued that Jewish political and social equality would come only with political change in Germany itself, not with Jews giving up elements of their religion. Indeed, for Holdheim to have laid his hands upon what he believed to be the Jewish essence would have been a contravention of his hierarchy of values, which set religion, as he understood it, above practical considerations. Quite early in his career he wrote to "thinking Israelites" in his congregation in Schwerin, "Religion cannot possibly, and should not, submit to the needs of the age, else the needs of the age will be raised to the status of religion."[6]

Holdheim's critics further held that even if he was not willing to give up a piece of Judaism for a political purpose, perhaps he was willing to do so because of its conflict with current culture. Was Holdheim trying to reshape Judaism to fit a zeitgeist that was penetrated by the reigning cultural ideal known in Germany as *Bildung*, a concept that contained within it higher education and a culturally imbued character? He was clearly aware of the charge, which did have some validity, especially in his early writings. But he would not admit to it, and later in his career he denied it forcefully—for example, in a sermon to his congregation where he weighed the contemporary *Bildung* disadvantageously against Jewish tradition. From the pulpit he exclaimed, "How distant is our time, with its widely praised *Bildung*, from the spirit of Moses," which was ready to make every sacrifice and which can give heart to "our enervated age."[7] At least in this sermon, it was not the age that was to instruct Judaism, but Judaism was to instruct and inspire the age.

Holdheim was willing to allow that the laws of the Rabbis had validity in their time, that when they were compiled they may even have been progressive. Nonetheless, a severe gap yawned between their time and the present. It was unconscionable to distort the historical truth and suggest that the ancestors were moderns before their time. In his view, modernity was not an extension of the Middle Ages, but a rupture from it. Moreover, it had reached a higher level than that represented by the traditional texts, even, in its totality, by the Bible. Holdheim expressed his view most strongly when he famously wrote, "The Talmud speaks with the ideology of its own time, and for that time it was right. I speak from the higher ideology of my time and for this age I am right."[8] That was not an egotistical statement. Holdheim did not regard himself as the shaper of his age, but rather as someone who was fortunate enough to be immersed in it.

Perhaps Holdheim's most significant break from the chain came with his insistence upon a non-halachic Judaism. In his view, Jewish law had no role in Diaspora Judaism. Law was the proper domain of the secular state, while religion devoted itself to personal and social morality, to the spirit and the heart. To be sure, traditional Judaism had likewise recognized that law lay within the domain of the state and that in conflicts between state law and halachah the state's authority held precedence. As the broadly accepted principle had it, *dina d'malchuta dina*, "the law of the state is law [also for us]." However, regrettably, even in nineteenth-century Europe, after its component states had increasingly abolished the medieval system of legal autonomy for Jewish inhabitants, certain legal functions had remained delegated to the Jewish communities. In particular, these included laws pertaining to marriage, divorce, and inheritance. Even liberal rabbis were called upon to act with legal authority in these areas. Holdheim, unlike his colleagues, wanted to place all legal affairs, without exception, in the hands of the state. Religion, he believed, was not at all about law, but about religiosity. At one time, the Jewish religion had been the law of a Jewish state. Hence, at that time it made sense for Judaism to develop a legal system. But with the destruction of the theocratic state, the dispersion, and the establishment of Jewish communities in non-Jewish lands, Jewish law had become out of place, and rabbis had no business being legal administrators.

No less radical was Holdheim's approach to the religious authority of Jewish texts. In the course of his life, he progressed from accepting the authority of the entire Jewish textual tradition to accepting less and less of it. First he secularized the medieval Jewish codes, then the Talmud, and finally the Bible. All, he came to believe, were humanly created documents. But where, then, did religious authority lie within Judaism? Where could he locate it? His response, disruptive in its time, would soon gain ever more sway within the Reform Movement. Ultimate authority, he came to believe, lay in no text whatever, but rather in the conscience of the individual Jew. In his inaugural address in Berlin, he expressed his view clearly: "Conscience is that indubitable revelation of religion to which Judaism attaches its teaching. . . . Every revelation must be authenticated through the inner voice of conscience."[9] Holdheim thus replaced heteronomy of text with autonomy of person in Reform Judaism. Obedience to law became obedience to the dictates of conscience or—in the case of religious services—obedience to a deepening aesthetic sensibility.

With authority lodged firmly within each individual—though it could be transferable, in part, to Reform rabbinical leadership—Jewish tradition no longer fit the paradigm of the chain. It now became more like a treasure chest that contained precious jewels (inspirational texts) but also much dross. In Holdheim's view, a Jew's religious conscience did not necessitate neglect of the Rabbis' finest creations. One might draw inspiration from tradition, he told the Reform Congregation, as long as one did not try to relive it, to draw an earlier age out of its time into the present.[10] Instead one needed to learn how to choose (knowledgeable choice, it would later be called), and surely in his role as rabbi, Holdheim intended to provide guidance so that commonality of choice could, in time, create renewed community. It is misleading to suggest that Holdheim rejected the Talmud; he simply wanted to accept it and other traditional texts, including the Bible, not in their entirety as intrinsically authoritative documents, but selectively, choosing from within them whatever values possessed continued relevance and inspiration.

Holdheim's selectivity extended, as well, to forms of religious observance. Although in his early years he did not eliminate the physical celebration of holidays, he did, already then, tell his first community, in Frankfurt-on-the-Oder, that while the celebration of holidays remained of great importance, their significance lay not in their being divinely commanded but in their ability to strengthen and renew religious life.[11]

Those customs and ceremonies that failed to reach the soul were not worthy of survival. Rituals were not ends in themselves; they were pathways to religious exaltation.

In its essence, religion was a matter of soul. It expressed itself in words, for the most part, and not in the performance of ritual acts. The Berlin Reform Congregation managed without shofar, *etrog*, or *lulav*. The members celebrated not the holidays as such, but rather the idea of each holiday. Theirs was intended to be an inward celebration, not an external one. Religious reflection replaced religious rite. For the Reform Congregation, performance of a ritual act stood in contradiction with its fundamental conviction, which claimed inwardness as its exclusive and solely justified principle.[12] Not surprisingly, prayer was almost exclusively in the German vernacular, for how could a language that was not understood enter the heart? What mattered for Holdheim were not the forms of religion but its essential content, its ethical monotheism. In his eyes, that fundamental idea of Judaism corresponded to "an ideal universalism" that not only was adequate to every age, but rose above every time and place.[13]

In its essence, Judaism was for Holdheim as much eternal and unchanging as Judaism in its traditional totality was for the champion of Neo-Orthodoxy in Germany, Rabbi Samson Raphael Hirsch. Its universal content demanded preservation. Forms, on the other hand, were never of the essence and hence were properly subject to alteration. They were not ends in themselves, but only means toward spiritual ends, in relation to which their effectiveness could be measured. Since in Holdheim's time more and more Jews worked within the general economy, and hence had to labor on Saturdays, Holdheim's congregation came to the conclusion that the principal service of the week should be held on Sundays, when all would be able to be present. What mattered, after all, was not the day of the week but that there be one day of rest and reflection. In this regard it is important to note, however, that Holdheim vigorously denied that such changes resulted from the desire to be more broadly accepted in non-Jewish society. It was not because Christians went to church on Sundays that Jews should go to synagogue on that day.[14] As we have noted, Holdheim stressed that political considerations would never determine his Judaism. Neither would imitation of non-Jews. Whatever reforms he favored, he did so because he believed that without them Judaism would not easily survive in the modern world.

What held for Jews in Germany, however, did not hold for Jews still living in a traditional Jewish society, such as the Jews in Poland. In a different social and intellectual context, there was no need to change practices, no need for reformers to propagate their views among Jews who faced no conflict with modernity.[15] Nor was it necessary to adopt the notion that Jewish identity was nothing more than a religious confession. And that was true even if you lived in Berlin. Speaking to his Reform Congregation in 1853, he said, "We cannot imagine a Jewish faith without the Jewish people that suffered and endured on its account, for which a thousand of martyrs gave their lives."[16] He was even willing to use the term "nationality" with regard to the Jews as long as that term was understood not in political terms but as an ethnically particularized expression of religion.[17]

The Jewish people, in Holdheim's view, was characterized by its bearing a universal message of liberty. Hence its religious strivings should be aimed at advancing the moral cause of humanity as a whole. Holdheim directed his Judaism outward and extended its sanctity beyond ethnic borders. Just as God was not understood as the God of Israel alone, so, for Holdheim, was the sacred community of Israel not set apart from the sacred community of humanity, nor the covenant between God and Israel from the covenant between God and humankind. Hence the covenant of circumcision lost its centrality. The sacred particularities of the worship service, limited as they were in his congregation, set Jewish religious practice apart, but they paled in significance before the holy moral law of humanity.[18]

Thus Holdheim was not averse to inserting yet another disruption into the steady course of religious reform. He argued for the religious equality of Jewish women more than did most of his Reform colleagues, and he officiated at interfaith weddings.

Holdheim's most frequent criticism of the traditional Judaism anchored in the Talmud pertained to the status of women. He called attention to a double sexual standard for the two sexes. While a Jewish woman was expected to remain fully loyal to her husband, a Jewish man was permitted to have intercourse with a a unmarried non-Jewish woman. Divorce was not possible without the permission of the husband. Therefore, not only did all Jews require emancipation from the inequality to which they had been subjected by the state, but also Jewish women required emancipation from Jewish law. It was not possible to avoid the conclusion, Holdheim argued, "that in Talmudic Judaism women occupy a religious position that is deeply subordinated beneath that of men. Only the altered religious consciousness of the present, set against that of the Talmud, has freed them from it. . . . So long as our religious institutions rest on Talmudic principles, women will, with respect to religious practice, factually have to tolerate a lower status, whose disadvantages they feel the more painfully when a lively sense of their religious maturity awakens within them."[19]

Where Holdheim thought that women were treated especially badly was in the traditional wedding ceremony. The manner in which it had long been practiced was not only, to Holdheim's dismay, inappropriately a legal act, but it also diminished the full humanity of the bride. Even so intrepid a reformer as Abraham Geiger, when he presided at weddings, had left the Jewish marriage ceremony essentially unchanged. As late as 1870, Geiger wrote that the bridegroom should speak both for himself and the bride. "The chaste bride, who has already more whispered than audibly spoken her 'yes,' should not have to speak and act publicly, but rather attend the words of her husband with a soulful look as she eagerly stretches out her finger so that the ring can be placed upon it. For the future, as well, the husband will be the one who gives, the wife the one who receives."[20] That was not at all the way that Holdheim thought it should be. The wedding ceremony, he believed, should be egalitarian. In a pamphlet he issued as early as 1845, he argued against current usage whereby "the man acquires the woman with her consent or, if she is underage, with the consent of her father, as an object is acquired, without, on her part, also acquiring the man."[21] This was not only unfair to the bride, but the very idea of one person acquiring another was morally offensive. However, if properly altered, the wedding ceremony could be made egalitarian. It could also be made to include a non-Jewish partner along with the Jewish counterpart.

Holdheim believed not only that a marriage ceremony should be equal with regard to the roles assigned to each member of the couple, but that it should be fully universal, since Judaism, after all, was in its essence a universal religion.[22] During the brief period when civil marriages were allowed in Prussia, at the middle of the nineteenth century, Holdheim was therefore willing—perhaps even eager—to officiate at the corresponding religious ceremony. The prohibition of outmarriages, he maintained, referred to foreign nations and not to foreign faiths. Moreover, the Rabbinic injunction to marry only Jews rested on the notion that the Jewish people possessed an exclusive sanctity, an idea that Holdheim believed modern Jews had outgrown.[23]

For what he referred to as a "mixed marriage," Holdheim developed an original ritual that not only gave the bride an egalitarian role unprecedented in any previous form of Judaism, but was also fully universal in its content. Although we do not possess copies of the ritual itself, it is easy enough to reconstruct it from Holdheim's description. In his view, two values within the ceremony were central: sanctification and love. With regard to the former, he thought it demeaning to the bride that the groom alone should declare, as in the traditional ceremony, that his bride was sanctified to him. How could the groom have the audacity to declare for his beloved that she was now sanctified to him, that is, his possession? Should she not have the right to declare for herself to whom she was sanctified? At the very least, the words should be spoken in complementary fashion, as well by the bride as by the groom. She would declare that the groom was likewise sanctified to her. But the problem was deeper. Does one individual at all have the right to speak for another? Properly, each partner should speak for himself or herself, actively sanctifying the speaking self to the other, who received it.

To remove the commercial or legal function of the ceremony, Holdheim abolished the presentation of a ring by either party. The wedding ceremony, like worship in the synagogue, was to consist of words, neither legal formulas nor even symbolic acts. There was also no need for a chuppah. Holdheim thought the bridal canopy "partly superfluous," partly—and somewhat strangely—also out of keeping with the couple's "delicacy of feeling."[24]

Not surprisingly, Holdheim also objected to the traditional reference to "the laws of Moses and Israel." He did so for two reasons. As we have seen, he regarded marriage as not a matter of religious law. The ceremony should not resemble a legal transaction but rather be an elevation of love. In addition, he did not want to tie the marriage bond narrowly to the Jewish tradition by reference to Moses and Israel. That issue became directly relevant when he performed a mixed marriage.

Thus, we may assume that as the officiating rabbi at a ceremony where one member of the couple was not Jewish, Holdheim asked each partner speak the following simple sentence (of course, in the vernacular): "I wish to be sanctified to you according to the laws of God." ("Laws" here, of course, means God's moral laws.) Following this brief exchange of vows, Holdheim would then deliver his wedding sermon, which, on one occasion, included the following passages—which were hardly in keeping with his reputation as a severe rationalist:

> Love alone stands as life's most elevated moral value and does not require support from a [particular] faith. Judaism teaches the one God and the one love. . . . One God in heaven and one love in the heart. . . .
>
> In truth, it is the most elevated triumph of religion that a noble, warm feeling wins out over cold reason, the heart over the head, rapture [*Begeisterung*] over spirit [*Geist*], love over opinion. However different you may be with regard to religious denomination, your fortune will remain undimmed if only you will be one in your love, undimmed though outside your home you attend different houses of worship, if only your domestic devotion is a common one. Even if your paths to heaven diverge, if only on earth you will walk together on the path of virtue, you will then meet one another at its goal. . . .
>
> And though there be no tangible altar erected here upon which you have exchanged your vows, though external signs and symbols are lacking that are intended to remind you of God's presence, you nonetheless know that His all-seeing eye penetrates within, that His paternal heart accepts your holy vows. And in order yet more forcefully to recall [God's] holiness I stand here in His name to sanctify and bless your bond, and to beseech from God's grace the most elevated of blessings, that of peace.[25]

Though Rabbi Samuel Holdheim disrupted the course of the Reform Movement in his time, fiercely dividing opinion among his colleagues because he told unpleasant truth, radically set individual choice against authoritative text, and raised the religious status of Jewish women, today his views find broad acceptance, even as they continue to stoke controversy.[26]

NOTES

1. Note the title of Holdheim's essay: *Die Religionsprincipien des reformierten Judenthums* [The principles of religion in reformed Judaism] (Berlin, 1847).

2. Yet, with the inconsistency that often characterized his writings, Holdheim, at least once, argued for the historical prevalence of Jewish religious reform, which would give his own views some rootage in the past. In a sermon to the Reform Congregation in Berlin, he urged his listeners to be "careful with your judgment of the past. You will find that, as old as Judaism is, that old is the history of its development, that old is the reform of Judaism." He was even willing to raise up the Pharisees as early examples of religious reform and deem his enemies modern Sadducees. See his *Die Erhaltung des Juden-thums im Kampfe mit der Zeit. Ein Bild aus der Vergangenheit belehrend für die Gegenwart* [The preservation of Judaism in conflict with time: A picture out of the past for the edification of the present] (Berlin, 1851), 10–11.

3. See Samuel Holdheim, *Das Religiöse und Politische im Judenthum* [The religious and political in Judaism] (Schwerin, 1845), iv.

4. Heinrich Graetz, *Tagebuch und Briefe* [Diaries and letters], ed. Reuven Michael (Tübingen, 1977), 146.

5. Heinrich Graetz, *Geschichte der Juden* [History of the Jews] (Leipzig, 1870), 11:565.

6. Samuel Holdheim, *Vorträge über die mosaische Religion für denkende Israeliten* [Lectures on the Mosaic religion for thinking Israelites] (Schwerin, 1844), xiv.

7. Samuel Holdheim, *Sechs Predigten* [Six sermons] (Berlin, 1863), 71.

8. Quoted in Michael A. Meyer and W. Gunther Plaut, eds., *The Reform Judaism Reader: North American Documents* (New York: URJ Press, 2001), 13.

9. Samuel Holdheim, *Antrittspredigt bei dessen Einführung in sein Amt als Rabbi-ner und Prediger der Genossenschaft für Reform im Judenthum zu Berlin* [Inaugural sermon on the occasion of his installation in his position as rabbi and prea-cher of the Berlin Reform Congregation) (Berlin, 1847), 8.

10. Holdheim, *Antrittspredigt*, 7.

11. Samuel Holdheim, *Die Einsegnung des Neumondtages* [The consecration of the new month] (Frankfurt-on-the-Oder, 1837), 19.

12. Holdheim, *Die Religionsprincipien*, 13.

13. Samuel Holdheim, *Die erste Rabbinerversammlung und Herr Frankel* [The first rabbinical conference and Mr. Frankel] (Schwerin, 1845), 18.

14. For Holdheim's argument, see Meyer and Plaut, *The Reform Judaism Reader*, 14–15.

15. Samuel Holdheim, *Der religiöse Fortschritt im deutschen Judenthume* [Religious progress in German Judaism] (Leipzig, 1840), 5.

16. Samuel Holdheim, *Predigten über die jüdische Religion* (Berlin, 1853), 148, as cited in Ralph Bisschops, "Samuel Holdheim and Sigismund Stern," in *Redefining Judaism in an Age of Emancipation: Comparative Perspectives on Samuel Holdheim (1806–1860)*, ed. Christian Wiese (Leiden, 2007), 273.

17. Samuel Holdheim, *Jakob und Israel. Predigt* [Jacob and Israel: A sermon] (Schwerin, 1841), 17. Jews have their own liturgy, a product of their history. It does not mean that Holdheim was a nationalist but that all Jews had a common ethnic root and despite universal aspiration were nonetheless in certain respects particular.

18. Samuel Holdheim, *Gemischte Ehen zwischen Juden und Christen* [Mixed marriages between Jews and Christians] (Berlin, 1850), 64.

19. Samuel Holdheim, *Die religiöse Stellung des weiblichen Geschlechts im talmudischen Judenthum* [The religious status of the female sex in Talmudic Judaism] (Schwerin, 1846), 77.

20. Abraham Geiger, "Die Versammlung zu Leipzig und die zu Philadelphia" [The Jewish assemblies of Leipzig and Philadelphia], *Jüdische Zeitschrift für Wissenschaft und Leben* 8 (1870): 12.

21. Samuel Holdheim, *Vorschläge zu einer zeitgemässen Reform der jüdischen Ehegesetze* [Suggestions for a contemporary Reform of Jewish marriage laws] (Schwerin, 1845), 13.

22. As a universal religion, Holdheim thought that Judaism should also be capable of attracting people of a different faith. See Bisschops, "Samuel Holdheim and Sigismund Stern," 245.

23. Holdheim, *Gemischte Ehen*, v, 4.

24. Holdheim, *Vorschläge*, 27.

25. Samuel Holdheim, "Traurede bei Einsegnung einer Mischehe" [Wedding charge in blessing a mixed marriage], in Holdheim, *Predigten über die jüdische Religion. Gehalten im Gotteshause der jüdischen Reform-Gemeinde zu Berlin*, vol. 4, *Fest-und Gelegenheitspredigten* (Berlin, 1869), 213–14. Toward the end of his life, Holdheim wrote a work in Hebrew titled, in brief, *Maamar HaIshut* [Essays on matrimony] (Berlin, 1861). Published posthumously, it includes, on page 41, the following hopes for (presumably fully Jewish) wedding couples (note the references to *Shechinah* and chuppah): "The most elevated of ties is that which unites soul with soul, spirit with spirit, so that they become a single body in their love for each other, and tranquility reign between them,

so that His *Shechinah* dwells within them and within their home. And they become helpmates one to the other, God assisting them to perfect their souls in morality, modesty, and avoidance of sin. And they raise up boys and girls to Torah, to chuppah and to good deeds, so that the people of God, His progeny and His covenant, grow like a verdant olive tree that ceases not to bear fruit."

26. A largely different and more extensive recent study of Holdheim may be found in Michael A. Meyer, "'Most of My Brethren Find Me Unacceptable': The Controversial Career of Rabbi Samuel Holdheim," *Jewish Social Studies* 9, no. 3 (Spring/Summer 2003): 1–19.

12

Sephardism and Modernity
Jewish Communities in Flux

Rabbi Marc D. Angel, PhD

M Y GRANDFATHER, Marco Romey, used to tell us of his experiences
as a young Sephardic bachelor newly arrived from Turkey to Seattle. He and the few other young Sephardim had arrived during the first
decade of the twentieth century. They went to an existing Ashkenazic
synagogue, assuming they would find welcome among fellow Jews; but
instead of welcome, they were greeted with suspicion. Were they really
Jews? They didn't have "Jewish" names; they didn't speak or understand
Yiddish; they never heard of gefilte fish! Even when the Sephardim
showed their prayer shawls and recited Hebrew prayers, the Ashkenazim
were not convinced.

It took a generation or two for Ashkenazim and Sephardim to begin to
reconnect after centuries of separation during the long diasporic exile.
Until the late nineteenth and early twentieth centuries, the Ashkenazic
world of Europe had little interaction with living Sephardim. And the
Sephardic/pan-Sephardic world, concentrated, for the most part, in
Muslim lands, lived in its own cultural bubble. The two communities
developed along different historic lines; although sharing the same
religion and peoplehood, they were, to a large extent, strangers to each
other.

Sephardim: Preliminary Definitions

My grandparents were members of the Sephardic communities of Turkey
and the Island of Rhodes. Those communities harked back to the Jews of
medieval Spain (*Sepharad* in Hebrew), many of whom found haven in the
Ottoman Empire following the expulsion of Jews from the Iberian Pen-

insula in the late fifteenth century. Their language was Judeo-Spanish. Their religious practices and customs followed the Sephardic traditions as codified by Rabbi Joseph Karo in his *Shulchan Aruch* and other great Sephardic halachic authorities. They prayed according to the classic Sephardic rite, including the kabbalistic texts that were incorporated over the centuries.

While most of the Sephardim lived in the lands of the Ottoman Empire, a smaller group settled in Western Europe and the Americas. These "Western Sephardim" were Jews or descendants of Jews who had been forcibly converted to Catholicism in Spain and Portugal but who eventually were able to return to Judaism. They established communities in such places as Amsterdam, Paris, Bordeaux, Bayonne, London, Hamburg, and, beginning in the seventeenth century, the Americas. The Western Sephardim were quick to adapt to the lands of their dispersion and developed their own distinctive patterns of Jewish life.

Although the term "Sephardic" literally refers to Jews of medieval Spanish background, it has more generally come to include those communities that followed the patterns of Sephardim, such as halachic practice, liturgical rituals, and religious customs. Thus, Jews of the Middle East and North Africa—even those not "Sephardic" genetically—have become part of the Sephardic world culturally. The late Dr. Henry Toledano referred to these communities as "pan-Sephardic." This chapter will be considering disruptions in the Sephardic/pan-Sephardic world as of the mid-nineteenth century and will be using the term "Sephardic" to refer to the entire pan-Sephardic Diaspora.

Disruption One: Confronting Modernity and Westernization

The Western Sephardic experience was unique among the Sephardic communities. Western Sephardim have been described as the first "modern" Jews, in that they generally flourished in relatively free societies. They valued general as well as Jewish religious education. They spoke the languages of the lands in which they lived. They advanced economically and professionally. Their synagogues were marked by a high sense of aesthetics and decorum.

The Western Sephardic communities were governed by rabbis and laypeople who strove to maintain classic religious traditions. But as members became increasingly receptive to the freedoms of Western culture, individuals strayed from halachic observance. The "establishment" had to deal with growing numbers of Jews who were lax in their observance and others who left Judaism altogether. Notorious examples of defectors included Benedict Spinoza of seventeenth-century Amsterdam and Benjamin Disraeli of nineteenth-century London.

Western Sephardic leadership worked diligently to adapt religious traditionalism to the challenges of modernity. In seventeenth-century Amsterdam, Rabbi Menasseh ben Israel published books in Spanish and Portuguese in order to provide religious guidance to newly returning Conversos. Dr. Isaac Cardoso of eighteenth-century Verona wrote powerful tracts defending Judaism from Christian attacks and misrepresentations. Grace Aguilar of nineteenth-century London wrote important works stressing the spiritual qualities of Judaism and refuting pervasive anti-Jewish stereotypes fostered by Christian society. Rabbi Eliyahu Benamozegh of nineteenth-century Livorno wrote extensively on Jewish ethics, the universal messages of Judaism, and the spiritual foundations of Judaism. In twentieth-century America, the Western Sephardic religious leadership included such figures as Rabbis Henry Pereira Mendes and David de Sola Pool of New York and Sabato Morais of Philadelphia.

Yet, for a variety of reasons, the Western Sephardic communities have diminished in numbers and influence. Over the centuries, many Western Sephardim became acculturated in their adopted societies. While the traditionalists succeeded in maintaining their communities for centuries, a gradual erosion in membership and commitment set in. The Sephardim, along with their fellow European Jews, suffered catastrophic losses during the Holocaust and have been unable to regain their former vitality.

The Western Sephardic congregations in South America and the Caribbean declined due to assimilation, migration out of the region, and other factors. In North America, the Spanish and Portuguese synagogues of New York and Philadelphia continue to adhere to the Western Sephardic rite in prayer, but very few members are actually of Western Sephardic birth. The synagogue in Newport, Rhode Island, is basically an Ashkenazic congregation, and the synagogues in Charleston and Savannah have joined the Reform Movement. Overall, until the mid-nineteenth century, the Western Sephardic congregations were the mainstream of American Jewry, but they were eclipsed by Ashkenazic influences beginning in 1840 with the dramatic increase of immigration of Ashkenazic Jews. Thus, the Western Sephardim today form a minuscule percentage of Sephardic Jewry, and in spite of their many historic achievements, the disruptions of modernity and Westernization have reduced this group dramatically.

Sephardim in Muslim Lands

The Sephardic/pan-Sephardic communities of the Muslim world are not monolithic, and each community has a history of its own. Until the mid-nineteenth century, most of these Jews lived in self-contained communities governed by traditional Jewish law. They were a tolerated minority, sometimes enjoying relative freedom and prosperity and sometimes suffering discrimination and poverty.

The forces of Westernization and modernization began to emerge in the mid-nineteenth century. The Ottoman Empire made a series of reforms, known as Tanzimat, between 1839 and 1876. These reforms aimed at adopting European-style government and stimulating the economy. Jews in the Ottoman Empire gained new freedoms, and the educated and affluent classes were drawn to the progressive policies. Although the masses of Jews lived within the traditional framework, cracks in the old system began to develop.

During the course of the nineteenth century, the Ottoman Empire was in the throes of decline, ceding much territory in the process. Greek independence brought significant changes for the Sephardim of Greece. In the early twentieth century, with the rise of Kemal Ataturk, Turkey experienced a strong surge of nationalism. As the century progressed, the Jews of Turkey—along with other minorities—were drawn into the Turkification process, moving away from former traditional patterns that had characterized their communities for centuries.

In the 1860s, the Alliance Israélite Universelle[1] began a major educational endeavor that aimed to bring modern, French-style schools to communities throughout the Middle East and North Africa. Between 1862 and 1914, Alliance schools could be found in Morocco, Tunisia, Libya, Egypt, Syria, Turkey, Iraq, and Iran. By 1900, Alliance Israélite

Universelle was operating one hundred schools, with a combined student population of twenty-six thousand. In 1912, the Alliance had seventy-one schools for boys and forty-four for girls, with schools in such places as Baghdad, Jerusalem, Tangiers, Istanbul, Beirut, Cairo, Damascus, Salonika, and Rhodes.

The impact of these schools was significant. While the existing traditional schools were almost exclusively open to boys, the Alliance provided education to thousands of girls. While existing traditional schools focused heavily on teaching religious texts, the Alliance schools offered an expansive general education. Parents who wanted their children to advance socially and economically were attracted to the opportunities that the Alliance schools offered.

The Alliance schools were met with mixed responses. Some strongly opposed them as a threat to traditional religious life. The emphasis on French language, literature, and culture was seen as undermining Hebrew and religious Jewish studies. But for others, these schools offered a path for educational and economic progress. Graduates of the Alliance schools played increasing roles in transforming and modernizing their communities.

Some Alliance students went on to pursue advanced studies in Paris and elsewhere. Many had their eyes opened to the possibility of emigration where new opportunities beckoned. For the female students, the Alliance provided a framework for life beyond the role of wife, mother, and homemaker. Students were often taught by highly educated female teachers, who themselves served as role models. Subtly, and not so subtly, the patterns of traditional life were undergoing change.

The success of the Alliance schools led the existing traditional schools to upgrade their own educational program. In order to attract students, the communal schools began to offer classes in languages and general studies; they also improved their methods of teaching Hebrew and religious studies.

While the forces for Westernization and modernization were seeping into the Jewish communities of Muslim lands, larger external factors also came into play. Many of the lands in which these Jews lived were coming under the control and influence of European colonial powers. Egypt was under British control from 1882 until 1956. Sudan was a British colony from 1899 to 1956. Britain also was the colonial power for Jordan, Palestine, and Persian Gulf nations. French colonies included Tunisia (1881–1956), Algeria (1830–1963), Morocco (1912–56), Syria (1918–46), and Lebanon (1918–43). Italy controlled Libya (1911–51) and the Island of Rhodes (1911–44).

Many of the Jews living in these lands identified with the European powers. They worked in their consulates, learned their languages, adopted their style of dress, and so on. To the often downtrodden Jews, the European colonizers seemed to offer a higher culture with more opportunities for advancement. But as Jews "Europeanized," they also tended to move further away from traditional religious observance. The rabbinic establishment that had governed the Jewish communities for centuries was gradually losing the adherence of modernizing Jews.

From the early twentieth century, migration of Sephardim from their native lands grew significantly. The spirit of change had taken hold. Many were drawn to the Land of Israel. Many others were attracted to the United States. Some found their ways to Western Europe, the south of Africa, and cities of Latin America. The migration pattern was not only a result of the confrontation with modernity, but was also stimulated by the desire to escape the dire conditions in their homelands—poverty, natural disasters, and wars.

Reactions to the Disruptions of Modernity

Rabbinic leadership in the Sephardic/pan-Sephardic communities reflected different attitudes. The traditionalists—steeped in a kabbalistic/midrashic Judaism—felt deeply threatened by the Westernizing/modernizing influences. They sought to maintain the premodern ways of their communities. They were intellectually and emotionally unequipped to provide enlightened guidance to the growing numbers of Jews who were becoming alienated from the status quo and who were attracted to the freedoms and opportunities of modernity.

Albert Memmi, one of the great intellectual figures of twentieth-century France, grew up in the Jewish ghetto in Tunis. After attending a French high school, he went on to Paris for advanced studies. He eventually sought to identify with the Tunisian national movement but was rejected because he was a Jew. In his book *The Liberation of the Jew*, he describes his malaise: "When we graduated from the lycee in Tunis many of us decided to cut ourselves off from the past, the ghetto and our native land, to breathe fresh air and set off on the most beautiful of adventures. I no longer wanted to be that invalid called a Jew, mostly because I wanted to be a man; and because I wanted to join with all men to reconquer the humanity which was denied me."[2] Memmi, who died in 2020 at the age of ninety-nine, seemed never to have been able to make peace with his Jewishness.

Elias Canetti (1905–76) was a Bulgarian-born Sephardic Jew of the Judeo-Spanish tradition. Yet his upbringing was far from traditional, and his mother went so far as to feed him ham as a way of ridding him of past claims of Judaism. Through his various writings and teachings, he had a significant impact on general intellectual life and was awarded the Nobel Prize for Literature in 1981, largely in recognition of his major work *Crowds and Power*.

Rene Cassin (1887–1976) was born into the Sephardic community in Bayonne, France, and grew up in Nice. He became a political activist and was coauthor of the Universal Declaration of Human Rights issued by the United Nations. He was awarded the Nobel Peace Prize in 1968. He identified strongly with the work of the Alliance Israélite Universelle and served as its president from 1943 to 1976. Yet his personal life was well removed from traditional religious belief and observance.

Memmi, Canetti, and Cassin represent a Sephardic intellectual class that contributed greatly to general society but who removed themselves from the traditional life of Sephardic Judaism. With the rise of modernity, acculturated Sephardim advanced in many fields and in many lands; but in the process, many drifted away from traditional Jewish living.

The Sephardic rabbinic establishment could not hold back the forces of modernity and westernization. But there were important religious leaders who responded creatively and intelligently to the new challenges and who succeeded in maintaining tradition-based communities.[3] The rabbis of Morocco maintained close ties and held rabbinic conferences in which they dealt with the issues facing their communities. Rabbi Benzion Uziel (1880–1953) was the Sephardic chief rabbi of Israel from 1939 until his death in 1953. His extensive writings, including impressive volumes of responsa (*Mishp'tei Uziel*), had considerable influence throughout the Sephardic world and beyond.

Rabbi Uziel's religious worldview, characteristic of much of the Sephardic rabbinic community, was reflected in a letter he wrote to the leadership of the Alliance Israélite Universelle.[4] While recognizing the importance of students learning both religious subjects and general studies, he stressed the need to master Hebrew as well as the language of the land in which they lived and at least one European language. The goal of Jewish education should be clear: to raise children faithful to their people and to their Torah, people who would be useful to their families, their people, and society. Rabbi Uziel insisted that general subjects be taught by religious teachers. Otherwise, a spirit of secularism would enter the children's hearts, leading them away from the very principles for which Jewish schools stood. If modern-day Jews thought that their children could achieve success only by receiving an exclusively secular education, they were in fact sacrificing their children's spiritual lives. There was no necessity to do so, since one could attain worldly success while remaining deeply steeped in Torah tradition.

Traditional Communal Framework

Religious leaders throughout the Sephardic Diaspora felt that the Jewish people could best be served by remaining faithful to its own distinctive way of life. To them, Reform was a surrender to the whims of European modernity, and it could only lead to a breakdown in Jewish religious life.

Whereas the issues of emancipation and enlightenment led to the formation of religious movements within Ashkenazic Jewry, Sephardic Jewry did not fragment itself into Orthodox, Conservative, Reform, or other movements. Ashkenazic Jewry was torn by feuding among the ideological movements. It established separate communities, institutions, even cemeteries. Sephardic Jewry was spared this internecine denominational struggle.

Certainly, not all Sephardic Jews adhered to the details of traditional halachah. Laxity in observance was growing. A lessening of reverence for rabbinic authority was apparent in many communities. Yet, the religious intellectuals, as well as the masses, were desirous of maintaining a traditional framework for their communities. The Sephardim found a modus vivendi characterized by respect for tradition and tolerance for those whose observance of halachah fell short. Whereas some individuals might not be personally observant, the synagogue and community structure were to operate according to halachah.

Disruption Two: Confronting the Ashkenazim

The Sephardic/pan-Sephardic communities were learning to cope with the challenges of modernity and westernization. They were dealing with the influences of the Alliance schools, the impact of the colonial European powers, the changes in their educational system, the new opportunities for girls and women, the growing laxity in religious observance, and the alienation of some of the best and brightest intellectuals.

But the Jewish communities of the Muslim world were to undergo massive disruptions over which they had little or no control. Large-scale migration from these communities was evident from the early twentieth century. Thousands of young people were seeking new opportunities in the United States. Many others were attracted to the idealism of returning to the Jewish homeland. With the establishment of the State of Israel in 1948, vast numbers of Jews from North Africa and the Middle East migrated there—often driven from their homes by anti-Israel Muslim governments. Indeed, Jews of the Sephardic/pan-Sephardic world came to be the majority of Jews in Israel. In 2021, there are very few Jews still living in the former communities in North Africa and the Middle East.

As Sephardim came into contact with the Ashkenazic-dominated communities in the United States, Israel, and elsewhere, they now had to face a new set of disruptions. Among their problems was dealing with negative stereotypes prevalent in the Ashkenazic community.

When Sephardim were arriving in the United States in the early decades of the twentieth century, they came to be labeled as "Oriental Jews." Indeed, they themselves assumed this designation, and some of their early organizations were the Federation of Oriental Jews, Oriental Hebrew Association, Oriental Israelite Fraternity, and others. Moise Gadol, editor of the Ladino newspaper *La America*, established the Oriental Bureau of HIAS in 1911.[5]

Why would the term "Oriental" be applied to Jews from Turkey, the Balkans, Greece, and Syria? Apparently, it was to distinguish this group of Jews from the more cultured "Western" (also referred to as Occidental) Jews. After all, Western civilization was deemed to be the most advanced. The "Orientals" were Eastern, backward, uncultured by Western standards. So Ashkenazim (and Western Sephardim too) could separate themselves from the lower-status newcomers by applying a term that then had negative connotations.

A similar situation arose in Israel. Jews from Muslim lands were termed *eidot haMizrach*, "Eastern tribes." It is as though normative Jews are simply Jews, that is, Ashkenazim; but Sephardim/pan-Sephardim are broken into Eastern compartments—interesting (and sometimes troublesome) Jewish exotica. The late Dr. Daniel Elazar noted the prejudicial use of the term. He pointed out that the Jews of North Africa should hardly be referred to as "Easterners" when all of Morocco is farther west than London, and most of North Africa is farther west than Poland. The appellation is obviously not related to geography, but to "the mobilization of loaded terms to advance a convenient Ashkenazic myth in a situation where to be Western is often synonymous with being modern. And since virtually everyone wants to be modern, this myth gives the Ashkenazim a significant psychological advantage over the Sephardim."[6]

I remember as a student at Yeshiva College in the early 1960s that an emissary from Israel addressed us about the need for us to make *aliyah*. He spoke with dread about the possibility of Israel being overtaken by the Mizrachim (Eastern) immigrants from Arab lands. He urged Western *aliyah* in order to maintain Israel as a modern democracy. He verbalized a common fear/prejudice: the Sephardim/pan-Sephardim were not "us"; they were foreigners with low Eastern culture. They could not be trusted to become westernized, certainly not right away.

These anti-Sephardic notions were held in spite of the fact that many of the Sephardim spoke Spanish, French, Italian, and other European languages; that many had received "Western" education in the schools of the Alliance Israélite Universelle and in the general schools run by the European colonial powers in their lands; that many, even of the less educated and less affluent classes, had a rich religious and cultural heritage that had sustained their communities for centuries. Were the poorer and less educated Sephardim in worse conditions than the Ashkenazim of the shtetls of Eastern Europe?

The pervasive prejudice against the "Oriental" Jews, the *"eidot haMiz-*

rach," was not always overt and conscious. It was not necessarily meant to be malicious. But, in fact, it served to undermine the status of Sephardic/pan-Sephardic Jews. The Jewish schools almost totally ignored the existence of Sephardim—their history, culture, traditions. At best, they would introduce a Sephardic song or describe a Sephardic food. Generally, Sephardic tradition was either ignored, misrepresented, or confined to the areas of folklore/music/food.

Sephardic rabbis in Israel were relegated to lower positions with lower pay than their Ashkenazic peers. Rabbi Chayim David Halevi, late Sephardic chief rabbi of Tel Aviv, was active in an association of Sephardic rabbis between 1953 and 1959, known as Agudat HaRabbanim Ha-Sephardiyim b'Yisrael. The group fought for proper recognition by the Ashkenazic rabbinic establishment. In those days, Sephardic rabbis were not allowed to sign simple documents attesting that a person was married or single. While Ashkenazic rabbis were appointed as chief rabbis of cities and received commensurate compensation, Sephardic rabbis, for the most part, were only appointed as rabbis of communities (*rabbanei ha-eidah*) and received lower salaries. Once the basic objectives of the Sephardic rabbinic group were achieved (by 1959), the group disbanded.

The frustrations of the Middle Eastern/North African immigrants were many. They were often settled in remote towns and villages. Many lived in *maabarot*, tent cities, until real housing could be found for them. Their children were not expected to attend academically advanced schools or universities. Their economic situation was problematic, since many positions in government and business were granted by *proteksia*, favoritism by those in power to people of their own backgrounds.

While the Sephardim did indeed make considerable progress in adapting to life in Israel, the underlying social and economic problems could not be ignored. In 1971, a group of Israeli-born Jews of North African and Middle Eastern backgrounds created the Black Panthers party. Its goal was to promote social justice for their communities and to combat their perception of widespread discrimination against them. They brought their concerns to public attention through demonstrations, media events, and political action.

Early in the 1970s, Soviet Jews began to arrive in Israel in large numbers. The Israeli government worked energetically to absorb these new immigrants, who needed housing, jobs, social services, education for their children, and so on. The North African and Middle Eastern Jews could not help but note the difference between how poorly they were treated in comparison with the Soviet immigrants. In spite of general progress, frustration and discontent persisted.

Sensing an anti-Sephardic attitude among the Ashkenazic rabbinate, especially in Chareidi circles, Rabbi Ovadia Yosef spearheaded the establishment of the Shas political party in 1984. The goal was to assert Sephardic rights throughout Israel and especially in the religious realm. Shas became a political power with the election of its party members to the Israeli Knesset. Shas expanded its network of schools and yeshivot and won the support of many Sephardic/Middle Eastern voters—even those who were not themselves Chareidi in outlook or observance.

In the United States, Canada, Europe—wherever they settled in the Diaspora—North African and Middle Eastern Jews faced the usual challenges of immigrants, but they also faced problems in their relations with the existing Ashkenazic establishment. Their Jewishness was questioned; their "Oriental" or "Eastern" backgrounds were deprecated; their traditions were ignored or relegated to the domain of folklore. But within several generations, most of these Jews progressed professionally, economically, and socially. As Sephardim and Ashkenazim grew more accustomed to each other—and married each other—the old alienations and stereotypes diminished.

The situation in Israel has also improved over the generations, especially given the advancement of Sephardim in all areas of Israeli life. Marriages between Sephardim and Ashkenazim have become much more common, and the merger of cultures has become more prevalent, especially in the non-Chareidi segment of the population. Yet, Jews of North African and Middle Eastern backgrounds still feel pangs of discrimination and negative stereotyping.

Sephardic immigrants, whether in Israel or the Diaspora, had to deal with serious disruptions as a result of moving into new lands. Their former communal structures and religious patterns were dislocated and not fully or easily replicated in their new homes. The Jewish establishment operated on the assumption that normative Jews and Judaism were Ashkenazic, that Sephardim needed to "Ashkenazify" in order to become modern and acceptable. It was as though Sephardic history came to an end hundreds of years ago and nothing of real significance occurred among them for the past few centuries.

Whether in Israel or the Diaspora, Sephardim had to deal with a sort of identity crisis. They no longer had the calm confidence of living in societies that accepted and valued them and their traditions. If their children attended Jewish schools, they were taught normative Ashkenazic Judaism. Their own rabbis—especially those of the new generations—were becoming "Ashkenazified." They adopted Ashkenazic practices and even dressed in the black hats and frock coats of the Ashkenazic rabbinic establishment.

In responding to the challenges, some Jews of North African and Middle Eastern background literally changed their names so as not to be identifiable as Sephardim. Others tried to blend into the Ashkenazic majority in whatever ways they could. Sephardic yeshivah students and rabbis began to identify with the Chareidi Ashkenazic rabbinic leadership. Rabbi Ovadia Yosef was a strong voice on behalf of maintaining Sephardic halachic teachings; yet much of the Shas leadership dress and speak pretty much like Ashkenazic Chareidi rabbis.

Another trend has also emerged in which Sephardim fully accept their backgrounds and embrace an almost "tribal" devotion to the particular customs of their past communities. These Jews take pride in being loyal to the rites and practices of the Jews of Morocco, Syria, Turkey, Iraq, Yemen, etc. Instead of backing away from these traditions, they proclaim them proudly and energetically.

Even the term *Mizrachim* has been turned on its head by some of the more militant Sephardic groups. Instead of being a source of derision, being "Eastern" has become a positive value in modern times. Eastern Jews can claim an indigenous connection to the Land of Israel, even more than Jews of European background. With the growing intellectual trend toward multiculturalism and diversity, the Mizrachim are feeling a new sense of importance in the Jewish world, especially in Israel. Being "Western" is not necessarily viewed as an asset.

Disruption Three: Confronting the Future

At present, the Sephardic/Ashkenazic rift is still evident, especially in Israel. The *Jerusalem Post* reported in 2021 that Miri Regev, a member of the Israeli Parliament for the Likud party, was seeking to become the party leader and to move on to become prime minister. Regev was born in the southern development town of Kiryat Gat to immigrants from Morocco, Felix and Marcelle Siboni. She declared that "the time has come to have a Sephardi Prime Minister and that the Likud rank and file must vote this time for someone who represents their class, their ethnicity and their agenda."[7] Regev and the leadership of the Shas party continue to stoke the ethnic pride of the Sephardim and position themselves as alternatives to the Ashkenazic establishment.

"Ethnic" politics is obviously still a factor in Israel. This is evident not only among Jews of North African and Middle Eastern descent, but also among others, including Russian Jews and Anglo-Jews. In the short term—at least for another generation—ethnic divisions and divisiveness will flourish.

But will these ethnic divisions continue indefinitely? What will the terms "Sephardic" and "Ashkenazic" mean one hundred years from now? How many Jews will be "pure-blooded" Sephardim or Ashkenazim?[8]

The Ashkenazic world, although still tending to emphasize Sephardic folk qualities, is also coming to appreciate Sephardic intellectual traditions, rabbinic teachings, and religious worldview. Scholars are increasingly researching and publishing articles and books exploring the Sephardic experience in the lands of North Africa and the Middle East.

Change is inevitable. Although we are not prophets, we can envision a Jewish world a century from now that has moved beyond ethnicity. Our great-great-grandchildren will descend from Jews of many diasporic backgrounds. They will have a mixture of Sephardic/Ashkenazic genes (and other genetic components drawn from converts to Judaism and from Jews who do not neatly fit into Sephardic/pan-Sephardic or Ashkenazic compartments). Aside from genetics, they will also be drawing on a wide range of intellectual and cultural traditions. Hopefully, they will draw on the best of all our traditions and live a happy, wholesome Jewish life free from ethnic strife.

I suspect that one hundred years from now there will still be groups of tightly knit Chareidim and Chasidim. There may also be groups of ethno-centered Jews who tenaciously cling to particular traditions. But most Jews, whether in Israel or the Diaspora, will be sharing in a more general Jewish culture that combines elements from many traditions.

The Sephardic/pan-Sephardic Jews of today need to identify and promote positive elements of their history and culture that are worthy to be transmitted to future generations. The day will surely come when all Jews—of whatever background—will come to view each other as "us"—as one people with a shared history and shared destiny. Instead of ethnic rivalries, prejudices, and stereotypes, we will ultimately emerge as a "homogenized" Jewish people, proudly and happily composed of many diverse elements.

(If I may dare to add, I think that not only will ethnic divisions become increasingly irrelevant, but the division of Jews into religious "streams" will also decline. A century from now, I don't think it will be important for Jews to identify as Orthodox, Conservative, Reform, Reconstructionist, Renewal, or any other such subdivision. Rather, Jews will make their own free and independent decisions as to what to believe and observe, where and how to pray, etc. We will still have a wide range of opinions and plenty of controversy, but it will be in the realm of personal choice rather than institutional rivalries.)

Thus, the third disruption of the Sephardic/pan-Sephardic world is actually a disruption for all Jewry. It is a disruption—or rather a transformation—brought about by the coming together of Jews of all backgrounds, by intergroup marriage, by growing understanding and appreciation of the history and cultures of each of our diverse communities.

Our goal as a Jewish people should be to draw on all the strengths of all our communities and to work toward a Jewish peoplehood that is inclusive, diverse, strong, and healthy.

Notes

1. See Andre Kaspi, ed., *Histoire de l'Alliance Israélite Universelle: De 1860 a Nos Jours* (Paris: Armand Colin, 2010).
2. Albert Memmi, *The Liberation of the Jew*, trans. Judy Hyun (New York: Orion Press, 1966), 22.

3. Among this group were Rabbi Israel Moshe Hazan (1808–1963), born in Izmir, who served Sephardic communities in Rome, Corfu, and Alexandria; Rabbi Yehuda Yaacov Nehama (1825–99) of Salonika; Rabbi Yosef Hayyim (1835–1909) of Baghdad; Rabbi Eliyahu Hazzan (1846–1908), who served the communities of Tripoli and Alexandria; Rabbi Reuven Eliyahu Israel (1856–1932), last chief rabbi of the Island of Rhodes.

4. Benzion Uziel, *Mikhmanei Uziel* (Tel Aviv: Ha-Poel Ha-Mizrachi, 1939), 517.

5. Gadol later abandoned the term "Oriental" not only because he thought it was pejorative, but because he thought the public used the term specifically to relate to Asians.

6. Daniel Elazar, *The Other Jews: The Sephardim Today* (New York: Basic Books, 1988), 24.

7. Gill Hoffman, "Miri Regev Announces Run for Prime Minister: Stop Voting for 'White People,'" *Jerusalem Post*, August 15, 2021.

8. With each passing generation, Israeli Jews of various backgrounds are marrying each other and moving away from strict ethnic boundaries. Their children grow up in homes of mixed cultural/religious traditions. In the Diaspora, where Sephardim are a relatively small minority within the overall Jewish population, it is fairly common for Sephardim to marry Ashkenazic or other Sephardic Jews of different background.

FOR FURTHER READING

Angel, Marc D. *Foundations of Sephardic Spirituality: The Inner Life of Jews of the Ottoman Empire.* Woodstock, VT: Jewish Lights, 2006.

———. *La America: The Sephardic Experience in the United States.* Philadelphia: Jewish Publication Society, 1982.

———. *Loving Truth and Peace: The Grand Religious Worldview of Rabbi Benzion Uziel.* Northvale, NJ: Jason Aronson, 1999.

———. *Voices in Exile: A Study in Sephardic Intellectual History.* Hoboken, NJ: Ktav, 1991.

Chouraqui, Andre. *Between East and West.* Philadelphia: Jewish Publication Society, 1968.

Elazar, Daniel. *The Other Jews: The Sephardim Today.* New York: Basic Books, 1989.

Kaspi, Andre, ed. *Histoire de l'Alliance Israélite Universelle: De 1860 a Nos Jours.* Paris: Armand Colin, 2010.

Laskier, Michael. *North African Jewry in the Twentieth Century.* New York: New York University Press, 1997.

Stillman, Norman. *The Jews of Arab Lands in Modern Times*. Philadelphia: Jewish Publication Society, 2003.

Zohar, Zvi. *Rabbinic Creativity in the Modern Middle East*. London: Bloomsbury Press, 2013.

13

The Pittsburgh Platform of 1885
The American Reform Rabbis' Declaration of Independence

Rabbi Kari Tuling, PhD

IN 1885, A GROUP OF REFORM RABBIS met in Pittsburgh to create a statement of principles for the emergent American Reform Movement. Only eight points long, this document represented a key moment of disruption; Isaac Mayer Wise later referred to it as a "declaration of independence."[1] Wise himself had long tried to keep the various streams of American Judaism together as one unified movement and as such was somewhat ambivalent about the Pittsburgh Platform when it was first articulated. He was indeed right about its ultimate effect, however: this document marked the point when those various streams diverged and became separate movements. The differences could not be breached, as the ideological and theological differences were too great.

Still relevant to the Reform Movement's own self-understanding, the text of the Pittsburgh Platform appears on the website of the Central Conference of American Rabbis (CCAR), the rabbinical organization of the Reform Movement, in order to provide a sense of that body's history. Given this document's significance, it is worth reproducing both the CCAR's introduction and its eight points in full here:

> Convening at the call of Kaufmann Kohler of New York, Reform rabbis from around the United States met from November 16 through November 19, 1885 with Isaac Mayer Wise presiding. The meeting was declared the continuation of the Philadelphia Conference of 1869, which was the continuation of the German Conference of 1841 to 1846. The rabbis adopted the following seminal text:

1. We recognize in every religion an attempt to grasp the Infinite, and in every mode, source or book of revelation held sacred in any religious system the consciousness of the indwelling of God in [humanity]. We hold that Judaism presents the highest conception of the God-idea as taught in our Holy Scriptures and developed and spiritualized by the Jewish teachers, in accordance with the moral and philosophical progress of their respective ages. We maintain that Judaism preserved and defended midst continual struggles and trials and under enforced isolation, this God-idea as the central religious truth for the human race.

2. We recognize in the Bible the record of the consecration of the Jewish people to its mission as the priest of the one God, and value it as the most potent instrument of religious and moral instruction. We hold that the modern discoveries of scientific researches in the domain of nature and history are not antagonistic to the doctrines of Judaism, the Bible reflecting the primitive ideas of its own age, and at times clothing its conception of divine Providence and Justice dealing with men in miraculous narratives.

3. We recognize in the Mosaic legislation a system of training the Jewish people for its mission during its national life in Palestine, and today we accept as binding only its moral laws, and maintain only such ceremonies as elevate and sanctify our lives, but reject all such as are not adapted to the views and habits of modern civilization.

4. We hold that all such Mosaic and rabbinical laws as regulate diet, priestly purity, and dress originated in ages and under the influence of ideas entirely foreign to our present mental and spiritual state. They fail to impress the modern Jew with a spirit of priestly holiness; their observance in our days is apt rather to obstruct than to further modern spiritual elevation.

5. We recognize, in the modern era of universal culture of heart and intellect, the approaching of the realization of Israel's great Messianic hope for the establishment of the kingdom of truth, justice, and peace among all [humanity]. We consider ourselves no longer a nation, but a religious community, and therefore expect neither a return to Palestine, nor a sacrificial worship under the

sons of Aaron, nor the restoration of any of the laws concerning the Jewish state.

6. We recognize in Judaism a progressive religion, ever striving to be in accord with the postulates of reason. We are convinced of the utmost necessity of preserving the historical identity with our great past. Christianity and Islam, being daughter religions of Judaism, we appreciate their providential mission, to aid in the spreading of monotheistic and moral truth. We acknowledge that the spirit of broad humanity of our age is our ally in the fulfillment of our mission, and therefore we extend the hand of fellowship to all who cooperate with us in the establishment of the reign of truth and righteousness among men.

7. We reassert the doctrine of Judaism that the soul is immortal, grounding the belief on the divine nature of human spirit, which forever finds bliss in righteousness and misery in wickedness. We reject as ideas not rooted in Judaism, the beliefs both in bodily resurrection and in Gehenna and Eden (Hell and Paradise) as abodes for everlasting punishment and reward.

8. In full accordance with the spirit of the Mosaic legislation, which strives to regulate the relations between rich and poor, we deem it our duty to participate in the great task of modern times, to solve, on the basis of justice and righteousness, the problems presented by the contrasts and evils of the present organization of society.[2]

These eight points of the Pittsburgh Platform provide insight into the pressing issues of the day and offer us a window into the emerging theological views of the nineteenth-century American Reform rabbis. Let us consider each point, one by one.

The opening statement, offered in point one, is particularly interesting because of its clear sense of pluralism: it provided a sharp answer to Christian supersessionist claims that Judaism has remained a relic of the past with no future of its own. This point also offered up an early articulation of American pragmatism; keep in mind that when this text was written, neither of William James's religious masterworks *The Varieties of Religious Experience* (1902) or *The Will to Believe* (1896) had yet appeared.[3] Nonetheless, this first point contained that same American pragmatic sensibility as is found in James's works.

Point two, arguing "modern discoveries of scientific researches in the domain of nature and history are not antagonistic to the doctrines of Judaism," reflected the need to respond to the problem of miracles within the biblical text. Contemporary scientific ideas included Darwin's theory of evolution, an idea that profoundly shook the foundations of biblical belief when it was first articulated in *The Origin of Species* (1859). Further, Julius Wellhausen's momentous book of biblical criticism, *Prolegomena to the History of Israel* (1878), had been translated into English a few years earlier and offered what is known as the documentary hypothesis regarding the Bible's origins.[4] The Bible's mythic telling of Israelite history and religion was greatly at odds with the scientism of the era. The rabbis gathered in Pittsburgh wished to emphasize Judaism's continued relevance even in light of the latest scientific discoveries, a point that resonates in our day as well.

To understand the theology of the next few points of this platform, we should consider the work of the German philosopher Immanuel Kant (1724–1804), the most influential of the Enlightenment thinkers, because many of these points emerged as arguments and counterarguments to the philosophical currents of his day. In his *Religion within the Boundaries of Mere Reason* (*Die Religion innerhalb die Grenzen der bloßen Vernunft*, 1793), Kant outlined what he thought was wrong with most religious observance and attempted to sketch a version of religion that might be compatible with reason. In so doing, however, Kant also reflected many of the prejudices of his time and place, particularly with regard to Judaism. His deployment of these prejudices made it much harder to achieve Jewish integration into European society; it also made it more difficult for Jewish research and Jewish ideas to be accepted into academic circles. Kant's influence was as widespread as it was deeply penetrating; his ideas dominated intellectual and political discourse throughout the nineteenth century. It is, in fact, difficult to overstate Kant's influence in that era, as his ideas were held in such high esteem.

Kant specifically opposed the practice of using revelation as the basis of law, which is why his work presented such a core problem for halachic thought. It is not that Kant objected to lawfulness or to religion; rather, he argued that the individual must rationally accept the principles of ethics, internalize them, and self-legislate them as one's duty, as opposed to following the laws because they were issued by an authority. For Kant, the individual should take on the role of lawgiver, acting in the manner of God, legislating duty as a moral imperative. An individual should then freely choose to do one's duty and should feel compelled to do so without needing the incentives and disincentives of an external law. In fact, strictly speaking, for Kant, an act was not considered to be ethical if it was performed for the purpose of deriving any kind of gain, even if that gain was something ostensibly good, such as seeking favor in the eyes of God. His philosophical ideas meant that the structures of Jewish law appeared to be particularly problematic to those hoping for greater Jewish integration into European culture.

In Kant's view, Judaism was wholly a historical (and not ideal) religion, one that had strayed from its early awareness of "the good principle" and had degenerated into a dry legalism. On this basis, Kant drew a sharp contrast between Judaism and Christianity regarding the issue of autonomy. He suggested that Judaism, in the time of the Jewish commonwealth, had been a political entity with a set of civil laws. These laws included ethical statutes, such as the prohibitions against stealing and against murder, but they were not actually ethical because they had been organized around a system of cultic ritual. In Kant's words:

> The *Jewish faith*, as originally established, was only a collection of merely statutory laws supporting a political state. . . . Strictly speaking, Judaism is not a religion at all but simply the union of a number of individuals who since they belonged to a particular stock, established themselves into a community under purely political laws, hence not into a church.[5]

The heteronomous nature of Jewish law disqualified it from claiming any moral good that might be achieved by its regulation of behavior, because it did not create a context in which a person could make a purely autonomous choice to take on these requirements as duties.

Kant's theological challenge to the Jewish community required an answer. Coming a century later, the Pittsburgh Platform offered an American Reform Jewish response. The authors did so in bold terms, briefly and clearly: "We recognize in the Mosaic legislation a system of training the Jewish people for its mission during its national life in Palestine, and today we accept as binding only its moral laws, and maintain only such ceremonies as elevate and sanctify our lives, but reject all such as were not adapted to the views and habits of modern civilization." In other words, they agreed that the laws unrelated to ethics were of a specific time and place, but they rejected the notion that these laws do not qualify as truly ethical simply because of their origins.

With regard to the fourth point, "all such Mosaic and rabbinical laws as regulate diet, priestly purity, and dress originated in ages and under the influence of ideas entirely foreign to our present mental and spiritual state," we again turn to Kant to explicate the underlying concerns. Kant made a distinction between the religions of "rogation" (i.e., asking or making supplication) and "moral" religions. Most religions, in his estimation, fall into the former category. As Kant argued:

> All religions, however, can be divided into *religion of rogation* (of mere cult) and *moral religion*, i.e. the religion of *good life-conduct*. According to the first, the human being either flatters himself that God can make him eternally happy (through the remissions of his debts) without any necessity on his part *to become a better human being*; or else, if this does not seem possible to him, that God himself *can make him a better human being* without his having to contribute more than to *ask* for it, and, since before an omniscient being asking is no more than *wishing*, this would amount in fact to doing nothing, for, if improvement were a matter of mere wishing, every human being would be good.[6]

Kant's position here was that prayer as such is akin to magic, in that it expresses a wish that reality be changed in some fundamental way. The one who offers prayer is intending, in Kant's view, to have God intervene and remove all guilt or to see to it that guilt is no longer necessary. Kant therefore objected to the idea that one might become a better person without any struggle or difficulty. Kant contrasted the religions of rogation with his own rationalist understanding of Christianity:

> According to moral religion, however (*and, of all the public religions so far known, the Christian alone is of this type*), it is a fundamental principle that, to become a better human being, everyone must do as much as it is in his powers to do; and only then, if a human

being has not buried his innate talent, if he has made use of the original predisposition to the good in order to become a better human being, can he hope that what does not lie in his power will be made good by cooperation from above.[7]

In his religious thought, Kant emphasized the need to struggle, and he viewed prayer as a request to avoid such difficulties. Repentance, in fact, was a problem for Kant, inasmuch as he had difficulty reconciling (a) the need for free will as the basis of moral accountability and (b) the human tendency toward evil. Kant therefore argued that the one who prays might think that God would step in and make up the difference between the sinner's striving to be good and the actual moral value.

Kant also objected to the creation of a structure for church (or synagogue) leadership, in the form of priests or other religious professionals. He referred to this role as "priestcraft" and made it clear that such activity is not desirable: "*Priestcraft* is therefore the constitution of a church to the extent that a *fetish-service* is the rule; and this always obtains wherever statutory commands, rules of faith and observances, rather than principles of morality, make up the groundwork and the essence of the church."[8] It should be noted here that Kant also explicitly associated the negative aspects of "priestcraft" with Jewish ritual. He did not claim that Christianity was completely free of such wasted effort; however, Judaism, in his estimation, was nothing more than statutory laws and cultic ritual, with no concern for morality.

Kant's challenge here also required a response. One possibility would have been to agree with Kant's denunciation of ritual: as we see in the Pittsburgh Platform, the Reform Movement at that time had no regard for the value of ritual for the sake of ritual and sought only those expressions of Judaism that emphasize universal ethics—a position that echoed aspects of Kant's thought. Theologically speaking, however, the strongest, fullest liberal response came about three decades after the Pittsburgh Platform, from the pen of the German Jewish scholar and neo-Kantian philosopher Hermann Cohen; his masterwork *Religion of Reason Out of the Sources of Judaism* was published posthumously in the year after his death in 1918. Cohen did not argue for traditionalism in its full expression; to the contrary, he was in favor of a modernized Judaism. At the same time, he also saw a need to defend Jewish ritual practice against the charges leveled by Kant.

In responding to Kant's position, therefore, Cohen argued the following: (1) the Israelite sacrificial cult represented one step of many toward an ever-higher understanding of God; (2) the prophets were indeed the catalyst for the evolution for this process; (3) in contrast to Judaism, Christianity adopted a number of patently mythic elements, to its detriment; and (4) Judaism therefore has a better claim to the designation "religion of reason."

More specifically, Cohen argued that Christianity took a step backward when it tied its narrative of redemption to the sacrificial system, to achieve expiation through vicarious sacrifice. Cohen wrote, "It is a tragedy of monotheism that precisely the attribute of God's goodness, the forgiveness of sin, has endangered pure monotheism through the concept of the son of man. It endangers the concept of God as well as that of [hu]man[ity]."[9] In the view of Jewish studies scholar Avi Bernstein-Nahar, this position was taken in direct response to Kant's negative assessment of Judaism: "As a rejoinder to Kant, Cohen's *Religion* was a no-holds-barred attack on Christian supersessionism in general, and Kant's invidious distinction between Judaic legalism and Protestant morality in particular."[10] Cohen proposed a different understanding of repentance—one that was built upon the Jewish sources but was also innovative. In Cohen's view, the Christian concept of expiation through sacrifice was too closely tied to the ancient idolatrous practices of sacrifice. Rather than moving past the literal understanding of sacrifice—that is, toward the twin ideas that God rather than the priest grants atonement and the idea that the congregation is the necessary context for achieving this sense of atonement—Christianity was stuck in the literalism of needing God's punishment for sin. For Cohen, the need for punishment originated in the sinner, not in God. God's holiness necessarily precluded the need for punishment. And an ideal—for God is indeed an ideal—cannot demand human or animal sacrifice. Therefore, the sacrifices must have been done in order to appease human needs.[11]

Thus, in explaining how Judaism had a better claim to the designation "religion of reason," Cohen began with a Talmudic concept called *sh'gagah*, the accidental or unintentional sin. Specifically, he was referring to the idea that an *intentional* sin might be reckoned by God to be *accidental* if a person makes a concerted and wholehearted attempt at repentance.[12] If the sin was accidental, then it was necessarily forgiven. But the individual was not able to achieve this understanding on his or her own; the community's presence was needed, as was God's forgiveness. In Cohen's words:

> To err, to go astray, is [hu]man[ity]'s lot, but therefore *sh'gagah* is the limit of [hu]man[ity]'s fault. Whenever this limit is overstepped, only God knows what happens to [hu]man[ity]. Human wisdom is at a loss in the presence of the possibility of *evil* in [hu]man[ity]. The Day of Atonement maintains the fiction of the unshakable moral preservation of everything human: all [hu]man[ity]'s sin is *sh'gagah*. Therefore God can forgive without relinquishing his justice.[13]

This arrangement sidestepped the difficulty that Kant faced in reconciling free will with God's forgiveness: if humanity was born with evil in its heart, then there was no basis for moral accountability. Cohen objected, rather, by arguing that Kant's approach did not acknowledge the goodness of God in creating humanity as pure souls. God's love is such that any sins we might commit should be reckoned as accidental. All we need to do is turn and repent: "It is the essence of God to forgive the sin of [hu]man[ity]. This is the most important content of the correlation of God and [hu]man[ity]. Through goodness the result of this correlation becomes clarified and distinguished."[14] The correlation between God and humanity is the expression of the eternal hope of messianic redemption that is always present, because of God's goodness. In Cohen's words:

> Therefore no special *arrangements* in God's essence are necessary for the forgiveness of sin. Creation and revelation are the sufficient preconditions; they both create the holy spirit of [hu]man[ity]. And this holy spirit, whose self-preservation is accomplished by self-sanctification, is entirely secured against relapse into sin through God's goodness, whose particular task is forgiveness.[15]

We are, in essence, already forgiven even before the act of turning toward God.

Cohen argued for a more nuanced approach to the question of ritual than was offered by the rabbis of the Pittsburgh Platform roughly three decades earlier. Over the next century, the Reform Movement shifted its understanding of ritual and became more open to those rituals that were not exclusively ethical in their origins. At the time of the Pittsburgh Platform, however, the rabbis were interested in jettisoning anything that felt medieval or otherwise might appear "backward" in the American context.

The fifth point of the Pittsburgh Platform reflected the anti-Zionism of the American Reform Movement at the time. Much of the early political Zionism, particularly before the establishment of the State of Israel, focused on creating a "nation like any other nation" rather than a spiritual and religious homeland for Jews, an idea that found greatest resonance in Eastern Europe. Similar to the Jews of Central Europe, the American Jewish community did not experience the same kind of persecution and prejudice that made early Jewish nationalism such a compelling argument in Eastern and Central Europe. In fact, in the American context, this kind of political concern was much less urgent. As the historian Michael Meyer explains:

> The United States enshrined in its constitution the political equality for members of all religious groups for which European Jews were still struggling, in part by giving evidence for their modernity. Moreover, American Jewry was not forced into a narrow economic structure, nor did it possess the comprehensive corporate structure of its European counterparts or an authoritative rabbinate of the old style. From the start, American Jews were integrated into the general socio-political life to a degree that was only partially achieved in Central Europe even after a long process of modernization.[16]

Though the integration of the American Jewish community was imperfect at times, American Jews had genuine reason to feel at home in America. Eventually, however, rabbinical voices within the Reform Movement shifted their stance, even before the State of Israel was created, in response to events in Europe, as the need for a safe haven for Jews became more pressing.

The sixth point of the Pittsburgh Platform returned to the pluralism of the first point: "We recognize in Judaism a progressive religion, ever striving to be in accord with the postulates of reason.... Christianity and Islam, being daughter religions of Judaism, we appreciate their providential mission, to aid in the spreading of monotheistic and moral truth .... We extend the hand of fellowship to all who cooperate with us." This point likely reflected the convening rabbis' feeling of being at home in America: here it is indeed possible to create interfaith coalitions, though true cooperation occurred much later, after the Second World War. Note also, however, that it stated directly (contra Kant) that Judaism is indeed a religion—and a progressive one, at that.

The seventh point is also a rejoinder to Kant, for he had (wrongly) claimed that Judaism was not actually a religion in part because Jews did not believe in any kind of afterlife. As the seventh point stated point-blank: "We reassert the doctrine of Judaism that the soul is immortal." The next portion of this point, however, was a restatement of a once-radical Reform position. It had emerged in the decades prior, in response to ongoing scientific discoveries: "We reject as ideas not rooted in Judaism, the beliefs both in bodily resurrection and in Gehenna and Eden (Hell and Paradise) as abodes for everlasting punishment and reward." In earlier decades, this idea was radical enough to cause a congregation to consider firing their rabbi if he were to affirm this idea in a sermon. By the time of the Pittsburgh Platform, however, it had become much more common to explicitly acknowledge this belief.

Finally, we come to the eighth point: "In full accordance with the spirit of the Mosaic legislation, which strives to regulate the relations between rich and poor, we deem it our duty to participate in the great task of modern times, to solve, on the basis of justice and righteousness, the problems presented by the contrasts and evils of the present organization of society."

According to Jewish law, it is not possible to be ethical without giving to the poor; even the poor are expected to give to the poor, for it is considered an expression of human dignity to be able to fulfill one's ethical obligations in full. Hermann Cohen, for example, suggested that ethics should not merely be an ideal but also a call to action. As Cohen wrote, "It must not be a matter of indifference whether my morality and all [humanity's] morality remain dutiful striving only, sufficient in itself; rather, I have to take an interest in the question of whether the *ideal* has life and actuality."[17] In other words, an ethics that remains merely an ideal is no different than good intentions in the absence of action. Purity of intention, for example, is insufficient when addressing the concrete reality of feeding the poor. The mere intention to do something ethical sometime in the future is of little consequence to the one who is hungry right now. In this regard, Judaism prescribes specific moral actions that directly affect the welfare of others and articulates a concern for the weakest members of society, such as the widow, the stranger, and the orphan. The suffering of the stranger is both a demand and an opportunity for the discovery of the ethical self. As we see here, in both the Pittsburgh Platform's statement and Cohen's philosophical explanation, the Reform Movement's deep concern for alleviating poverty has a long history, rooted as it is in a theology of social action.

In the creation of the Pittsburgh Platform, the gathering of Reform rabbis demonstrated their willingness to step up and boldly state foundational principles. Though some of these points have changed in the intervening decades (for example, the Reform Movement has since reaffirmed the need for ritual and has also changed its basic stance with regard to political Zionism), this document charted a clear vision of a vital and energized American Reform Judaism, one that was genuinely willing to wrestle with the larger questions of meaning and practice in the context of emerging scientific and philosophical ideas. It was truly a "declaration of independence" for the nascent Reform Movement, a point of disruption that allowed for building something new.

NOTES

1. Stephen D. Temkin, *Isaac Mayer Wise: Shaping American Judaism* (Oxford: Littman Library, 1992), 289.
2. "Declaration of Principles: 1885 Pittsburgh Conference," CCAR, https://www.ccarnet.org/rabbinic-voice/platforms/article-declaration-principles/.
3. "No American has matched William James (1842–1910) in the breadth and depth of his psychological studies. . . . James was, in fact, the sponsor of an important American school of thought, of philosophy, known as pragmatism. In essence, he insisted that thinking is meant to be a prelude to and

a guide for action, that ideas and beliefs and values—what is called truth—
must pass the muster of significance, of consequence: a nuts-and-bolts
working test" (Robert Coles, introduction to *Selected Writings: William James*
[New York: Book-of-the-Month Club, 1997], xii).

4. The documentary hypothesis names the theory that the Hebrew Bible was
written by a series of editors—identified by the initials J, P, E, D, or R—
rather than by God.

5. Immanuel Kant, *Religion within the Boundaries of Mere Reason and Other Writings*, ed. and trans. Allen Wood and George di Giovanni (Cambridge: Cambridge University Press, 1998), 130.

6. Kant, *Religion*, 71.

7. Kant, *Religion*, 71; emphasis added.

8. Kant, *Religion*, 174.

9. Hermann Cohen, *Religion of Reason Out of the Sources of Judaism*, trans. Simon Kaplan (Oxford: Oxford University Press, 1994), 211.

10. Avi Bernstein-Nahar, "In the Name of a Narrative Education: Hermann Cohen and Historicism Reconsidered," in *Hermann Cohen's Ethics*, ed. Robert Gibbs (Leiden: Brill, 2006), 160.

11. These passages have been drawn from *Religion of Reason Out of the Sources of Judaism*, which is Cohen's masterwork. To get an overview of his thought, see Hermann Cohen, *Writings on Neo-Kantianism and Jewish Philosophy*, ed. Samuel Moyn and Robert S. Schine (Boston: Brandeis University Press, 2021).

12. See Babylonian Talmud, *Rosh HaShanah* 17b and *Yoma* 86b.

13. Cohen, *Religion*, 223.

14. Cohen, *Religion*, 213.

15. Cohen, *Religion*, 213–14.

16. Michael A. Meyer, *Judaism within Modernity: Essays on Jewish History and Religion* (Detroit: Wayne State University Press, 2001), 324.

17. Cohen, *Religion*, 21.

FOR FURTHER READING

Batnitzky, Leora. *How Judaism Became a Religion*. Princeton, NJ: Princeton University Press, 2013.

Beiser, Frederick C. *Hermann Cohen: An Intellectual Biography*. Oxford: Oxford University Press, 2018.

Diner, Hasia R. *The Jews of the United States, 1654 to 2000*. Berkeley: University of California Press, 2004.

Ellenson, David. *After Emancipation: Jewish Religious Responses to Modernity*. Cincinnati: Hebrew Union College Press, 2004.

Langton, Daniel. *Reform Judaism and Darwin: How Engaging with Evolutionary Theory Shaped American Jewish Religion*. Berlin: De Gruyter, 2019.

Meyer, Michael A. *Response to Modernity: A History of the Reform Movement in Judaism*. New York: Oxford University Press, 1988.

Moyn, Samuel, and Robert S. Schine, eds. *Writings on Neo-Kantianism and Jewish Philosophy*. Boston: Brandeis University Press, 2021.

Sarna, Jonathan. *American Judaism: A History*. New Haven: Yale University Press, 2019.

Wenger, Beth. *History Lessons: The Creation of American Jewish Heritage*. Princeton, NJ: Princeton University Press, 2012.

14

Power, Pragmatism, and Peoplehood
Mordecai Kaplan's Radical American Judaism

Rabbi Michael Marmur, PhD

N° PERSON HAS HAD A MORE CONSEQUENTIAL IMPACT on American Judaism than Mordecai Kaplan (1881–1983). His views on God, denominations, peoplehood, election, community, creativity, Zionism, education, prayer, and more have made a profound impression on the American Jewish experience. In his foundational 1934 work *Judaism as a Civilization*, he described and critiqued the main versions of Judaism as he saw them—Reform, Conservative, and Neo-Orthodox—and set out the need for a radically new approach to being a modern American Jew.

Mordecai Menachem Kaplan was himself a modern American Jew—quintessentially modern, fervently American, wholeheartedly a Jew. The intersection of these key characteristics within Kaplan gave rise to a radical new approach, one that continues to reverberate decades after his death, and not only within the Reconstructionist Movement that he inspired.

Modern

A passionate advocate of science, rationality, democracy, aesthetics, and notions of progress and enlightenment, Kaplan was convinced that the changes wrought in the contemporary world were irrevocable and fundamental in nature. For the first years of his life, in Lithuania (which he left at the age of eight), and then in the United States, Kaplan lived a conventionally pious Jewish life, steeped in the practices and acquainted with the doctrines of traditional Orthodoxy. As he was to recall some decades later, he came to a point of crisis when he had become disqualified, in my own mind and conscience, to function as an Orthodox rabbi, [as] the informal instruction which I had been receiving from the late Arnold B. Ehrlich . . . finally shattered my belief in *Torah min Ha-Shamayim*. The traditional outlook which I had acquired from my Jewish Seminary, was entirely dispelled. Simultaneously, however, with the loss of my Orthodox perspective on Judaism, there was forming in my mind, with the aid of what I learned from Ahad Ha'am, on the one hand, and from Matthew Arnold on the other, together with the aid of my post-graduate studies in philosophy, sociology and education, a new perspective on Judaism."[1]

Mordecai Kaplan was a modernist in the sense that once he had been exposed to critical modes of thinking, previously held beliefs were untenable because they had become implausible. In the terminology of later theorists, Kaplan experienced in his own life a disenchantment, an understanding that the structures of myth and argument used to bolster a traditional worldview had crumbled. Rather than dispense with his Jewish commitments, he sought new ways of preserving and strengthening them.

Kaplan's mention of Arnold Ehrlich (1848–1919) in the passage quoted above is telling. Ehrlich, who had come to America at age thirty, was a Jew of immense learning, schooled both in the classical texts of Jewish tradition and in contemporary literature and thought. Kaplan recalls that Ehrlich "taught me to penetrate through the vast layers of traditional commentaries to the rock-bottom original intent of the biblical authors. In doing so, he undermined my belief in the Mosaic authorship of the Torah and in the historicity of the miracles."[2]

The other figures mentioned in Kaplan's recollection of his modernist awakening conform, each in his own way, to this pattern—individuals prepared to stand outside accepted norms in pursuit of truth. Ahad Ha'am (the pen name of Asher Ginsberg, 1856–1927) offered a post-Enlightenment critique of traditional Jewish structures of thought and institutions of life and pioneered a cultural Zionist sensibility. While political Zionists were preoccupied with changing the physical condition of the Jews, the cultural Zionists focused more on such questions as the promotion of Jewish values, the Hebrew language, and the like. From the English poet Matthew Arnold (1822–88), Kaplan took an aesthetic and ethical appreciation of Hebraic culture and the rejection of religion founded on miracles in favor of religion founded on its natural truth.[3] Prominent among other giants of European modernity who exercised a palpable influence on Kaplan was Émile Durkheim (1858–1917); traces of his sociological method are to be found throughout Kaplan's work.

Common to all these influences is the legacy of Baruch Spinoza (1632–77), the philosopher whose ideas contributed much to the rise of a modern sensibility.[4] Spinoza was prepared to risk opprobrium and even excommunication for the sake of truth as he saw it. Kaplan's own approach privileged the continued flourishing of the Jewish people to a greater degree than Spinoza, but he nonetheless held him up as a beacon of creativity.

In *Judaism as a Civilization*, Kaplan outlined three essential characteristics of modern thought: reliance on the scientific approach for knowledge, human welfare as the criterion of the good, and an emphasis on aesthetic experience and creativity. He regarded these three developments as elemental and foundational but was not unaware of their potential threat to the established order of Jewish life and to the prospect of Jewish continuity. His entire project can be seen as a response to this challenge: how to articulate a vision for Jewish life in line with the insights and dictates of modernity, that is, how to ride its wave and not be drowned by it.

Kaplan was convinced that modernity represents a paradigm-changing challenge: "Our Jewish life is as unlike the life of our grandparents as the automobile is unlike the buggy. Therefore, we should not expect Jewish life to operate on the basis of wants which they felt, but which we do not feel."[5] Rote repetition of beliefs and practices from an earlier time with no attempt to understand and express them in a new way is, Kaplan argued, a strategy that was bound to fail.

Kaplan went beyond presenting traditional Jewish ideas in terms palatable to a modern sensibility. Indeed, he regarded such a cosmetic procedure as futile and intellectually dishonest. Rather, he was convinced that the modern and the contemporary had to provide the backdrop for any compelling version of Judaism. In a telling diary entry, he wrote:

"Perhaps if I worked hard enough . . . I might succeed in proving that our salvation lies in learning what to live for in the here and now, whether as Jews or as members of any people."[6] Salvation is not to be earned by escaping the contemporary, but rather by finding a way truly and fully to occupy it. In his pragmatic optimism, his belief in democracy and progress, his embrace of science and history, and his conviction that civilization is molded in the encounter with the here and now, Kaplan was a thoroughgoing modernist.

America

Kaplan believed that America was founded on modernity's finest principles and that it could become a vehicle for their advancement. As he recorded in his diary in 1918, "To love America is simply to love myself, for it is only in this blessed country that I could have achieved what I most value in myself, relentless honesty of mind. The Jewish people gave me the problem to work on, but only America gave me the means, the leisure and the freedom to understand the problem."[7]

America did more than provide the conditions for Kaplan's work to flourish. He also thought directly about the religious, political, and cultural significance of America in religious terms, as exemplified in his 1951 compilation *The Faith of America: Prayers, Readings and Songs for the Celebration of American Holidays.* In a 1960 work, he declared that the task for American Jews is "to promulgate an indigenous civic religion for the American people that shall act as a unifying influence, uniting all Americans regardless of race, creed, or status, without being authoritative or coercive."[8]

Kaplan contended that the challenge of America would demand that every sinew be strained for Jewish life to prevail and flourish. He penned these prescient words in 1934:

> It is by no means a foregone conclusion that Judaism in America is destined to live. It all depends upon what the next generation will do. Already the maelstrom of life is about to tear up Judaism by the roots, and nothing less than a heroic effort will prevent it from being swept away completely. If Jewish endeavor be merely haphazard and impelled by blind habit, Judaism's day in America is done. But, if that endeavor be directed by an alert intelligence

and a high idealism, Judaism will live.[9]

The maelstrom of life to which Kaplan refers here is presumably the particular circumstances of life in that era, including the impact of assimilation and the Depression. Judaism would need to find a response to the challenges posed by the loosening of traditional ties, the growth of extremist political movements, the risks of financial adversity, and more. American thinkers such as Josiah Royce (1855–1916), Ralph Waldo Emerson (1803–82), and William James (1842–1910) and American Jewish leaders such as Cyrus Adler (1863–1940) helped provide a distinctly American stamp to Kaplan's approach. No influence was greater on him than that of John Dewey (1859–1952), as can be adduced from Kaplan's entry for June 2, 1952, the day after Dewey's death:

> I am indebted to him for the method of thought and world outlook that have enabled me to make sense out of the buzzing confusion of the various modern attempts to fill the vacuum created by the desuetude of tradition. Dewey has helped me arrive at a pragmatic reinterpretation of Bible and Rabbinics. His principle that "an activity which does not have worth enough to be carried on for its own sake cannot be an effective preparation for something else" has encouraged me to conceive of Judaism as a this-worldly civilization.[10]

Dewey's willingness to approach traditional problems with unconventional categories of thought as well as his clarity and directness, his commitment to democracy and rationality, and a preference for pragmatics over metaphysics—these and other qualities of Dewey found their way into Kaplan's discourse.

In Kaplan, Jewish thought found a distinctively American voice. He eschewed abstruse philosophical formulations and picayune legalisms in favor of a pragmatic and organic worldview. Rather than attempting to squeeze reality into existing categories of thought and practice, Kaplan understood that these categories would need to bend and grow, as they have done in the past, to meet the contours of a new day. He accused the Jewish establishment of failing to appreciate the enormity of the challenge: "Most Jewish leaders, whether lay or religious, act as though the structure of Jewish life may have been somewhat shaken, but not as though it were in danger of collapsing. Either they are unconcerned about the future of the Jewish people, or they fail to realize that *the inevitable consequence of the generally accepted version of democratic nationalism is to render Judaism superfluous to the Jew.*"[11]

Kaplan felt blessed to be an American, but he also appreciated that the social and ideological processes he saw unfolding placed Jewish continuity in peril. The internal logic of what he describes here as democratic nationalism encourages citizens to commit their energies to the social collective at the expense of parochial commitments. In his understanding, continuity would only be ensured through flexibility, engagement, and vitality; nostalgia, inertia, and complacency will not be equal to the task.

Mordecai Kaplan called for Jews to maintain their distinct commitments as a people, a civilization, situated both within the wider American context and the wider Jewish world. In Kaplan's reading, the Judaism of the Old World had been predicated on authoritarian and hierarchical assumptions. In order to achieve a successful transition to the New World, radical reconstruction would be called for. None of the available options—among them intransigent resistance to change, vapid declarations of liberal slogans, abandonment of Jewish identity—were attractive to Kaplan. He believed that the challenge and promise of modernity and America demanded that Judaism bring all its powers of radical creativity to bear.

Jew

Kaplan was aware that the implications of his radical views might be construed as a death sentence for Jewish continuity. After all, if the truths of bygone eras were exposed as specious or at least unsupportable in our present time, why continue practices whose rationale was now defunct?

> The answer is that, as Jews, we feel impelled to maintain the continuity and growth of the Jewish people. There can be no ultimate good or salvation for us, either as individuals or as a group, unless we are permitted to express ourselves creatively as Jews. The conditions essential to our salvation must therefore *include* those which enable us to experience continuity with the Jewish past, as well as make possible a Jewish future.[12]

This expression, "the conditions essential to our salvation," is pure Kaplan. He adopts a traditional religious concept and translates it into a modern sociological context. Jews cannot realize their salvation if they are cut off from the continuity of Jewish history. They need to be rooted in the Jewish past in order to realize a meaningful future as Jews. Thoroughly modern and proudly American, Kaplan was convinced that the way to express these commitments, the way to live in dignity and solidarity with all peoples, was to live fully within one's own identity. Tired distinctions between religious and national dimensions of this identity were no longer fit for purpose. Top-down authoritative theologies based on the notion of a supernatural commanding God could no longer be accepted and were to be replaced with the notion of Judaism not as a creed but as a "civilization, centered in loyalty to the body of the Jewish people throughout the world" and expressed through "autonomous institutions of learning, congregations and societies."[13]

Judaism had to be set on a new footing. "The modern Jew cannot… look to the Torah as a source of authority, in the sense that whatever it permits is right and whatever it forbids is wrong. He reverses the process and says, '*Whatever is right should be incorporated into our Torah, and whatever is wrong should be eliminated from our Torah.*'"[14] While the Conservative Movement presented itself as the continuation of the age-old process of Jewish law, Kaplan (who taught in the seminary of that movement for decades) believed that the authoritarian system of Jewish law should be replaced by a much more democratic approach, in keeping with acceptable American norms. The Judaism of tomorrow would be committed to the eradication of inequalities and social ills for all and would rid itself of parochialism and chauvinism.

Kaplan was a Hebraist and a Zionist, and much of his energy was devoted to questions of Jewish education. He was convinced both of the significance of perpetuating Jewish life and of the impossibility of fulfilling this task without a high degree of Jewish literacy. The core motivation for seeking to advance Jewish life, its value proposition, was that one's Jewishness is part of who one is:

> The value of Jewish tradition to the modern Jew is not dependent on its assertion of superiority over other traditions. . . . Whether

good, bad, or indifferent from a moralistic standpoint, the Jewish tradition—with its heroisms and events, its laws, struggles, tragedies, defeats, dreams, and yearnings—constitutes the actual experiences of the people. Jews should want their children to weave these experiences into their own world, to appropriate them as an integral part of their own consciousness.[15]

For Kaplan, a Jew is a Jew not as a result of some supernatural status awarded from on high, but as a sociological and psychological fact. The motivating factor in Jewish identity was not perceived by Kaplan as a revelation or a doctrine, but as an energy, combined with a deep sense of Jewish pride. Already in a diary of 1914 he writes, "The dynamic force in Judaism is none other than the socio-psychic vitality of the Jewish people. The problem, therefore, cannot be reduced to a question of preserving certain abstract concepts whether they belong to the past or present. Our only concern is that the Jewish people be worthy of being Israel."[16]

The key aspects of Kaplan's approach stem from the intersection of these three foundational aspects of Kaplan's make-up—modern, American, and Jew. His views were more radical and unsettling than most, as his 1945 excommunication surely illustrates.[17] The fact that Kaplan came from the heart of the Orthodox consensus and moved away from it by the power of his convictions made his thought more threatening than that of an outsider. Like Spinoza in seventeenth-century Amsterdam, Kaplan challenged Orthodox beliefs concerning the election of the people Israel, the nature of divinity, and the sanctity of the Bible. Both looked to the well-being of society as a whole, Jews and non-Jews alike. The wording of Kaplan's excommunication provides powerful testimony to the impact his views had on the Orthodox establishment of his day:

> The leaders of the people, rabbis of Greater New York and surroundings, heads of yeshivos, Hasidic leaders, and scholars from the great yeshivos of this community, gathering together . . . because of the terrible scandal done in a high-handed and openly insolent manner by a certain person called Dr. Mordecai Kaplan, in publishing a new monstrosity by the name of *Siddur Tefihlos* in which he demonstrated total heresy and a complete disbelief in the God of Israel and in the principles of the law of the Torah of

Israel—and the future of a heresy that continues like this who can contemplate?—therefore, it has been decided unanimously . . . to excommunicate him and to separate him from the community of Israel until he fully repents in accordance with law and custom.[18]

Kaplan knew viscerally that the life he imagined for the generation of his grandchildren would be modern and enlightened, American and democratic, and thoroughly Jewish. He applied his formidable analytical capacities to thinking through what would have to change in order for this result to become possible. His radical conclusion was that a reconstruction of Jewish life was called for, one in which the metaphysical basis of the old paradigm was replaced with new ideas, new liturgies, new theologies.

Power, Pragmatism, Peoplehood

Three important words in Kaplan's vocabulary were *power*, *pragmatism*, and *peoplehood*. In an essay on Jewish ethics, Kaplan asserted that "life is inherently power."[19] It's not that we live according to the dictates of raw power alone: the rational and universal dimensions of our existence give form to the content of human life, while the spiritual and eternal dimensions give it purpose. Nonetheless, Kaplan does believe that we are part of a system of being animated by energy. It is in this context that his conception of God can be best understood.

Kaplan strove to imbue the word "God" with a meaning that could work in the contemporary American context. Kaplan's God was not a supernatural personality casting a divine hand upon human affairs so as to influence history. Such a notion, he thought, was no longer supportable to those who had become exposed to modern concepts of rationality, causality, and science. He was not compelled by the notion of some abstracted philosophical source of ethical obligation, described by many of liberal Jewish thinkers under the clear influence of Immanuel Kant. Rather, he proposed a God of progress, a process unfolding through human history, a power conducive to salvation. He employed the term "soterics" from the Greek term *soteria*, relating to the doctrine of salvation—the power moving individuals and society toward a better tomorrow.

Throughout the many decades of his active career, Kaplan staunchly rejected the claim that this emphasis on power and process was tantamount to atheism or that it was a total break from previous Jewish attempts to describe divinity. In a 1956 work, Kaplan developed his argument: "What are life, knowledge, goodness, if not processes? They are certainly not beings or entities. Since God is life, knowledge, goodness, what else can He be but a Process?"[20] In the spirit of his comment, made in conversation in the early 1970s, that "my conception of God is entirely derived from social psychology,"[21] Kaplan's God was an expression of the human will to live and to strive for the betterment of the world. As human beings become aware of themselves as persons, they also "become cognizant of the help of a Power or powers to conquer obstacles."[22] That which is most distinctive about the self comes to be known as soul, and the power or powers become known as God.

It might be imagined that an approach influenced by pragmatism and sociological theory would advance a form of moral relativism, but this was not the case. In one of the central paradoxes of his approach, Kaplan rooted his ethics in his naturalist conception of God. Kaplan's theology was radical, but it was firmly rooted in a conception of God calling out for moral action, even if this God was not the fierce parent or personalized legislator imagined in former times:

> To believe in God is to be sure of the distinction between good and evil. We then know the difference between conscience and the fear of what others may think of us or do to us, if we do not behave in the way they should like. We then recognize in the urge to decency an inherent sense of responsibility, by which we share in the creative activity of God. Every experience of success in overcoming the misery of cowardice, envy, hate and greed is an experience of God. Faith in God is faith in the possibility of such achievements, without which we inevitably sink into moral defeatism.[23]

Kaplan's pragmatism leads him away from abstruse philosophical speculations and toward the question of how beliefs and practices serve the social good, how ideas are to be understood in the context of human relations and natural conditions. In an important passage in *Judaism as a*

Civilization, Kaplan sets out how tradition could be understood in pragmatic terms:

> We must evolve a method of interpretation which, though it regard the traditional religious teachings and institutions as a product of social life, reflecting the limitations of the various periods of their origin, will yet discover to what extent these teachings and institutions made for faith, salvation and loyalty. By this means the pragmatic implications of the traditional teachings will be revealed and developed. Thus the forgotten mood of a people's civilization can be recaptured and given a "spiritual contemporaneousness."[24]

New values would have to inspire continuing the ancient rites and customs. They would no longer be understood as mitzvot commanded by a supernatural divine personality, but rather as folkways (close in meaning to the Hebrew *minhag*, often translated as "custom") and *sancta*—the persons, events, texts, places, concepts, and actions sanctified by a particular civilization. "To make revitalization possible, the *sancta* of religion must be reinterpreted in each generation so that their meanings are relevant to the needs of that generation. *Tradition must not be a source of authority*, imposing restrictions on the creativity of later generations, *but a source of wisdom and moral awaking new creative powers*. When *sancta* have become meaningless, they cease, in the nature of the case, to be *sancta*."[25]

Rather than restrict Judaism within the unsuitable confines of the term "religion," Kaplan preferred the expansive notion of civilization. Judaism is what happens when the Jewish people responds with creativity to the challenges of the day. Such a definition leads to a position both more traditional and more radical than some other expressions of modern non-Orthodox Judaism: more traditional because in Kaplan's reading the folkways and *sancta* are not to be discarded lightly; more radical because his understanding of their source and purpose was less warm and fuzzy, less platitudinous, and less pious than some of the other ideas on offer in the marketplace of modern Jewish ideas.

Mordecai Kaplan believed that a process (which he called revaluation) could ensure the continued vigor and relevance of Jewish life for a new generation. If Reform spoke of the doctrine of informed choice, whereby every aspect of traditional practice would be held up to examination and only those aspects that stood the test of credulity and ethical probity would make the cut, Kaplan's approach was to embrace a broad swath of practices and to seek to reinterpret them in light of our contemporary commitments.

Many scholars think the word "peoplehood" was coined by Kaplan.[26] In any case, it was he who brought it into parlance and gave it currency. Like God, it was to be understood and explained in pragmatic terms. Any notion that the Jews enjoyed divine favor was to be rejected as meaningless. Kaplan's God did not have favorites and did not make choices. In specifically Jewish terms, peoplehood implied the acknowledgment of their status as "an international people with Israel as its cultural center."[27] To live out this peoplehood did not mean rejection of the other culture in which one lived, but it did demand the acquisition of a level of cultural literacy (including a focus on the reborn State of Israel and the Hebrew language), to facilitate meaningful engagement with one's Jewishness. This cultural literacy projects Judaism not only as a system of rites and customs, not only as a bookshelf, but rather Judaism in all its complex manifestations—Judaism as a civilization: "The alternative to regarding Judaism as a specific tradition which consists of supernaturally revealed laws and teachings is to regard Judaism as a civilization which is both the product and the incentive of the will to live as a people."[28]

There is one belief characteristic of traditional Judaism that Kaplan insisted could not be reinterpreted, but instead had to be rejected, and this was the notion that the Jewish people was chosen by God. The doctrine of election was objectionable on rational theological grounds, just as it had been for Spinoza three centuries earlier. Spinoza's naturalism, like Kaplan's trans-natural position, could make no sense of the idea that God chose this or that people. "The idea of Israel as the Chosen People must . . . be understood as belonging to a thought-world which we no longer inhabit."[29] In Kaplan's view, the idea that the Jews were chosen by God was to be rejected both on rational and on pragmatic grounds, and in its stead he proposed the more innocuous concept of vocation. By this term he meant dedication to the civilization of one's people not for reasons of chauvinism or exclusion, but in order "to promulgate, by its way of life, the truth of the universal presence of God in all religions, and the universal obligation of every man to use his traditional *sancta* for glorifying not merely his own people or church, but mankind as a whole."[30]

In my reading, Kaplan was alarmed at the possibility that Jewish nationalism could yield the perverse fruits visible in other twentieth-century nationalisms. This may well have strengthened his conviction that any trace of a doctrine of divine election must be eradicated and that his espousal of a version of Ahad Ha'am's cultural Zionism should be embraced. He hoped that Jewish expressions of peoplehood would be a gateway to a truly universalist worldview: "That the Jewish people, through its present struggle for existence, should help to eliminate the dross of collective selfishness and sacred egoism from modern nationalism, and render it essentially a means of social creativity and individual betterment would, indeed, be a vindication of the divine right of peoples to retain their individuality."[31]

Kaplan spearheaded the idea of the Jewish center. Building Jewish life exclusively around the synagogue was no longer a feasible option. Instead, Jewish centers should cater to the needs of the community far beyond the liturgical and ritual domains. To some degree, the Jewish community in North America and elsewhere, not least in the synagogues themselves, has been Kaplanized. Wherever macrame, Yiddish, racquetball, and services are on offer, traces of Kaplan's vision of community can be found.

Mordecai Kaplan believed that the world was moving inexorably away from the obscurantism of the past—we can but wonder what he would have made of developments in America and around the world of recent decades. His copious writings, stretched as they are over many decades, demonstrate a consistent vision: "The segment of the Jewish people which still subscribes to the supernaturalist version of Jewish history is rapidly diminishing. However, given the humanist version of Jewish historic group consciousness and conscience, the most important activity for Jews to engage in would be to proceed with its formal self-reconstitution as a self-governing, self-educative and self-perpetuating people."[32]

"A self-governing, self-educative and self-perpetuating people"—to this vision Kaplan dedicated his prodigious energies. Many of those who rejected him with ferocity are more Kaplanian than they might care to admit. He was by any measure a disruptive presence in American Judaism. More than a voice of disruption, Kaplan was a power that makes for reconstruction.

NOTES

1. See Jeffrey S. Gurock and Jacob J. Schacter, *A Modern Heretic and a Traditional Community: Mordecai M. Kaplan, Orthodoxy, and American Judaism* (New York: Columbia University Press, 1997), 33.
2. Mordecai M. Kaplan, "The Way I Have Come," in *Mordecai M. Kaplan: An Evaluation*, ed. Ira Eisenstein and Eugene Kohn (New York: Jewish Reconstructionist Foundation, 1952), 289.
3. Meir Ben-Horin, "Defining God: Arnoldian Elements in Kaplan's Theology," *Jewish Social Studies* 43, no. 3/4 (1981): 189–214.
4. For an excellent exposition of Spinoza's influence on Kaplan's thought, see Shaul Magid, "The Spinozistic Spirit in Mordecai Kaplan's Revaluation of Judaism," *Modern Judaism* 20, no. 2 (2000): 159–80.
5. Mordecai M. Kaplan, *The Future of the American Jew* (New York: Macmillan, 1949), 13.
6. From February 27, 1946. See Mel Scult, *The Radical American Judaism of Mordecai M. Kaplan* (Bloomington: Indiana University Press, 2014), 159–60.
7. Riv-Ellen Prell, "America, Mordecai Kaplan, and the Postwar Jewish Youth Revolt," *Jewish Social Studies: History, Culture, Society*, n.s., 12, no. 2 (2006): 158.
8. Mordecai M. Kaplan, *Dynamic Judaism: The Essential Writings of Mordecai M. Kaplan*, ed. Emanuel S. Goldsmith and Mel Scult (New York: Schocken Books; Reconstructionist Press, 1985), 169.
9. Mordecai M. Kaplan, *Judaism as a Civilization: Toward a Reconstruction of American-Jewish Life* (Philadelphia: Jewish Publication Society, 1994), 81.
10. Scult, *Radical American Judaism*, 83. There are many books and articles outlining Dewey's significance. For an outstanding example of his approach, see John Dewey, *Democracy and Education: An Introduction to the Philosophy of Education* (New York: Macmillan, 1916).
11. Kaplan, *Future of the American Jew*, 107.
12. Kaplan, *Future of the American Jew*, 179.
13. Mordecai M. Kaplan, *A New Zionism* (New York: Theodor Herzl Foundation, 1955), 112.
14. Kaplan, *Future of the American Jew*, 382.
15. From Kaplan's 1970 work *The Religion of Ethical Nationhood*, quoted in Kaplan, *Dynamic Judaism*, 206.
16. Mel Scult, *Judaism Faces the Twentieth Century: A Biography of Mordecai M. Kaplan* (Detroit: Wayne State University Press, 1993), 180.

17. See Zachary Silver, "The Excommunication of Mordecai Kaplan," *American Jewish Archives Journal* 62, no. 1 (2010): 21–48.
18. Text of the Decree of Excommunication: https://kaplancenter.org/believing/the-excommunication-of-mordecai-kaplan/herem-text/.
19. Quoted in Kaplan, *Dynamic Judaism*, 174.
20. From *Questions Jews Ask*, quoted in Kaplan, *Dynamic Judaism*, 74.
21. Mordecai M. Kaplan and Arthur A. Cohen, *If Not Now, When? Toward a Reconstitution of the Jewish People* (New York: Schocken Books, 1973), 113.
22. Kaplan, *Future of the American Jew*, 171.
23. Kaplan, *Future of the American Jew*, 202.
24. Kaplan, *Judaism as a Civilization*, 386.
25. Kaplan, *Future of the American Jew*, 49.
26. See Noam Pianko, *Jewish Peoplehood: An American Innovation* (New Brunswick, NJ: Rutgers University Press, 2015).
27. From *Questions Jews Ask*, quoted in Kaplan, *Dynamic Judaism*, 57.
28. Kaplan, *Future of the American Jew*, 377.
29. Kaplan, *Future of the American Jew*, 211.
30. Kaplan, *Future of the American Jew*, 230.
31. Kaplan, *Future of the American Jew*, 93.
32. Kaplan and Cohen, *If Not Now*, 30–31.

For Further Reading

Goldsmith, Emanuel S. "Mordecai M. Kaplan's Synthesis of Judaism and American Religious Naturalism." *American Journal of Theology and Philosophy* 11, no. 1 (1990): 5–23.

Goldsmith, Emanuel S., Mel Scult, and Robert M. Seltzer, eds. *The American Judaism of Mordecai M. Kaplan.* New York: New York University Press, 1990.

Kaplan, Mordecai M. *The Purpose and Meaning of Jewish Existence: A People in the Image of God.* Philadelphia: Jewish Publication Society, 1964), 196.

———. "The Way I Have Come." In *Mordecai M. Kaplan: An Evaluation*, by Ira Eisenstein and Eugene Kohn, 283–321. New York: Jewish Reconstructionist Foundation, 1952.

Pianko, Noam. "Reconstructing Judaism, Reconstructing America: The Sources and Functions of Mordecai Kaplan's 'Civilization.' *Jewish Social Studies: History, Culture, Society*, n.s., 12, no. 2 (2006): 39–55.

PART FIVE

Contemporary Innovations

15

The Breakup
Rethinking American Jewish Literary History

Adam Rovner, PhD

J EWISH AMERICAN literary critic Leslie Fiedler claimed in a well-
known essay, "The Breakthrough" (1958), that Jewish writers had
only first begun to "play a critical role in the total development of American literature" in the 1930s.[1] The vanguard he noted as having played
this role included Michael Gold, Henry Roth, and Nathaniel West.
After glossing some of the early work of these authors in the first part
of his essay, Fiedler turned to consider his own time period, the 1950s.
He contrasted Jewish writers representative of the "simple-minded lib-
eral-middlebrow,"[2] including Budd Schulberg (*What Makes Sammy Run*),
Irwin Shaw (*The Young Lions*), and Herman Wouk (*The Caine Mutiny*),
with the "highbrow," which included Saul Bellow, Bernard Malamud,
and Delmore Schwartz. Both the middlebrow and highbrow authors had
made a "breakthrough" in the postwar era, Fiedler opined, but only the
highbrow authors really mattered to the "total development of American literature." All nine of these representative middle- and highbrow
Jewish writers from the 1930s and 1950s are men—as are twenty-five of
the twenty-seven others Fiedler mentions by name in his essay. Fiedler's
assumptions have become so authoritative that they have prevented many
critics and readers from considering the significant role Jewish literature
played in the "total development of American literature" even before the
postwar era. In tracing the impact of Jewish authors on American readers, my purpose throughout this chapter will be to demonstrate how the
consumption of Jewish fiction by non-Jewish Americans disrupts both
the history of American Jewish social influence in the twentieth century
and the understanding of how Americans encountered Jews after the

age of immigration. The mass circulation of Jewish fiction has been overlooked by mainstream Jewish literary historiography. This chapter offers a broader conception of the historical processes of Jewish fiction's dissemination as a way to consider what has been both included in and excluded from an always evolving American Jewish self-understanding.

Fiedler axiomatically asserts that although "the thirties mark the mass entry of the Jewish writer into American fiction . . . there are no major triumphs."[3] Fiedler's claim that there were "no major triumphs" in the decade is puzzling given that he praises *Call It Sleep* lavishly in the same piece. Still, his explicit contention is that a hierarchy of aesthetic achievement—"major triumphs"—may be objectively determined; his implicit supposition is that the corpus of what comprises American fiction can be readily identified. In other words, Fiedler suggests by his selection of authors that American fiction must be written in English, and he assumes that aesthetic class systems can be confidently identified (e.g., middlebrow versus highbrow; minor triumphs versus major triumphs). Indeed, Fiedler clarifies that writers representative of the middlebrow, while they might be committed to the "high-minded literature of social reform,"[4] cannot escape their prevailing assent to bourgeois values and the pieties of "whatever is thoroughly unexceptionable."[5] However, those writers who occupy the highbrow terrain are characterized by "attitudes of dissent" that render them "more closely kin . . . to European intellectuals than to more traditional American writers."[6] Thus Fiedler's exploration of American Jewish novelists leads him to conclude that the more they dissent from bourgeois values, the more elevated their achievements, and the more precisely they evoke a European sensibility. There is an irony in his assessment that Jewish American literature is better when it is more European, but this of course accords precisely with Fiedler's preferred aesthetics.

Fiedler's historical approach to the period of the 1930s through late 1950s and his assumptions about the hierarchy of the American Jewish literary system still exert a powerful influence. Troubling ideologies lie behind Fiedler's normalization of distinctions between the middlebrow and the highbrow, ideologies that still dominate criticism of American and Jewish arts and letters.[7] One of the problems with an uncomplicated identification and concomitant celebration of the highbrow is that readers and scholars thereby miss an entire set of Jewish American texts.[8] To remedy this absence, I would like to break with Fiedler's elitism and focus on popular Jewish literature of the 1930s, specifically those works considered middlebrow, or what Gordon Hutner has referred to less pejoratively as "better fiction."[9]

Better fiction disrupts the idea of what sort of fiction matters and influences readers. It may not be the "best" fiction or attain the status of "high art," but it is also not formula fiction or pulp fiction. Better fiction was certainly not considered impoverished by editors, publishers, critics, reviewers, translators, and hundreds of thousands of readers at the time of its appearance. Better fiction is just that: it is better than formula or "genre" fiction, though typically not considered as enduring as the highbrow "classics" or "masterpieces" we so often venerate. Of course, classics only rarely achieved popularity in their day and are often rediscovered by later generations of scholars and teachers, who then canonize them. By definition, novels that endure, novels that transcend their particular era or context, are anomalous. They cannot, therefore, be broadly representative of an era, either aesthetically or ideologically.[10] As a set, better fiction exists as more representative of an era than classics. Therefore, the set of better fiction has much to teach us about the concerns, demands, values, and ideologies of the past—as well as of the ideologies of those who have demeaned or ignored better fiction over the decades.

But how can researchers and scholars of Jewish literature determine the set of better fiction—Jewish fiction—from nearly one hundred years ago? How can those interested in the history of Jewish letters adequately define what constitutes better fiction in a manner that prevents the intrusion of our contemporary, subjective prejudices? One answer is to use the selection lists of Book-of-the-Month Club, which served as the most significant arbiter of better fiction in its day. As historian of reading William St. Clair has indicated, "Any study of the consequences of the reading of the past ought to consider the print which was actually read, not some modern selection."[11] By exposing the ideologies that undergird the aesthetic valuations that have been in place since Fiedler's seminal essay, we can extrapolate a political economy of middle-class Jewish fiction in the American 1930s and disrupt an aesthetic that obscures how Americans encountered Jewish figures (both authors and their characters). A politi-

cal or ideological economy of reading "trac[es] the effects of the governing structures [e.g., management, trade, prices, distribution] on texts,
books, access, readerships, and consequential mentalities."[12] Exploring
how these "governing structures" inform the "total development" of the
American literary system shows how Fiedler and his heirs provided only
a very partial understanding of the Jewish "breakthrough" in American
letters. Uncovering the rich seams of Jewish fiction that run through the
American literary landscape allows us the opportunity to grapple with
complex questions of class as well as gender; popular fiction has long
been seen as déclassé ("middlebrow") and typically has been gendered
female. The overlap in these categorizations is itself indicative of troubling ideologies and worthy of disruption.

The majority of American readers of the 1930s belonged to households
that were economically sufficient—at least enough to allow for leisure to
read—though prone to downward social mobility during the Depression years. These readers were reasonably well educated and sought to
demonstrate their aesthetic discrimination. Their class aspirations likewise indicated a growing convergence between education and prosperity
in the United States. This market share, this broadly socially conformist
demographic, defined the membership of the Book-of-the-Month Club
in those years. The original chairman of the selection committee of the
Book-of-the-Month Club, Yale professor and influential editor Henry
Seidel Canby (1878–1961), described the typical club reader as someone
"who has passed through the usual formal education in literature . . . who,
without calling himself a *litterateur*, would be willing to assert that he was
fairly well-read and reasonably fond of good reading."[13] Canby uses the
masculine pronoun to characterize his average club subscriber, but we
can credibly deduce that a large percentage—if not the majority—of club
members were, in fact, women.

Book-of-the-Month Club membership was profitably recruited
from sales lists that included "buyers of the better magazines, gift-shop
mail-order buyers . . . students in charm and glamour courses, alumni
of most colleges, high school teachers, and principals."[14] Since women
would be well represented on such lists, many subscribers were assuredly
female. Though data is not available for the 1930s, women made up the
majority of club subscribers through the 1940s and much of the 1950s.[15]

Likewise, the Book-of-the-Month Club adhered to a distribution model—the mail-order "club"—that had targeted American women, especially housewives, since the 1880s.[16] One reason middlebrow fiction has largely been dismissed from critical consideration may be its strong historical and social connection to women and their reading practices.[17]

Much like parlor book clubs today, Book-of-the-Month Club members read family sagas, regional realism, melodramas, as well as nostalgic historical fiction. Club selections of inarguably American fiction in the long 1930s—which I define as lasting from January 1930 to the US entry into World War II in December 1941—provide familiar examples of better fiction and of its representative genres: Willa Cather (*Shadows on the Rock*, 1931, and *Sapphira and the Slave Girl*, 1941), Pearl S. Buck (*The Good Earth*, 1931, and *The Patriot*, 1939), Margaret Mitchell (*Gone with the Wind*, 1936), John Steinbeck (*Of Mice and Men*, 1937), Richard Wright (*Native Son*, 1940), and William Saroyan (*My Name Is Aram*, 1941). These authors are all recognizable names today, and their works sometimes appear in high school and college courses. Work by women writers is much in evidence on this highly abbreviated list. Note as well that multi-ethnic writing and international perspectives emerge into the mainstream with works by the African American Wright, the Armenian American Saroyan, and Pearl S. Buck, whose purportedly ethnographic novels of China captivated readers for decades.

In fact, of the ninety-nine works of fiction distributed by the Book-of-the-Month Club from 1930 through 1941, thirty were by women authors, or approximately 30 percent.[18] The presence of female and minority voices in club selections questions the received wisdom that women's writing was nearly invisible on the American scene of the era. Women's writing and ethnic literature are not absent in the set of middlebrow fiction; it is the set of middlebrow fiction that has been absent from critical consideration. The welcome move to expand the canon to include more works by women looks a bit belated, not to say chary, when nearly one-third of those featured by the club were women and when successful Jewish women writers (like Vicki Baum) of the 1930s continue to be excluded from most discussions of Jewish literature. This is despite the fact that two of Vicki Baum's novels were club selections from the 1930s, not to mention novels by two other once-popular writers from the period, Vera

Caspary and Leane Zugsmith. But my focus is on the near-total neglect within literary studies of the set of better fiction. Thus, it is not so much a particular woman writer who has been marginalized by American and American Jewish literary historiography as it is writers—both male and female—who were thought to have appealed to women and whose taste was equated with bourgeois values.

During the long 1930s, the Book-of-the-Month Club featured ten novels by Jewish writers, or approximately 10 percent of its total selections.[19] These novels are Joseph Roth's *Job* (1931), a recasting of the biblical narrative in twentieth-century Russia and America; Vicki Baum's genre-establishing *Grand Hotel* (1931), as well as another technically accomplished work of intersecting fates, *And Life Goes On* (1932); Franz Werfel's epic novel of the Armenian genocide, *Forty Days of Musa Dagh* (1934), and his modern fable of faith, *Embezzled Heaven* (1940); Robert Nathan's apocalyptic *Road of Ages* (1935); Bruno Frank's fictional biography, *A Man Called Cervantes* (1935); Arnold Zweig's brilliant World War I novel, *Education before Verdun* (1936); Sholem Asch's magisterial life of Jesus, *The Nazarene* (1939); and Arthur Koestler's anti-Stalinist novel, *Darkness at Noon* (1941).

Not all the Jewish authors listed above may be said to have written "Jewish fiction." Dan Miron suggests that a work may be considered Jewish if it "evinces an interest in or is . . . conditioned by a sense of *Judesein*, being Jewish, or is being read by readers who experience it as if it showed interest and were conditioned by the writer's being Jewish."[20] I recognize that it is more than a little ironic to use a term inspired by Heidegger to define Jewish literature; nonetheless Miron's shorthand remains profitable. Four of these novels (Joseph Roth's *Job*, Nathan's *Road of Ages*, Arnold Zweig's *Education before Verdun*, and Asch's *The Nazarene*) focus on identifiable Jewish characters exclusively or predominately. Asch's *The Nazarene*, for example, offers a detailed life of Jesus within a frame story describing the relationship between a young Jewish scholar and an antisemitic philologist in late 1930s Poland. Touching on similar themes, Nathan set his *Road of Ages* in a near-future 1930s after all Jews throughout the world are expelled from their own countries and doomed to wander in a massive caravan to a kind of reservation established for them in the Gobi Desert. Zweig also touches on the theme of social antisemitism in *Education before Verdun*, which presents a Jewish soldier's adventures and misadventures in World War I; the club edition of the novel features a postscript written by Zweig that describes his flight from Nazi Germany and resettlement in Haifa. An additional two (Baum's *And Life Goes On*, which focuses on an unhappily married woman whose platonic relationship with a Jewish shopkeeper sets in motion her desire to change her domestic life, and Werfel's more problematic *Embezzled Heaven*, which depicts a Jewish convert to Catholicism in a negative light) feature Jewish characters in subordinate roles that are nonetheless crucial to the narrative. Werfel's *Forty Days of Musa Dagh*, while not depicting Jewish characters, was received at the time of its publication as an allegory of Jewish vulnerability to Nazism.[21] Thus, depending on how we count, between 4 percent and 7 percent of the entire Book-of-the-Month Club fiction selections for the long 1930s may be thought of as conditioned by Miron's sense of *Judesein*. This may not be a high percentage, but even at the lower figure of 4 percent, it remains higher than one would expect from 1930s America, a period characterized by casual and institutional antisemitism. The significance of Jewish writing among Book-of-the-Month Club selections suggests that the club and its judges helped facilitate the integration of Jewish culture into the American mainstream, perhaps even promoting acceptance of Jews and Jewish norms among the aspirational classes of the American heartland.

The list of ten Jewish writers and their works also reveals the cosmopolitan overtures of the Book-of-the-Month Club and the diasporic nature of Jewish literature. Of these ten novels, only two (*Road of Ages* and *The Nazarene*) were not written in German originally. This fact in and of itself remains significant, as it demonstrates that an American readership was ready, or at least was judged as ready, to abandon anti-German sentiment during the interwar era. Asch's *The Nazarene* was composed in Yiddish but not published in that language until 1943 (*Der man fun Natsres*).[22] Nathan, a commercially successful American author who was born into New York's Sephardic aristocracy, wrote in English. At the time of the distribution of their work through the Book-of-the-Month Club, Asch and Nathan were living in America and writing for American audiences; thus, we can inarguably refer to them as Jewish *American* writers.[23] One can understand the reluctance to include a novel—even one written

in Yiddish—about the life of Jesus in the Jewish American canon.[24] Then
again, what could be more American than an immigrant Jewish author
penning a best-selling novel about a Jewish boy whose mother thought
he was God? Those works that would have been most identifiable to
readers in the 1930s as Jewish American fiction *at the time* (e.g., works by
Asch and Nathan) are precisely those absent in Jewish American literary
historiography.[25]

Just how broadly did these Book-of-the-Month Club selections penetrate the American market and allow readers to identify what Jewish
fiction might be? Estimates are readily available. Club membership rose
nearly fourfold from 93,660 in 1930 to 362,585 at the close of 1939.[26]
Members were required to purchase four books per annum, though they
could purchase more. Assuming completely randomized selection criteria, this yields the statistical likelihood that any given book was chosen
in any given month as one in three (for a club minimum requirement of
four books purchased over twelve months). We can then estimate that
perhaps 31,220 members would have purchased *Job* in 1930, and perhaps
120,861 members would have purchased *The Nazarene* in 1939. These
rough figures are in line with documented publisher print runs to meet
consumer demands in the middle of the decade. For example, Knopf
printed 62,500 copies[27] of Nathan's *Road of Ages* in 1935, when club membership approached 137,000.[28] If anything, my estimated figures for distribution of titles through the club may be conservative.[29]

Book-of-the-Month Club members who did indeed purchase and keep
these selections would likely have had only perfunctory personal contact
with Jews and little knowledge of Jewish life. American Jews clustered
overwhelmingly in cities in the 1930s. The club targeted those Americans
who did not live in major metropolitan areas, simply because those individuals were not served by bookstores. In other words, the seven works I
identify as Jewish fiction distributed by the club in the 1930s were more
than likely purchased in the heartland of America, not its cities. Statistics
from 1930–31 indicate that 32 percent of the entire US population lacked
access to a bookstore, while two-thirds of all US counties lacked any sort
of book outlet at that time.[30] A Book-of-the-Month Club executive confirmed that fully two-thirds of members lived in towns or rural areas.[31]
We can therefore conclude that Jewish fiction enjoyed broad distribution

throughout the 1930s in the American heartland due to the club. Thus, despite what the prevailing historiography implies, neither Jewish writers nor Jewish subject matter was ghettoized by tastemakers or readers in the 1930s. It was the better fiction consumed by the middle class that was scorned by a metropolitan and often anti-bourgeois elite. Fiedler's so-called breakthrough looks far less noteworthy when one considers the massive distribution of Jewish better fiction—the middlebrow he disdains—throughout the United States in the 1930s.

In 1926, the Book-of-the-Month Club was launched by three business and publication veterans: Robert K. Haas, Maxwell Sackheim, and Harry Scherman. All were Jewish, which indicates the importance future sociological studies of Jewish Americans in the book industry may hold. Club selections, however, were made independently by a five-person selection committee headed by Henry Seidel Canby. While not avant-garde in his tastes by any means, Canby was profoundly concerned with choosing literature of aesthetic merit that reflected the modern world of club readers. The other four members of the original committee were Vermont novelist, feminist, and activist for racial justice Dorothy Canfield Fisher; the politically progressive newsman William Allen White, from Kansas; journalist Heywood Broun, who was a vocal socialist and member of the Algonquin Round Table; and the prolific New York writer and editor Christopher Morley. Interestingly, Canby, Canfield Fisher, and Morley shared a Quaker background.

The men and women on the Book-of-the-Month Club selection committee, commonly referred to as "the judges," helped guide and shape the sensibilities of its readers across the United States throughout the long 1930s. Radway suggests that we view the committee's literary selections as "an exercise in social training and pedagogy."[32] The values the judges attempted to pass on to their rural and exurban readers as part of this "social training" may be determined implicitly. All of the judges were politically liberal, if not clearly leftist. Though none of the judges were Jewish, several possessed a philosemitic streak. They tended to promote racial justice, greater gender equality, and what we might today term multiculturalism. The club also established a "Foreign Advisory Committee" in 1929. The role of this international group of authors was to recommend European works to the American judges for consideration.

The members of the Foreign Advisory Committee were Arnold Bennett and H. G. Wells (England), Thomas Mann (Germany), André Maurois (France), Arthur Schnitzler (Austria), and Sigrid Undset (Norway). Two of these members had been awarded the Nobel Prize in Literature, Undset (1928) and Mann (1929), and were literary celebrities at the time of their appointment to the Foreign Advisory Committee. Another two of the members were Jewish, Maurois and Schnitzler, though only the latter may be said to have dealt with identifiably Jewish characters in his fiction. The influence of these international advisors on the American judges remains unclear, yet given the many works translated from the German, it is plausible to assume that Mann and to a lesser extent Schnitzler (d. 1931) helped to bring German-language works to the notice of club judges. With the outbreak of World War II, the Foreign Advisory Committee was disbanded.[33]

German-language Jewish fiction migrated into the American literary mainstream via translation; this mainstream already sustained American Jewish writers working in English (and Yiddish). The aesthetic and thematic influence of German fiction on American letters of the period remains intriguing. After all, it was Fiedler who proposed that 1950s American highbrow literature evinced the values that he imagined European writers to possess. The source for those values—the "attitudes of dissent" Fiedler vaunted—might logically be found in the European literature American authors would have been exposed to through translation and mass circulation. It may even make *more* sense to consider much read, much discussed, and much disseminated non-English language Jewish novels such as *Job*, *Education before Verdun*, and *The Nazarene* as representative of American tastes and values of the 1930s than it does to consider anomalous, little read, little reviewed, and barely circulated American literary works. In other words, Joseph Roth's German-language immigrant epic *Job* might be more representative of American literature's political economy than Henry Roth's immigrant epic *Call It Sleep*.

A masterpiece, *Call It Sleep* (1934) appeared a decade after Jewish immigration to the United States had all but ceased in the wake of the Johnson Immigration Act (1924) and the earlier Johnson Quota Act (1921). *Call It Sleep* was, in this way, socioculturally belated in comparison to earlier, more naturalistic and much more popular works on the theme, like *Job*. Henry Roth's own novel disappeared from view after a small print run and was not resurrected until the mid-1960s, in large part due to the efforts of Fiedler and Alfred Kazin, who both praised the novel in an *American Scholar* forum (1956) dedicated to "the most neglected books of the last twenty-five years."[34] Today, *Call It Sleep* is an especially revered canonical work, valued for its multilingual tour de force.[35] We too need to adopt a capacious understanding of Jewish American literature, one that embraces the set of better fiction written in a multitude of languages, translated into English, and then widely disseminated across the United States.

The predominant national approach to Jewish American literature of the 1930s—emphasis here on the nominalized *American*—exists in tension with the cosmopolitanism of the most representative Jewishly inflected works of that era, which I have identified from the set of Book-of-the-Month Club selections. Simultaneously, the established canon of 1930s Jewish American literature—Gold, Henry Roth, West—asserts anti-bourgeois values that were antagonistic to pervasive American bourgeois values, precisely those middlebrow values we see reflected in the better fiction of the club. To clarify: those texts taken by Fiedler in the 1950s (and others) to epitomize Jewish American literature in the 1930s are not only aesthetically anomalous in comparison to the most circulated works of Jewish literature of the era, but they are also ideologically inimical to the better fiction most consumed by readers at the time.

Therefore, it is not surprising when we turn to the so-called breakthrough period of the 1950s to see that two of the authors Fiedler most associates with the middlebrow—Schulberg and Wouk—appear as Book-of-the-Month Club selections. Those most identified with the highbrow—Bellow, Malamud, Schwartz—are all absent from club lists. Most scholars of Jewish American fiction ignore Schulberg and Wouk (not to mention Shaw) and valorize Bellow, Malamud, and Schwartz. Perhaps the highbrow authors are indeed better; perhaps they simply reflect the "attitudes of dissent" defined by Fiedler and others as axiomatically worthy of critical consideration. But this prejudice means that the history of Jewish American literature misses an entire system of literary works, the middlebrow, and excludes the most representative elements of Jewish American literary taste and experience, as well as marginalizing fiction written and largely consumed by women.

American Jewish literary criticism has typically treated the aesthetics of fiction as an index to the ideologically sanctioned values of a social elite. That is, such criticism purports to discover the sociopolitical beliefs and norms its practitioners—scholars, critics, authors—endorse in the fictions these selfsame scholars, critics, and authors value. Bluntly put, fiction is judged to be "good" to the extent it reifies the political and social values of its adjudicators. This is not surprising; the landscape of contemporary literary criticism often treats the aesthetic as an index to ideology[36] or, more grossly, subordinates the aesthetic to ideology. Academics tend to believe that aesthetic value is a product of social construction, and so we defer to our ideological values, such that we advocate for our tastes based on progressive notions of marginality, hybridity, class, gender, sexuality, race, ethnicity, and of course, the "attitudes of dissent" that so enraptured Fiedler. Yet we often fail to recognize that our ideologies are subject to the same historicism and social construction. In casting a skeptical eye on professional prejudices, I want to shine light on the erasure of a set of texts and their attendant reformist values. Scholarly disinterest in middle-class better fiction is no less revealing of an otherwise concealed social reality than is our appreciation of a few avant-garde or *engagé* masterpieces.

But what if we were to reverse this operation? What if we used social forms—the political economies of fiction and the ideological economies of scholarship that valorize dissent *contra* bourgeois values—as an index to those aesthetic forms that are consequently disadvantaged or privileged? Perhaps such a criticism would allow our scholarship to migrate toward a more comparative conception of American Jewish literature that treats not only the loftiest works, but also the most representative. Doing so may allow us to make greater sense of the existing canon and allow for a more informed revision and reshaping of our ever-evolving American Jewish culture. This may indeed be the next disruptive breakthrough.

NOTES

1. Leslie Fiedler, "The Breakthrough," in *Recent American Fiction: Some Critical Views*, ed. Joseph J. Waldmeir (Boston: Houghton Mifflin, 1963), 84.
2. Fiedler, "The Breakthrough," 105.
3. Fiedler, "The Breakthrough," 84–86.
4. Fiedler, "The Breakthrough," 100.
5. Fiedler, "The Breakthrough," 99.
6. Fiedler, "The Breakthrough," 105.
7. By the 1970s, Fiedler had reconsidered this elitism and was championing popular literature, or in his terms, "commodity literature." Fiedler in fact notes the 1930s as a period of great expansion in popular literature in the United States. Fiedler, "Giving the Devil His Due," *Journal of Popular Culture* 12, no.2 (Fall 1978): 197–207. See also Fiedler, "Towards a Definition of Popular Literature," in *Superculture: American Popular Culture and Europe*, ed. C. W. E. Bigsby (Bowling Green, OH: Bowling Green University Popular Press 1975), 29–38.
8. Gordon Hutner makes the point that works of bourgeois fiction "go missing as a class and as a genre." I prefer the data processing term "set," precisely because it avoids any economic ("class") or literary ("genre") shadings. See *What America Read: Taste, Class, and the Novel, 1920–1960* (Chapel Hill: University of North Caroline Press, 2009), 4.
9. Hutner, *What America Read*, 1.
10. See Sacvan Bercovitch, "The Problem of Ideology in American Literary History," *Critical Inquiry* 12, no. 4 (1986): 631–53.
11. William St. Clair, "The Political Economy of Reading," in *The Reading Nation in the Romantic Period* (London: Cambridge University Press, 2007), 3.
12. St. Clair, "Political Economy of Reading," 6.
13. Quoted in Joan Shelley Rubin, *The Making of Middlebrow Culture* (Chapel Hill: University of North Carolina Press, 1992), 98.
14. Charles Lee, *The Hidden Public: The Story of the Book-of-the-Month Club* (New York: Doubleday, 1958), 138.
15. Club data indicates that female members were in the majority for nine years between 1947 and 1958, so it is reasonable to assume that women represented a considerable share of the members in the previous decades as well. See Lee, *The Hidden Public*, esp. 148–49.
16. Rubin, *The Making of Middlebrow Culture*, 108.
17. See Hutner, *What America Read*, 134.
18. See Lee, *The Hidden Public*, 164–74.
19. Data from "List of Selections, Dividends, and Alternates, 1926–1957," in Lee, *The Hidden Public*, 161–94. I have not included Book-of-the-Month Club "dividends" (giveaways) in my accounting, but have included "alter-

nates." Lee does not include collections of short stories by a single author or Virginia Woolf's biography of Elizabeth Barrett Browning's cocker spaniel, *Flush*, in his determination of fiction selections, while I have done so.

20. Dan Miron, *From Continuity to Contiguity: Toward a New Jewish Literary Thinking* (Stanford, CA: Stanford University Press, 2010), 405.

21. See Louis Kronenberger, "Franz Werfel's Heroic Novel," *New York Times*, December 2, 1934, BR1–2.

22. See Melissa Weininger, "A Question of Truth: Form, Structure, and Character in *Der Man Fun Natseres*," *Hebrew Studies* 56 (2015): 367–76, for more on Asch's novel and its publication history.

23. Vicki Baum immigrated to the United States in 1932 and after World War II wrote in English. Incidentally, Asch and Nathan later became good friends. See Robert Nathan, "Judaism and the 'Lost' Intellectuals," *Jewish Forum*, September 1952, 129–30.

24. Asch (1880–1957) was born in Poland but immigrated to the United States in 1914 and was later naturalized. He then returned to Poland in the 1920s and resided there for most of the 1930s before returning to the United States as antisemitism grew. The massive success of Asch's *The Nazarene*—transgressive by the standards of normative Jewish literature—holds out an interesting point of comparison to Isaac Bashevis Singer's later success in translation, particularly in terms of Singer's own transgressiveness.

25. In the period 1975–2016, many articles appearing in *Studies in American Jewish Literature* reference the canonical works of Michael Gold or Henry Roth. Not a single article is devoted to Sholem Asch's most popular novel, and Robert Nathan is never even accorded a mention.

26. Lee, *The Hidden Public*, 62, 70.

27. Data graciously provided by Dr. Josh Lambert.

28. The end-of-year Book-of-the-Month Club membership for 1935 was 137,010, according to Lee, *The Hidden Public*, 70.

29. For example, while Book-of-the-Month Club membership in 1940 was at least as high as the 1939 end-of-year total (362,585), Wright's *Native Son* sold an astounding 215,000 copies within three weeks after its selection. See Janice Radway, *A Feeling for Books: The Book-of-the-Month Club, Literary Taste, and Middle-Class Desire* (Chapel Hill: University of North Carolina Press, 1997), 287.

30. Lee, *The Hidden Public*, 26.

31. Lee, *The Hidden Public*, 27.

32. Radway, *A Feeling for Books*, 262.

33. Lee, *The Hidden Public*, 35.

34. Fiedler, "The Most Neglected Books," *The American Scholar* 39 no.2 (Spring 1970): 478; and Alfred Kazin, "The Most Neglected Books," 486.

35. See Hana Wirth-Nesher, *Call It English: The Languages of Jewish American Literature* (Princeton, NJ: Princeton University Press, 2008).

36. Cf. Caroline Levine, *Forms: Whole, Rhythm, Hierarchy, Network* (Princeton, NJ: Princeton University Press, 2015), 22.

Sincere thanks to those who have commented on drafts of this piece and helped me refine my thinking: Clark Davis, Hanan Hever, Josh Lambert, Michael Weingrad, and attendees of the Yale Conference on Modern Hebrew and Jewish Literatures (2018).

16

Liturgy as an Instrument of Intellectual Change
Between Comfort and Disruption

Rabbi Sonja K. Pilz, PhD

IN 2007, *MISHKAN T'FILAH* began to replace the rows of *Gates of Prayer* volumes on the shelves of Reform synagogues and homes throughout the United States, Canada, and to some extent, Australia, South Africa, and Europe. The new book was heavy, bulky, and comprehensive. It was beautiful in a very unassuming manner, and among the wealth of readings, poems, and meditations, almost all readers could find something that appealed to them. Excitement and pride seem to have paved the way for the then-new prayer book and its two later siblings, the golden and silver shining volumes of *Mishkan HaNefesh*, the High Holy Day prayer books published in 2015 by the same publishing house, CCAR Press, under the auspices of the Central Conference of American Rabbis (CCAR).

Not even the most critical observer of these changes could have called them "disruptive." For sure, none of these three volumes has functioned as an instrument of intellectual change. They could not have possibly done so because they were the very products of not only the intellectual changes that marked the previous decades of the Reform Movement, but also the intellectual universe that makes up the so-called Western world.[1]

At this juncture, allow me take a step back to provide some context. To do so, I want to bring into focus one of the most remarkable *sugyot*[2] of the Talmud I have ever come across. In the Babylonian Talmud, *P'sachim* 106a, we read:

Rav Ashi [a great Rabbinic authority in fourth-century Babylonia; presumably, the first editor of the Babylonian Talmud] once came to the city of Mechoza. They asked him, "Would the master do the *K'dushah Rabbah* for us?" And they brought him a cup of wine. He thought to himself, "What is the *K'dushah Rabbah?*" Then he said [to himself], "Well, since the wine requires that from all the blessings there are that I first say *borei p'ri hagefen*, I will start with that one." He said *borei p'ri hagefen* and expanded on it. He saw an elderly man bend over and drink [presumably, in response to the blessing and expansion he had just delivered], and he said the following verse about himself: "The wise one has his eyes in his head" (Ecclesiastes 2:14) [meaning: "Wise is the man who uses his eyes to discern the expectations of his environment"].

From this *sugya* we learn not only that the exact text of our prayers remained somewhat fluid for centuries (a topic of hot debate in the last decades of the last century!), but also something essential about the dynamics of liturgy itself: it must, by its very nature, entail enough of the known, familiar, and comfortable—in short, the "expected"—to give the *k'hilah* (community) of our people the sense that it is both authentically "Jewish" and coming from a place of personal integrity. Our liturgy unfolds and shifts within certain structures and patterns: morning, *Musaf*, afternoon, and evening services, quotes from the Scripture, Rabbinic blessings, private and medieval *kavanot*[3], Chasidic sayings, and Jewish poetry from the early biblical verses to the contemporary, all mirror and echo each other, shape our expectations as people who pray, and make the small changes we embrace even more exciting. Think, for example, about the strong reactions that a slight change to the name of God in a well-known blessing may evoke, even if just in its translation!

The centuries that followed Rav Ashi's innovations have not broken with this paradigm;[4] since the beginning of Rabbinic Judaism, our liturgy has been characterized by a delicate balance between the yearning for utmost historical authenticity and the need to respond to the ever-changing worlds of our praying people. For centuries, the task of the rabbis was not to create new prayers and liturgy. Instead, they were to allow for and confirm new liturgical expressions already found and created by the people (through liturgical hybridity,[5] liturgical creativity, or a mixture of both) by determining whether any given new liturgical expression contravened prevailing halachah or whether it could be brought into harmony with it.

With the emergence of non-halachic movements and the heightened sensitivity for human needs also manifesting in most halachic movements, the paradigm, after centuries, began to shift. Modernism, feminism, and then postmodernism have changed not only the content, but also the very making of Jewish liturgy, echoing the changes in thought and practice taking place in the broader society. For the sake of outlining these changes, I will compare below the last two generations of Reform prayer books regarding the process and practice of their making: the *Gates* series and the *Mishkan* series.

The Gates Series

The liturgy of the *Gates* series may not seem disruptive today, but like every renewal in a liturgical space, including the *New Union Prayer Book* (the subtitle of the *Gates* series), it caused its share of antagonism. Liturgical changes are always hard to make, often more for aesthetic than intellectual reasons. As the weight, color, design, and tone of a book changes, people lose the tacit sense of familiarity and comfort that takes years to build.[6]

The *Gates* are an eight-volume compendium, from Shabbat services to High Holy Day observance to a volume of prayers and liturgies for the Reform Jewish home. The books were published by CCAR Press between the mid-1970s and 1980s, a decade of enormous cultural change.[7] They are very similar in structure, tone, and theology—a fact that should not be surprising given the fact that they all are the product of a single person, Rabbi Chaim Stern, whose goal it was to "birth . . . a new liturgy for the Reform community of the future."[8]

Who was Chaim Stern? Born in Brooklyn, New York, in 1930, Stern was a prolific, deeply learned rabbi who had spent part of his career in London serving the Liberal Movement. While living in England, Stern had been a part of the production of *Gates of Joy*, the British prayer books for the Liberal Movement, and he had published his own books as well.[9] His experience and scholarship, as well as his seemingly never-ending energy and dedication, made him a perfect candidate for a job the American Reform Movement was seeking to fill when he was back in the United States: an individual rabbi, rooted in scholarship and gifted with poetic and liturgical sensitivity and creativity, to reshape the liturgical life of the Reform Movement in the United States and beyond. And Stern went to work!

What is remarkable about the creation process of the *Gates* series is that the books are, even with a certain amount of peer reviewing and changing,[10] "in largest measures"[11] the writing of a single person. Even though the books build on the heritage of American Reform Judaism,[12] every word in them is Stern's language.[13] The names and descriptions for God used in the different sets of services offered in the books blossom from Stern's theologies and range from covenant theology to the early beginnings of process theology. The atmosphere evoked by the prayers and liturgies reflected Stern's own religious sensitivities, which he laid out in separate services to reflect the theological diversity within the Reform Movement of the time.

In the introduction to *Gates of Prayer*, he wrote:

> We are a diversified people. Within our Reform community are proponents of many viewpoints. There are disagreements among us on many issues. It is our hope that *Gates of Prayer* will unite us all in worship. We do not assume that all controversy is harmful; we do not presume to judge which controversy is not "for the sake of Heaven"; still less do we wish to stifle the expression of views sincerely held. Therefore, in this prayerbook, we have followed the principle that there are many paths to heaven's gates, that this prayer and that one, this service and that one, may both have the power to lead us to the living God.[14]

The Reform Movement and Chaim Stern himself knew that the Reform Movement of his time, maybe more so than ever before, was "diversified"—a term that must be interpreted in all its tension as both "divided" and "pluralistic"—in its theologies and political standpoints. His books responded to the many liturgical innovations of other movements and faiths at the time by inviting more active participation and using poetic language; they also attempted to create a container for a plurality of opinions, styles, and needs that might have otherwise led to the division of the very Movement itself. This strategy was employed again by the editors of *Mishkan T'filah* roughly forty years later for the very same reasons. Even so, with the publication of the *Gates* series, the Reform Movement sought to create unity and social cohesion by creating a unified and unifying liturgy—a strategy that the *Mishkan* series would abandon entirely. It is worth quoting Stern's original writings in full to give the reader an impression of the overall tonality of his prayers and meditations. What follows are two meditations on the candle lighting on Friday nights that are included in *Mishkan T'filah*[15] and continue to be read widely to this day:

> As these Shabbat candles give light
> to all who behold to them,
> so may we, by our lives, give light to all who behold to us.
>
> As their brightness reminds us
> of the generations of Israel who have kindled light,
> so may we, in our own day, be among those who kindle light.

And:

> O Source of light and truth,
> Creator of the eternal law of goodness,
> help us to find knowledge by which to live.
> Lead us to take the words we shall speak
> into our hearts and our lives.
>
> Bless all who enter this sanctuary in need,
> all who bring the offerings of their hearts.
> May our worship lead us to acts of kindness, peace and love.

And so, for forty years, the majority of American Jews grew accustomed to the sound and sensuality of Stern's work, as well as its gravitas and beauty, its wholesome dignity, and its emphasis on historic continuity and contemporary mission. Its unbroken, calm tone was carried beautifully when spoken by the sonorous voices of still mostly male senior rabbis on Friday nights and at High Holy Day services, while candles were lit in shimmering spaces and the members of the choir got ready to sing, and the congregation would dutifully speak their parts of the responsive readings.

The Mishkan Series

Roughly forty years passed. It is an interesting fact in itself that after forty years—the duration of our people's wandering through the wilderness, the duration of one generation's active memory[16]—the movement seemed to have sensed that the time had come to make a change.

By the mid-1990s, when the CCAR began its work on *Mishkan T'filah*, the Reform Movement had been ordaining women rabbis for more than twenty years. Those women had changed the look, the sound, the overall structures, and the theologies of Reform congregations and congregants. Like many other American communities, American Reform Jews had become more pluralistic, more feminist, more sensitive to questions of egalitarianism and equity, and to a certain degree, more open to sharing the words of "others" from the bimah.

A product of and witness to those cultural shifts, the process of creating the first volumes of the *Mishkan* series looked quite different than it had looked for the *Gates*. Instead of being the product of a single, male mind, the *Mishkan* volumes, beginning with the publication of *Mishkan T'filah* in 2007, are the outcomes of years of intense committee work. It took twenty years to publish *Mishkan T'filah*, which was even more collaborative than the later *Mishkan HaNefesh*. The committees as well as committee members involved (altogether sixty-three people!) changed over the course of those years. At the heart of the books, however, lies a vision both aesthetic and decisive in content, both simple and extremely radical:

- Each double-page spread of *Mishkan T'filah* is divided into a right page (traditional prayers, transliterations, and semi-literal translation) and a left page (alternative prayers, poetry, and reflections).
- Each double-page spread of *Mishkan T'filah* thus turned into a dialogue of different styles, voices, and also theologies. In *Mishkan T'filah*, atheism and pantheism are to be found right next to orthodox monotheism; voices of doubt speak up right next to voices of trust and hope.

The vision behind these choices was to give clergy members and readers/pray-ers an opportunity to create the service closest to their hearts, even as they were intuitively embracing texts that were the most in sync with their own theology, mindset, or spiritual needs.[17] After years of extensive committee, editorial, and design work, the first draft of *Mishkan T'filah* was ready—to be sent to selected congregations all over the country in the form of a preview bundle in order to receive feedback, make more adjustments, and then, finally, go to print.[18] Its publication was accompanied by countless conversations and teachings at meetings and conferences, as well as a weekly essay on its prayer texts, poetry, and possible musical settings, in "Ten Minutes of Torah," an email newsletter published by the Union for Reform Judaism (URJ), later published in part as *Divrei Mishkan T'filah: Delving into the Siddur*, by Rabbi Richard S. Sarason.[19]

To what degree can a prayer book be considered disruptive? To what degree might it possibly reflect the intellectual changes and ruptures of its time?

Mishkan T'filah was very quickly embraced by the American Reform community. How could it not be? It was created, adapted, and produced by a community of teachers, rabbis, cantors, and congregants at the heart of the Reform Movement. Its very goal had been to reflect the community in its current state of mind and spiritual place. Difficulties in navigating this extensive and quite large and heavy book were overcome by clergy members who found the voices of their own teachers between its covers, who could trust in the intention of the book to preserve the texts by Chaim Stern with the most emotional connections, and who relied upon the contemporary lyrics of the most common Reform synagogue songs.[20] Thus, *Mishkan T'filah* reflected the state of the entire Reform community as perhaps no book has done before: it is a theologically pluralistic, poetic, politically liberal, liturgically flexible and creative prayer book that gleans its core theological messages from contemporary rabbis, poets, and activists.

The golden and silver siblings of *Mishkan T'filah*, the High Holy Day prayer books *Mishkan HaNefesh*, continued this trajectory, while reinserting into the Reform liturgical repertoire some of the organically neglected traditional sections. This change toward tradition reflects accurately a moment in time in which American Jews as a whole, and the Reform Movement is no exception, sought greater historical authenticity and highly personalized spiritual expression at the same time.[21] This is just one of the many ways in which the zeitgeist (the widely shared theological, spiritual, political, and aesthetic preferences within the Movement) crafted the liturgy of its current prayer books—like *Mishkan T'filah*, *Mishkan HaNefesh* is the product of a widely shared effort.[22] Thus, the *Mishkan* series fulfilled its intended task. Opening their covers, the majority of readers and pray-ers will find their own beliefs, doubts, and aesthetic preferences reflected and expressed by the liturgies the books present.

Nevertheless, embedded in the very process of creating the books is a radical editorial decision: *Liturgy created to reflect the current moment cannot, by definition, be intellectually or spiritually challenging or disruptive.* At their very core, the books are meant to be as comforting and familiar sounding as possible. What is lacking, in all the books, is a vision of what the Reform community might—and maybe should—become, or what else it could be at this moment in time and in the future. Since 2020, ethics violations have brought to light great imbalances in power in all three major institutions of the Reform Movement—Hebrew Union College–Jewish Institute of Religion, the CCAR, and the URJ and its summer camps. The very human need to care for and support the familiar and comfortable might have led to a situation in which new, unfamiliar, and at times challenging voices from within and outside our community have been ignored, belittled, and even silenced.

The lack of vision embedded in the very editorial process of liturgical publication has been counterbalanced continuously by additional publications of CCAR Press, most presently by the publication of *Mishkan Ga'avah*,[23] a compilation of liturgies and prayers that gives voice to the LGBTQ+ community within and outside the Reform Movement, and the *Shabbat Table Cards*[24] for Friday night home rituals. However, the books proved to have additional lacunae.

Almost exclusively, the books reflect a white, Ashkenazic, American tradition—in the midst of an increasing awareness of the racial and cultural diversity of American Jews. While nothing is wrong with preserving and celebrating white Ashkenazic ethnicity and its tradition, it is time to make space for other ethnicities and traditions next to it. The family histories of Jews living in the United States today do not solely tell a story of European descent. They are vastly diversified due to factors such as different migration histories, interreligious marriages, conversions, adoptions, and simply the hybridization of Jewish tradition thanks to open resources both online and in person.

God is referred to as "the Eternal" and "Sovereign," but never in more (gender-)fluid, creative terminology—even after more than decades of influence from and of feminist theology in other spaces and liturgy. It was in 1996 that Marcia Falk published the first edition of *The Book of Blessings*,[25] now published by CCAR Press. Her book marks a turning point in the liturgical God-language of American Jews, even though exploration had started long before this date. Different Jewish communities have found their ways to address and turn to God, seeking to connect to all of God's faces. In order to truly welcome all Jews into our synagogues and Zoom rooms—and to deepen our understanding of the Divine—we have to make space for their names of God.

Also, the praying community is not depicted as a diverse group of people of different political, gender, sexual, race, and body expressions—in the midst of a time of heightened polarization. The books, in all their literary and theological diversity, express a specific political view, tell a specific kind of Jewish history, and speak in some voices but not in others. It is difficult for our leadership, but also for each of us individually, to fully acknowledge the fact that there are people, members of our communities, who are radically different from us. The Reform Movement is home to Republicans and Democrats, born Americans and immigrants, white, Brown, Black Jews, Asian, and Latinx Jews, LGBTQ+ and straight Jews, cis, trans, and nonbinary Jews, Persian and Maghrebi Jews, old Jews and young Jews, angry Jews and Jews seeking comfort . . . the list could go on forever. To truly learn from each other, to truly find God in the faces of all of us, we need to find liturgical forms and languages that confront and challenge us to find God in the face of every single one of us.

Traditional liturgy that might challenge contemporary theological assumptions has been omitted (e.g., we, the pray-ers, are continuously referred to as God's partners, but never as God's servants, subordinates, or flock)—in the midst of a wide search for deep, authentic, personal, home-based, spiritual authenticity. However, we have learned at this point that not every Jew comes to synagogue in order to be called to volunteer in an ongoing battle for the good in the world—even in partnership with God. Often, people pray in order to feel embraced by a fatherly/ motherly figure; often, people pray to find guidance in dedicating their lives to the service of a purpose (or an entity) that is holier and bigger than themselves and their own lives. Often, people pray in order to see their own brokenness reflected in the words of other Jews who came before them, or who live right next to them, in order to feel less alone. Both books make little room for voices of despair, accusation, shame, depression, confusion, and loneliness. In a time of increasing awareness of the mental health struggles of so many of our members, especially of the younger generation, our liturgical language must make space for the tired and scared, not only for God's confident partners.

The liturgical translations of both books still echo the sonorous, all-knowing voice of Rabbi Chaim Stern. While the theological content has shifted, the reader and pray-er find little language that might disrupt or challenge their spiritual selves. We, very much still living in the aftermath of the Holocaust and shaped by the traumas of increasing environmental, social, and financial instability, have not created liturgies that reflect those very cornerstones of life in the twenty-first century.

Next Steps

To what degree can—or should—liturgy be disruptive? Many regular pray-ers come to synagogue looking for a home, a sense of belonging, comfort, to be seen. While sermons and *iyunim*[26] might be disruptive at times, the recurring liturgies of almost any Jewish service bring about, by their very nature, a sense of continuity and tradition, even if the tradition is only several years old. By definition, Jewish liturgy thus creates tradition through repetition and similarity; intellectual disruption is not part of the standard Jewish liturgical recipe.

What if we wanted to lean into this challenge? What might the creation of an intellectually and spiritually challenging siddur look like? Let me engage you in a thought experiment—and let's assume for this experiment that the Reform Movement will continue in its current structure for years to come. Right now, the Reform Movement has a complex and multilayered identity. While many in the leadership still remember the grand tonality of Chaim Stern's liturgies, the Movement has grown accustomed to the pluralistic voices of *Mishkan T'filah*. Already now, many of our rabbis and members seek out and absorb theologies and practices from within the realm of other Jewish movements (from the very traditional world to the very experimental), as well as from other faith traditions (from Christianity to Buddhism). The younger generation is shaped by the social agenda of this day and by a growing understanding that even given the relative religious openness of the Reform Movement, still, many Jewish identities, some of them evolving as we speak, have not been given their spaces yet (to name just a few: Jews of Color, Native American Jews, nonbinary Jews, and Jews with different abilities and disabilities—and yes, feminist Jews). Less and less does mere location determine synagogue affiliation and belonging, and a growing number of Jews have reevaluated their priorities around physical, mental, and spiritual needs. In another twenty years, we might very well expect the members/affiliates/visitors of and to the Reform Movement to be even more diverse in identity, taste, and body/mind constitution. Instead of making this increasing diversity our defining characteristic, we might opt to intentionally define—and then shape—a vision not only for what we are, but also for what we ought to be as a community defined by its religious belief and belonging.

What might the next liturgical process look like?

1. Technology is never a driver, but always a factor in creating both new comforts and new challenges. Through whatever medium we will pray together, my best guess is that it might give us possibilities for an even more enhanced liturgical fluidity—both on the side of the creator of liturgies and rituals (namely, clergy members and other spiritual leaders), and also on the side of the prayers—through changing liturgical formats in specific communities, and through individualized, additional texts, notes, and possibly personal prayers and home rituals. All these changes, however, will only increase comfort and not disruption.

Here are some ideas to give more space to the disruptive potential of our liturgy:

2. The Reform Movement could select a core group of four or five rabbis and cantors trained in theological thought

not only to define the core elements of a Jewish theology reflecting the then-current state of the Movement, but also to develop a vision for the desired theological identity of the Movement—a vision, similar to the vision of our clergy and lay leaders, that inspires hope, endurance, strength, humor, sweetness, connection to the communities of the past and present, and beauty.

3. The above group of people could hand over the project to two or three artists of words, visuals, and potentially sound. This is a step of trust and submission—and a step necessary to allow for the unexpected and disruptive to happen; artists will not necessarily find the same words of comfort as clergy. They do, however, excel in exposing the radical truths of their time. What words and images (and sounds) might they use to disrupt our comfort? What ways to challenge our beliefs about ourselves, the Reform Movement, and the world we live in? Liturgy could provide forms and words to the formless and unspeakable. At its best, it could make both thinkable and doable what might have otherwise been simply overwhelming or even confusing. In order to free this potential, clergy, the guardians of tradition, must hand it over.

Let me come back to the story of Rav Ashi with which I opened this chapter, as it is the backbone of the vision I just outlined. Imagine you are a stranger entering the space of another (Reform) community. You step into the space, and the congregational leader, who has not given out all the honors yet, turns to you, the visitor, and asks you to lead the congregation in a core section of liturgy. You might feel nervous about the integrity of your own custom, or you might be nervous about whether you will be able to meet the spiritual needs of the gathered community. How personal would your prayers need to be to truly reflect not only who the community is, but also where you yourself are coming from and the person you might want to become? How communal must the liturgy you are about to share be in order to create a space of familiarity and comfort for those with whom you are gathered? The truth about the potential of our prayers to be both comforting and disruptive may lie between those two questions.

NOTES

1. Among those changes are our increasing wrestling with the pluralities of personal, theological, and spiritual truths we are living with—both a product and possibly the end of postmodern thinking, research, conversation, and writing. For an introduction to postmodernism, see Christopher Butler, *Postmodernism: A Very Short Introduction* (Oxford: Oxford University Press, 2002).

2. A *sugya* is a passage in the Talmud, typically comprising a detailed proof-based elaboration of a mishnah and replete with debates and exchanges by the Rabbis of the Talmud.

3. *Kavanot* are meditations designed to deepen and direct a prayer experience.

4. To trace this paradigm through the centuries, it might be helpful to consult the following books: Naftali Cohn, *The Memory of the Temple and the Making of the Rabbis* (Philadelphia: University of Pennsylvania Press, 2013); and Ruth Langer, *To Worship God Properly: Tensions between Liturgical Custom and Halakhah in Judaism* (Cincinnati: Hebrew Union College Press, 1998).

5. Simcha Fishbane, "In the Absence of Ritual: Customs of the Holiday of Shavuot," *Maqom* 22 (Spring 2012): 1–42.

6. To this day, a newly revised version of the "old" *Union Prayer Book* of 1892 is published by the Chicago Sinai Congregation and the Society for Classical Reform Judaism for those who were unwilling to adapt to the changes introduced by the *Gates* and the *Mishkan* series.

7. Ely E. Pilchik offers his thoughts on the three great "stumbling blocks to prayer" of the time: the trauma of the Holocaust, the experienced economic abundance of the time, and the perceived coldness of science making faith unnecessary (*Gates of Understanding* [New York: CCAR Press, 1977], 105–10). We may want to add the founding of the State of Israel, feminism, and sexual liberation to his list.

8. Lawrence Hoffman, "Introduction: The Liturgical Question," in *Gates of Understanding*, 3.

9. See online, "Chaim Stern," Jewish Virtual Library, https://www.jewishvirtuallibrary.org/stern-chaim.

10. The Liturgical Committee of the CCAR at the time comprised ten members and their chairman, Robert I. Kahn (1967–73), and his successor, Stanley Dreyfus (1973–79). Even though its members provided feedback and sought out the feedback of many other rabbis, cantors, and laypersons, they were not involved in the writing of the prayers themselves.

11. Hoffman, "Introduction: The Liturgical Question," 8.

12. Namely, the prayer book *Olat Tamid* (1872), published by David Einhorn, the following *Union Prayer Book* (1895), and *Service of the Heart*, a British publication from 1967.

13. This was possible, in part, not only because Chaim Stern was a prolific writer. At the time, it was also possible to adapt preexisting texts quite freely as long as they were referenced correctly (which they were in *Gates of Understanding*, the explanatory volume accompanying the *Gates* series, 182–269)—a liberty of which Stern made ample use.

14. Chaim Stern, introduction to *Gates of Prayer* (New York: CCAR Press, 1975), xiii.

15. *Mishkan T'filah: A Reform Siddur* (New York: CCAR Press, 2007), 121.

16. Jan Assmann, *Cultural Memory and Early Civilization: Writing, Remembrance, and Political Imagination* (Cambridge: Cambridge University Press, 2007), e.g., 196.

17. The members of the editorial committee who shepherded the book's publication came to call the vision one of "integrated theology"—the integration of several kinds of theologies right next to each other. See Edwin Goldberg and Elaine Zecher, "CCAR Press Author Interview: Rabbis Goldberg and Zecher on 'Because My Soul Longs for You,'" Ravblog, October 6, 2021, https://ravblog.ccarnet.org/2021/10/ccar-press-author-interview-rabbis-goldberg-and-zecher-on-because-my-soul-longs-for-you/.

18. *Mishkan HaNefesh*, the two-volume set of High Holy Day prayer books, did not nearly take as much time to produce but followed the vision of *Mishkan T'filah*.

19. Richard S. Sarason, *Divrei Mishkan T'filah: Delving into the Siddur* (New York: CCAR Press, 2018).

20. Additionally, the Reform Movement begun to publish a series of *Visual T'filah*, which allowed congregations to gather and pray from the book without having to lift their physical weight and without getting too overwhelmed by its wealth of liturgical choices and additional readings. *VT* was created by Rabbi Dan Medwin, until 2021 the director of digital content at the CCAR.

21. Sarason, *Divrei Mishkan T'filah*, x.

22. The publication of *Mishkan HaNefesh* took seven years from the first meeting to the publishing date in 2015, including many rounds of feedback and piloting. The recently published Israeli Reform prayer book *T'filat HaAdam* followed in the procedural footsteps of its American counterpart. Also in Israel, the prayer book was created through committee work. Editorial decisions were made based on numerous rounds of feedback.

23. Denise Eger, ed., *Mishkan Ga'avah: Where Pride Dwells* (New York: CCAR Press, 2020).

24. *Shabbat Table Cards* are available on www.ccarpress.org.

25. Marcia Falk, *The Book of Blessings: New Jewish Prayers for Daily Life, the Sabbath and the New Moon Festival* (Boston: Beacon Press, 1999; Reform Judaism Publishing ed., New York: CCAR Press, 2017).
26. In this context, an *iyun* is a brief insight or exploration during a worship service of a prayer, idea, or event.

17

Reform Jewry Sings a New Song
Disruptions and Innovations

Cantor Evan Kent, DMA

I WAS ONE OF THOSE children who enjoyed going to Shabbat evening services. There was comfort in the music supplied by a choir and organ, and even though I barely understood the prayers, the synagogue environment and the familiar faces of adults and other children made me feel welcome and at ease. My mother and father, sitting next to me, helped me follow along in the prayer book, and I would count the pages from the beginning of the service until its conclusion. With an organ reverberating through the sanctuary and a choir hidden from view, we sang songs like "God Is in His Holy Temple" and "Father Hear the Prayer We Offer." At the conclusion of the Shabbat service, Rosalie Wetzler, the synagogue organist, would slide back the screen that hid her and the four-voice choir from the congregation, and she and the black-robed quartet would wave to the congregation. The partition would then slide back, and just as mysteriously and magically the choir and Rosalie would disappear.

A few years later, the choir and Rosalie were moved from behind the partition to a corner near the front of the sanctuary. Soon after that, the little *Union Prayer Book* with its maroon silk bookmark was replaced by the very large *Gates of Prayer*, and eventually the *Union Prayer Book for High Holidays* (also with a maroon silk bookmark) was put aside, and a new book from Britain, *The Service of the Heart*, was used for Rosh HaShanah and Yom Kippur.

That synagogue on the South Shore of Long Island was the epicenter of my family's life. My parents were on the board, my father was the youth group director and confirmation class teacher, my mother was president of Sisterhood, and my friends and I knew every inch of the synagogue building, the adjacent school building, and all the hiding spots for an after-service game of hide-and-seek. Men wore suits and ties to services, women wore dresses and often hats, and ladies from the Sisterhood with white gloves helped pour tea and serve cakes and cookies after the services were over. It will sound cliché, but Temple Sinai of Bay Shore, Long Island, was like a second home.

Eventually the quartet disappeared, but Rosalie the organist remained. She now accompanied student cantors from the Hebrew Union College–Jewish Institute of Religion (HUC-JIR), who sang some of the old familiar melodies but also new songs, unfamiliar songs. I did not know it at the time, but I was witness to the beginnings of a liturgical and musical revolution within Reform Judaism.

This chapter illuminates a series of disruptions that changed and continue to change the music in the Reform Jewish synagogue. Although I am not a musicologist, ethnomusicologist, historian, or sociologist, I do have a unique perspective regarding this phenomenon, as I grew up in the Reform Movement and for twenty-five years served as the senior cantor of Temple Isaiah, a Reform Jewish congregation in Los Angeles. As an adolescent, I was an avid participant in Jewish youth groups, conclaves, retreats, and camping. Additionally, I have been on the faculty of HUC-JIR for over a quarter century. These vantage points have afforded me a unique perspective to both witness these societal interruptions and also be a participant in the following series of disruptions that have changed (and continue to change) the sound of liturgical music in the Reform synagogue:

1. The popularity of the Jewish summer camp and the emotional, social, and cultural impact it had on generations of Jewish adolescents.
2. The development of a Jewish folk-rock-pop style, with Debbie Friedman as the leader of this movement.
3. Demographic changes in the Reform Jewish community.

A New Way of Thinking

To best understand these events and how they have impacted and continue to impact the musical environment in the Reform synagogue, I turn to the philosophical work of Gilles Deleuze. Deleuze asks us to see processes such as politics, economics, social, and cultural structures in a new way, to discard previous linear and hierarchical thinking, and to try a new approach. Deleuze employs the image of a tree as a metaphor for our current attempts to understand these large societal structures and phenomena.

Deleuze explains that a tree is rooted in one place, not moving. The roots eventually give way to the trunk of the tree, the trunk to the branches, and the branches to the leaves. There is a clear beginning, middle, and end, with a definite hierarchy. Instead of thinking of the disruptions in synagogue music as a linear, hierarchical, historical progression, like a tree, I propose we look at these disruptions as presented by Deleuze: the rhizome.[1]

Rhizomes are all around us: potatoes are rhizomes, grass is a rhizome, tubers are rhizomes, ginger grows as a rhizome. Rhizomes are extremely chaotic and unpredictable root structures growing in a way distinctly different from a tree. These rhizomes have no defined beginning or end, and at any moment the rhizome can shoot a new root out of its side in a completely different direction. These new roots can then produce roots of their own that in turn produce other roots. Eventually, these roots systems form networks of root systems, and then these random root offshoots often connect one network of roots to another network of roots. According to Deleuze, this image of the rhizome is a more accurate metaphor to describe how thoughts, ideas, and political and cultural movements all connect.

Disruption 1: Summer Camp

If I were hard-pressed to identify only one disruption that had the power to change the music of the Reform Jewish synagogue, it would be the "magic" of the Jewish camp experience. This camp magic seems to be rooted in the 24/7 atmosphere, where the environment, Jewish values, the connection to Israel, and the culture and beliefs of Judaism are part of everyday living. Michael Zeldin claims that the success of Jewish summer camp magic relies on three distinctive elements: charismatic people, intense identification with a larger group, and the reenactment of camp ritual. Zeldin also states that it was this summer camp magic that

helped facilitate "friendships that have lasted a lifetime" and was responsible for shaping personal, communal, and professional identity.[2] Amy
Sales and Leonard Saxe also acknowledge this camp magic. The essen-
tials include (a) a rural setting, (b) a self-contained environment, (c) a
phoenix-like, intentional community that is re-created each summer,
and (d) camp-specific rituals, norms, and behaviors that are passed from
one generation of campers to the next.[3]

The common element for all attempting to define this magic is the
existence of ritual at Jewish summer camp, and the distinguishing characteristic of camp ritual that is communal song. Sales and Saxe observe,
"Song is used to bring order to chaos in the dining hall, to build community, and to create spiritual moments. It brings groups together, it
energizes, it creates mood."[4] Judah Cohen notes that communal singing
at camp provides campers with a sense of community and religious identity.[5] It is communal song that is fundamental to this camp magic.

My own research into the communal song at Jewish summer camp[6]
indicates that the communal singing at summer camp, be it at prayer
services, song sessions, a *Havdalah* campfire, or a rousing hand-clapping
version of *Birkat HaMazon*, serves as a disruption (in the most positive
way) that heightens individual "Jewishness" and serves as a mechanism
for creating Jewish community and deepening attachment to the Jewish
community. The feelings, emotions, and connections campers receive
from these musical camp experiences become physically, emotionally,
and psychologically embodied and persist through the campers' entire
lives. They recall their experiences with great fondness and pass these
memories on to their children, who often become campers themselves.
The magic of communal song is so strong that decades after campers
have left camp, the sounds, tastes, smells, and sensations from their summers away linger in their minds and souls.

Jewish summer campers return to their congregations and seek these
all-encompassing, embodied, and lasting experiences while attending
prayer services at their home congregations. From my own experience
as a synagogue cantor, these campers often returned dismayed, disap-
pointed, or disheartened that the "regular" Friday night service could
not be like camp. Campers often wondered:

1. Why do I have to get dressed up?
2. Can you sing the new melody we learned this summer for *L'cha Dodi*?
3. We think it would be great to dance during services!
4. How come when I come to services here, I don't feel anything, but Friday night at camp was sooo special?

Some campers felt shut out, but others persisted and tried to bring a bit of that camp magic into the then-normative Friday evening service. One eager camper brought her guitar into my office and taught me what she had learned that summer. During the ensuing years, she joined me on the bimah on multiple occasions and eventually attended rabbinical school. Another group of campers approached me and the rabbis and asked if the ancestral mothers could be included along with the ancestral fathers in the *Avot*, the first prayer in the Shabbat *Amidah*. I, along with the rabbis and educators, considered and studied the request, and a short while afterward a new version of the *Avot* was pasted in the copies of the currently used prayer book, *Gates of Prayer*.

These returning campers were also instrumental in helping institute other liturgical changes, such as the singing of the *Mi Shebeirach* and the addition of *iyunim* and *kavanot* (introductions to prayers). Services became less formal, and eventually Friday night services were moved to an earlier time to accommodate families and allow time following services for congregational dinners.

Did a few teenagers returning from camp really propel all these changes? The answer is a qualified yes. The summer camp experience is a node of a rhizome that then crosses its roots with a rhizome we may call "the synagogue," and these rhizomes then expand on preexisting systems.

Disruption 2: Debbie Friedman (1951–2011)

In late December 2010, I sat in an Italian restaurant on Westwood Boulevard with my husband, Rabbi Don Goor, two congregants from Temple Isaiah in Los Angeles, and acclaimed Jewish singer-songwriter Debbie Friedman. Debbie had recently moved to Southern California, and we were in the middle of collaborating on the semester ahead at the

Los Angeles campus of the HUC-JIR. This dinner was just days before Debbie was to leave for the Limmud adult-learning retreat in the UK, and she shared her plans for teaching and song sessions there. As we sat around plates of pasta and glasses of wine, Debbie shared her vision of liturgy and music at the Los Angeles campus and how excited she was to continue her work with the HUC-JIR students.

That was the last conversation I had with Debbie. She returned from Limmud and died shortly thereafter from complications from pneumonia. There is a terribly sad irony that Debbie Friedman's *yahrzeit* coincides with Shabbat B'shalach, also known as Shabbat Shirah—the Shabbat on which synagogues worldwide chant the portion describing the Exodus from Egypt. At her funeral, acclaimed singer-songwriter Craig Taubman began the funeral with an *a cappella* rendering of her composition "Sing Unto God" (1972). The song that helped launch her career was now being sung to accompany Debbie as she was brought to her eternal resting place.

We all *knew* Debbie; that's just who she was. When she sang, we felt as if she were singing to us individually. Even in a room of thousands, the plaintive quality of her voice reached out across the stage and the lights and entered the deepest part of your soul. She had a huge personality, and she embraced everyone. Her songs were like those nodes on the rhizomic piece of ginger: they have spread far and wide and intersected with the voices and songs of future generations of singer-songwriters.

I cannot speak for Debbie posthumously, but I think she would be amused that she is listed as one of the "disruptions" in this chapter. And, she would look at me, roll her eyes, laugh, and say, "Yeah. That's me. The big disruption." Her self-effacing personality aside, Debbie Friedman single-handedly precipitated major changes in the way we think about synagogue liturgies and communal singing in the Reform synagogue.

Friedman's early career was fostered by mentors and teachers from the Mount Zion Reform community in Minneapolis, summers at the Kutz Camp Institute, and a six-month trip to Israel in 1969. While at Kutz, Friedman developed her songleading and songwriting skills. It was also at Kutz where she was mentored by such luminaries as composers Michael Isaacson and Lazar Weiner. During the six months at Kibbutz Yifat, Friedman gained fluency in Hebrew and fell in love with the country and people of Israel. These three locales, though separate and distinct, were a formidable force in Friedman's development as both a singer and songwriter.

Friedman's rise to prominence occurred in May 1972 with the presentation of her *Sing Unto God* service at Mount Zion. The Friday night service was composed of eleven liturgical selections basically following the outline for Friday evening worship as presented in the *Union Prayer Book*, the prayer book then used throughout the Reform Jewish community. Although Friedman could not read music, she had trained a local high school choir through rote repetition to learn the melodic lines, harmony, and Hebrew text. The service was eventually recorded, distributed, and served as a way for Debbie's music to be more widely disseminated.[7]

Deleuze writes how music can "deterritorialize" and decenter,[8] and in the case of the *Sing Unto God* service, Friedman decenters the *Union Prayer Book* liturgy. She takes the canonic prayers and verses of the prayer book and recasts them for a new generation. Although some have derided Debbie's lack of musical training and criticized her songwriting technique by referring to her compositions as "tunelets" and "ditties,"[9] there is actually an unaffected sophistication in the way she melds together words and music. In "Sing Unto God," for example, Friedman features a shifting rhythmic drive that makes the song engaging for both the listener and the singer. "And Thou Shalt Love" (the English interpretation of the *V'ahavta*) contains a melody that builds slowly with a sequential gradual rise in pitch and a climactic triplet figure on "and do all of Thy commandments" to emphasize these words.

Friedman's disruption of Reform Jewish liturgy is especially apparent in her continued attempts to give voice to the biblical women who have often been minimized and relegated to the margins of our tradition. In "Miriam's Song" and "Devorah's Song," Friedman expands on the biblical narrative and extols the virtues of these matriarchs.

In "Miriam's Song," Friedman provides us with a multi-verse midrash on the role of Moses's sister Miriam at the time of the Exodus. Her musical midrash is based on the verses coming immediately after the Song at the Sea. In the Torah we read, "Then Miriam the prophet, Aaron's sister, picked up a hand-drum, and all the women went out after her in dance with hand-drums. And Miriam chanted for them" (Exodus 15:20–21).

In her now well-known lyrics, Friedman creates not only a song, but a beautifully envisioned midrashic biblical scene:

> And the women dancing with their timbrels
> Followed Miriam as she sang her song
> Sing a song to the One whom we've exalted.
> Miriam and the women danced and danced
> the whole night long.
> And Miriam was a weaver of unique variety.
> The tapestry she wove was one which sang our history.
> With every thread and every strand
> she crafted her delight.
> A woman touched with spirit,
> she dances toward the light. (Friedman 2013)

Friedman was not only a composer, but a storyteller, and the rhizomic tendrils extending from the song are extensive. In my congregation (and others), "Miriam's Song" provided opportunity for seemingly spontaneous dancing as women (and some men) of all ages linked arms and danced through the sanctuary celebrating the moment of the Exodus. "Miriam's Song" is transformative not only because of the midrashic text giving voice to female empowerment, but also because it legitimized dancing and other physical expressions in the sanctuary as a valid part of worship. Similarly, in "Devorah's Song," Friedman amplifies the voice and the story of the prophet Devorah:

> Arise, arise, Devorah
> Arise, arise and sing a song
> Arise arise, Devorah
> *Uri, uri dabri shir*
> Devorah the prophet was a judge in Israel
> She sat beneath her palm tree on a hill
> And people came from everywhere
> Just to hear her judgments honest and fair
> Devorah the prophet, Devorah a mother in Israel. (Friedman 2013)

Through Friedman's lyrics and music, the prophet Devorah becomes contemporary, vibrant, jumping off the page, and once again presents a female role model who, like Debbie Friedman herself, forged new pathways and whose prophecy echoes continually.

As in other works, Friedman utilizes English and Hebrew text together seamlessly—as a work of dynamic art—influencing an entire generation of singer-songwriters. Rabbi Danny Freelander noted that in this use of the languages together, Hebrew and English created "a tipping point in contemporary Jewish music, a profound change that has created the sound and substance of American Judaism today. My life—our lives—have been spiritually enriched by her contributions, which will continue to bless as future generations sing her songs and perceive their origin as 'traditional.'"[10] Rhizomes of female empowerment entwine themselves around those tendrils of vernacular language mixed with Hebrew and essentially help to create a new art form.

"L'chi Lach" functions as a midrash on the biblical story of Abraham's journey. Here again, Friedman asserts a woman's voice: that of the unvoiced Sarah by presenting the midrashic command *"l'chi lach."* A continually rising vocal line provides us with a sense of direction and a feeling of moving forward. The story of our ancestors is also one of perseverance; such a vocal line demands a bit of tenacity from amateur singers, as the musical range pushes the natural limits of what might be considered appropriate for congregational singing. And yet, as it is sung, we don't give up; rather, we, like Abraham and Sarah, journey forward. Friedman is making a subtle yet radical statement when she asks us to sing *"L'chi lach."* The biblical text has been reimagined and reenvisioned, and the words *l'chi lach* indicate to both singer and listener that we all belong, that we all have a place in our communal storytelling, and that we are all part of the greater Jewish journey. The rhizomes of "Miriam's Song," "Devorah's Song," and *"L'chi Lach"* spread far and wide, creating a space for women and encouraging other singer-songwriters to compose songs expressing inclusivity.

Of all of Friedman's compositions, it is Debbie's interpretation of the traditional prayer for healing, *Mi Shebeirach*, that may have the most lasting impact on the liturgies and music in the Reform synagogue. In traditional settings, the *Mi Shebeirach* for healing is a short prayer interpolated as part of the service for the reading of the Torah. Friedman changed this. She, along with Rabbi Drorah Setel, wrote a new *Mi Shebeirach* that combined English and Hebrew and included the ancestral Matriarchs alongside the Patriarchs. Friedman and Setel's *"Mi Shebeirach"* was originally written in 1987 for a *Simchat Chochmah* (Joy of Wisdom) ceremony in honor of Marcia (Marty) Cohn Spiegel, a feminist activist who had raised issues of alcoholism, addiction, and domestic abuse within the Jewish community. As Spiegel was about to turn sixty, she wanted a ceremony focusing on her own need for personal healing. According to Greg Drinkwater, writing in *American Jewish History*, "Cohn Spiegel, active in a Conservative synagogue and thus familiar with the traditional *Mi Shebeirach* blessing, asked Friedman to write a new version for her, and Friedman agreed, turning to Setel for help. As Friedman and Setel wrote the new song, multiple contexts and goals informed their work. Through this song, they would affirm Cohn Spiegel's need for her own emotional healing, while also providing a Jewish source of support for others experiencing emotional, spiritual, and physical pain."[11] Although others had written blessings for healing or had adapted the traditional *Mi Shebeirach* prayer for healing services, the Friedman version is probably the best known and has had the most lasting impact.

When Friedman sang *"Mi Shebeirach,"* she would ask those gathered to provide names in the interval between the first and second verse. This practice of calling out names is also often augmented with the reading of a list of names of all those in need of healing. As a congregational cantor for twenty-five years, I had a unique perspective regarding the power of this moment. The singing of *"Mi Shebeirach"* with the recitation of names was an earnest endeavor, with worshipers patiently waiting until the rabbi's gaze met their eyes as a signal to call out a name if warranted. People would often weep as they called out the name of a family member or friend. A friend would reach over and clasp their hand or put an arm on their shoulder. In that moment of praying for healing, the sanctuary was transformed: prayer became real and vivid, God was present, and individual worshipers became a community.

Although healing centers and healing rituals had existed in some communities, the Friedman setting of *"Mi Shebeirach"* made the possibility for healing rituals and prayers to enter the liturgies of a greater number of Reform synagogues. Debbie's *"Mi Shebeirach"* gave us permission to acknowledge our own frailties and weaknesses and especially to understand how healing of body and spirit is not the same as curing physical ailments.

The rhizomes sent forth from Debbie Friedman's guitar, voice, ingenuity, and vision have expanded way beyond prayers for healing. Friedman's songs and prayers provided a gateway into liturgy and ritual previously not open to liberal Jews. The ways we currently pray and, in my opinion, even our current prayer book, *Mishkan T'filah*, have been influenced not just by her music, but by the type of community she provoked in the most positive way.

I was witness to Debbie's captivating presence and songs many, many times at conferences, study retreats, prayer services, and concerts; she enabled the environment of *communitas*[12] in which members of the group coalesce, feel invigorated, and empowered. The newest generation of Jewish singer-songwriters now interlace their tendrils and roots with those of Debbie Friedman's and will continually empower these singing communities and expand the boundaries of Jewish song and liturgy.

Disruption 3: Changing Communities

I am standing on the bimah on a Friday night, and the rabbi and I are leading opening songs and psalms to begin ushering in Shabbat. I see that the sanctuary is partially filled with new members and those we call the "Friday night regulars," and as my eyes scan across the sanctuary, encouraging the congregation to join in song and prayer, I come to the realization that this congregation in which I am now standing is not the same congregation I stood in front of when I first joined the clergy team at Temple Isaiah in 1988. An entire generation has passed on. The seats where the "regulars" sat have been taken over by other members. When I began my tenure, there were women who were called *bubbe* and grandfathers were *zayde*, and there were a few congregants who had grown up speaking Yiddish. But these *bubbes* and *zaydes* are now long gone, and there are few congregants who know more than a few Yiddish expressions.

There are more intermarried families. There are non-Jews. There are more single people. There are a few gay men who come to services with their children. There are Persian Jews. And there are Israeli families of Sephardic heritage. I look down at my music, and the author of the song is listed as "traditional"; and as I sing, I ask myself, "Whose tradition is this? Who in this increasingly diverse congregation is represented by this so-called tradition?" This epiphany was the beginning of my attempt to find music that might better represent the multicultural community I was now serving as cantor. This disruption of demographics is a disruption I believe will spread rhizomes for decades to come.

Recent reports on the Jewish community by American Jewish Population Project[13] and the Pew Research Center[14] confirm my observations that the Jewish community has appreciably changed. The percentage of non-white Ashkenazic Jews has increased, and particularly among Jews under the age of thirty, 28 percent identify as non-white. But just as the congregation has changed, so has the leadership. There are non-Ashkenazic rabbis, cantors, synagogue leaders, and congregational presidents. Arya Marvazy, senior director of programs at the Jews of Color Initiative, concurred with my observation and felt that especially in Los Angeles, more Persian Jews are affiliating with Reform congregations, and this creates "greater diversity in the synagogue space."[15]

I created a challenge for myself: to find a way to create a synthesis of sounds, a musical palette reflecting the congregation's diversity, history, long tradition of musical excellence, and a forward-facing aesthetic embracing a new cultural reality. Simultaneous with this realization, a benefactor came forward and provided the funding for an instrumental ensemble for Friday night services. I was also blessed by rabbinic colleagues who encouraged me to find "our sound"—a synthesis of rhythms, melodies, and harmonies that was unique to the synagogue. I was very fortunate to be joined in this musical and liturgical pursuit by an incredible pianist/music director, a multi-woodwind player (flute, clarinet, saxophone), and a percussionist who played both hand drums and drum set. As we began planning services, we sought to create a fusion of sounds embodying Middle Eastern rhythms and jazz-inflected harmonies. I sought to find a musical-liturgical vocabulary that was inviting and inclusive, but also simultaneously honored multiple traditions.

I wondered if this musical grappling was my own issue or whether it extended to other cantorial colleagues—especially cantors of Mizrachi and Sephardic backgrounds. I discovered I was not alone in this quest and that many of my cantorial associates have sought to bring non-

Ashkenazic sounds and rhythms into their services as a way of honoring their own specific backgrounds and heritage while also responding to changing community dynamics.

Even though Cantor Donna Azu comes from a Persian background, she grew up attending Ashkenazic synagogues. She only truly began to explore Persian song and chant while in cantorial school and researching her master's degree thesis. Although she has introduced only a few Persian melodies to her congregation, they are "very open to new music . . . and learning more about other Jewish communities." She has successfully included melodies from Nava Tehila congregation in Jerusalem and told me that "although these melodies aren't Persian, they do have a Middle East flavor."[16]

Others, like Cantor Galit Dadoun, who grew up in a North African home in Israel, realized her congregation had little knowledge of "other Jews—Sephardic, Mizrachi. . . . Every time I find something that has an accessible melody influenced by Sephardic or Mizrachi melodies, I will incorporate it, but . . . I do most of my exploring and learning from people like [cantorial colleague] David Berger, and Israelis nowadays who write in that style. I add a lot of 'Israeli' to everything I do because I have a personal preference, but also I find Israelis write to the words better."[17] The American Reform synagogue, however, is for the most part an Ashkenazic-centered movement, and often this stifles those who are desirous of sharing their treasured cultural melodies and chants. Cantor Aviva Marer, who grew up in a family of Bene Israel Jews from India and has a strong sense of personal identity and cultural pride, expressed her personal ambivalence in presenting Mizrachi music to her congregation due to fear of "othering" herself and feelings of personal reluctance. "But I also wonder how much of it has to do with the Ashkenazi-centric cantorial education HUC offers. Aside from one class in Ladino, we really didn't explore world Jewry much at all. That said, I will also own the fact that I have very few memories of tunes or melodies that I knew growing up. . . . Also, please know that every rabbi I have worked with thus far has always been extremely supportive and encouraging of me exploring more Sephardic music. It is my hesitancy, not theirs."[18]

Liturgical and musical change takes time. It often takes years for these musical rhizomes to spread their roots. Deleuze called this idea of eventual rhizomic change "becoming." The concept of *becoming* is a recurring and salient theme in the work of Deleuze and Guatteri.[19] This *becoming* is the notion that an entity is always in a state of flux, continually changing, always emergent. According to Deleuze, all the elements of a system or assemblage (as Deleuze calls it) do not act as a coordinated whole, but rather all the elements interact with other elements and create new entities. This *becoming* or emerging is visible and audible in the liturgical and musical changes we are currently witnessing in the contemporary liberal synagogue, and this disruption to the demographics of the Reform Jewish community is a disruption that will continue to spread rhizomes, tendrils, and tubers through our musical liturgies for decades to come. As the community in the liberal synagogue continues to diversify, the music and liturgies will also be impacted to reflect the increasingly varied population sitting in the pews.

Cantors like Jaqueline Rafii are determined to make this Deleuzian "becoming" a reality. In her master's thesis she expresses how all Jews must expand their understanding of each other's cultures and embrace the idea of Jewish community as a global community:

> Beyond preserving this music, I realized there would be value in disseminating it to Jewish communities around the country—whether Persian, Ashkenazic, Sephardic, Mizrahi, or otherwise. I had observed a gap in general American Jewish knowledge about the customs, music, and history of non-Ashkenazic Jews, and I felt an urge to research and bring awareness to the rich wellsprings of the many diverse cultures within the Jewish family. I believed integrating global melodies into services and programs, perhaps even gradually making them a normative part of the menu of offerings to American Jewish communities, would help promote understanding, unity, and connection among Jews of all backgrounds.[20]

Cantor Rafii reminds me that this embrace of new melodies from unfamiliar cultures both by congregations and those cantors, cantorial soloists, and music directors who want to share them is often a slow and uncertain process. Sometimes, even when we have good intentions, our attempts are thwarted. Often that "becoming" does not happen even when we want it to.

In the fall of 2012, I stood on the bimah at Royce Hall, the large theater on the UCLA campus, where Temple Isaiah held their High Holy Day services, and began the first of three repetitions of *Kol Nidrei*. This would be my last time singing *Kol Nidrei* as the cantor of the synagogue, because in July 2013 I, along with my husband, Rabbi Donald Goor, would be moving to Jerusalem, Israel. I could feel the support from my fellow clergy, the large volunteer choir, and the thousands of congregants gathered for this most sacred moment. The first recitation of *Kol Nidrei* was beautiful—with choir, cello, piano. Then came the moment for the second repetition. I turned the page in my loose-leaf binder of music, and then I looked at my accompanist. In a stage whisper, I said, "I can't do it."

"What do you mean you can't do it?"

"I can't sing this . . ."

"*Kol Nidrei*? You have to sing *Kol Nidrei*."

"No—the Yemenite version I prepared and rehearsed . . . I just can't do it."

"Sing something else . . . you have to sing something . . ."

In the huge binder of High Holy Day music was an *a cappella* setting of the "traditional" *Kol Nidrei*, and that is what I sang.

I got cold feet.

I chickened out.

I had wanted to share with the congregation my growing appreciation for the depth, breadth, and tradition of Jewish music beyond the sounds of Eastern and Western Europe. I also wanted to express the cultural reality of how the Temple Isaiah community had changed over my twenty-five years. I thought I would use this Yemenite chant for *Kol Nidrei* to demonstrate these changes in a tangible, musical way.

I never sang that *Kol Nidrei*.

I had not done my homework. This Yemenite rendition of one of our most hallowed prayers could have been the culminating moment after months of congregational education through musical sermons, workshops, and bulletin articles. I could have reached out to colleagues, congregants, and scholars to share wisdom about the styles and sounds of non-Ashkenazic music with my congregants and laid the groundwork for liturgical and musical expansion.

But I did not.

After living in Israel for almost a decade, I am surrounded daily by the melodies, songs, and chants representative of the scope of Jewish culture. These songs are on the radio and on television. They blare from the speakers of passing cars on the street. The rhythms and musical modes of the Middle East reverberate through the *shuk* as the merchants call out the price of melons and tomatoes and the prayer chants resound from the synagogues in my neighborhood. And on Saturday evening the Orthodox men gathered in my building's lobby to chant *Havdalah* sing a somewhat hazy version of the melody made famous by Debbie Friedman. The mixture of east and west, ancient and modern is unavoidable, and it reaffirms my belief that we are more musically interconnected than ever. The rhizomes weave themselves around each other and make new connections that in turn make even newer connections.

More than ever, I'm ready to sing that Yemenite version of *Kol Nidrei*.

NOTES

1. For a more detailed description of a "rhizome," see Gilles Deleuze and Felix Guattari, *A Thousand Plateaus: Capitalism and Schizophrenia*, trans. Brian Massumi (Minnneapolis: University of Minnesota Press, 1987), 3–25.

2. Michael Zeldin, "Making the Magic in Reform Jewish Summer Camps," in *A Place of Our Own: The Rise of Reform Jewish Camping*, ed. Michael M. Lorge and Gary Phillip Zola (Tuscaloosa: University of Alabama Press, 2006), 90, 87.

3. Amy Sales and Leonard Saxe, *How Goodly Are Thy Tents: Summer Camps as Jewish Socializing Experiences* (Waltham, MA: Brandeis University Press, 2003), 46–49.

4. Sales and Saxe, *How Goodly Are Thy Tents*, 84.

5. Judah M. Cohen, "'And the Youth Shall See Visions': Songleading, Summer Camps, and Identity among Reform Jewish Teenagers," in *Musical Childhoods and the Cultures of Youth*, ed. Susan Boynton and Roe-Mon Kok (Middletown, CT: Wesleyan, 2006), 178.

6. Evan Kent, "So Much More than Kumbaya: Music at Jewish Summer Camp and the Formation of Jewish Identity" (doctoral dissertation, Boston University, 2013).

7. For a fuller discussion on the *Sing Unto God* service and Debbie Friedman's early life, see Judah Cohen, "Sing Unto God: Debbie Friedman and the Changing Sound of Jewish Liturgical Music," *Contemporary Jewry* 35, no. 1 (April 2015).

8. Deleuze and Guattari, *A Thousand Plateaus*, 296–97.

9. See, for example, Eliyahu Schleifer, "Current Trends of Liturgical Music in the Ashkenazi Synagogue," *The World of Music* 37, no. 1 (1995): 68.

10. Debbie Friedman, *Sing Unto God: The Debbie Friedman Anthology* (New York: Freda and Cheryl Friedman and Transcontinental Music, 2013), xiv.

11. Gregg Drinkwater, "Queer Healing: AIDS, Gay Synagogues, Lesbian Feminists, and the Origins of the Jewish Healing Movement," *American Jewish History* 104, no. 4 (2020): 619.

12. Victor Turner, *The Ritual Process* (New Brunswick, NJ: Aldine Transaction, 1969), 96–97.

13. Leonard Saxe et al., *American Jewish Population Estimates: Summary & Highlights 2020*, American Jewish Population Project, Brandeis University, revised May 18, 2021, https://ajpp.brandeis.edu/us_jewish_population_2020.

14. Pew Research Center, *Jewish Americans in 2020*, May 11, 2021, https://www.pewresearch.org/religion/2021/05/11/jewish-americans-in-2020/.

15. Arya Marvazy, personal correspondence, December 31, 2021.

16. Cantor Donna Azu, personal correspondence, December 29, 2021.

17. Cantor Galit Dadoun, personal correspondence, December 24, 2021.

18. Cantor Aviva Marer, personal correspondence, December 28, 2021.

19. Deleuze and Guatteri, *A Thousand Plateaus*.

20. Jaqueline Rafii, "Music of an Ancient Jewish Family: Recovering, Preserving, and Disseminating the Prayer Music of Persian Jews" (Academy of Jewish Religion, master's thesis, 2021).

18

The Gender Revolution
Disruptions of Jewish Feminism

Rabbi Elyse Goldstein

WHEN I WAS GROWING UP in the 1960s, the notions of a female rabbi, a female Israeli Supreme Court judge, or an Orthodox synagogue where women read the Torah from their side of the *m'chitzah* were either impossible dreams or ridiculous scenarios. I never once saw a woman ascend the bimah of my Reform temple in Forest Hills, New York, except to light the Friday night candles; even the mothers of the bat mitzvah girls sat in the pews while the fathers proudly had an *aliyah* to the Torah.

In 1968, when I was thirteen years old, I was the only girl in my Reform religious school class who chose to have a bat mitzvah instead of a "sweet sixteen." I will never forget the moment I ascended the bimah, read my portion, and opened my speech. I pushed the prepared text aside—the text that had been written for me by my rabbi—and began to speak extemporaneously. I explained how meaningful and important the day was for me, and then I announced that I wanted to become a rabbi. My family gasped. The cantor broke into tears. And then the rabbi *literally* fell off his chair. When he regained his composure, he announced into the microphone on his side of the bimah, "No, no, of course she means she wants to be a *rebbetzin*." "But no!" I said into the microphone on my side of the bimah, "Let my husband be the *rebbetzin*; I'm going to be the *rabbi!*"

Gales of laughter follow in this cute and true story. But for me, it wasn't intended to be funny. In fact that announcement would be the beginning of a lifetime of not only explaining and justifying and figuring out what it means to worship and lead *in spite of* my gender, but also as much *because of it.* I didn't know then what it would mean to break a glass ceiling. I was only thirteen and I wanted to change the world. Then, my intention was highly personal, totally individual. I never thought that women becoming rabbis would shake the very foundations of Judaism, question every assumption of Jewish life that was based on patriarchal power, or challenge what it meant to be a Jew altogether. I didn't realize then that I was in the middle of a quiet revolution, one that would not remain quiet but would eventually echo into the pages of the prayer book, the board rooms of major Jewish organizations, the seminaries, the yeshivot, and the Israeli government, all within the next generation.

In the years following my bat mitzvah declaration, Sally Priesand and the first generation of female rabbis were ordained, women became cantors and synagogue presidents, and liturgy changed not only to include the Matriarchs but eventually to incorporate the gender-neutral Hebrew of Marcia Falk and the feminine presence of the *Shechinah*. We started singing songs of Miriam in summer camp, learned Talmud from Orthodox women, introduced the notion of female spirituality, made lace tallitot, and redefined sexual politics. We felt empowered to create midrashim with biblical women named and unnamed, to take on the traditional meaning of the *mikveh* and reappropriate it to a feminist agenda, and even to invoke the name of the Goddess. We reclaimed and recast scores of different rituals and questioned the hierarchical nature of those rituals and the community that owned them. We challenged the Israeli public to rethink the lines between religious and secular, and we brought the issues of childcare, domestic abuse, violence against women, and power imbalances in the Jewish organizational world to the fore.

Indeed, Jewish feminism has brought the largest-scale disruption in Judaism since the 1800s, when Emancipation allowed Jews to leave the ghetto and Reform Judaism attempted to find a way to help Jews navigate this new world. As Emancipation challenged the role that Jews could play in secular society, Reform Judaism challenged the role that secular concepts could play in Judaism. In the 1960s, feminism continued to interact with both of those challenges. First, it continued to expect that core concepts of the secular world—equality of the sexes, in this case—would find a home within Judaism. This notion that secular ideas and values can inform a Jewish community without destroying it may have begun with Emancipation, but it was truly tested when the Jewish feminist movement revealed the gap between the growing secular leadership opportunities for women and the lack of Jewish leadership opportunities for women. Second, it continued to expect that the role of the Jewish woman in religious society would mirror the role that all women began to see themselves playing in secular society, that is, as equal partners in every aspect of life.

The scope of feminist disruptions within Judaism was very broad. It began with the ordination of women, which questioned previous assumptions of male authority. That revolution led to significant challenges to our previously male-identified rituals, to the ritual garb that identifies "the Jew," and finally, to our male God-language—and with that, inevitably, to our core theology.

Rabbinic Authority

The most significant disruption occurred in 1972, when the standard images and expectations of Jewish leadership were shattered by the public ordination of Rabbi Sally Priesand by Hebrew Union College–Jewish Institute of Religion (HUC-JIR), the seminary of the Reform Movement. Since the early nineteenth century, Reform Judaism had, at least on paper, ensured the religious equality of women. The American introduction of the ceremony of confirmation for both girls and boys in 1846 by Max Lilienthal in New York City attested to the growing religious emancipation of women; he saw no reason to exclude girls from the new rite.[1] As early as 1851, Isaac Mayer Wise had removed separate seating from his synagogue, Anshe Emeth in Albany, New York.[2] In the 1850s, reforming rabbis were arguing for the ceremonial religious equality of women; the abolition of *chalitzah*, a ceremony freeing a woman from marrying her dead husband's brother (or closest male relative); and the rejection of the status of *agunah*, a woman unable to remarry because of her husband's unwillingness or inability to grant her a Jewish bill of divorce. All these reforming discussions, however, were based on the assumption that men would continue to govern decision-making bodies in the Jewish world. Since men made the rules, men could bend them or even break them so as to "allow" women's entrance into such male bastions as bar mitzvah or *aliyot* to the Torah. This entrance was limited to what the male leadership felt was still proper for "ladies" of that era. It was not until the 1920s that the question of whether such opportunities for equal religious expression might lead women to enter the echelons of rabbinic leadership was formally debated.[3]

As historian Pamela Nadell has expertly and carefully traced, the path toward female ordination in the United States faced many of its own disruptions.[4] In 1919, a woman named Martha Neumark began to study at the Reform rabbinical seminary. In 1921, she was allowed to lead a High Holy Day congregation, thus marking her entrance into the paraprofessional rabbinic world. The occasion prompted Kaufmann Kohler, then president of Hebrew Union College (HUC), to form a faculty committee to study the feasibility of ordaining women. The report emerged officially in 1922, at a conference of the faculty of HUC, and revolved around three themes. The first was halachic, and the rabbis studied whether Jewish law might permit such ordination. The second was sociological, and the rabbis wondered whether women could retain their devotion to home and family within the difficult and laborious tasks of the rabbinate. The third was communal, and the rabbis worried whether ordaining women would create an irreparable schism within the larger community. Despite these concerns, the faculty of the seminary voted in favor of women's ordination. However, a few months later, the lay Board of Governors, with whom the final decision rested, rejected the vote and restricted ordination from HUC to men only. Though women attended the seminary as students from as early as 1900, they were not to be ordained. It was in Nazi Germany that the first woman actually held a rabbinic title. In 1935, Regina Jonas, a student at the liberal seminary in Berlin, was empowered with a special diploma to "hold rabbinic office." She ministered to her people first in Berlin and then in the Terezin concentration camp and died in Auschwitz in 1944. Twenty-eight years after her death and fifty years since the seminary faculty had formally agreed to ordain women, Sally Priesand became the first woman to be granted *s'michah*, official ordination, from the faculty and lay body of a major rabbinic seminary. It took the merging of the 1960s counterculture, the women's liberation movement of the early 1970s, and the personalities of Priesand, the president of HUC-JIR, Nelson Glueck, and the HUC-JIR faculty of the time to move fully from the *idea* of religious leadership

THE GENDER REVOLUTION 283

for women to the *practice* of it. This disruption changed the face of Jewish authority forever.

The Reform Movement knew there would be implications of Priesand's ordination. Indeed, the Reconstructionist Movement soon followed suit, with the ordination of Sandy Eisenberg Sasso in 1974, and the Conservative Movement ordained Amy Eilberg in 1983. Today even the Orthodox Movement deals with the demands of its own female leadership. A New York–based yeshivah, Maharat, ordains Orthodox women, who can take the title Maharat (*Morah Hilchatit Ruchanut Toranit*, translated as "Torah-based, spiritual teacher according to Jewish law"), or Rabbanit, or despite facing strong opposition, Rabbi.

Female rabbis often bring their feminist concerns into their work, along with a sense of collective responsibility as women. What were once considered solely women's issues, belonging to the Sisterhood or women's auxiliaries, are now discussed from the bimah and at conferences of major mainstream Jewish organizations. In sermons and study groups, the female characters of the Bible are studied, examined, and dissected. The issues of sexual harassment and power hierarchies in organized Jewish life have come to the forefront. Gender stereotyping in textbooks is being analyzed and corrected. The presence of women in positions of religious and communal authority, influence, and decision-making has pushed what have been previously identified as "marginal" issues into the consciousness of the mainstream.

Ritual

We love and crave rituals because they are reassuring, predictable, familiar, and time-tested. They remind us of our past and point the way to the future. They tell us who is in and who is out, and who or what is most important to us. Rituals remind us of where our community and family boundaries lie. Even as we come to expect a birthday cake, or anniversary roses, or Thanksgiving turkey as a part of the rhythm of the cycles of a secular year, so too do rituals inform us of our religious tradition's values and expectations and the rhythm of its year. We instinctively understand that ritual behaviors tend to be experiences not of intellect but of heart. They generally do not shock, provoke, or discomfort us. And when and if they do, we face them slowly and with some trepidation. We wonder how to reappropriate and reclaim them without having to throw them out and start from scratch.

Rituals are practices or customs that accompany times of transition and demarcate religious ceremonies. Given the depth of connection people have with the Jewish rituals of their upbringing and the ways in which they are entrenched in how we emotionally connect with Judaism, we can see wherein lies the challenge of creating new rituals that speak to contemporary women. Jewish women simply do not have a religious, customary observance or practice for the processes specific to female bodies and activities traditionally connected to female behavior. Jewish feminism allowed us to ask ourselves whether we should create such "new" traditions and what to do with the ritual gaps many women felt when it came to some of the most significant moments of female lives. We asked: What should be our template? Who will decide if it "works"? Will our children and grandchildren find it normative?

Rituals serve to provide mechanisms for people to process transitions, some of which are powerful and positive (for example, birth, partnership, historical victory) and others that are meaningful but negative (for example, death, divorce, historical calamity). The disruption of feminism both names transitional moments to which Judaism has historically not attended—for example, the onset and the continuation of menstruating, childbirth, lactating and weaning, aging—and also elevates them as both physically and spiritually meaningful and significant. The creation of rites for those neglected transitions—both reclaiming "found" rites and inventing new ones—seems itself disruptive work.

Yet, newly created rites were not fully disruptive, first, because we come from a long and hallowed Jewish heritage that keeps adapting without losing its central character and, second, because our spirituality has become increasingly broad and global, so "new traditions" actually no longer seem such an oxymoron. For example, Passover seders have new Haggadot and new tunes, but they follow the same basic lines as seders have historically. In part because of a post–World War II willingness to adapt and incorporate new experiences, like celebrations of the State of Israel and memorials for the Holocaust, Jews have learned from each other across the world. In the twenty-first century, Jewish rituals are often driven by what we can find on the internet and put together as a hodgepodge of sources from everywhere both inside and outside of Judaism. Our denominational communities interact with each other more and more, and Jews connect both formally and informally with other religious communities all the time. It would not be unusual for a largely Ashkenazic community to sing *Ein Keiloheinu* in Ladino and serve up a Yemenite challah for Shabbat. Feminists who found themselves searching for rituals for historically ignored moments set up such paradigms for adapting rituals already in place. Though caught between the old and new, we live in a dynamic tension that both helps us create and yet ensures we not wander too far off the Jewish map.

Jewish feminism sought to close the gap between the received and the as yet unknown by investing our rituals with authority and gravitas, for example, insisting a baby-naming ceremony for a girl be seen as a covenantal service (called *b'rit habat* [plural, *b'rit banot*], the covenant of girls) and encouraging—even requiring—it to be performed on the eighth day. So common did this ceremony become, sometimes moving from the home to the sanctuary of the synagogue, that soon the Conservative Movement followed suit in normalizing birth rituals for Jewish girls. Today, the Orthodox world also regularly celebrates the birth of a Jewish girl with some kind of ceremony. Jewish feminism created that space for a new ritual and eventually turned the ceremony into an expectation.

The same process occurred for a girl becoming bat mitzvah; the ceremony received parity only when feminists insisted on moving it to Saturday mornings, when it had previously been more of a Friday night celebration, without a Torah reading. Jewish weddings changed their look as well, as brides began to circle their grooms and both partners smashed a glass at the end. The traditional text under the chuppah that sealed a wedding—"Behold, you are consecrated to me"—now said by both partners, rather than just the husband, and the oft-used substitute phrase "I am my beloved's and my beloved is mine" was moved to another part of the ceremony rather than left to be the woman's non-halachic legal bond.

The questions that Jewish feminism posed about ritual soon moved beyond whether we need rituals that "balance the scale" or that are "equal" to the traditional rituals that have been celebrated for or performed by boys and men. In the liberal movements, we continue to answer that question with egalitarian adaptations of traditional ceremonies. However, feminists also inquired about female agency, the autonomy of experience and the references Jewish rituals incorporated. In asking a new set of questions, Jewish feminists wondered how to invent entirely new rituals. If we choose to be inventive, what will "female" rituals look like? Will they focus on biological womanhood—menstruation, childbirth, lactation—or on a more inner sense of womanhood, or as is increasingly important now, should Jewish ritual not be defined by physicality? What would inventive feminist rituals look like beyond the once-accepted gender binary, identified through biology?

We learned in the early phases that imitative rituals can be extremely meaningful and satisfying. They fulfilled the need for balance. They addressed the exclusive maleness of so much of our traditional life-cycle events. They "normalized" the entrance of women into the public religious life of the community. They made the tradition confront the spiritual needs of women and included women on every level into the dramatic and sacred moments of life.

But we learned that on another level, imitative rituals alone do not satisfy. They say nothing about women qua women. They do not mark the unique moments that happen only to women. They do not bond us with other women in a historical way. They wrap women in male imagery, making women "honorary men" for the moment. They express Judaism in ways that still are male ways of envisioning the universe, male ceremonies imagined and invented by men. They are still largely male answers to the question "How shall we mark this moment?" Inventive rituals reimagine, start from scratch, and have no historical bounds or expectations, no communal sanctions or standards. They ask, "Is there something uniquely female about this act, about this object?" By definition, they are probably not traditional. Feminism made us look up and notice that there are no rituals to imitate for first menstruation, for menopause, for lactation and weaning, for pregnancy, infertility, miscarriage; for divorce, for children leaving home, for hysterectomy, for mastectomy, for rejoining the workforce after spending years at home; for rejoicing in the company of women, for forming bonded friendships, and for caring for an elderly parent.

We learned that inventive rituals are also risky. They are not linked to thousands of years of practice. They do not look like what our ancestors did. One ceremony does not necessarily link to the next, as bar mitzvah links to chuppah. And we miss the knowledge and linkage that past generations have performed similar rituals to mark similar times of life and events. Many of the early new rituals that Jewish feminism invented assumed heterosexuality, heterosexual marriage, and childbearing as a norm. And many of these ceremonies are still eclectic, individualized, hard to find, and promulgated mostly in "women's" books, in Rosh Chodesh groups, and among women rabbis, found on internet search engines.

The feminist disruption of ritual also led to a questioning of previously understood male rituals like bar mitzvah, and certainly the current controversies around circumcision—the ritual of *b'rit milah* as well as the actual medical cutting—can be found also in feminist writings and thought, since feminism has required Jews of all denominations to question the precise meaning and intentions of all rituals, especially those that include the body and bodily autonomy.

Ritual Garb and Objects

It is not surprising then that when women clergy began role modeling on the bimah and women started taking public and significant ritual roles, we also began to question why lay people could not take on the traditional male garb they began to see their female rabbis don. Women's tallitot and women's *kippot* started to appear at conventions and online, proliferating greatly when the market share for Judaica included women buying for themselves. Miriam's cups to hold water during the seder, in memory of Miriam's well, are now common. There are female *sof'rot* (Torah scribes) now writing *sifrei Torah* (Torah scrolls) and mezuzot, as well as even making the parchment for these scrolls, and congregations specifically seek out these female scribes to commission them in a kind of correction for past male hegemony over the production of these objects. Even before the time these ritual changes were coming into play in North America, a group centered in Israel but with international membership called Women of the Wall (*N'shot HaKotel*) started demanding the right to wear tallitot, *t'fillin*, and *kippot* and to read Torah on the women's side of the Western Wall. Beginning in 1988 and echoing their North American and Western European counterparts, they too deemed it normative for women to take on this ritual garb and to proudly wear *t'fillin*, tallit, and *kippah* without needing to ask permission from any authority. This group gained momentum through the Reform Movement and even began marketing their own tallitot, designed especially for them by renowned Judaica artist Yair Emanuel of Jerusalem and crafted in Israel, which feature the four Matriarchs adorning the four corners of the *tzitziyot* (fringes.)

The purple and turquoise "A Woman of Valor" tallit, with the words of Proverbs 31 embellishing the neck piece ("A woman of valor, who can find?")—the poem recited traditionally by men to their wives on Friday nights—shows we have reinterpreted even the most traditional words into what could be called a feminist reappropriation. While one could say that commercialism on its own does not demonstrate progress, there is a ubiquity of ritual garb specifically made for women that marks a threshold and that is a demonstration of the incredible flexibility that feminism shows in reaching back to traditional forms and making them a powerful, meaningful, and relevant touchstone for women in new and important contexts.

Now imagine being in a synagogue, watching a female rabbi preside over a bat mitzvah celebration, both the young woman and her clergy wearing hand-dyed silk tallitot in pastel colors and lace *kippot*, while the mother wears a Women of the Wall tallit with the four Matriarchs at the corners, the sister of the bat mitzvah is called up for an *aliyah* with her female partner, and they are all reading from a Torah scroll that has been scribed by a woman: you have a good visual of the ritual disruptions feminism has created.

God-Language

Language both reflects and creates reality. When I was growing up, a firefighter was a fireman. If a woman held that job, we called her a "lady fireman" because we could not picture how a fireman could be anything but a man. Since language reflects reality, the vocabulary of a woman functioning in that job reflected the paradox of a woman doing a man's job; therefore, she was a "lady fireman." But language also creates reality. I knew I couldn't be a fireman, because a fire*man* is a *man*.

While most of us believe that the language of the prayer book is mainly metaphorical, some of it is indeed literal. When the siddur indicates Shabbat is like a bride, it is using a simile. But when it declares, "God creates light," the language in the siddur is literal. Through feminism we began to understand that our theological language also created a reality, that *imitatio Dei*— to be like God—was understood as exclusive to men; for if God the Father is our highest ideal, is not then maleness itself the ideal?

As Jews, we find ourselves engaged with the God of the Bible, whether we personally believe in a supernatural Being, or a spiritual force, or some amorphous indefinable personal connection to the universe. As children, that God of the Bible is taught to us through stories, and we come to know God as a King, a Father, an all-powerful and mighty Being, mostly referred to as "He." As adults, we are invited to redefine, reevaluate, and reshape our beliefs from those that we held in childhood. Feminism rejected simplistic childhood images. Our spiritual experience and, thus, our spiritual vocabulary were challenged to increase and broaden, and with it, so was the language of prayer. Feminism challenged the absurd notion that language does not matter, for it posited and then demonstrated that intertwined with male metaphors for God are also fundamental issues of male dominance and male authority.

It is extremely difficult to speak about God in a concrete way. We accept that human language is, by definition, limited. But our prayer language is even more limited by the common use of the male gender for God. While medieval Jewish philosophers such as Maimonides championed an invisible, incorporeal God and rejected the anthropomorphism of the Bible as a mere projection of human need, the representation in the Torah of God as male, if not physically then in terms of imagery, has been a dominant theme throughout time. The image of God's maleness in the text is expressed not only through the male pronoun, but through many male characteristics: God as a "man of war" (Exodus 15:3), a shepherd (Psalm 23), king (Psalm 10), and father (Jeremiah 3 and 31). In Jewish liturgy, the standard formulation for all blessings has been "Lord, King of the world."

Language can be poetic, esoteric, or symbolic in nature, but it is never arbitrary; "chair" means chair and not table. When we say "moon," we mean moon, not sun. So, male images of God served as "models of" and "models for." They served as models of the past male hierarchy and models for the continued male hierarchy. Even today, male imagery of God continues to shape the way we think about God, Judaism, and the role of men and women in the religious sphere. While people rightly protest that symbols are not reality but only symbols, through centuries of familiarity, symbols lose their transparency and come to be seen as descriptive of, and not merely as metaphors for, reality.

What we say about God colors what we say about ourselves on a personal level. Jewish feminism questioned the root assumptions and root beliefs about God and the resulting hierarchical nature of our religion; so it also challenged the language of those beliefs. It confronted the root conceptions, and the root comfort, of God as Father.

Since English is a non-gendered language, feminists first substituted neutral terms for God; "Ruler" was used for "King," "Parent" substituted for "Father." We spoke of God as "God" instead of either "He" or "She." However, we now realize that such neutralization works only when the listeners divest themselves of all male stereotypes and archetypes, so that the word "parent" does not automatically conjure up a father, either heavenly or human. We saw that neutral language only works when it doesn't let us hide.

We then boldly included the use of "She," to point out the anthropomorphism and ultimate blasphemy of centuries of using "He." The threat of being labeled a "pagan" for the use of "She" or female God imagery stifled and squashed early serious discussion of such options, and it pointed to our own deep discomfort with the notion of ultimate female authority. Hebrew, however, is a gendered language. As with changing "He" to "She" in English, we started doing the same in Hebrew and changed the masculine gendered Hebrew of *baruch atah* to the feminine form of *b'ruchah at*. We experimented by switching back and forth during one service or by using feminine in one service, masculine in the next. Marcia Falk produced groundbreaking work in *The Book of Blessings* (2007), which offered a new Hebrew that renders blessings not only in a non-gendered way, but also in a non-hierarchical way. No longer did she use the "Blessed art Thou, Lord our God, King of the universe" formula. Instead, she suggested "We bless the Source of Life" (in Hebrew: *n'vareich et m'kor hachayim*). The word "we" in Hebrew takes neither the male nor female form; it is a truly "neutral" pronoun. Rather than God remaining the distant King, or becoming a Queen, God became the Core of Life, the Fountain of Life, and other more imminent (inner) rather than transcendent (outer) idioms. Her use of language moved the language of prayer not only away from gender, but also away from traditional formulations of God as over us, reigning supreme, and demanding our praise.

We also added *Shechinah* to our roster of God language. *Shechinah* literally means "dwelling" and appears as a name for God's presence in Rabbinic literature beginning in the second century CE. The Talmud mentions God placing "His *Shechinah*" in the midst of Israel (Babylonian Talmud, *Sanhedrin* 39a) and of the *Shechinah* resting upon individuals when they study Torah (*Pirkei Avot* 3:7). Depicted often as luminous light, the *Shechinah* shines with God's radiance; it is a manifestation of divinity to indicate God's presence at a given place. Medieval Jewish philosophers describe the *Shechinah* as a separate entity itself, created by God. With the development of the Kabbalah, Jewish mysticism, the *Shechinah* takes on definite feminine characteristics. In the late twelfth and thirteenth centuries, the *Shechinah* begins to be described as princess, daughter, and the feminine principle in the world. Jewish feminists rediscovered and retaught *Shechinah* as a powerful feminine model already within Judaism. Here were our ancient goddess symbols of moon, mother, water, earth, all embodied in our own authentically Jewish symbol.

Feminism asked us a series of powerful and important questions: How much are we willing to change the Hebrew when it comes from the Torah? And how do we write prayers that express a woman's experience of spirituality? Would they be distinctly "female"? Could men say them? Would the structure of a woman's prayer book, written only by women, be different? What about those who identify as nonbinary, as neither male nor female speaks to them or for them?

The disruption of patriarchal notions and language for God was a tidal wave. As God concepts changed, our concepts of ourselves as Jews had to change. As birth and moon and mothering imagery were introduced by Jewish feminists, we began to wonder about what it means to be *b'tzelem Elohim*, made in that divine image. Male and female were they created—or is there a nonbinary creation as well? As feminists began to write theology, beginning with Judith Plaskow's groundbreaking book

Standing Again at Sinai: Judaism from a Feminist Perspective (1991), we corrected the patriarchy of traditional Jewish thought and created our own
brand that took into account not only feminist but also ecological and
political concerns. We gained a new theological vocabulary, losing God
the Father and expanding both our vocabulary and our imagery of the
Divine. Feminism also suggested that the very model of Jewish prayer in
general—a group of people all saying the same thing at the same time,
things someone else has written for them—may be an outdated, patriarchal model.

Conclusion

No Jew today, even the most isolated or extremist one, is free from the
influence of feminism, even if only to have to justify a "traditional" position. Whereas in the last generation the feminist position might have
seemed marginal and threatening, today congregations must explain
why the women in their synagogue do not participate ritually or publicly,
why there are no women's voices at the Torah study they frequent, and
why their view assumes heterosexuality or male privilege. That Jews of
every denomination are in dialogue with these questions proves that
the questions have entered mainstream Jewish consciousness and have
become part and parcel of the wider view of the community. The fact that
young rabbis no longer struggle with finding women's voices in the text
or in the classroom, but instead have set upon the task of redefining the
entire rabbinate itself as a result of sensitivity around gender, proves just
how wide and how deep the conversation has become.

The disruptions that early Jewish feminism provoked have so clearly
entered our conversation that the tone and content of Jewish life have
been forever altered. The "Jew" we had grown accustomed to identifying
as the man with long side curls and a fur hat shares the stage with the
woman with a pink tallit. And it continues to morph into the androgy-
nous or genderqueer or trans Jew, leaving us with no stereotypical way to
identify the image of a "typical Jew."

As with the ordination of women, the ordination of openly gay, lesbian, and transgender rabbis in the liberal movements has shaken all
our assumptions about gender, sexuality, and religion. A new generation
of thinkers has challenged us: Should feminism by definition widen the

conversation about gender altogether? What is a gender? What does being "feminine" or "masculine" mean? Does our biological sex or the genitalia we were born with define us as Jews?

The Jewish feminist revolution began with equal-access feminism: women wanted to have the same opportunities and the same religious responsibilities as men. Second-stage Jewish feminism went further to challenge the theological language in describing God and to shake our foundational assumptions about women, men, and the whole halachic system. It questioned the hierarchies of synagogue life, the language of the prayer book, and the nature of the prayer itself. That there is a changing table in the men's room of a synagogue is no accident. That there are liberal *mikvaot* where both men and women immerse for all manner of events is because of a seismic change in attitude.

Third-stage Jewish feminism is being born as I write, as the disruptions of feminism help lead the way for the current disruptions of queer inquiry and of nonbinary sensitivity. Indeed, the feminist disruption in the Jewish world in every category—ritual, prayer garments, language, worship, leadership, theology—caused an awakening of awareness to gender and its politics that now continues to animate Jewish life, scholarship, thought, prayer, and practice. Simply put, once we began questioning the role of being female in the way we envision Judaism, the question of any and all gender-specific roles, assumptions, expectations, definitions, and significance in what a Jew practices, how a Jew prays, and what a Jew wears or looks like would have to follow. And indeed they have. In this way, Jewish feminism not only disrupted but also created a new space where all Jews, indeed all seekers, could find a home.

NOTES

1. See David Resnick, "Confirmation Education from the Old World to the New: A 150 Year Follow-Up," *Modern Judaism* 31, no. 2 (May 2011): 219.

2. Jonathan Sarna, "The Debate over Mixed Seating in the American Synagogue," in *The American Synagogue: A Sanctuary Transformed*, ed. Jack Wertheimer (New York: Cambridge University Press, 1987), 362–94.

3. In 1897, following the success of the Pavilion of Religions at the World's Fair in Chicago and the formation of the National Council of Jewish Women, Rabbi Emil Hirsh organized the first American debate on the topic of female

ordination. Invitees to the symposium "Women in the Synagogue" included
Henrietta Szold, Ray Frank, and others. Please see Jewish Women's Archive,
"Symposium on 'Woman in the Synagogue': Contributions from Henrietta Szold, Hannah G. Solomon, and Ray Frank," https://jwa.org/media/
symposium-on-woman-in-synagogue-contributions-from-henrietta-
szold-hannah-g-solomon-and-ray-fr.
4.   See Pamela Nadell, *Women Who Would Be Rabbis: A History of Women's Ordination, 1889–1985* (Boston: Beacon Press, 1999).

FOR FURTHER READING
The flowering of Jewish feminist scholarship is a huge part of the disruptions I
have described. Where once all text was viewed through the eyes of men and the
male experience, we now have the opportunity to hear the voices and be inspired
by the insights of women and the female experience.

WORKS ON JEWISH FEMINISM (ANNOTATED)
Adler, Rachel. *Engendering Judaism: An Inclusive Theology and Ethics.* Boston: Bea-
con Press, 1999: An invaluable read into the deepest, core questions that
Jewish feminism created.
Goldstein, Elyse. *New Jewish Feminism: Probing the Past, Forging the Future.* Wood-
stock, VT: Jewish Lights, 2008: Exploring the disruptions this article sug-
gests, in more detail.
Płaskow, Judith. *Standing Again at Sinai.* New York: HarperOne, 1991: The book
that first brought the "feminist revolution" into Jewish thinking.
Ruttenberg, Danya. *Yentl's Revenge: The Next Wave of Jewish Feminism.* Seattle: Seal
Press, 2001: A younger generation tackles the questions their Jewish feminist mothers raised.

WORKS OF JEWISH FEMINIST BIBLE COMMENTARY
Cohn Eskenazi, Tamara, and Andrea L. Weiss, eds. *The Torah: A Women's Com-
mentary.* New York: CCAR Press; Women of Reform Judaism, 2008.
Frymer-Kensky, Tikva. *Reading the Women of the Bible: A New Interpretation of Their
Stories.* New York: Schocken Books, 2004.
Goldstein, Elyse. *The Women's Haftarah Commentary.* Woodstock, VT: Jewish
Lights, 2008.
———. *The Women's Torah Commentary: New Insights from Women Rabbis on the 54
Weekly Torah Portions.* Woodstock, VT: Jewish Lights, 2000.

19

Moving Beyond Post-Holocaust Theology
Critical Theory as a New Paradigm

Rabbi Jason Rodich

How does our largely nontheological generation find spiritual and ethical resources in our tradition to confront a world that seems so uncertain? From the vantage point of my pulpit in San Francisco in 2022, I worry that the Reform Judaism that we teach American Jews often fails us. I know that it sometimes fails me. In a difficult world in which meaning is so often elusive, how might Reform Judaism continue to assert that life is, in fact, deeply meaningful? How might it assert that how we love, argue, celebrate, and protest, how we are sick and die and mourn, how we are in human relationships, and what we eat and say and do all matter profoundly? Our approach to religion must make Judaism our partner in constructing meaning and ethics and serve as an inquiry into life's most demanding questions. I suggest that critical theory, a mode of social inquiry that aims to critique society and expand human liberation, might serve as an important framework for Jewish theology today.

Today, North American Reform Jews occupy a religious paradigm deeply influenced by the Holocaust and the establishment of the State of Israel, despite Reform Judaism's roots in the intellectual milieu of nineteenth-century Germany. The religious universalism and broad idealism of the pre–World War II era was brutally refuted in the wake of the ideology of hatred and death of the National Socialists and other Fascist regimes. Evil knocked at the doors of great hope and optimism; the utopian and Romantic ideals of nineteenth-century Reform Judaism collapsed along with Jewish communities of Europe.

Beautifully and redemptively, in the second half of the twentieth century new thinkers living primarily in the United States and Israel, including survivors of the Holocaust, reconstructed Jewish thought in ways that responded to this collapse and even challenged reactions in Jewish thought rooted in trauma.[1] These postwar leaders understood that much was at stake and that Jewish tradition must change or, more specifically, ways of understanding and theorizing the tradition needed to change.

Abraham Joshua Heschel taught us about the power of awe, Emmanuel Levinas exposed us to the spiritual demands of the other, Emil Fackenheim instilled in us the religious obligation to remember, and Maurice Eisendrath demonstrated the power of protest. Regardless of their denominational affiliations, their thinking flowed into the Reform Movement and helped us grapple with questions that earlier modern thought could not. For example, Reform Jewish institutions embraced the Zionism they had previously rejected and cast it as a modern and rational form of salvation. In that move, they accepted ethnic and national pride alongside the extreme universalism of Reform's founding leaders. Communal participation and eventually certain rituals such as wearing a tallit were restored to Reform practice, in the spirit of Heschel's insistence that *kavanah* (intention) be centered in Jewish religious practice.[2] All of this helped to usher a traumatized people into a new era with a sense of Jewish religiosity still intact, or at least available, that could make meaning of the recent past but more importantly operate with questions of the present and future in focus.

Once again, Jews, along with all of humanity, find ourselves in a new era, and we need to be brave enough to do as the post-Holocaust theologians did: propel ourselves forward in order to offer current Reform Jews meaningful religious life that articulates a sense of meaning and holiness for our chaotic world today.

I contend we need a new universe of thought, what Rabbi Rachel Adler calls a *nomos*, in which we conceive of Jewish theology today.[3] We are now in an era that is shaped by several new and demanding factors that are different from the difficulty of developing a relationship with God after the Holocaust. The post-Holocaust generation of thinkers courageously reimagined Jewish spirituality for their generation, and we must do so for ours.

I write from specificity. I am a forty-year-old gay rabbi serving at a large congregation in San Francisco. Certainly, my concerns are not universal, though I do not think they are unique. Within our congregation, in addition to the full range of pulpit responsibilities, I lead a community of hundreds of young adults ages twenty-one to forty, in a city that is currently an epicenter of global business because of our proximity to Silicon Valley. In other words, San Francisco is and is not representative of the full Jewish world, but without question, it is a place to which Jews from all over the world come because of its economic opportunity and cultural vibrancy.[4]

What I observe in my community is that there is very little faith in God per se and that religious practice is minimal for many of my congregants. Indeed, one of the fundamental questions that emerged in Jewish thought after the Holocaust, the ontological question of the possibility of God's existence in the face of such wickedness, does not seem to be the framing question for a relationship with God today. For many of my congregants God does not really exist at all or, at least, not in any way that the classical tradition understands God. And yet, there remains a rather firm commitment to Jewish identity and Jewish community as expressed through participation in life-cycle events, enrollment of children in religious school, social programs, and occasional attendance at prayer services. There is assuredly a heartfelt commitment to the Jewish project. Yet, if a transcendent God is no longer tenable and, as I will argue, postmodern and nuanced ideas of God are not well taught or transmitted, then what is the philosophical foundation that supports our tradition? Are we merely standing on ceremony and vague notions of tradition?

What, then, is the Judaism that we transmit from generation to generation today? In our prayer books, it can appear as though we still ascribe to a classical theology that God will heal the sick, remove evil from our midst, and free the captive. The contemporary alternative readings are mostly unserious attempts to rework theology and often seem to avoid it altogether, and one wonders what to make of these words in a world in which the captive remain captive, the sick still die, and most significantly, evil seems to, once again, be knocking at the doors of hope and possibility. It is not clear to me to what one turns in our Reform liturgy to make sense of, for example, the rise of fascism, endless gun violence, or the climate crisis if one does not actually believe in the God described there. One can speak vaguely of intention or meditation or a feeling of spirituality, but I don't see how these ideas really function as a critical life resource when they are not rooted in a theological framework in which the worshiper believes.

There are certainly many important newer thinkers, both within the Reform Movement and beyond, including beloved teachers of mine whose work has been personally transformative, such as Rabbis Benay Lappe and Rachel Adler. Even so, the innovations of some of our best contemporary religious thinkers (many of whom are women and queer people) have not been able to make structural changes to the praxis of Judaism. I fear that, in part, despite being a movement committed to ongoing change, we are in many ways not open and at risk of fossilization.

The post-Holocaust thinkers had a similar problem on their hands. They understood that classical Jewish theology could not stand up to the demands of their questions and their pain when theodicy (the justification of an omnipotent God's goodness, i.e., the Holocaust was not God's failure) was impossible for most Jews. While much of their work is still critical for us (like Heschel's articulation that Shabbat is a "palace in time"), we do not truly internalize their wisdom if we overly rely on the philosophical labor of that generation when our needs are not the same and especially when we face a world in crisis.[5] There remains an ideological chasm between the world out of which post-Holocaust theological innovations emerged and the reality that many of us live in today. In my experience, Reform rabbis and educators continue to teach thinkers like Heschel while largely ignoring the contributions of more recent thinkers.

Where does this leave us? Rabbi Rachel Adler offers us narrative theology and a reworked approach to halachah rooted in a feminist ethic of inclusion and deep respect for the other, while Rabbi Bradley Artson offers us a Jewish form of process theology that posits God as a culminating sum of human choice and natural processes.[6] Through Svara, her queer *beit midrash*, Rabbi Benay Lappe insists that one not need to be a rabbi or scholar to possess the keys to the textual tradition—I've watched more than one young person break into tears at the joy of stepping into the role of interpreter of the tradition. But does fresh thinking about Jewish spirituality, in a holistic and structural way, shape our lives in liberal Judaism? *What do we believe in?* Do we have a methodology by which we might create and disseminate new theological approaches? Reform Jewish thought at its best embraces the need to continually change the ways in which we understand our tradition. If we ever think we've fully come to a complete and immutable answer, we have probably abandoned something core to the Reform Movement's philosophical commitments.

To make this concrete, allow me to explore a few examples of how this moment demands a new chapter of Jewish thought. The first is the staggering rise in global conflict and authoritarian governments. In the previous generation, the simultaneous establishment of the State of Israel and the unprecedented rise to power of American Jewry gave American Jews a sense of hope that was perhaps not so different from the utopian dreams of Reform's early founders in Germany. In recent years, however, we have borne witness to the rise and mainstreaming of American and European white nationalist movements.[7] American Jews watched young white men carrying torches and shouting "Jews will not replace us" and then watched their president fail to condemn them and even appear to curry their favor. In Israel, despite overall strong support among Reform Jews, the chasm between American progressive values held dear by many in the Reform Movement and Israeli state policies vis-à-vis the disenfranchisement of Reform Jews and Jews of Color and violations of Palestinian human rights grows wider. In other words, the causes for hope for the previous generation are now, for some, the very source of concern about the future. Do the modern American and Israeli nation-states reflect the religious understanding of Zion after all? Did this post-Holocaust Jewish world we built actually save us?

Another reason for the need for new Jewish thought is more personal and immediate: We are not who we used to be. While some Reform Jews still debate the merits of interfaith marriage, many in our communities are fully embracing multireligious households and are not waiting for rabbis to give the green light about raising children who are, for example, both Jewish and Hindu. The once controversial notion of patrilineal descent (now known as equidescent) is now commonplace, and the questions that it raises are increasingly irrelevant for most Reform Jews.

We are more diverse than ever before.[8] Despite that diversity, we fail to offer a thought framework that can accommodate and account for (and celebrate) the reality of many people's lives. What does it mean, for example, for a white male rabbi to insist that for him to perform a marriage, the couple must agree to raise their children exclusively Jewish when the non-Jewish partner is a woman of color from Asia who wants to pass on her heritage to her children? Is the notion of one religion and one practice practical for the family? Does this demand fit into a theological framework that American Reform Jews largely accept? In what ways does this demand for fidelity to Judaism also reify racist and colonial structures, and to what extent is it rooted in a fear of loss rather than a hope for what might be?

It is in this light that I offer *theory* as a spiritual resource and philosophical approach in place of theology. I am arguing for a post-theological and deeply spiritual and intellectual Jewish practice.

What, in this context, is theory? Beyond the plain meaning of theory as a supposition for how something works, I first encountered theory as a concept as an undergraduate at The New School in New York, studying critical theory with a focus on feminism and critical race theory (long before these became right-wing talking points). In those Greenwich Village classrooms, I discovered critical theory as something that was, in retrospect, sacred. The *Oxford English Dictionary* defines "critical theory" as "a philosophical approach to culture, and especially to literature, that seeks to confront the social, historical, and ideological forces and structures that produce and constrain it."[9] The term is applied particularly to the work of the Frankfurt School.[10] Many of the scholars of the Frankfurt School were themselves Jewish by religion, culture, or descent, including Hannah Arendt, Walter Benjamin, and Theodor Adorno. I learned critical theory as a *practice*, as a way of interrogating the world of meaning around us to understand it, to make it more just, and to re-create meaning and purpose as our understanding of ourselves and the universe evolved.

The word "theory" has its etymological roots in the ancient Greek word *theōría*, meaning "contemplation, speculation, a looking at, things looked at."[11] If many (most?) Reform Jews, as I contend, can no longer accept a theistic source of power as a source for truth, ethics, and meaning making, perhaps in our generation we might find a sacred reverence for our greatest human gift: our ability to think with our own minds and remake ourselves and the world, seeing this as sacred without becoming arrogant.

Theory, at its best, is never only about contemplation, and I am not calling for an ivory tower Judaism or a belief in humans as God. Quite the opposite: we need Judaism to nurture us and help us be our best, loving, and ethical selves. Theory can be, for example, the work of understanding and enacting the classical theological categories of creation, revelation, and redemption, while also freeing us to forge new categories that help us articulate ethics and meaning in our lives.

If we, as critical theory supposes, are creators of a reality (which is always contingent) through speech and signs or through, as Judith Butler contends, performance, then when we think critically about our lives and our world, we become partners of one another in a sacred act of creation. How, for example, might prayer ritual be structured to help us navigate this?

When we engage in critical thought, questioning ourselves and each other, putting all assumptions on the table, are we not seeking a kind of revelation? By this, I mean a revelation that builds upon the legend of Sinai to a commitment for ongoing truth seeking and mind changing rather than to things we cannot accept as true. Torah teaches us that our ancestors were transformed by the ancient Revelation and covenant making, and we, too, might be transformed again and again as we see our world through a critical lens. Perhaps most significantly, theory can lead to redemption. As we theorize—as we constantly reimagine ourselves and our world—what evil and injustice might we undo in the process?

Theory as sacred practice is a refocusing of Jewish religious life on the process rather than on ultimate answers. For example, instead of asking what Judaism says about what happens after we die, we might ask about what it means to live and die in our tradition or what it means to have ancestors and what ethical demands those ancestors make of us.

At stake is a theological orientation that I suspect many gave up decades ago or never actually embraced. Liberal Jews have floundered in learning to talk about theology in a sophisticated way. Post-Holocaust thinkers ushered in a new era of thought that radically departed from the theodicy that came before it, working to save Judaism for Jews. We have a new challenge and the same obligation. The Pew Research Center's report *Jewish Americans in 2020* found that only 25 percent of American Jews believe in God, and this number is inclusive of Orthodox Jews, who likely make up a large portion of that 25 percent.[12] And yet, many Jews continue to seek connection with our tradition and with one another. Reform Judaism needs to once again lead a reform of Judaism. We need ritual and religious practices that are in line with who we *actually* are today, even as we remain firmly rooted in our past. We need a philosophical foundation for that practice that does not rely on mental gymnastics or metaphor to make Judaism work in our lives. If we are people who don't believe in a deity as "*Avinu Malkeinu*, our Father our King," then why are we saying this? Metaphor can bring us only so far. We require a grounded thought framework that we might embrace and that might embrace us, in our need for options, in our commitment to the rational. Without this, I fear that the possibility for Jewish religious life will shrink away for even more Jews, as what we offer seems farther and farther from the love, joy, pain, and heartbreak of our lives.

NOTES

1. See, for example, "Auschwitz or Sinai" by Rabbi David Hartman, who argues that Revelation at Sinai, not survival of genocide, should be the organizing principle of the Jewish people: Hartman, "Auschwitz or Sinai," Shalom Hartman Institute, February 1, 2013, https://hartman.org.il/auschwitz-or-sinai/.
2. Abraham Joshua Heschel, *Moral Grandeur and Spiritual Audacity: Essays*, ed. Susannah Heschel (New York: Farrar, Straus and Giroux, 1997).
3. Rachel Adler, *Engendering Judaism: An Inclusive Theology and Ethics* (Boston: Beacon Press, 2005), 34.
4. According to the San Francisco Jewish Community Federation and Endowment Fund's 2021 "A Portrait of Bay Area Jewish Life and Communities" population study, the Bay Area is home to approximately 350,000 Jews, the fourth largest Jewish population in the United States; https://jewishfed.org/sites/default/files/An_Integrative_Report_from_the_Bay_Area_Jewish_Community_Study.pdf.
5. The Pew Research Center's 2013 study notes that one-third of Jews born after 1980 say they have no religion, compared to just 7 percent for those born before 1927. Pew Research Center, *A Portrait of Jewish Americans*,

October 1, 2013, https://www.pewresearch.org/religion/2013/10/01/
jewish-american-beliefs-attitudes-culture-survey.

6. Rabbi Bradley Artson on process theology: "Process theology recognizes
    every 'thing' is really a series of events across time, a process, that emerges
    in relationship. We are each a process, and creation is a process. God is a
    process; revelation is a process. All emerge in relationship, meaning that
    no thing can be understood in isolation. . . . But God's power is not coer-
    cive and not all powerful. God cannot break the rules or unilaterally dic-
    tate our choices. Having created and then partnered with this particular
    cosmos, God is vulnerable to the choices that each of us makes freely as
    co-creators" (Alan Brill, "Interview with Rabbi Bradley Artson on Pro-
    cess Theology," *The Book of Doctrines and Opinions: Notes on Jewish Theology
    and Spirituality* [blog], May 1, 2018, https://kavvanah.blog/2018/05/01/
    interview-with-rabbi-bradley-artson-on-process-theology/).

7. In this example, I am thinking about groups in the United States such as the
    Proud Boys and others who participated in the Charlottesville riots in 2017
    or in violent and lethal attacks on synagogues (in 2018, 2019, and 2022) and
    in Germany the right-wing nationalist party Alternative für Deutschland
    (AfD).

8. In the 2017 "A Portrait of Bay Area Jewish Life and Communities," com-
    missioned by the Jewish Community Federation of San Francisco, the
    Peninsula, Marin and Sonoma Counties, the study found that "25% of Bay
    Area Jewish households include a respondent or spouse who is Hispanic,
    Asian-American, African-American, or of mixed or other ethnic or racial
    background (other than white). For those ages eighteen to thirty-four, the
    corresponding percentage is 38%; for those ages thirty-five to forty-nine,
    it is 27%. One-in-ten households include a respondent who is lesbian,
    gay or bisexual. Lesbian, gay or bisexual respondents are most numerous
    in San Francisco—one in five" (https://www.readkong.com/page/bay-
    area-jewish-life-a-portrait-of-and-communities-3254790).

9. *Oxford English Dictionary Online.*

10. The Frankfurt school refers to a group of intellectuals at Goethe University
    in Frankfurt during the interwar period who took up the project of creat-
    ing new social theory to help explain and imagine justice for the difficult
    world in which they lived. They offered a new thought framework that was
    at once credible as well as hopeful. For a robust exploration of critical theory
    and the Frankfurt School, see James Bohman, "Critical Theory," in *Stanford
    Encyclopedia of Philosophy*, ed. Edward N. Zalta, Spring 2021, https://plato.
    stanford.edu/entries/critical-theory/.

11. *Oxford English Dictionary Online.*

12. Pew Research Center, *Jewish Americans in 2020*, May 11, 2021, https://www.
    pewresearch.org/religion/2021/05/11/jewish-americans-in-2020/.

20

Holocaust Testimony
Listening, Humanizing, and Sacralizing

Stephen D. Smith, PhD

THE EVENTS OF THE HOLOCAUST will one day slip from living memory into history. It is only a matter of time. And yet, more than any other historical event that preceded it, the history of the Holocaust has been told through the eyes of those who lived it, even though it represents the deaths of those who did not survive.

Jewish deaths are more than a tally of corpses; people were murdered *because* they were Jews. Their deaths represent the fact that *being* Jewish constitutes a mortal threat. The witness of the survivor is about the survival of the Jewish people, which is an extension of the sacred traditions of Jewish liturgy and lore from the inception of the biblical narrative. No threat to the existence of the Jewish people was greater than the threat of the Nazis. For Jews, Holocaust testimony is existential, historical, metaphorical, and sacred. The attack on the Jewish community was an attack against all Jews, and therefore testimony is a reminder of the sanctity of Jewish life. The Holocaust also has universal application. If the genocide of the Jews was a failure on the part of humanity, Holocaust testimony is also a reminder about the sanctity of all life, relevant to all people.

The witnesses of the Holocaust have left a treasure trove of insights, information, and personal reflections that allow us to reexperience what happened as if we had been present. The German perpetrators meticulously documented when the trains bound for the death camps departed and how many Jews were being shipped in the wagons. At first, this dramatically insufficient historical data was all that historians had to work with to reconstruct the past. Today, thanks to the courage of those who were victims of the Nazi genocidal assault on the Jews, we now have tens of thousands of personal recollections of Jews who were *inside* the wagons when the doors were slammed shut. The time they took and the pain they endured to write and record and remember now make it possible to journey inside those wagons with them and to know in great detail what it was like to be there. As Zoe Waxman points out in her careful study *Writing the Holocaust: Identity, Testimony, Representation*, testimony gives meaning to history.[1]

Jews began to write down their experiences during the Holocaust from the start. Perhaps because Jews are a highly literate people, understand the long arc of history, or understood the Holocaust's severity more than anyone else, Jews who were trapped in the ghettos of Europe facing inevitable death feverishly wrote down their experiences for an unknown future audience. As soon as the concentration camps were liberated, the surviving victims immediately began to testify to their experiences.[2] Thousands of testimonies were collected by hundreds of volunteers in the 1940s.[3] Then followed a period of relative silence for approximately forty years, culminating in an explosion of publications, oral history projects, memorial museums, and education programs in the 1990s, which have continued through today. All these projects brought the personal experience of surviving victims of the Holocaust to long overdue public attention.

Holocaust testimony typically describes events in the past, but it constitutes much more than mere historical documentation. It goes to the very heart of existence for those who survived. They do witness what happened, but they also name those who did not survive as a memorial to their cruelly foreshortened lives. Survivors create a bridge between past and future, allowing those of us who did not experience their trauma to understand something of its meaning for humanity today. Surviving victim of the Holocaust and Nobel Peace laureate Elie Wiesel sees testimony not only as a bridge to the past, but as an extension of the survivors' very survival: "Rejected by mankind, the condemned do not go so far as to reject it in turn. Their faith in history remains unshaken, and one may wonder why. They do not despair. The proof: they persist in surviving— not only to survive but to testify."[4]

Witness is their being, but for their witnessing to have any meaning, it must translate into some form of changed behavior in those who hear it. Anita Lasker-Wallfisch was in the orchestra in Auschwitz-Birkenau and directly saw the sadistic bestiality of the Nazis. In my many conversations with her, she has always urged me not to give the German authorities credit for creating the factories of death as if it were some kind of technological achievement. "They were not clever; they were ludicrous, stupid idiots!" she puts it bluntly. She also expresses deep disappointment about how we have yet to apply any knowledge we have gained from listening to testimony. As she first exclaimed in her 1996 book *Inherit the Truth*, "I thought that our suffering was atonement for all time and that generations to come would be free from prejudice forever. Alas! I was wrong."[5] She is still saying it today.

So how do we translate the past into the present in a meaningful way? Will what we say about the past when the eyewitnesses of the Holocaust are no longer present suffice to hold us to account? The first thing to consider, of course, is that the Holocaust has a different meaning to Jews than to non-Jews. The ramifications for a Jewish audience listening to testimony are clear: all Jews without exception were marked for death. As such, every story is highly personal. The Holocaust remains an assault on the identity of all Jews up to and including the present day. Emil Fackenheim responded to this ongoing trauma through his so-called 614th commandment, "not to hand Hitler a posthumous victory" through the diminishment of Jewish identity. He sees the remedy of this lingering threat through the *reinforcement* of Jewish identity following the Holocaust.[6] In a similarly charged way, Primo Levi puts the need for memory of the Holocaust at the same level as the central prayer in the Jewish liturgy, the *Sh'ma*, recited daily by Jews the world over. In his poem "Shema," Levi describes the dehumanization of Jews during the Holocaust, then challenges his reader with an almost verbatim quote from the *Sh'ma* in the final part of the poem:

> Consider this has been:
> I commend these words to you.
> Engrave them on your hearts
> When you are in your house, when you walk on your way,
> When you go to bed, when you rise.
> Repeat them to your children.
> Or may your houses crumble,

> Disease render you powerless,
> Your offspring avert their faces from you.[7]

Levi's paraphrase of Deuteronomy 11:13–21—which warns against being "lured away" lest "God's anger. . . flare up against you"—suggests that if Jews do not remember, they will be cursed. The threat of the curse provides pretext to engrave the memory of the Holocaust "on your hearts." The injunction for Jews to pray three times daily is echoed by Levi in that divine retribution will follow should they fail to acknowledge the Holocaust. Levi replaces the acknowledgment of divine presence with remembrance of the suffering of Jews, in what he refers to as "the memory of the offense."[8] The significance of ending his poem "Shema" with the threat of a curse is paradigmatic of the curse against Amalek in Deuteronomy 25:19. It is not enough that Amalek's name be blotted out, but also one must remember why Amalek was cursed for all time.[9] Levi reminds his readers to keep the attempt to remove the memory of Jews from history ever present. He implies that testimony has near sacred status, which is echoed by Elie Wiesel, who says that testimonies are a canon of contemporary Jewish texts to be revered, to inspire, reveal, and warn.[10]

As is evident in the chapters in this volume, this is not the first time that the memory of Jewish destruction has taken on sacred meaning. And due to anti-Jewish violence over many centuries, there has been unfortunate reason to write about atrocity. In an article about Holocaust memory, David Roskies argues that "the greater the perceived destruction, the greater the effort to preserve every documentary scrap. That is precisely why the *sheymes* which normally refers to material containing the name of God and therefore not to be destroyed may also be applied to material written in the time of persecution, deserving special status."[11] Roskies awards the *Oneg Shabbat* Archive in the Warsaw Ghetto Talmudic status and describes Emmanuel Ringelblum's work in founding, maintaining, and ensuring the preservation of the archive as akin to the work that Rav Ashi accomplished with the Talmud. Further, Roskies suggests that the texts preserved from the Warsaw Ghetto hold a sacred quality. They are not God-given revelation, but rather authoritative texts that derive their authority "from the dead, whose deeds they chronicle; from those who preserved and buried every scrap of evidence . . . and from the living who publish, teach and translate these memorial texts."[12]

In an influential essay, George Steiner takes the sacred nature of first-person Holocaust narratives and applies it to texts written both during and long after the events were over: "The only completely decent "review" of the *Warsaw Diary* or of Elie Wiesel's *Night* would be to re-copy the book, line by line, pausing at the names of the dead and the names of the children as the orthodox scribe pauses, when re-copying the Bible, at the hallowed name of God."[13] Steiner's reference to the *sofrim* whose sacred duty is to ensure the correct and kosher rewriting of Scripture transforms historical and literary texts into sacred writings. Applying such reverence to narratives about the Holocaust sets the tone for a thoughtful reading of them. Nevertheless, readers do need the literacy to read critically if they are to learn from them fully. Readers need to be able to distinguish types of texts and not assume that because the subject matter is about the Holocaust, the text itself is untouchable.

Steiner's proclamation of the inherent holiness of testimony inadvertently makes writing about the profane sacred. Though he does clarify that his reverence is directed toward memory of the victims, any text about the Holocaust by default contains what Primo Levi refers to as "the memory of the offense," that is, the memory, however sacred, still includes the criminal acts contained within it.[14] Applying sacrality to testimony places it outside of historical and literary review, and therefore out of reach. There is more to learn from testimony when we have critical methodologies at our disposal. It is clearly not the intent of the authors who write to elevate such heinous acts; on the contrary, much like *M'gillat Esther* read at Purim, testimonies exist to explain the unspeakable acts of cruelty that Nazism carried out and how those who share it survived. Distinction also needs to be drawn between Adam Czerniakow's *The Warsaw Diary*, a primary source written at the time in the ghetto, and Elie Wiesel's *Night*, which is exegetical creative literature written ten years after the events. Though Wiesel is a surviving victim, writing about sacred matters does not elevate the narrative of *Night* beyond critical review. Testimony is fundamentally a polemic, as it is both an implicit and explicit denunciation of the motivation and actions of the Nazis. As such, it makes the point that the evil that was perpetrated did not prevail. Testimony given by surviving victims is by default salvific in some measure, because each person who witnesses has outlived the Nazi regime.

As time passes, the temptation to mythologize such memorial texts becomes greater, particularly when they are translated, edited, and read by audiences decades or generations after their occurrence.[15] Holocaust testimony is a form of "historical exegesis."[16] As Yosef Hayim Yerushalmi observes, this aligns well with Jewish memory, which is predisposed to reflecting the past through meta-historical myth rather than dry history. He observes that meaning is most likely to be derived from the Holocaust, "not at the historian's anvil, but in the novelist's crucible," thereby implying that interpretative storytelling allows the facts to speak more intelligibly than can data alone.[17] And so "the question is not whether the Holocaust will become a myth, but what kind of myth it will become."[18] Being aware that there is a need to make sense of the Holocaust and that doing so will lead to its mythologization is critical to the study of Holocaust testimony itself. Testimony contains factual information but is not limited to facts. It is the personal interpretation of experience provided in narrative form and therefore provides meaning in addition to facts. The need to create meaning from the Holocaust can easily lead to simplified redemptive (or anti-redemptive) conclusions.[19]

The vast corpus of survivor literature and audiovisual testimony bequeathed to us ensures a wealth of source material well beyond the life of the surviving victims themselves. Much of the material we have amassed is mainly documentary in nature—if exegetical at times—and requires us to find an interpretative framework in which it might be read, taught, or communicated through a variety of genre and media. The many volumes of documentary material may appear to guard against its own mythologization, but counterintuitively, the opposite is true. From the mass of Holocaust historical data, "heroes" and "villains" have emerged. They help us understand a complex past but also lead to the ossification of that past into a standardized, ritualized, homogenized, polarized, and sterilized account.[20]

Notwithstanding the long history of Jewish literature and liturgy that has reinterpreted destruction across the generations, Holocaust testimony has become a new genre of Jewish literature. Because of the direct assault on Jewish identity waged by the very nature of National Socialism, testimony is imbued with a sacral duty toward the dead and what their deaths represent to living Jews and surviving victims. Most Jews murdered by the Nazis did not have the dignity of a personal burial site. The dehumanization of the Holocaust reduced victims to numbers and suspended the rites of death and mourning. In many cases, establishing where and when a victim died remains impossible. Because there was no burial, the victims have no headstone with their name, date of birth, and the day they died, which also means they have no *yahrzeit*. While Yad Vashem has successfully collected names of almost five million Jewish people murdered during the Holocaust, testimony may be the only place the deceased victim's identification is preserved beyond their name. Arek Hersh regularly states in public that as the sole survivor of his family, he feels the duty to speak of them as a means of memorialization.[21] University of Southern California's Shoah Foundation has amassed approximately two million names extracted from testimonies in which the interviewee mentions a person. This number does include all the names they mention—such as friends and acquaintances and children born after World War II—but conservatively contains over a million names of people memorialized through their testimonies.

For all people to learn from testimony, there must be common understanding about what testimony means. Such a discussion has the unfortunate consequence of creating a crisis of witness, because there is a fundamental dilemma around both what is said and what can be understood when one listens to Holocaust testimony. The dilemma of Holocaust witness is the mandate from the dead to witness their deaths; thus, the surviving victims have borne witness to the world. In so doing they have described something that is impossible for most of us to comprehend. They struggle to find words to describe experiences to people who did not live through such extraordinary events. To try and explain this dilemma, Lawrence Langer quotes surviving victim Magda F., who said, "To understand us, somebody has to go through with it. Because nobody, but nobody fully understands us. You can't. No [matter] how much sympathy you give me . . . you're *trying* to understand me, I know, but I don't think you [can]. I don't think so."[22] I will try to rephrase what Magda said: To understand an event, one must live through it. Since only the surviving victims have lived through the events of the Holocaust, nobody else can understand them. It does not matter how much sympathy the listener might feel. However hard they might try to comprehend, it is just not possible to do so.

The danger of this dilemma is twofold: to make sense of it one must simplify it, and simplifying the impossible lends itself to mythologization. A good example of how historical events are mythologized as sacred memory events can be found in the Haggadah. When the Israelites departed from Egypt, there were many thousands of individual experiences, but only one narrative prevailed. Imagine how different the Passover seder would be if we had all those individual stories. What has survived is the mythologized and sacralized liturgy that gives a unifying narrative and provides coherent meaning. The tradition of metaphorical memory that Yerushalmi identified within Jewish culture leans into a mythological and simplified version that is easy to pass down. Such mythologization has some advantages, not least because it avoids the past being lost altogether and creates a single truth that everyone agrees upon. But it also turns the past into an object of history. We must ask each other: how do we break the deadlock of the dilemma and learn to listen without feeling the need to mythologize and simplify? The surviving victims have fulfilled the mandate to remember the dead. Our roles as the witnesses to the witnesses require that we do not objectify them as artifacts of history, but instead keep their memories alive as subjects to *encounter*. The dilemma of witness is broken when the listener knows that it will not be possible to understand the entire meaning of what has been said, but nevertheless is still willing to encounter the witness and struggle with their testimony.

When we think of archives, we imagine objects—documents, photos, artifacts, and testimony. Sometimes they are physical, and now, more often than not, they are digital. We go to the archives to research the objects within it. Once discovered we curate and reassemble the data we find there. We may layer on our own analysis of the past, provide critical analysis of the sources themselves, or disseminate the objects for the purposes of public education. Whatever we decide to do with what we find, we treat the data therein as objects.

Now imagine for a moment that the many archives of Holocaust testimony are not objects of the past, but subjects in the present—people who have shared their lives, whom you can still encounter.

This is in keeping with Jewish philosopher Martin Buber, who reconceived of the notion of encounter with deity; he described transforming the relationship from *I-It*, in which God is an object, to *I-Thou*, in which God is a co-subject. This results in a deeper understanding of deity in relationship to the individual in the present. In Buberian ontological philosophy, I-It objectifies the experience of the other, turning them into a thing. I-Thou subjectifies the other, creating a relationship. Using the Buberian I-Thou construct when listening or reading testimony, the listener no longer objectifies the experience of the witness or the form of their words. Instead, they "stand in relation" to the one who is witness to the events and respects the essence of their being.[23]

With remarkable insight, surviving victim of the Holocaust and psychologist Dori Laub identified that the dehumanization of Jews during the Holocaust eliminated the form of intimacy that stems from being recognized. Radical dehumanization meant that there was no one to whom another could say "thou."[24] In other words, the complete objectification of Jews meant there was virtually no one to whom a victim could turn and reach out and be seen as fully human. For Laub, testimony is the way to provide a missing "thou"; it is a rehumanizing path through which surviving victims can convey their inner memories of loss and pain to a trustworthy and humane listener. Testimony is not text, therefore; it is an extension of the life of the individual, an invitation to encounter who they are through what they share.[25]

In a similar vein, Karl Jung conceives of identity as being in two parts—the *persona* is what one sees and experiences of a person's identity from the outside looking in, and the *individual* is the living experience of the person from the inside out. By rethinking testimony as a *relationship*, it becomes possible to see beyond the *persona* (object) and experience the *individual* (subject) through *encounter*. Applying Buber and Jung's ideas to testimony allows us the opportunity to alter the subject-object relationship of "I-It" to "I-Thou"; the testifier and the listener reframe their relationship into a subject-subject encounter of mutual learning and coexistence. This mode of encountering testimony does not require the eyewitness to be present or alive. It is a mode of literacy, through which we are able to listen to or read first-person narratives as an extension of the life of the individual at the time at which they told it.

When the object of history becomes a new subject in the present, testimony may be reconsidered as a *type of relationship*, rather than as a *form of representation.* Buber stated that "all actual life is encounter" wherein "nothing conceptual intervenes, between I and You, no prior knowledge and no imagination."[26] Through an encounter with a person who lived through the past, mythologization is not possible; the listener ceases to need metaphorical meaning from the past when listening to the perspective of the subject in the present.

In an I-Thou encounter, there are no preconditions. The witness does not need the listener to understand, because the listener and the witness have each other's full attention. The listener does not demean or objectify the surviving victim as a thing-in-itself, because they fully recognize the humanity of the individual who is sharing the most painful moments of their life. The fear of being misunderstood and the likelihood of being misrepresented are both removed when they encounter humanity in each other.

There is real application for a Buberian reading of testimony after the inevitable end point of living eyewitness testimony. Marianne Hirsch refers to the period after the surviving victims are no longer alive as "postmemory."[27] At that point, their lives will be in the custodianship of society. It is also the time when testimony will most likely be canonized and turned to liturgical myth. In a bid to identify where the place of the Holocaust lies within public conscience in the future, Holocaust scholar Lawrence Langer has asked, "To whom shall we entrust the custody of the public memory of the Holocaust?" He continues, "To the historian? The critic? The poet, novelist or dramatist? To the surviving victim? Candidates abound, all in search of a common goal: the detour that will, paradoxically, prevent us from being led astray. . . . In some way too, with the exception of surviving victims, all are witnesses to memory, rather than rememberers themselves."[28]

The somewhat arbitrary list of individuals who could step in to maintain the function of witness are just examples of the many possible mediators of witness. The digital age has already lent itself to a confusing cacophony of voices representing the next generation of witnesses to the Holocaust. Such a cacophony has some merits in prolonging and extending the re-representation of witness; however, multiple voices will also complicate, occlude, or conflate the nature of the Holocaust with many convenient contemporary interpretations. This is not to deny the importance of having multiple voices or many points of view, but to alert ourselves to the potential misuse of memory. If memory is to be abused, it may be safer to create a unifying and simplified narrative upon which everyone can agree, to avoid the misappropriation of memory.

But before we fall back on a simplified version of the past, Jewish tradition has another tried and tested antecedent that can support ongoing discussion of highly complex debate. Wiesel reminds us that the oral tradition of Talmudic debate passes down through generations as a tradition of learning from "mouth to ear, from eye to eye."[29] He is referring mainly to the process of transmitting the message, but there is another aspect to notice. It took several hundred years of detailed debate before the Talmud was codified. To this day, the names of the Rabbis who struggled to interpret the Torah for their present day exist in our present, even though they died over sixteen hundred years ago. When reading the Talmud, we *encounter* the Rabbis as co-subjects in the present. Let us apply that same *kavod* (honor) to Holocaust testimony. We can and should continue to encounter them as living people, long into the future. We become witness to their act of witness.

The questions remain: who are the witnesses of the future, and can anyone be a witness to the Holocaust? Henry Greenspan reflects that there is a process of listening to surviving victims and entering the process of intellectual and emotional discourse in a bid to learn from the "memory of the Holocaust with the meaning of a single life."[30] This engagement of learning from one life at a time produces witnesses of the witness. The original witness provides not only the facts of history, but also what the experience has come to mean in the life of that one individual. Not all testimony is a simple narrative. It can contain many contradictions. When an individual testimony is set alongside testimonies of others, there are many points of difference in terms of what was experienced and what it has come to mean for the surviving victim who is sharing a life story. Greenspan believes it might be possible to inhabit the many contradictions—its "principles of incoherence"—so that we, too, must participate in the struggle to witness and to becoming, to a certain degree, "fellow recounters."[31] The incoherence and contradictions are not a danger to Holocaust memory. Instead, they show the human nature of the events, the struggle to describe them, and they guard against oversimplification.

But we also must be comfortable living with neither knowing nor understanding everything.

With the passage of time and the transmission of memory, the sense of personal connection and hence, to some degree, the authority with which one can speak become diminished with each generation of witness. Still today, surviving victims carry the responsibility of witnessing for those who cannot—the dead—and give testimony about their own experience. They are the first link in a chain of witness after those who did not survive. We are the inheritors, the next link in the chain. Like the ongoing debates of the Talmud, continuity is established when we enter the conversation with those who will never hear a surviving victim's testimony firsthand.

Whatever the consequences of the eventual and inevitable death of the surviving victims, they will one day die, and their memories will die with them. At that point, whatever has been collected will be completed by default. Testimony will continue to have impact within the unfolding contemporary context if we allow it to do so. The trajectory of Holocaust memory will be carried through the chain of witness, in which the testimonial narrative will cease to grow, but its effects will continue to be felt if the entire corpus moves from object to subject when the last surviving victim dies. This is a powerful disruption in the Jewish journey through history whose consequences cannot yet be understood—even as we struggle to rehumanize the dehumanized. Maybe this is one way for us to address the fear the Elie Wiesel stated: "Somewhere in my novels I have tried to imagine being that last survivor. I do not want to be that survivor. I'm afraid of that survivor, of his vision. I'm afraid of the madness that would invade him, weigh upon him, to have so much knowledge, and to know that, with him, all this knowledge will go down, will go out."[32]

Notes

1. See introduction in Zoe Waxman, *Writing the Holocaust: Identity, Testimony, Representation* (London: Oxford University Press, 2012).
2. I use the term "surviving victim" rather than "survivor" because I want to always be reminded it was not inevitable that they would survive and that their victimization goes on in their memory even if they did physically survive.

3. See the excellent book that details how survivors tried to document their own story by Laura Jockusch, *Collect and Record! Jewish Holocaust Documentation in Early Postwar Europe* (New York: Oxford University Press, 2012).

4. Elie Wiesel, *One Generation After* (New York: Random House, 1970), 40.

5. Anita Lasker-Wallfisch, *Inherit the Truth: A Memoir of Survival and the Holocaust* (London: Giles de la Mare, 1996), 13.

6. The 614th commandment was said to be heard coming from Auschwitz: "Jews are forbidden to hand Hitler posthumous victories!" See Emil Fackenheim, *God's Presence in History* (New York: New York University Press, 1970), 84.

7. Primo Levi, *Collected Poems* (London: Faber and Faber, 1992), 9. The poem is dated January 10, 1946. It is a paraphrase of Deuteronomy 11:13–21, which warns against being "lured away" lest "God's anger . . . flare up against you." The threat of the curse then provides the pretext to "teach them [these words of Mine] to your children, and speak of them when you sit at home, and when you go on a journey, when you lie down and when you rise up, (*The Authorised Daily Prayer Book of the United Hebrew Congregation of the Commonwealth* [Cambridge: Press Syndicate of the University of Cambridge, 1992], 68–69).

8. When describing the memory of the offense, Levi struggles with the indelible nature of the memory that the offense of torture and persecution forces upon its victims and at the same time recognizes the "drifting" of memory that inevitably takes place over time.

9. Isabel Wollaston, *A War against Memory: The Future of Holocaust Remembrance* (London: Society for Promoting Christian Knowledge, 1996), 12.

10. Elie Wiesel, *A Jew Today* (New York: Vintage Books, 1979), 238.

11. David Roskies, "The Library of Jewish Catastophe," in *Holocaust Remembrance: The Shapes of Memory*, ed. Geoffrey Hartman (Oxford: Blackwell, 1994), 33.

12. Roskies, "Library of Jewish Catastophe," 33.

13. George Steiner, *Language and Silence: Essays on Language, Literature and the Inhuman* (New York: Atheneum, 1977), 168.

14. Primo Levi, *The Drowned and the Saved* (London: Abacus, 1989), 11–21.

15. Sara Horowitz, "Voices from the Killing Ground," in Hartman, *Holocaust Remembrance*, 42.

16. James E. Young, *Writing and Rewriting the Holocaust: Narrative and Consequences of Interpretation* (Bloomington: Indiana University Press, 1988), 11.

17. Hayim Yosef Yerushalmi, *Zakhor: Jewish History and Jewish Memory* (New York: Schocken Books, 1989), 98.

18. I first heard Jonathan Webber say this during a field trip to Poland in 1992 when I was a graduate student. It has stayed with me ever since and

informed much of my thinking about how we treat the past through our many representations.

19. For an excellent introduction to the memory and myth of Auschwitz see Jonathan Webber, *The Future of Auschwitz: Some Personal Reflections*, Frank Green Lecture 1 (Oxford: Oxford Centre for Postgraduate Hebrew Studies, 1992).

20. For example, "Auschwitz" has become shorthand for the Holocaust itself; when "ghettos" are referenced, the little boy with his hands up in the Warsaw Ghetto is almost invariably used as a visual reference; *Schindler's List* has become a synonym for the rescue of Jews by courageous non-Jews; Anne Frank supplants all children in hiding.

21. Stated on numerous occasions witnessed by the author, in public lectures about his life and experience during the Holocaust.

22. Lawrence Langer, *Holocaust Testimonies: The Ruins of Memory* (New Haven: Yale University Press, 1991), xiv.

23. Martin Buber, *I and Thou*, trans. Walter Kaufmann (New York: Charles Scribner's Sons, 1970), 60.

24. Dori Laub and Shoshana Felman, *Testimony: Crises of Witnessing in Literature, Psychoanalysis and History* (New York: Routledge, 1992), 82.

25. See my forthcoming book, *The Trajectory of Holocaust Memory: The Crisis of Witness in Theory and Practice* (London: Routledge, 2023).

26. Buber, *I and Thou*, 62.

27. Marianne Hirsch, *The Generation of Postmemory: Writing and Visual Culture after the Holocaust* (New York: Columbia University Press, 2012).

28. Lawrence Langer, *Holocaust Testimonies; The Ruins of Memory* (New Haven and London: Yale University Press, 1991), 39.

29. Wiesel, *One Generation After*, 15–16.

30. Henry Greenspan, *On Listening to Holocaust Survivors: Recounting and Life History* (Westport, CT: Praeger, 1998), 27.

31. Greenspan, *On Listening to Holocaust Survivors*, 28.

32. Elie Wiesel, in conversation with Stephen Lewis, in *Art out of Agony: The Holocaust Theme in Literature, Sculpture and Film*, by Stephen Lewis (Montreal: CBC Enterprises, 1984), 160.

21

Inclusive Judaism
A Vision for the Future

Rabbi Nora Feinstein

I N HIS INTRODUCTION to this volume, my rabbi and teacher Stanley
Davids asks, "Can we embrace disruption while holding fast in more
than a pro forma manner to precious continuity? Can there be a future
without a coherent past? Can there be a future without an openness to
disruption? Will our tradition ultimately be re-formed into obsolescence? What lies beyond the next corner?"

I want to add my own rhetorical question to Rabbi Davids's: How
could we possibly capture the multivocal sweep of Jewish history, texts,
tradition, and communities in a single volume? The answer is that we
cannot, for no single volume, however exhaustive, could ever hope to do
full justice to a tradition as ancient, rich, and multifaceted as Judaism.
And that, in a way, is the point. This volume's privileging of certain perspectives over others and its inevitable inadequacies and shortcomings
themselves attest to the work that remains to be done in order to compose texts and construct communities reflective of Judaism's diversity
and multivocality. For all that this volume has accomplished, its most
important contribution, to my mind at least, is to inspire further investigation of chains of disruption and continued transmission of Jewish
tradition into the future.

My main aim in this retrospective is not to point out this volume's
shortcomings. Rather, I set out a vision for what an inclusive Judaism's
responses to change might look like moving forward. In this sense, I
hope that this survey contributes not only to the preceding chapters of
this volume, but to the dialogue and action that it aims to foster.

Inclusive Judaism: A Positive Vision for the Future

Recognizing those people who have been disregarded, itself a disruption to extant norms and narratives, provides us with the opportunity to strategize about inclusion—that is, how to stretch the tent to invite the voices that even this kind of volume seems to ignore. Therefore, rather than dwell on those perspectives not given adequate attention in this volume, I want to ask what a truly inclusive Judaism might look like. Acknowledging those who have too often been excluded from the dominant narratives of our tradition is an important starting place, but it is hardly sufficient. We also need to ensure that their voices are not silenced and suppressed going forward.

The social scientist James C. Scott speaks of a culture's public and hidden transcripts—that is, the official record of a particular people and the record of all those whose voices have been silenced, dismissed, and lost.[1] There are sparkling moments of breakthrough—disruptions—when the hidden transcript, the stories of the long-quieted voices, collides with the public one. Those are moments in which narratives radically rupture. And that seismic shift can be destructive or redemptive for a culture's public transcript.

A truly inclusive Judaism would draw inspiration from instances of disruption and breakthrough, centering those voices and perspectives that are too often ignored or silenced. Thankfully, there are individuals and organizations who, at this very moment, are engaged already in the vital work of centering those whose voices have been and still are, to a large extent, marginalized. They are showing us ways to reconcile the public and hidden transcripts. In a much-beloved talk about her work with Svara, the "traditionally radical yeshiva dedicated to the serious study of Talmud through the lens of queer experiences," Rabbi Benay Lappe teaches that in such moments, which she characterizes as instances of "crash," we have three options as human beings: we can "cling to the story as though nothing happened, discard it altogether, or integrate the old with the new and adapt."[2] She argues that queer and marginalized folks have been the harbingers of future Jewish culture. She is not alone in her efforts to both enrich and complicate our collective story. There are amazing organizations and innovators throughout the Jewish world educating other Jews on how best to build new communities or retrofit existing ones to be more inclusive, equitable, and accessible. They are engaged in work that is both reparative and visionary.

Textual and Historical Precedent for Inclusion

There is, I want to suggest, textual and historical precedent for including the voices and perspectives of those neglected both on the page and in our communities. After a very famous disruption, the destruction of the Second Temple in Jerusalem in 70 CE, the Rabbis reimagined Judaism for a radically altered world. In the Rabbinic understanding, after the Temple was destroyed, prophecy ceased. No longer the purview of the biblical prophets, prophecy was instead left in the hands, as the Rabbis put it, of babes and fools (Babylonian Talmud, *Bava Batra* 12b). This view, classically understood, symbolizes the Sages' attempt to discount those claiming to be arbiters and transmitters of tradition other than themselves. By shunting prophets into a category of marginalized folks—children and fools—people without full autonomy and status as adult Jews, the Rabbis deride and delegitimize anyone seeking to call themselves a prophet.

While prophecy qua prophecy may have ceased when the Temple was destroyed, the people's relationship to God—to the Divine—did not. Rather, the focus shifted to the transmission of tradition through the sacred endeavors of studying and teaching text. In such a way, the practices of interpreting and studying Jewish sources in order to derive a sense of meaning from our collective canon—probing the relationship between Jewish people, Jewish practice, and Jewish wisdom—became constitutive of Jewish life itself. They became the sacred, connective tissue of Jewish life—an inheritance that is on proud display in the preceding chapters.

But what if we took seriously the above claim that prophecy—recast as wisdom, vision, and inspiration—can be found in the hands of children and fools? What if we looked to the people in the next generation and on the margins of present-day Jewish communities as sources of insight? What if we studied those ideas about the future and perspectives on the past and present that shake us from our complacency, rouse us from our soporific status quo? What would it mean for us to liberate ourselves from preconceived notions about whose voices matter and where divine inspiration can be found?

To be sure, we remain constrained by a textual interpretive chain that has, like so many cultures, been dominated by a small number of voices, reflecting the privilege historically granted to those permitted to study, teach, and transmit the tradition. Nevertheless, there have always been those on the margins of our physical spaces and in the margins of our texts whose voices have been hidden from the public record, but whose stories and lives shape our own. How we include those past, present, and future voices offers an opportunity for transformation of our tradition and our communities, an opportunity for richer understanding, and an opportunity for new, better stories and storytellers.

Imagining an Inclusive Judaism: Stumbling Forward

There's another line from Talmud echoing throughout the pieces in the volume, as they explore the disruptions that shape the stories and histories of the Jewish people: "A person can only stand on words of Torah by stumbling over them" (Babylonian Talmud, *Gittin* 43a). *Torah* can mean many things to many people; its definition is neither limited to the Pentateuch nor meant to refer specifically to the Written and Oral Torahs. Literally, *Torah* means "instruction" or "source of wisdom." Arguably, *Torah*, this core Jewish term, need not be restrictive or limited; it is, at its core, capacious and expansive.

Many people are demonstrating new ways to live out Torah every single day in all manner of Jewish spaces. These individuals stand firmly on the foundation of our tradition even as—or perhaps because—they stumbled on the path to get there. They struggled with the interpretations of Torah they encountered along their way. And, in response to their subsequent offerings, others will stumble; they will question their sense of Judaism and will quite often have their assumptions upended. Encountering others will lead to continued disagreements about the correct interpretation of Torah; they will ask what and who merits inclusion in Jewish community. There will be failed experiments in living out these interpretations of stumbled-over Torah. Communities and institutions that are unable to adapt to cultural pendulum swings and the exigencies of people's lived experiences and identities will fade.

Our tradition—an inheritance of humans wrestling for sacred truth—will continue to stand and be made stronger if we recognize that we must, necessarily, stumble over and grapple with the limitations of our texts and the boundaries of our communities again and again. Inevitably, new leaders, institutions, and interpretations will emerge from people experienced in stumbling and learning who are equipped to lend a hand to others as they bumble through their own learning journeys. A willingness to traverse difficult terrain will prove essential, for what we are prepared to call Judaism and whom we are prepared to receive as Jews must necessarily evolve.

As other authors in this volume have shown, the interrelation of tradition and change in the engagement of Torah—a hallmark of Jewishness—itself emerged from disruption. Our texts reflect our urge to see ourselves in our shared narratives, to see ourselves in our people's story. In the Mishnah, *Pirkei Avot* starts with its own genealogy and details the process by which Torah wisdom passed from Moses to Joshua, Joshua to the elders, the elders to the prophets, the prophets to the Great Assembly, and from them to subsequent generations. The ability to see oneself as part of the chain of transmission of Torah from Revelation at Sinai, in other words, establishes one's legitimate authority as an interpreter of Jewish tradition.

Grappling with the process by which tradition absorbs or resists change limns our sacred texts and subsequent commentaries. Indeed, the first post-prophetic teaching of the Rabbis in *Pirkei Avot* comes from the Sages of the Great Assembly: "Be deliberate in judgment; develop many students; and make a fence for the Torah" (1:1). I want to suggest that these three teachings in fact provide guiding principles for imagining an inclusive Judaism moving forward.

Be deliberate [or: patient] in judgment: On the one hand, do not be hasty to dismiss innovative ideas as purely disruptive to our notions of who Jews are and how they engage Jewishly. On the other hand, do not idolize innovations as the lodestar. Many ideas parading as innovations may simply be loud and flashy distractions from the crucial, unrelenting, and Judaism-sustaining work of building inclusive and nourishing communities.

Concomitantly, or conversely, as an innovator or a fan of innovative disruptions, be patient with those who are reluctant, dismissive, or seemingly unwilling to adapt to changes. Learning and evolving takes time; the pace of change may not be as quick as some might hope or think necessary. Nonetheless, we all must remember and remind one another that Judaism is a communal project. As such, "doing" Jewish as a group requires more than being Jewish and/or reflexively perpetuating the Judaism that we first encountered or with/in which we were raised. Judaism asks us to be judicious, intentional, and thoughtful about our lived expressions of Jewishness as individuals and as communities.

Living a vibrant Jewish life with others requires buy-in and contributions from diverse people and stakeholders over a long period of time. Judging others who live and enact their Judaism differently than we do is natural, but it can also be destructive. Others' views of Judaism, of themselves, and of the world may be different from our own. Those divergent views likely have important lessons to teach us about ourselves, our tradition, and our history. Emerging changes, both those that appear disruptive and those that seem innovative, deserve our attentive care and humble learning posture as individuals and as collectives.

Develop many students: See those drawn to Judaism and Jewish learning as precious and necessary to the survival of Judaism. In the Koren commentary on this mishnah, the editors write, "Transmission of Torah/wisdom is best accomplished when taught to many students rather than confined to an elite group of scholars. The sages had keen awareness that great students may be found in all strata of society, and that everyone should have access to as excellent an education as possible."[3]

The people poised to guide Judaism into and through the next disruptions, and into and through the next centuries, may be people who come from unexpected places and backgrounds. And we need to be attentive to their Torah wisdom, even and especially when it threatens our sense of boundaries and our sense of what is or is not Judaism.

Make a fence for the Torah: Boundaries, in some measure, are a necessary precondition of community. If everyone belongs, no one belongs. And yet, to fixate on the fence is to the detriment of the Torah it is designed to protect. Broadening access to Torah by including and listening to voices previously excluded from the interpretive chain necessitates a measure of discomfort. The sociologist Tressie McMillan Cottom teaches that discomfort is actually the visceral experience of pluralism.[4] Judaism will survive so long as we are willing to live with the discomfort entailed by a plurality of expressions and a diversity of communities.

Judaism has a profound offering at a moment when our world seems to privilege speaking with only those with whom we agree, gathering— in person or virtually—only with those who make us feel comfortable. Judaism asks us to question received truths, not only the Torah but also the fences and institutions set up to enable access to that Torah.

Conclusion

In the introduction Rabbi Davids asks, "Can we embrace disruption while holding fast in more than a pro forma manner to precious continuity?" As you made your way through this volume, perhaps you, like me, have come to see or have been reminded of the ways in which continuity and discontinuity are mutually reinforcing.

Each of us brings our stories to the page before us—whether it is a page of this volume or a page of another text in the Jewish canon. What a blessing these encounters are, for they offer an opportunity to consider how our personal narrative intersects with our evolving public transcript. I leave this particular text as I began: curious and hopeful, prepared to embrace and learn from disruptions, for that is the only way Judaism continues. I wonder what our world could look like if we were less concerned about Jewish continuity, less invested in those innovations that serve to perpetuate the status quo and maintain systems of power, and more curious about discontinuities and disruptions poised to create sustainable, necessary, and nourishing changes in, to, and for our Jewish communities. This change will take time. This change will take us. The future is waiting. Will you join me?

NOTES

1. James C. Scott, *Domination and the Arts of Resistance: Hidden Transcripts* (New Haven CT: Yale University Press, 1992).
2. Benay Lappe, "An Unrecognizable Jewish Future: A Queer Talmudic Take,"

Eli Talks, May 29, 2014, https://youtube.com/watch?v=CBWIER_GQY.

3.   Jonathan Sacks, trans., and Marc Angel, commentator, *The Koren Pirkei Avot* (Jerusalem: Koren, 2015), 5.

4   In an interview with Ezra Klein, Cottom said, "Broadening access doesn't mean that everybody has the experience that I, privileged person, had in the discourse. Broadening it means that we are all equally uncomfortable, right? That's actually what pluralism and plurality is. It isn't that everybody is going to come in and have the same comforts that privilege and exclusion had extended to a small group of people. It's that now everybody sits at the table, and nobody knows the exact right thing to say about the other people" ("Transcript: Ezra Klein Interviews Tressie McMillan Cottom," *New York Times*, April 13, 2021, https://www.nytimes.com/2021/04/13/podcasts/ezra-klein-podcast-tressie-mcmillan-cottom-transcript.html).

Afterword

Leah Hochman, PhD

THE LAST SEVERAL YEARS have reinforced for me the wisdom of the blessing "May you live in uninteresting times." Though often identified as an "ancient Chinese" curse ("May you live in interesting times"), the phrase itself derives much more recently from its use by British diplomats in the early twentieth century. The sentiment, along with the myth of its attribution and the reality of its origin, provides a metaphor for the chapters throughout this volume. Each of the "disruptions"—from the biblical period to the present day—represent some aspect of either an unexpected or anticipated "interesting time"—in the wake of which Jews were forced to respond in practical, spiritual, and intellectual ways. In general, changing registers of politics, financial and physical security, religious innovation, and clashing social orders sparked different kinds of Jewish reactions to those disruptions. Though constant with regard to a commitment to Torah (in the broadest sense, as a central narrative) and a shared history, Jewish response was neither uniform nor monolithic. Over time, stories about Jewish action or inaction, ideas formulated in the wake of those stories, and deeply held opinions about both those stories and ideas have formed. In trying to understand our own experience, the authors whose work appears in this volume have looked backward into our people's history in order to make sense of our current very interesting time.

Throughout this collection, contemporary rabbis and scholars (and rabbi-scholars) have explored how those initial responses sparked secondary responses sometimes decades, sometimes centuries later. Secondary reactions provoked other mechanisms or strategies of change. Rather than a clear and distinct line of Jewish development, we have read that Jewish religious practice and belief are a product of fits and starts, actions and reactions, bumpy transitions and deep disruptions. As has hopefully become clear, disruptions are seldom moments of immediate transformation and are more often an unfolding of long processes of understanding, reconciling, rejecting, reorienting, and otherwise making meaning out of "interesting" times. Doing so is Jewish instinct: we have embedded transformative and traumatic experience in our liturgy, in our texts, in our self-understanding, in our theology, and in our ritual behaviors. And we have built upon those experiences to help us face other, similar moments. Turning trauma into meaningful acts of intention (*kavanah*) and steadfast expressions of belief (*emunah*) is a millennia-old practice. Thus, the initiatives born out of disruptive events have led to the fostering and development of a rich fabric of Jewish thought, practice, and action that was neither inevitable in its outcome nor capricious in its trajectory.

The truism that change is inevitable runs throughout the essays of this book. Often Jewish history is approached with assumptions about origins, and historicity is quickly assigned to events. The contributors to this volume have invited us to slow down those expectations and reinvestigate the influence of Jews who and key moments that have come to frame the understanding of why and how Judaism developed the way it has. They walk us through different "interesting" moments in history in which Jews have lived and thrived. In doing so, they have queried contemporary assumptions about those moments, the contexts in (and out of) which they occurred, and the repercussions—happy or otherwise—for the development, evolution, and practice of Judaism.

One such moment that has always captured my attention is the shift from the medieval to the modern period. Though in classes I can delineate behaviors and belief systems between the two (beautifully described in the chapters by Tamar Marvin, PhD, on Maimonides and Rabbi Kari Tuling, PhD, on the Pittsburgh Principles), I know the change in perspectives and worldviews was the result of many smaller moments of personal experience, joy, and sorrow. Personal memoirs are treasure troves of such information, like the one written by Glikl bas Judah Leib—more commonly known now as Glueckl of Hameln (1646–1724)—who started her story in 1691. Having lost her husband of twenty-nine years to a mortal injury two years earlier, the widow with twelve surviving children worked through her grief by writing about her life.[1] In the wake of the Thirty Years' War (1618–48), she witnessed travel restrictions, expulsions, robberies, murder, the fervor of belief in Shabbetai Zvi, trade, and the ravages of plague. She described a picture not only of the disruptive world around her, but also of her self-understanding, marked by her unyielding belief in personal integrity, unwavering devotion to Torah, and a deeply personal understanding of a transcendent and impersonal God.

Tellingly, Glueckl's story begins not with her, but with her grandparents and great-grandparents. Her maternal grandmother, widowed herself by an incidence of plague and mourning several children, fled her infected house and lived as a refugee in an outside shelter. Upon returning home, she found it stripped utterly bare. With hard work, tenacity, and deep belief, she provided for her surviving children and built a new life. Decades later, while living with Glueckl's family in Hamburg, her grandmother took charge of caring for the sick and injured refugees of terrible violence in Ukraine known now as the Chmielnicki Massacres (1648). With the same resolve and stubbornness she used to survive her own tragedy, Glueckl's grandmother cared for these Jews who boarded inside people's homes—"neighbors," fellow travelers in a life of insecurity. She climbed upstairs to the attic "three or four times a day, in order to nurse them."[2] In a throwaway line, Glueckl reminds her reader that they did not yet have hospitals. Glueckl and her sister both got the illness the refugees unintentionally brought with them, as did their grandmother, who did not recover. Her grandmother's experience was a defining one for Glueckl.

In her memoir, Glueckl draws on Judaism's attachment to memory and, through it, offers a way to identify with and learn from the events other people lived. Though she herself puzzles over her experiences, she intuits that what she has learned is valuable and that her future reader may come to know what she cannot. As a continuous narrative that stretches from one period of disruption to another, across centuries, Glueckl's memoir empowers us to look for meaning for ourselves even as we learn from her.

It took the experience of the global COVID-19 pandemic for me to understand how the traumas of Glueckl's grandmother's experience of loss, rejection, and disease were linked to Glueckl's own acute sense of loss, illness, and healing and—three hundred plus years later—my own. Rereading Glueckl's story reminded me that Jewish traditions do not gloss over the pain of a communal or personal crisis, the loss sustained in that crisis, or the fear that both inspire. Neither do those traditions glorify them. Rather, disruptive moments provide us with a rich and substantive bank of experiences out of which each person in his or her or their own time can make meaning, find resonance, and sustain faith. They also give us a sense of the choices Jews made, why they made them, and how those choices affect us today.

As one may have intuited, this project was born out of a curiosity—or, perhaps better described as a series of stacked curiosities—about how liberal Judaism developed the way it has. We wondered about the moments of its development and how the inconsistencies of key experiences in history contributed to the unique intellectual and spiritual responses of Jewish thinkers, believers, and leaders. Then, drilling down further, we asked more questions about which Jews influenced the trajectory of both majority and minority Jewish experience as well as when, how, and why certain Jewish voices grew loud enough to be heard centuries later. In what ways did those voices encourage—by design or by accident—others to experience or understand or synthesize in a manner similar to (or vastly different from) their own? In inquiring about the roads taken, we intended also to ask, which roads were left unwalked, and which paths remained unattended?

There is, however, a truism in the making of history: winners determine the narrative. The stories that get told (and retold) are generally those of the successors to those "winners." They shape the story of their own success through the backward gaze of "fate" or project the certainty of an outcome under the rubric of a divine providence that leans in their favor. As both Kristine Henricksen Garroway, PhD, and Jacob L. Wright, PhD, make clear in their respective chapters, the redacted texts of the Torah help construct a national ethic that privileges the prophetic and the priestly voices that subsequently become central foundational narratives for the establishment of the Israelite nation and *Am Yisrael* (the people Israel). The license to build a past to help understand and validate the realities of the present is a survival strategy used by every generation of Jews in every region of the Diaspora. Rabbi Joshua D. Garroway, PhD, describes how Paul traveled throughout the early Roman Empire, reread-ing the Hebrew Bible texts, deploying their message of redemption in order to give hope at a time of great despair. In their respective chapters on Rabbinic texts, both Gwynn Kessler, PhD, and Rabbi Candice Levy, PhD, show the multiple ways in which Talmudic voices excavate earlier texts to meet postbiblical challenges and construct productive means for understanding complicated expressions of Jewish religious selfhood and expectation. Deploying different approaches, each author shows how the Rabbinic construction of the Talmud weights the balance of diasporic realities with an established covenantal framework that requires belief in a divine plan and an expectation of spiritual redemption.

Unsurprisingly, that strategy is employed also by medieval inter-preters—mystics and rationalists alike—who contend with the prac-tical requirements of differing religiopolitical governing bodies while maintaining (and shoring up) belief in the God of Israel as interpreted and framed by the Talmudic age. The approach becomes clear also in the chapter from Rabbi Lawrence A. Englander, DHL, which carefully walks us through the "discovery" of the *Zohar* and its impact on the mys-tical tradition as a "lost" Rabbinic text. Similarly, Tamar Marvin, PhD, opens a window into Maimonides's firm faith in the truth of Rabbinic authority even as he creates an entirely new way of using and applying its insights. And we see the same tendency from North African rabbinic voices in the incisive reading by Michal Ohana, PhD, of the commen-tary that constructed a rich, deep, and provocative diasporic tapestry of post-Talmudic Judaism.

Of course, by their very nature, edited volumes must be selective in what they include and what they do not. We have tried to balance moments in Jewish religious and intellectual history that may be more familiar with those that may not be. Rabbi Stanley M. Davids's study of the conditions that prefigure Shabbetai Zvi's success and ultimate conversion to Islam is considered alongside the chapter by Rabbi Marc D. Angel, PhD, on Sephardic experience, religiosity, political activism, and social influence. The analysis by Yoav Schaefer of the philosophical revolutions precipi-tated by the respective works of Spinoza, Mendelssohn, and Kant comes into conversation with both the analysis by Michael A. Meyer, PhD, of Samuel Holdheim and the deep dive by Rabbi Kari Tuling, PhD, into the context out of which the Pittsburgh Platform was written.

Along the same lines, we have included some essays that look at familiar subjects using unfamiliar perspectives. The study by Adam Rovner, PhD, of American Jewish literature uses the Book-of-the-Month Club to trace trends of acceptance and assimilation in American society. Cantor Evan Kent, DMA, walks us through the major impact folk music, pioneered by Debbie Friedman and popularized at Jewish summer camp, has had on the liturgy in synagogues and the sound of American Judaism as a whole. The chapter by Rabbi Sonja K. Pilz, PhD, on the prayers written and collected in Reform prayer books, shows the immense spiritual and intellectual productivity of American Jewry in the late twentieth and early twenty-first centuries. And Stephen D. Smith, PhD, employs Martin Buber to invite the reader to engage with Holocaust testimony in an entirely new way.

We have also included essays that seek to investigate and reveal more about some of the ruptures of the last one hundred years. The discussion by Rabbi Michael Marmur, PhD, of the enormous bearing that Mordecai Kaplan's thought and practice has had on contemporary Jewry teaches us that what was once radical can, with time, become normalized. And that lesson is furthered by Rabbi Elyse Goldstein's intimate examination of the rise of Jewish feminism and its permanent improvement to expression and understanding of Jewish history, religiosity, and identification across denominations.

Despite this breadth of topics and themes, we know that our volume is both incomplete and imperfect. Rabbi Jason Rodich has offered us a substantive critique of how we have been caught in a reiterative cycle of self-understanding. And Rabbi Nora Feinstein has laid out a vision for future, inclusive disruptions. Both authors help us understand that if we can glimpse a disruption coming, we can influence its shape to our benefit. We know there are many other moments of disruption we have not included. Where we have given voice to viewpoints and leaders that may have otherwise been overlooked, we have also focused on recorded voices and not those whose actions and prayers had impact but have not yet been found by scholars. Unintentionally, this volume has contributed to a widespread tendency to emphasize certain voices and perspectives and marginalize and discount others.

Crucially, we have missed the opportunity to tackle other topics that have influenced Jewish life and Jewish expressions of belief. Among such a list are essays that look at questions of race, biology, and blood as a basis for anti-Jewish policies, antisemitic action, and intra-Jewish distinctiveness as well as the exercise of racist ideas and policies by Jews in and after the age of slavery. Though certain chapters gesture toward it, we do not devote one to the spread and growth of Chasidism in the eighteenth and nineteenth centuries, the halachic reactions to Chasidism in both Eastern and Central Europe, or the repercussions of ultra-Orthodox immigration to Israel and the United States in the mid-twentieth century. Similarly, we do not have a discussion of the growth and spread of Zionism or its counter anti-Zionism before or after the Second World War, or about the establishment of the State of Israel, or about Israeli society before and after the 1983 Israeli war in Lebanon. Also missing are discussions of the challenges of American civil society, identity politics, Jewish education, the impact of the 1970s and do-it-yourself Judaism, the role of super-philanthropists in shaping twentieth- and twenty-first-century Diaspora politics and demographic movement, denominational strife, environmental activism, the liberal acceptance of interfaith marriage and both matrilineal and patrilineal descent, the civil rights movement, the rise of Jewish spiritualism, and the fall of the Berlin Wall in 1989 and the subsequent breakup of the Soviet Union. There are, of course, many others. We hope future volumes will be able to address what we have not included here.

In acknowledging the shortcomings of this volume, I do not mean to undermine the importance of the fantastic contributions we have collected. Rather, I am enacting the important Jewish ethic to acknowledge when a work is incomplete and articulate what is left to do. Jewish history is long and complicated and has evolved through many an interesting time. We know that we have before us in the present, and will have in the future, new disruptions whose reverberations and ramifications are not yet knowable. Indeed, the slow but steady acknowledgment of the racial and ethnic diversity of Jews will lead to intentional rituals and liturgies written to include the experiences, viewpoints, and sensibilities of Jews of Color, who have long been marginalized by a majority white Ashkenazi narrative. Similarly, we will need to investigate the shifts in perception and allegiance of Jews in the Diaspora toward Israeli religion, society, and politics even as we contend with domestic and international pressures of rising antisemitism, white nationalism, and far left and far right critiques of the role of Jews in American society.

As we look toward the future, we know that as in the past, shifting demographics within distinct denominations will cause disruptions in communal leadership and philanthropic trends. And as definitions of those denominations continue to expand (or contract), further disruptions will erupt in how Jews define themselves as belonging to or moving beyond specific denominational ideology. And as definitions of selfhood, self-understanding, and identity become more fluid, so will the very nature of Jewish life, expression, and experience. Similar to the impact LBTQIA+ innovations have had on all spheres of liturgy, commentary, and interpretation, notions related to binary and nonbinary understandings of the individual will force Jews to act, react, and/or adapt their understandings of the Divine, each other, and ourselves.

Before us, of course, is the central disruption of the current decade, the pandemic caused by the contagion of the Sars-CoV-2 virus and its many derivations. The American death toll of over one million people is unfathomable. The trauma of all that loss—along with the intensity of the disruption to everyday life, Jewish educational structures, philanthropic and nonprofit support, financial advancement, mental health and emotional well-being, and the foundational institutions of Jewish life in the Diaspora—are not balanced by the blessings of Zoom *t'filah* (prayer) and joining congregations "from afar." And so, I return to the blessing with which I began: I hope that soon we will live in peace and health and a slightly more boring time.

NOTES

1. Glückel of Hameln, *The Memoirs of Glückel of Hameln*, trans. Marvin Lowenthal (New York: Schocken Books, 1977), 1. The original copyright dates to 1932, when Lowenthal first translated the memoir from a 1920 German edition offered by Alfred Feilchenfeld. The original Yiddish text had been transcribed by a descendant and held privately by the family until appearing in German first in 1896. Some of what I have written here appeared first in an HUC podcast. See https://collegecommons.huc.edu/bully_pulpit/off-script-episode-1/.

2. *The Memoirs of Glückel of Hameln*, 20.

Contributors

Rabbi Stanley M. Davids is a Phi Beta Kappa graduate of Case Western Reserve University and was ordained by Hebrew Union College–Jewish Institute of Religion (HUC-JIR) in 1965. Following his service as a chaplain in the US Army, he served as senior rabbi for congregations in Massachusetts, New York, and Georgia before retiring in 2004 as rabbi emeritus of Temple Emanu-El of Greater Atlanta. He was chair of the CCAR Israel Committee, honorary life chair of the Israel Bonds Rabbinic Cabinet, a life member of NFTY, international president of Alpha Epsilon Pi fraternity, and past national chair of the Association of Reform Zionists of America. Following his *aliyah*, he served for many years as a member of the Board of Governors of the Jewish Agency and as a member of the Zionist Executive of the World Zionist Organization. He continues to serve on the Board of Overseers of HUC-JIR's Los Angeles campus. With Rabbi Lawrence Englander, he was coeditor of *The Fragile Dialogue: New Voices of Liberal Zionism* (CCAR Press, 2018), and with Rabbi John Rosove, he was coeditor of *Deepening the Dialogue: Jewish-Americans and Israelis Envision the Jewish-Democratic State* (CCAR Press, 2020). Rabbi Davids and his wife, Resa, have three children and eight grandchildren.

Leah Hochman, PhD, directs the Louchheim School for Judaic Studies at the University of Southern California and serves as associate professor of Jewish thought at Hebrew Union College–Jewish Institute of Religion (HUC-JIR) in Los Angeles. She is the author of *The Ugliness of Moses Mendelssohn: Aesthetics, Religion, and Morality in the Eighteenth Century* (Routledge, 2014), the editor of *Tastes of Faith: Jewish Eating in the United States* (Purdue University Press, 2017), and the coeditor, with Rabbi Michael Marmur, PhD, of *Scriptions: Jewish Thoughts and Responses to Covid-19* (https://scriptions.huc.edu, 2021). Raised in the Seattle area, she earned her undergraduate degree at Pitzer College and both her MA and PhD in religion and literature from Boston University. After completing fellowships at Moses Mendelssohn Zentrum and the

Simon Dubnow Institute, she spent significant time in Berlin writing, researching, and teaching. Before joining the HUC-JIR faculty, she held positions at the University of Florida and Boston University.

Rabbi Marc D. Angel, PhD, is the founder and director of the Institute for Jewish Ideas and Ideals. He is the rabbi emeritus of Congregation Shearith Israel, the historic Spanish and Portuguese synagogue of New York City, and the author of numerous books and articles, many on Sephardic topics.

Rabbi Lawrence A. Englander, CM, DHL, is rabbi emeritus of Solel Congregation of Mississauga, Ontario, and is now adjunct rabbi of Temple Sinai in Toronto. He received his DHL degree in 1984 from Hebrew Union College–Jewish Institute of Religion in the fields of Jewish mysticism and Rabbinics. He is coeditor, with Rabbi Stanley M. Davids, of *The Fragile Dialogue: New Voices of Liberal Zionism* (CCAR Press, 2018). He has written a novel, *The Prince of Healers* (2021), based on the life of Moses Maimonides.

Rabbi Nora Feinstein lives in Washington, DC, where she serves as a rabbi at Sixth & I. Rabbi Feinstein previously worked at T'ruah: The Rabbinic Call for Human Rights. She holds bachelor's degrees from Barnard College and the Jewish Theological Seminary and received rabbinic ordination from Hebrew Union College–Jewish Institute of Religion in Los Angeles.

Rabbi Joshua D. Garroway, PhD, is the Sol and Arlene Bronstein Professor of Judaeo-Christian Studies at Hebrew Union College–Jewish Institute of Religion in Los Angeles. He was ordained at the Cincinnati campus of HUC-JIR in 2003 and then earned his doctorate at Yale University in 2008. His books *Paul's Gentile-Jews: Neither Jew nor Gentile, but Both* (Palgrave Macmillan, 2012) and *The Beginning of the Gospel: Paul, Philippi, and the Origins of Christianity* (Palgrave Macmillan, 2018) explore Paul's role in the origins of Christianity.

Kristine Henriksen Garroway, PhD, is professor of Hebrew Bible on the Los Angeles campus of Hebrew Union College–Jewish Institute of Religion. She is the author of *Children in the Ancient Near Eastern Household*

(Eisenbrauns, 2014) and *Growing Up in Ancient Israel: Children in Material Culture and Biblical Texts* (SBL Press, 2019). She is a regular contributor to thetorah.com.

Rabbi Elyse Goldstein was ordained in 1983 and has been breaking "stained glass ceilings" in Canada ever since. She served Holy Blossom Temple in Toronto, then Temple Beth David in Canton, Massachusetts, and then returned to Canada to found Kolel: The Adult Centre for Liberal Jewish Learning in 1991. In 2011, she founded City Shul, Toronto's downtown Reform synagogue. She has received the Covenant Award for outstanding Jewish educators and a Doctor of Laws, *honoris causa*, from Ryerson University in recognition of her path-breaking work in Canada.

Cantor Evan Kent, DMA, served Temple Isaiah in Los Angeles, California, for twenty-five years. In 2013, Evan made *aliyah*. Evan currently lives in Tel Aviv and is on the faculty of Hebrew Union College–Jewish Institute of Religion in Jerusalem and the Levinsky-Wingate College in Tel Aviv. Evan received a doctorate in music education from Boston University. His doctoral research examined how music at Jewish summer camps has impacted the development of Jewish identity.

Gwynn Kessler, PhD, is an associate professor in the Department of Religion and the director of the Beit Midrash at Swarthmore College. Dr. Kessler received her PhD in Rabbinics, with a specialization in midrash, from the Jewish Theological Seminary in 2001. Her research focuses on rabbinic interpretation of Scripture, or midrash, and more specifically on rabbinic theology and rabbinic constructions of gender and identity. She is the author of *Conceiving Israel: The Fetus in Rabbinic Narratives* (University of Pennsylvania Press, 2009) and the coeditor of *A Companion to Late Ancient Jews and Judaism* (Wiley-Blackwell, 2020). Dr. Kessler has previously taught at the University of North Carolina at Greensboro and at the University of Florida in Gainesville.

Rabbi Candice Levy, PhD, is the visiting assistant professor of Rabbinics at Hebrew Union College–Jewish Institute of Religion in Los Angeles. She was ordained at the Ziegler School of Rabbinic Studies in 2023 and received her PhD in Near Eastern languages and cultures from UCLA in 2013. Her dissertation, "Arbiters of the Afterlife: *Olam Haba*, Torah and Rabbinic Authority," examined rabbinic discourses of the afterlife as well as the complex interplay between rabbinic authority, Torah study, and theodicy, and the ancillary function of the afterlife for each of these.

Rabbi Michael Marmur, PhD, is an associate professor of Jewish theology at Hebrew Union College–Jewish Institute of Religion in Jerusalem. He is the author of *Abraham Joshua Heschel and the Sources of Wonder* (University of Toronto, 2016), and coeditor with David Ellenson of *American Jewish Thought Since 1934: Writings on Identity, Engagement, and Belief* (Brandeis University Press, 2020). His *Elements of a Jewish Theology: A Lexicon* is due for publication by Palgrave Macmillan in 2024.

Tamar Ron Marvin, PhD, is a scholar, writer, and educator currently based in Los Angeles. She holds a PhD in medieval and early modern Jewish studies from the Jewish Theological Seminary, a BA in literature and journalism from New York University, and is a rabbinical student at Yeshivat Maharat. She has taught in a number of university and Jewish settings, including American Jewish University, Hebrew Union College–Jewish Institute of Religion, and the Wexner Heritage Foundation, and has published her work in academic and broader media.

Michael A. Meyer, PhD, is the Adolph S. Oko Professor of Jewish History emeritus at Hebrew Union College–Jewish Institute of Religion in Cincinnati. He is the author or editor of a dozen books, including *Response to Modernity: A History of the Reform Movement in Judaism* (Wayne State University Press, 1995). His most recent book is *Rabbi Leo Baeck: Living a Religious Imperative in Troubled Times* (University of Pennsylvania Press, 2021) and his current project is a biography of Rabbi Alexander Schindler.

Michal Ohana, PhD, is a postdoctoral researcher at Martin Luther University of Halle-Wittenberg, specializing in Jewish thought and the intellectual history of the Jewish communities in North Africa in the sixteenth through twentieth centuries. Her first book, *Studies in the Thought of R. Shaul Serero: A Chapter in the History of Jewish Thought in Fez*, examines the thought of Shaul Serero, Fez's chief rabbi in the first half of the seventeenth century, and is published by Bar-Ilan University Press (2021).

Rabbi Sonja K. Pilz, PhD, earned her doctorate from the Department of Rabbinic Literature at Potsdam University in Germany and holds rabbinic ordination from Abraham Geiger College in Germany. Prior to becoming the spiritual leader of Congregation Beth Shalom in Bozeman, Montana, she worked for the Central Conference of American Rabbis as the editor at CCAR Press. Rabbi Pilz also taught at Hebrew Union College–Jewish Institute of Religion in New York and the School of Jewish Theology at Potsdam University. She previously served congregations in Germany, Switzerland, Israel, and the United States. Her work has been published by *Ergon*; *Liturgy*; *Worship*; the *CCAR Journal*; *Ritualwell*; and a number of anthologies. She lives with her husband and children in Bozeman, Montana.

Rabbi Jason Rodich is a dad, husband, and rabbi. Rabbi Rodich is interested in feminist and queer thought, the future of religion, poetry, ethics, and justice. Rabbi Rodich was ordained by Hebrew Union College–Jewish Institute of Religion in Los Angeles in 2014, is a recipient of the Wexner Graduate Fellowship, and attended the New School in New York, where he earned his BA in cultural studies and poetry.

Adam Rovner, PhD, is an associate professor of English and Jewish literature and the director of the Center for Judaic Studies at the University of Denver, where he has taught since 2008. His first book, *In the Shadow of Zion: Promised Lands Before Israel*, was published by NYU Press (2014). Adam's academic articles and general interest journalism have appeared in numerous outlets in the US and UK.

Yoav Schaefer is a doctoral candidate in Princeton's Department of Religion. His dissertation explores the early Jewish reception of Kantian philosophy, focusing in particular on Salomon Maimon's influential interpretation of the medieval Jewish philosopher Moses Maimonides. Before arriving at Princeton, Yoav earned a BA in social studies from Harvard University and studied Jewish philosophy and history at Tel Aviv University.

Stephen D. Smith, PhD, is a theologian who has dedicated his life to understanding the Holocaust and genocide. His focus has been on the power of personal narratives to provide insight as to the causes and consequences of genocide. He is the executive director emeritus of the USC Shoah Foundation, founder of the UK National Holocaust Centre, patron of the South African Holocaust and Genocide Foundation, and author of *The Trajectory of Holocaust Memory: The Crisis of Testimony in Theory and Practice* (Routledge, 2022).

Rabbi Kari Tuling, PhD, received rabbinic ordination in 2004 and earned a PhD in Jewish thought in 2013, both from the Hebrew Union College–Jewish Institute of Religion in Cincinnati. She has served congregations in Connecticut, Indiana, New York, and Ohio. She taught Jewish studies courses at the University of Cincinnati and the State University of New York, Plattsburgh, and courses in Jewish thought at Hebrew Union College–Jewish Institute of Religion in New York. Rabbi Tuling is a regular contributor to CCAR Press books and the *CCAR Journal*. Her book, *Thinking about God: Jewish Views*, was published by the Jewish Publication Society in August 2020.

Jacob L. Wright, PhD, is a professor of Hebrew Bible at Emory University in Atlanta, Georgia. He is the author of many books, the most recent being *Why the Bible Began: An Alternative History of Scripture and Its Origins* (Cambridge University Press, 2023). He also teaches an online course through Coursera ("The Bible's Prehistory, Purpose, and Political Future") that is free of charge to students.